The New Naturalist Library

A Survey of British Natural History

The Natural History of Orkne

Editors
Kenneth Mellanby, C.B.E., Sc.D.
S. M. Walters, M.A., Ph.D.
Professor Richard West, F.R.S., F.G.S.

Photographic Editor
Eric Hosking, O.B.E., F.R.P.S.

The aim of this series is to interest the general reader
in the wild life of Britain by recapturing the enquiring
spirit of the old naturalists. The Editors believe that
the natural pride of the British public in the native fauna
and flora, to which must be added concern for their
conservation, is best fostered by maintaining a high
standard of accuracy combined with clarity of exposition
in presenting the results of modern scientific research.

The New Naturalist

The Natural History of
ORKNEY

R. J. Berry, D.SC., F.R.S.E.

With 20 colour photographs, and
over 100 photographs and diagrams
in black and white

COLLINS
Grafton Street, London

William Collins Sons & Co. Ltd
London · Glasgow · Sydney · Auckland
Toronto · Johannesburg

First published 1985
© R. J. Berry 1985

ISBN 0 00 219062 1 (hardback edition)
ISBN 0 00 219406 6 (limpback edition)

Filmset by Ace Filmsetting Ltd., Frome, Somerset
Colour and black-and-white reproduction by Alpha Reprographics, Harefield, Midd
Printed and bound by Wm Collins Sons & Co. Ltd, Glasgow

Contents

Editors' Preface   9

Author's Preface   10

1. **Like Sleeping Whales**   13
   Islands and people
   Weather
   The natural history of Orkney

2. **Biological History**   26
   Land between Orkney and Caithness?
   The pattern of vegetation

3. **Rocks**   35
   Detailed geology
   The Ice Ages and after
   The coast

4. **Habitats and Vegetation**   48
   Man-made habitats
   The lowland zone
      Maritime habitats
      Lowland heath types
   Primula scotica
   Natural woodland and 'tree-less woodland' habitats
   Wetland and open water habitats
   Montane and upland habitats

5. **Sea and Shore**   87
   Shore biology
   Man and the sea
   The kelp industry

6. **Otters, Seals and Whales**   93
   Seals
   Whales
   Otters

7. **Freshwater Habitats**   110
   Lochs Harray and Stenness
   Other lochs
   Angling
   Streams
   Peat pools

Lagoons
Vegetation note
Amphibians
Change

8. **Terrestrial Animals**   124
Mammals
   North Ronaldsay sheep
   Other mammals
Lepidoptera
Other invertebrates

9. **Birds**   136
Changes in status
Coastal breeders
   Fulmars on Eynhallow
Inland habitats
   The moorlands
   Marshes and lochs
   Woodland
   Farmland
Orkney Hen Harriers
Present and Future

10. **Orkney Man**   163
Picts and brochs
The Vikings
Life in ancient Orkney
Mediaeval and modern Orkney
Life in recent centuries
Improved communications
Agricultural improvements
Agricultural practice
Man and the sea
The kelp industry
Orkney future

11. **Orkney Naturalists**   189

12. **Conservation, Development and the Future**   207
Oil reclamation
Seal-culling
Orkney and radioactivity
Fish farming
Kelp harvesting
The case for conservation

Getting about on Orkney   223

References and Further Reading   224

Bibliography   226

Appendix (Lists of Species)   236
    Myxomycetes
    Fungi
    Marine algae
    Characeae
    Lichens
    Mosses
    Liverworts
    Flowering plants and ferns
    Hirudinea
    Coleoptera
    Odonata
    Orthoptera
    Trichoptera
    Ephemeroptera
    Plecoptera
    Syrphidae
    Lepidoptera
    Arachnida
    Mollusca
    Birds
    Mammals

Index   303

Editors' Preface

With the successful publication in the New Naturalist Series, in 1980, of *The Natural History of Shetland* by R. J. Berry and J. L. Johnston, we hoped that a companion volume on Orkney would soon be produced. We were therefore delighted when Professor Berry, the senior author of the book on Shetland, intimated that he was prepared to tackle this task, especially since his own research was increasingly becoming concentrated on Orkney. We believe that he has now produced a very valuable work, which will be of much use to all those interested in Orkney, and in the ecology of islands in general. It is not just for the specialist but will also appeal to the casual visitor, who may skip some of the more technical sections and the species lists, though these will be greatly valued by other scientists interested in these fascinating islands.

Like Shetland, Orkney has been greatly affected by the discovery of oil in the waters near its coasts, and so the pressures on the wildlife have been greatly intensified. Professor Berry is fully aware of the dangers, and of the risks of accidents from oil spills. However, it is clear that the oil industry is aware of the damage to wildlife their activities could produce on land and in the sea, and that they are taking all reasonable precautions to safeguard the natural environment. It is a pleasure to acknowledge generous support from the Occidental North Sea Oil Consortium, which has made it possible to include the colour plates, which should do much to increase the appeal of this book.

Professor Berry has succeeded in presenting a comprehensive account of Orkney. He covers the flora and fauna of land and water and their development in the islands from the earliest times. He describes how man has wrestled with climate and land to exploit the natural resources of the islands, and traces the outcome of this from the prehistoric period, best known for striking sites such as Skara Brae, through to the coming of the Picts and the more violent happenings of the Viking invasion on to the present day. The islands came under the Scottish crown only in 1468, though contacts with Scotland for some centuries before that date were probably greater than those with the distant government in Scandinavia. Today, we are witnessing a further, and possibly even more traumatic change, not simply from the oil industry, but from population changes as an increasing number of 'strangers' settle in the islands, and, perhaps most serious of all, as developments in agriculture affect the whole landscape.

If nothing else, this account of wildlife as it exists today will be a valuable historical record. However, we hope that it will inspire those intent on conservation in Orkney, and also recruit many others to their cause, so that future generations can continue to enjoy all the plants and animals that have fired Professor Berry's enthusiasm and which he has so ably presented to us in this book.

Author's Preface

Fairly soon after the New Naturalist on the *Natural History of Shetland* was published, Robert Macdonald, then Natural History Editor of Collins asked me if I would write a complementary volume about Orkney. My immediate reaction was to refuse; I knew much less about Orkney than Shetland, and to cover Shetland properly, the writing had been a joint effort between Laughton Johnston (at the time the Nature Conservancy Council Officer in Shetland) and myself, with chapters by outside experts on geology, vegetation, Fair Isle, and the effects of oil. However, having talked with a group of Orkney Field Club members, including some of those most knowledgeable about Orkney natural history, I changed my mind, for four reasons:

1. My own research interests had moved from Shetland to Orkney, and I was becoming more and more fascinated by the county.

2. There were authoritative booklets available on the birds and the flowering plants of Orkney, but no general account of the islands' biology. In 1975 the Nature Conservancy Council (NCC) published the proceedings of a symposium on the *Natural Environment of Orkney* which contained much valuable information, but did not attempt to provide a complete coverage of Orkney natural history. There are some extremely good books on the history and geography of Orkney but they touch on natural history only in passing. There did not seem to be any single person likely to bring together the knowledge and understanding of Orkney natural history into one book, which, it was commonly agreed, was needed.

3. But the crucial factor, and the one that really made the book possible, was the cooperation of some of the best Orkney naturalists, who undertook to provide me with extended notes on subjects in which they were expert, and allow me to reword these in my own style. My name appears on the title page, but this book is truly a joint effort. There was a core which planned it from the start, and it is proper to acknowledge this. This group consisted of:

Miss Elaine R. Bullard, expert, even though amateur, plant ecologist and Orkney conservationist;
Dr Paul Heppleston, senior biology teacher at Kirkwall Grammar School, formerly with the Sea Mammal Research Unit of the Natural Environment Research Council;
Mr David Lea, formerly Orkney representative of the RSPB, and now responsible for the local guide organization, Go Orkney;
Mr Peter Reynolds, Assistant Regional Officer in Orkney for the NCC.

As well as their general involvement, Elaine Bullard was largely responsible for chapter 4 and part of chapter 10, Paul Heppleston for chapter 7, and Peter Reynolds for chapter 12.

Special thanks are due to Mr Eric Meek of Stenness, RSPB representative for Orkney, who has worked hard and long on both chapter 9 and the bird status list. His specialized knowledge of ornithological niceties has been invaluable.

In addition, other major help has come from Dr John Parnell of Queen's University, Belfast (chapter 3, on geology); Dr Alan Jones of the University of Dundee, Director of the Orkney Marine Biology Unit at Scapa (chapter 5, on the sea shore); Dr Bernard McConnell and the late Bill Vaughan of the Sea Mammal Research Unit (seals); Dr P. G. H. Evans, University of Oxford (whales); Professor Charles Gimingham, University of Aberdeen (vegetation); Ian Lorimer of Orphir (Lepidoptera); Mrs Sheila Spence of Harray (land mammals); and Mr Eoin Ross, formerly librarian at Kirkwall Grammar School (chapter 11, on Orkney naturalists). Other people who have contributed or helped include Dr Ian Baugh (NCC, Edinburgh); Dr Bill Bourne (Aberdeen); Dr James Cadbury (RSPB); Dr Olaf Cuthbert (Evie); Professor George Dunnet (Aberdeen); Professor Derek Flinn (Liverpool); Paul Harding (Biological Records Centre, Institute of Terrestrial Ecology); Mrs Jenny Moore (British Museum (Natural History)); Peter Leith (Stenness); Vincent Lorimer (Orphir), Mrs Nora McMillan (Merseyside Museum); Dr Peter Maitland (ITE); Jim Walker (Kirkwall); Colin Welch (ITE), and Douglas Young (North of Scotland College of Agriculture). Dr Morton Boyd, Director (Scotland) of NCC until 1985 supported the whole project, and gave permission to quote freely from the NCC's publication *Natural Environment of Orkney* (edited by Rawdon Goodier). I have quoted freely from many relevant publications throughout the book, and am grateful to the following for copyright permission: Mr G. Mackay Brown, Mrs M. Linklater, Orkney Islands Council, Mr R. P. Rendall, Social Science Research Council, and Cassell Ltd (publishers of Churchill's *History of the English Speaking Peoples*). Miss Gunnie Moberg of Stromness, Dr Charles Tait of Kirkwall, and members of Orkney Camera Club took considerable trouble in finding appropriate photographs; I am grateful too to the County Librarian for permission to reproduce photographs from the Kent Collection kept in the library in Kirkwall. Mr A. J. Lee drew all the figures.

A special word is necessary about chapter 10, on Orkney Man. More than anything else, Orkney is noted for its archaeological riches, and attracts scholars from far and near seeking a better understanding of the early history of man in north Britain. But this learned knowledge has hitherto been available almost entirely in inaccessible tomes. In 1982, with the help of Howie Firth of Radio Orkney and the financial support of the Nuffield Foundation, I brought together in Kirkwall a group of archaeologists, linguists, historians and anthropologists for a three day workshop in an effort to integrate the findings of the different disciplines which centre on man. The experts who met on that occasion included John Hedges (formerly Director of the North of Scotland Archaeological Unit, based in Orkney); Don Brothwell (Institute of Archaeology, London); Professors Gordon Donaldson (Edinburgh), Peter Foote (University College London) and Ronald Miller (Glasgow), and others. Their conclusions were published as the *People of Orkney* (1985) by the Orkney Press; chapter 10 is largely based on that book. My thanks are due to all who took part in the workshop, and contributed to enquiring who Orkney Man really is.

Finally and most importantly, the Occidental North Sea Oil Consortium agreed to subsidize publication in a most generous fashion, making possible a standard of illustration comparable to that in the *Natural History of Shetland*. It is doubtful whether the book would ever have appeared if this help had not been forthcoming.

It is said that Winston Churchill used to commission briefs from the greatest experts in the land for his historical books, and then rewrite them with his own coherence. That is the way this book has been written – or perhaps I should say, it is the way we have tried to write this book. While we are with Sir Winston, words he wrote in his Preface to the *History of the English-Speaking Peoples* are apposite:

'Our story centres in an island, not widely sundered from the Continent, and so tilted that its mountains lie all to the west and the north, while south and east is a gentle undulating landscape of wooded valleys, open downs, and slow rivers. It is very accessible to the invader, whether he comes in peace or war, as pirate or merchant, conqueror or missionary. Those who dwell there are not insensitive to any shift of power, any change of faith, or even fashion, on the mainland, but they give to every practice, every doctrine that comes to it from abroad, its own peculiar turn and imprint.'

Churchill was writing about Great Britain and its relationship to continental Europe, but his description fits remarkably closely to Orkney and its relationship with Great Britain. Here, then, is another story which centres on an island, or rather upon that group of islands which is Orkney, upon its biological past and present, and the multitudinous effects of its human inhabitants down the centuries.

R.J.B.

Like Sleeping Whales

CHAPTER I

The weather is good, if you like a temperate climate. Thermometer and baro-
meter measure our seasons capriciously; the Orkney year should be seen rather
as a stark drama of light and darkness . . . In the course of a single day you can
see, in that immensity of sky, the dance of sun, cloud, sea-mist, thunder, run:
the endless ballet of the weather.

George Mackay Brown, *An Orkney Tapestry*, 1969.

Most of Orkney is not spectacular and precipitous like its northern neighbours Shetland and Faroe, or like Skye and some of the Hebrides to the
south and west. The highest point (the Ward of Hoy) is only 1565 ft
(477 m) above sea level, and there is no land outside Hoy over 900 feet
(273 m). From the air the islands give a superficial appearance of a peaceful
agricultural undulation. From even further away an observer from a
satellite would see a central large island (always called the Mainland)
surrounded by nearly 100 other islands, ranging from skate-shaped Hoy,
down to mere tidal rocks (or skerries).

When I first visited Orkney, I thought it much duller in both topography
and biology than its Shetland cousin. But this first impression has proved

*Fig. 1
Looking from the
Mainland of Orkney
to Hoy across the
entrance to Scapa
Flow* (Photo: *R. S.
Moore*).

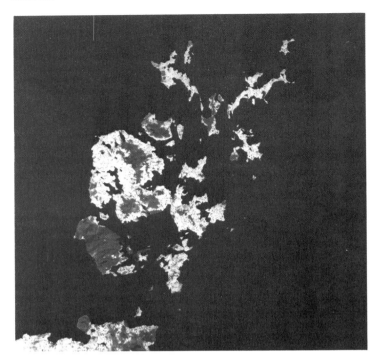

Fig. 2
Orkney as seen from
a satellite 560 miles
above the earth.

false: Orkney grows on one. The casual visitor who comes for a few days solely to see the spectacular archaeological monuments of Maeshowe or Skara Brae, or the naval and now oil developments of Scapa Flow, or the Hen Harrier, Orkney Vole or *Primula scotica*, will get a taste of the islands, but not an adequate flavour. Orkney reveals her charms gladly, but gradually, like a shy lover.

Bede described Orkney as 'lying in the ocean beyond Britain . . . at its back, where it is open to the boundless seas.' Like most early writers, he ignored the more distant Shetland; to him, Orkney was the *terra incognita* of the north. In somewhat more evocative words, Orkney is like a herd of sleeping whales, peaceful mounds with awful potentials. That is how George Mackay Brown imagined they appeared to the earliest colonists:

'The first Orkney peoples . . . sailed north into the widening light . . . Beyond the savage bulk of Cape Wrath there was empty ocean until in a summer dawn they saw the Orkneys like sleeping whales . . .'

Although the Latin word for a whale is *orca*, the islands are not named after whales, but probably from the Celtic *Inse Orc*, the Isles of Boars. The Orcs may have been a Pictish tribe which lived there. The suffix 'ey' is Old Norse for 'islands': hence Orkney, and properly not 'the Orkneys' or 'Orkney Islands'. The Roman author Diodorus Siculus (a younger contemporary of Julius Caesar) called the promontory where, he said, Britain terminated in the north, Orkan; and later Latin writers refer to Orkney under the plural of that name Orcades.

Fig. 3.
Map of Orkney.

Man arrived in Orkney around 3500 BC, more than two millennia after the Ice Sheet finally retreated from Scotland, and the islands have been linked and bound to human history ever since – Neolithic farmers, Bronze Age craftsmen, Iron Age builders, Viking warriors, Scottish adventurers, mediaeval traders, British servicemen, and many others. All of them have left their mark, most notably those who stayed to fight the land and the climate to herd animals and grow crops. For this reason the natural history of Orkney cannot be separated from its human history: the voles which are the prey of harriers and kestrels were brought by man over 4000 years ago (p. 126), and the Curlews which congregate on Orkney fields in their hundreds have increased as the hill land has been claimed by modern-day farmers.

But Orkney is not simply farmland. It is hill and moor, sea and dune,

Fig. 4.
An aerial view of the
South Isles of Orkney,
with the Churchill
Barriers, constructed
from concrete blocks
during World War II by
Italian prisoners of war
to keep enemy shipping
out of Scapa Flow. They
link Mainland (fore-
ground) with Laman,
Glimsholm, Burray and
South Ronaldsay;
beyond are the Pentland
Skerries with
Scotland in the far
distance (Photo:
Charles Tait).

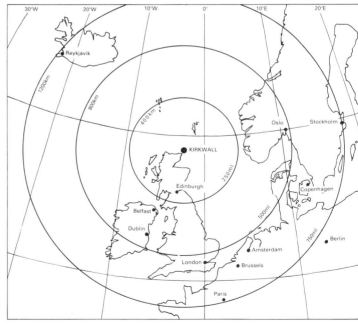

Fig. 5.
Distances of Orkney
from other places in
Europe. Norway and
Denmark are closer than
the English capital.

loch and marsh, water and sky in the fullest sense. Eric Linklater, himself an Orcadian wrote about it thus:

'There is, indeed, a power in the land, or in the broad sky enclosing it that may take perpetual captive those who are rash enough to open their eyes to the endlessly flowing line of its hills, their ears to the curlew's cry and the bourdoun of the sea, their hearts to the northern peace. On a fine morning, when the winds are still and the lakes relume an azure sweep of sky – vacant but for a curd of cloud, a mallard and its mate – there is a hush like the drifting of the young earth, not wakened yet, in the innocence of time . . . You too fall silent and catch with livelier ear the small bright talk of linnets in the heather, the creaking fall of a lapwing, the tentative voice of a plover or the thresh of a rising swan, and far away the Atlantic rolling its organ-tongue in a cavern of the western cliffs.'

Orkney lies between 58° 41′N and 59° 24′N latitude and 2° 22′W and 4° 25′W longitude. This means that it lies at approximately the latitude of Leningrad or the southern tip of Greenland. Kirkwall is nearer to Oslo than London, and, perhaps more relevantly, also closer to the Arctic Circle; it is more or less equidistant from Reykjavik, Stockholm, Berlin, Brussels, and Paris. It is as far from London as London is from Rome.

The county stretches 53 miles from south to north, and 23 miles from west to east, occupying about 240,000 acres (100,000 hectares). It is divided into about 70 islands (the exact number depending on the definition of when a rock is regarded as being an island), of which 18 were inhabited by 19,040 people at the 1981 census (plus another three islands with only light-house keepers). The main Shetland group lies about 50 miles north of North Ronaldsay, in the main Orkney group, with Fair Isle (which is part of Shetland) lying almost exactly half-way between Orkney and the main part of Shetland. The main island of Orkney is known as 'the Mainland'

It is impractical to give the detailed locations of all the places mentioned in the text of this book. Readers are recommended to refer to the Ordnance Survey 1:50,000 series sheets nos 5, 6 and 7, or Bartholomew's 1:100,000 sheet no. 61.

Fig. 6.
Looking northwards from John o'Groats across the unusually placid waters of the Pentland Firth to Stroma and Orkney (Photo: *R. J. Berry*)

(Pomona on some older maps), and contains more than half the land area, the only towns (Kirkwall and Stromness), and three-quarters of the population. A daily car ferry connects Stromness with Scrabster in Caithness, and there are regular flights to Inverness, Aberdeen and other Scottish cities from Kirkwall Airport. In every way, the Mainland dominates Orkney.

Islands and People

About 330 BC, a Greek explorer Pytheas of Marseilles circumnavigated Orkney and claimed to have sighted the edge of the world (*ultima thule*). On a clear day it is possible to see three points of land from the northern limit of Orkney, Fair Isle, Fitful Head, and Foula, all of them in Shetland. The most distant of these is Foula, which is therefore claimed by its inhabitants as being the 'edge of the world'. In AD 43 the Roman fleet of Claudius entered into a non-aggression pact with the Orcadians; Tacitus records in his *Life* of Agricola, that after the battle of Mons Graupius in AD 89, a Roman fleet subdued Orkney.

But all that was before even Orkney folk history. Later travellers left more detailed records, most notably among earlier visitors James Wallace in 1693 and John Brand in 1701. However the first complete description was by John Tudor in a book *The Orkneys and Shetland* (1883). He begins by describing the isolation of the Northern Isles, which is a part of their attractive mystery; and by drawing attention to misconceptions which are still common:

'Lying to the north of the most extreme northern point of the British Mainland, exposed to the full force of the Atlantic rollers and the hardly less turbulent surges of the wild North Sea, and surrounded by some of the fiercest tideways in the world, one cannot wonder that till comparatively recent years, the Orkneys and Shetland should to the average Englishman, or Scotsman too for that matter, have been geographical expressions and nothing more.

'Most people know better now-a-days: but still even educated people are apt to be somewhat confused in their ideas about the two groups, and to have a vague impression: that the Orkneys and Shetland are one and the same thing; that they consist of some scattered islands not much larger than the Scilly Isles; and that they are inhabited by a semi-civilized race, who live chiefly on sea-fowl and their eggs, and are in urgent need of missionaries to convert them from their semi-heathen practices.'

Weather

In general, the Orkney climate is remarkably equable; it can be described technically as 'hyperoceanic', a characteristic which it shares with the Western Isles and Shetland, and the peninsulas of the extreme west and north coasts of Scotland.

James Wallace in 1700 commented that 'notwithstanding this Country (Orkney) is so far removed to the North, the Air is temperate and wholsome, agreeing well with those Constitutions that can endure a little Cold.' Perhaps more accurately Hamish Blair, writing during the 1939–45 war, called it: 'All bloody clouds and bloody rains.' Stevenson's great lyric that has the lines, 'Blows the wind today, and the sun and rain are flying . . . Standing stones on the vacant wine-red moor . . . the houses of the silent vanished races . . .' might almost describe a typical Orkney day.

Fig. 7.
*Atlantic waves pound
the cliffs of Westray
one of the northern
Orkney isles, where a
lone Shag braves the
elements* (Photo:
Andrew Berry).

Much of lowland Orkney is described by meteorologists as 'fairly warm and rather dry', a category absent in Shetland and the Hebrides; this gives way at about 100 ft (30 m) to a 'cool and moist' climate, which occurs at sea level in Shetland and the west.

In Orkney, the most important factors are wind, which is felt to its full extent because of the smooth relief; and the long hours of daylight in summer (in midsummer, it is never really dark, whereas in midwinter the sun is above the horizon for barely six hours) (Fig. 4).

Perhaps the most surprising fact about Orkney weather is its mildness. During the months of December, January and February, the average daily maximum temperature in Kirkwall is similar to that in Edinburgh and

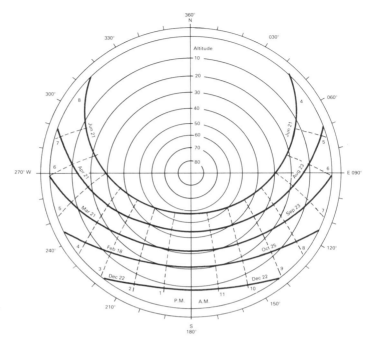

Fig. 8.
The height of the sun
at Kirkwall at
different times of
year. At mid-winter
the sun is above the
horizon for less than
six hours a day.

Glasgow, and less than 1°C lower than London, while the daily minimum in the same months is on average higher than in Edinburgh, Glasgow and London. The average date of the first air frost in Kirkwall is 20 November (earliest recorded 1951–1972, 13 October), and of the last 23 April (latest recorded 30 May). Snow or sleet falls on an average of 64 days a year, but rarely lies long. It is recorded as covering half or more of the ground at Kirkwall Airport on only 15 days a year on average (compared with 28 at Lerwick, in Shetland, 16 in Edinburgh, but only 12 in Stornoway and 4 in Tiree in the Hebrides). Not surprisingly, Lerwick temperatures are generally similar but slightly lower than in Kirkwall. The summers are cool, similar to Shetland, but also to Lapland and Alaska. Orkney has a growth season (mean temperature above 6°C) of five to six months, similar to the Pennine or Welsh plateaux. Lowland England has seven to eight months suitable for growing corn crops, and compared to this the Orkney climate is marginal, and can be disastrous in bad seasons.

The mean monthly temperatures in southern Greenland, the Falkland Islands, and South Orkney (which is part of the British Antarctic Territory) are given for comparison in Table 1. The enormous influence of the Gulf Stream is obvious. Port Stanley in the Falklands is cooler than Kirkwall, despite being more than 7° latitude nearer the equator (about the latitude of London in the northern hemisphere).

The other point to make about temperatures in Orkney is the comparatively small change between summer and winter. The difference between the average daily maximum at Kirkwall in January and in July is 9.6°C (9.3°C in Lerwick), whereas in Edinburgh it is 12.9°C, and 15.5°C at Kew.

Table 1   Average Monthly Temperatures °C – Mean of Daily Minimum and Maximum.

	Jan	Feb	Mar	Apr	May	Jun	Jul	Aug	Sep	Oct	Nov	Dec	Annual
Lerwick, Shetland 60° 8'N 1° 11'W	3.0	2.8	3.8	5.4	7.6	10.1	12.7	12.9	10.6	8.5	5.8	4.00	7.1
Kirkwall, Orkney 58° 59'N 2° 58'W	3.6	4.4	4.6	6.2	8.5	10.9	12.2	12.3	11.2	9.2	6.0	4.4	7.7
Cape Wrath, Sutherland 58° 37'N 5° 01'W	4.3	3.9	5.1	6.3	8.3	10.7	11.8	12.3	11.3	9.5	6.7	5.3	8.0
Stornoway, Hebrides 58° 12'N 6° 23'W	4.3	4.4	5.7	6.9	9.3	11.6	13.2	13.3	11.7	9.3	6.9	5.4	8.5
Lairg, Sutherland 58° 01'N 4° 35'W	1.1	1.7	4.1	6.5	8.9	12.3	12.7	12.7	11.4	8.1	3.9	1.9	7.1
Kew, London 51° 28'N 00° 10'W	4.2	4.6	6.7	9.4	12.4	15.9	17.6	17.3	14.3	11.1	7.6	5.4	10.6
Nanortalik, Greenland 60° 10'N 45° 05'W	-3.3	-2.4	-1.7	0.7	4.0	5.5	6.5	7.0	5.8	2.7	-1.0	-2.2	1.8
Stanley, Falkland Is. 51° 42'S 57° 52'W	9.0	9.4	8.4	6.0	3.8	2.3	2.1	2.6	3.5	5.6	7.5	8.4	5.7
Signy Is., South Orkney 60° 43'S 45° 36'W	0.7	1.1	0.4	-1.8	-6.1	-8.7	-10.4	-8.5	-4.7	-2.3	-1.1	-0.2	-3.5

Orkney has winter temperatures like those of the Black Sea, and summer ones like the White Sea.

The rainfall over most of Orkney ranges from 35 to 40 in (890 to 1020mm), more than Edinburgh and London, but less than Glasgow and Torquay. It is spread relatively evenly throughout the year (Table 2), with rain falling on a mean of 241 days each year, ranging from 16 days in each of the driest months of May and June to 25 days in December and January. Except in sea mist, visibility is extremely good. Temperature inversions are rare due to the small land area and frequent winds, so persistent fog is rare. The haars, cold sea mists which bedevil places along the Scottish mainland, are much less common in Orkney. Thunder only occurs on 4 or 5 days a year, compared with 7 or 8 days in Edinburgh and Glasgow, and 15 to 20 days in southern England. This means that lightning, and lightning-induced fires, are uncommon in Orkney. Even nearby Caithness has much more lightning than Orkney, due to convection currents over the land.

Orkney has more sunshine than Shetland, but less than most other places in Scotland (Fort William and Braemar have less than Kirkwall (Table 3)). But on the debit side, even Manchester has more hours of sunshine than Kirkwall (1334 hours as compared with 1179).

Finally, we come to wind, the most noticeable feature of Orkney weather. Gales may occur at any time of the year, although most commonly during the winter months (Table 4). The highest gust ever recorded in Britain at a low-level site was 136 miles per hour (61m per sec) at Kirkwall on 7 February 1969. A gale only slightly less ferocious removed 7000 poultry houses and 86,000 hens on 15 January 1952. Calm conditions are relatively infrequent (Table 5). Wind directions are fairly evenly distributed around the compass, although the commonest blow is from the quadrant between south and west. There is an increase of easterly winds during spring and early summer.

Table 2   *Mean Rainfall (inches)*

	Jan	Feb	Mar	Apr	May	Jun	Jul	Aug	Sep	Oct	Nov	Dec	Annual Total
Lerwick	4.52	3.31	3.09	2.71	2.20	2.20	2.53	2.76	3.75	4.44	4.63	4.44	40.49
Kirkwall	4.25	3.15	2.68	2.60	1.93	2.04	2.64	2.87	3.74	4.53	4.41	4.53	39.59
Cape Wrath	4.29	3.31	3.07	2.84	2.40	3.19	3.55	3.86	4.37	5.20	4.65	4.81	45.55
Stornoway	4.18	2.68	2.29	2.33	2.29	2.56	3.08	3.35	3.75	4.38	4.50	4.06	39.45
Lairg (Central Highlands)	4.02	3.23	2.68	2.88	3.27	3.11	3.59	4.33	3.59	4.14	4.18	4.57	43.58
Kew	2.14	1.55	1.46	1.81	1.81	1.72	2.44	2.24	1.98	2.25	2.45	2.06	23.95

Table 3   *Duration of Bright Sunshine (monthly total, in hours)*

	Jan	Feb	Mar	Apr	May	June	Jul	Aug	Sep	Oct	Nov	Dec	Annual Total
Lerwick	25	54	86	137	158	152	131	116	99	62	33	15	1067
Kirkwall	**33**	**63**	**99**	**152**	**163**	**160**	**138**	**127**	**107**	**74**	**39**	**24**	**1179**
Stornoway	37	66	108	153	186	173	132	135	106	76	48	26	1244
Edinburgh	41	68	99	149	176	183	169	147	120	91	52	37	1332
Kew	48	65	112	162	203	214	197	183	143	102	58	43	1529

Table 4   *Average Number of Days with Gales.*

	Jan	Feb	Mar	Apr	May	Jun	Jul	Aug	Sep	Oct	Nov	Dec	Annual
Lerwick	7.9	5.3	5.9	2.0	1.1	0.9	0.5	0.4	2.1	4.3	4.5	8.5	43.5
Kirkwall	**3.9**	**3.5**	**3.7**	**1.8**	**0.9**	**0.6**	**0.3**	**0.6**	**1.2**	**2.9**	**4.1**	**5.6**	**29.1**
Wick	2.1	1.5	1.7	1.1	0.2	0.1	0.2	0.3	0.7	1.3	1.3	1.9	12.2
Tiree	7.6	4.5	3.6	1.5	0.6	0.4	0.3	0.7	1.7	3.4	4.5	6.4	35.2
Leuchars (St Andrews)	2.1	1.2	1.3	0.4	0.4	0.4	0.1	0.2	0.6	0.8	0.8	1.3	9.5

Table 5 *Wind Strength*

Strength (Beaufort Scale)	0	1	2	3	4	5	6	7	8	9	9+
Wind speed (knots)	0	1–3	4–6	7–10	11–16	17–21	22–27	28–33	34–40	41–47	48+
% through year											
Lerwick	2.5	3.6	10.1	21.9	30.4	15.1	10.2	4.4	1.5	0.2	0.1
Kirkwall	2.8	5.7	10.8	22.6	31.3	14.1	8.5	2.8	1.0	0.2	0.1
Stornoway	5.8	7.5	7.7	15.2	26.3	16.4	12.0	5.9	2.6	0.4	0.1

The Natural History of Orkney

Geologically Orkney is an extension of Caithness, but the isolation and exposure of Orkney mean that there are fewer species of animals and plants there than might be expected if the Pentland Firth did not exist, and if Orkney habitats were more sheltered. This does not mean that Orkney is a biological desert – far from it – but it means that the stresses of natural selection and the vagaries of colonisation have affected the islands' flora and terrestrial fauna. The consequences of these pressures will appear during descriptions of different groups in the following pages.

Orkney's natural environment has been surprisingly neglected by naturalists when compared with other areas of the British Isles. *The New Orkney Book* (1966), produced by the Orkney Education Department as background material for use in Orkney schools compares the Orkney flora disparagingly with that of Sutherland. Orkney never had, for example, an ecologist of the calibre of C. B. Crampton, whose detailed descriptions of Caithness vegetation in 1908 provide an invaluable background to present-day studies. The Orcadian botanists of Crampton's time were primarily collectors and taxonomists, and their notes give little indication of vegetation types. Again, professional insect collectors visited Shetland regularly in the latter part of the 19th century, but paid relatively fleeting visits to Orkney. E. B. Ford comments in his New Naturalist on *Moths* that

'the moths of Orkney either resemble those of the mainland or are distinct forms: they are not generally transitional to the Shetland forms . . . however, we have far less information on the entomology of Orkney than of Shetland, for collectors who have penetrated so far tend to go on to the latter group where rare species and unusual forms are known to exist.'

Shetland has long been a mecca for ornithologists, but once again, bird-watchers have tended to bypass Orkney despite the fact that the group has the second biggest seabird colony in the UK (Westray) – only St Kilda has more birds – and 88 regular breeding species compared to 64 on Shetland.

Work carried out in Orkney has rarely appeared in accessible publications. The most important early work was Buckley and Harvie-Brown's *Vertebrate Fauna of the Orkney Islands* (1891), but this was not followed up until two local people produced short books in the 1970's, Eddie Balfour on *Orkney Birds* (1972) and Miss Elaine Bullard a *Checklist of Vascular Plants in Orkney* (1975). There are other works of course, ranging from Low's *Fauna Orcadensis* (written in the 1790s), to Robert Rendall's *Orkney*

Shore (1960) and William Groundwater's *Birds and Mammals of Orkney* (1974), but it is nonetheless true that Orkney has been much more poorly provided with natural history literature than most other parts of the United Kingdom. Certainly nowhere else as intrinsically interesting as Orkney is so starved of relevant writings.

The first comprehensive account of Orkney geology was published by Ben Peach and John Horne in 1880. This was followed up by a work by a native Orcadian who became Director of the Geological Survey of Great Britain, Sir John Flett. He supervised the preparation of the Geological Survey's *Memoir of the Orkney Islands*, published in 1935. This has been followed by the Geological Survey's volume on *Orkney and Shetland* (1976) in the British Regional Geology series, by a geophysical survey of Orkney (1968) and a *Geochemical Atlas for Orkney* (1978), which is relevant for agricultural analysis. The geochemical survey coincided with a more detailed exploration for uranium deposits which provided much local controversy, but little economic interest.

The first major publication on Orkney general natural history for nearly a century was the *Natural Environment of Orkney* (1975), the proceedings of a two day meeting sponsored by the Nature Conservancy Council. This present book depends heavily on that symposium, but it is also more inclusive. Its aim is to summarize as far as possible all that is known about Orkney natural history so that residents and visitors, amateurs and professionals alike will be guided and, hopefully, stimulated to learn more about 'the sleeping whales' that bask in the waters to the north of Scotland. There they will learn of the environment that shaped the Orcadian written about by Robert Rendall:

> *God, Who in days of old*
> *Created the sea*
> *And the skies – O there behold*
> *What beauties be –*
> *These treeless islands set*
> *Where the wild-goose flies,*
> *Lest men should e'er forget*
> *The sea and the skies.*

2 Biological History

The two horns of the Orkney South Isles enclosing Scapa Flow approach within six miles (ten kms) of the mainland of Scotland, with Hoy to the west and South Ronaldsay to the east. The Pentland Skerries and Stroma lie in the Pentland Firth itself. This turbulent channel has been a major factor in the misinterpretation of the Orkney fauna and flora, for it is uncertain when it came into being. During the Pleistocene, Orkney was fully glaciated. At the maximum glaciation, ice from Norway probably covered Shetland, Orkney, and Scotland; the final glacial period was a much more local affair, with ice passing over Orkney in a north easterly direction, and meeting the local Shetland ice cap between Orkney and Fair Isle. As the ice melted, the sea-level rose, and so did the land, released from the weight of overlying ice. Was there then a period when dry land existed between Caithness and Orkney, allowing the islands to be colonized by terrestrial organisms?

Fig. 10.
Southern Mainland
under cloud, looking
westwards towards
Hoy. (Photo:
Charles Tait).

If there was a land-bridge, its subsequent breaching would have isolated the Orkney populations, and they would now persist as relics of formerly much more widespread populations; if there was no post-Pleistocene land-bridge, the Orkney fauna and flora will have opportunistically colonized the islands at any time since the climate ameliorated, and hence will be much younger. Moreover, a colonizing group will almost certainly carry

less genetical variation than its ancestral population, and possess a different spectrum of inherited traits. It may then show a significant amount of differentiation by chance. This has happened, for example, with field mice (*Apodemus sylvaticus*) in Shetland and the Hebrides which are all more closely related to Norwegian animals than Scottish ones and which were once divided into three distinct species: *A. fridariensis* on Shetland, *A. hirtensis* on St Kilda, and *A. hebridensis* on many of the other Hebrides. It is now accepted that the field mice were carried to the different islands as commensals by human colonizers, and in some cases their establishment may have been comparatively recent.

Are the Orkney animals and plants merely survivors of those species which made their way across a land-bridge from Scotland – and therefore reflect no more than a typical segment of the north Scottish fauna and flora limited through extinction and the failure of late arrivals to get over the bridge – or are they a unique assemblage of colonists who have managed to reach the islands by a variety of means and establish themselves there?

The traditional understanding is that Orkney has a relict fauna and flora, but it is based on a mis-reading of biological facts rather than any geological evidence for a post-Pleistocene bridge. Most of the mis-reading can be laid at the feet of a distinguished mammalogist, M. A. C. Hinton, who worked at the Natural History Museum in London. He recognized that the Orkney vole has no living relatives in Great Britain. However he classified it as a close relative of an extinct vole, *Microtus corneri* which he believed to be widespread in the tundra of southern England during the Pleistocene. He argued that *M. corneri* followed the retreating ice-sheet northwards through England and Scotland, and into Orkney where it evolved into the Orkney vole, *M. orcadensis*. A subsequent wave of immigration brought another vole species, *M. agrestis*, across the land-bridge where the Straits of Dover are now, and this new vole (he believed) out-competed *M. corneri/orcadensis* which became extinct on the mainland of Britain. Because the Pentland Firth bridge had disappeared by the time that *M. agrestis* got to the north of Scotland, the Orkney voles were protected, and survived as a relict.

This story is recounted by Harrison Matthews (in his New Naturalist on *British Mammals*, 1952), although he obviously had doubts, because he notes, 'it may be the whole story, but on the other hand it may have to be modified in the future when more detailed research has been done on the genetics of voles.' However, geographers tended to be taken in by the biologists' assumptions. In the New Naturalist on the *Sea Coast* (1953), J. A. Steers writes,

'Probably the islands were separated from the mainland before the advent of the ice, but the depths in the Pentland Firth today suggest that eustatic movements of sea level would have been sufficient to cause a junction with the mainland, probably at the time the Dogger Bank was land. At this time *there must have been a connection to account for the similarity of fauna between the islands and the mainland* (my italics). The islands as we now see them are, therefore, of post-Glacial origin.'

More work on the genetics of Orkney voles has been done (p. 125), but other considerations show that Hinton's interpretation is wrong.

The Orkney vole is not in fact a distinct species, but belongs to *Microtus arvalis*, which is widespread in continental Europe. *M. arvalis* and *M. agrestis* live together over large areas of Europe; there is no reason to expect that *M. arvalis* would become extinct through competition with *M. agrestis* in Britain.

The range of *M. agrestis* extends further north in Scandinavia than that of *M. arvalis*. It would therefore be expected to colonize tundra habitats before *M. arvalis*. (*M. arvalis* is not related to a tundra living '*M. correri*'. Indeed, this latter species is a rather doubtful one: some of the fossil skulls attributed to it belong to a form called *M. oeconomus*, which does not now occur in Britain).

If the 'relict' theory is true, *M. arvalis* might be expected to be found on other islands which have been separated from Britain in post-glacial times. However, elsewhere in Britain it is found only on Guernsey (where it may indeed be a relict); it is not found, for example, on any of the Hebrides.

It seems almost certain that voles colonized Orkney by some other route than *via* Caithness. We do not know how they managed to get to the islands. Since their closest relatives today are in south east Europe, it seems likely that they were introduced by man, although it is not impossible that they arrived on a floating tree trunk or other form of raft. The method they used is irrelevant; the important point is that they cannot be cited as evidence for a land-bridge.

There are, not surprisingly, other geographical puzzles in the Orkney fauna, but it is the origin of the Orkney vole that has been the base for biological speculation about a land-bridge.

Land between Orkney and Caithness?

Is there geological evidence for a land-bridge? The two deep channels around Orkney (the Westray and Stronsay Firths separating the North Isles from the Mainland and Rousay, and the Pentland Firth), were once river valleys draining eastwards into a north-flowing river, and probably originated around the time of the volcanic episode in the Tertiary which produced the mountains of Skye and Mull. The Pentland Firth is not a recent breach in the Caithness rocks.

The Admiralty Chart now gives the depth of the Pentland Firth as 53 fathoms (105m). It is generally assumed that the rise of sea-level produced by the Pleistocene ice melting was about 300 ft (100m), which would imply that there might just have been dry land between Scotland and Orkney in post-glacial times. However, the Hudson Bay area of Canada seems to have risen more than 900 ft (300m) as a result of being relieved of an ice cap nearly two miles thick. Orkney never carried ice of this thickness, but an Orkney land-bridge cannot be ruled out.

The most direct evidence about a land-bridge comes from topographic studies of the sea-floor of the Pentland Firth. Most of the sea cliffs around Shetland continue down into the sea to a depth of about 45 fathoms (90m), where the sea-floor becomes flat. Around Orkney and westwards along the north coast of Scotland, the slope extends to 35 fathoms (70m). The sea rose so fast after the melting of the ice sheets of the last glacial period that little cliff erosion took place. The result was a coastline substantially as we know it today; the coast of north and north-east Scotland, Orkney and Shetland seems to have developed over a long period due to marine erosion at a number of levels within a height range of about 260 ft (80m) above the break of slope. The lack of any substantial wave-cut platform at

the present sea level proves that the present cliffs owe little of their retreat
to erosion by the sea at its present level. The current coastal profile was
largely created before the glaciation.

An interesting feature of the Caithness coast is a raised wave-cut rock
platform along the foot of the cliffs, about 10 ft (3m) above sea-level. This
is mostly substantial enough to protect the cliffs behind it from marine
erosion, and it carries beach material and relic stacks. A similar platform
occurs around Scapa Flow. This platform probably represents the main
late-glacial shoreline formed during the so-called Loch Lomond Readvance. It can only be the result of a unique period of marine erosion occurring during renewed glacial conditions after the last main glaciation. This
suggests that immediately after the main deglaciation, while the sea level
was still low, rivers cut into the valleys filled with glacial till. As the sea
level rose in response to the melting of ice elsewhere, these valleys filled
with mud and sand. The rate of isostatic rise of land as it was released from
the overlaying weight of ice increased and eventually matched the eustatic
rise of the sea (as water was freed by the melting of the ice) at about the
time of the Loch Lomond Readvance. The wave-cut platform was formed.
The isostatic rise continued as the eustatic rise decreased, with the net result
that sea-level fell again relative to the land. Peat started to form down to sea-
level. After some time, sea-level again rose and drowned peat in Caithness,
Orkney and Shetland. The still-rising sea is cutting into the wave-cut platform in the northern part of Orkney at the present.

It would be wrong to be dogmatic about the existence of a land-bridge:

Fig. 11.
Rock platforms
extend far out from
many of the islands;
at one time the whole
of Orkney was
attached to the north-
east corner of
Scotland (Photo:
R. S. Moore).

in the *Lepidoptera of the Orkney Islands* (1983), Lorimer quotes J. D. Peacock of The British Geological Survey as believing that 'it is highly unlikely Orkney was connected to the mainland after the arctic Loch Lomond Re-advance, 10,000 to 11,000 years ago,' while Bailey in his *Orkney* (1971) gives his opinion that the Pentland Firth remained dry land up to the Boreal period, about 9,500 years ago. All that it is safe to say is that any land-bridge cannot have persisted for long in conditions when animals and plants could pass over it.

The Pattern of Vegetation

The extreme oceanic conditions of the islands make it unlikely that the vegetation reached the climatic optimum of north western Europe five to six thousand years ago; they probably never advanced beyond the birch-hazel scrub typical of the mid Flandrian period. However, the presumed absence of grazing mammals and the unlikelihood of lightning-induced fires in summer, make it very possible for that scrub to have formed a low but almost complete cover from the shores of sea, lochs and fens to some way up the hills. Without a reasonably unbroken cover, trees, however small and scrubby, could not have survived, yet the widespread discoveries of hazel nuts show very clearly that they did. This low cover would have allowed the development of a rich understory of herbs, grasses, sedges and ferns, extremely vulnerable to fire and all very tempting to the domestic animals introduced by Neolithic man, the first traces of whom date from

Fig. 12. (opposite page)
On the northern shore of Westray the sandstone rocks form a series of flat beds into the Atlantic (Photo: *Rawdon Goodier*).

Fig. 13. (opposite page)
Land, sand and sea in Orkney (Photo: *R. S. Moore*).

Fig. 14.
Tundra on the Hoy hills, with Graemsay and Orkney Mainland in the background (Photo: *Rawdon Goodier*).

about 3500 BC. Above the tree line, the hills probably retained their post-glacial tundra-type vegetation which still persists in parts of Hoy, perhaps with a higher proportion of lime-loving plants (such as *Dryas*) which are scarce today. The many areas of fresh water would have been surrounded by willows and reeds and typical fen vegetation.

Direct evidence for this early scrubland is slight. Few C14-dated samples have been taken from deep peat and loch deposits (and only in such anaerobic conditions can such evidence survive); and in well-drained situations peat did not form, if at all, until long after man had lived and farmed in the islands. Most C14-dated pollen samples examined in Orkney have been taken from the much later blanket peat.

Whether it was man or climate that caused the birch-hazel scrub to decline is uncertain, although present opinion inclines to the former. Certain pollen studies indicate a largely treeless landscape since at least 4300 years ago (BP, or Before Present). The dating of a settlement at the Knap of Howar to 4800 BP puts the erection of these earliest known domestic buildings in Orkney very close indeed to the sudden decline of the birch/hazel scrub around 5000 BP, as dated from samples taken in the West Mainland. Possibly the transition from birch-hazel scrub occurred in two phases, with woody species disappearing first whilst tall herb and fern communities remained, followed by grazing and the change to pasture vegetation. Certainly it all took place over a short period of time. The presence of tree remains found preserved in peat below sea-level has not yet been satisfactorily explained.

The birch-hazel scrub declined less rapidly in more sheltered sites and sufficient pockets survived throughout the Neolithic period to permit some regeneration in the early part of the Bronze Age; one pocket still survives in Berriedale in north Hoy (p. 71).

Barley (in its primitive form as bere) and wheat were grown by the early inhabitants of both Knap of Howar and Skara Brae. They kept cattle, which were smaller than Neolithic ones elsewhere, almost equal numbers of sheep, which were probably not unlike the seaweed eating race still living on North Ronaldsay, and a few pigs. Animals were slaughtered young, presumably because it was difficult to provide winter feed. Birds and littoral molluscs were eaten. In the Skara Brae houses there are water-tight boxes which may have been used for keeping shell-fish until they cleared themselves of grit. The bones of large saithe and cod imply that the early Orcadians had boats good enough to fish some distance off-shore.

Neolithic Orkney had no blanket peat. C14 dates show that this began to form between 3000 and 3400 years ago. Thus there were nearly 2000 years between the disappearance of the birch-hazel scrub and the appearance of the now familiar 'grim and inhospitable' dark moorlands. Unfortunately, pollen analyses on this period are few in number. They indicate considerable differences from place to place and are generally unhelpful since a number of species are common to both the tall herb and fern communities which were (and are) the relics of the scrub understory, and to fen and pasture. It is therefore not easy to distinguish between these vegetation types. Weeds of cultivation were present, and there is an indication that heather tended to replace the lost scrub for a time, but was then replaced by grasses until just before the onset of peat when it expanded rapidly again.

At the beginning of this 'open' period there was a decline in ferns which are readily damaged by grazing; towards its end there was a short period of increase of such plants as Ribwort (*Plantago lanceolata*), Buttercups and some of the rosette-forming Compositae which are a strong indication of an increase in grazing pressure. There are also indications in the earliest blanket peat of burnings. Between about 3900 and 2900 BP the human population seems to have been relatively low. Fire and animals cleared the land of its earlier cover, the more open landscape removed shelter and made for a harsher climate – how much did this contribute to peat formation following the inevitable water-logging of tree-less soils and why did the human population apparently decline? It is interesting to note that recent studies on relict woodland in Hoy show a perfectly normal growth rate, so that present-day lack of trees in Orkney cannot be due to climate alone.

The Orkney landscape has been intimately influenced by humans ever since their first arrival. Nearly half the land area is improved pasture or agricultural land. But the unimproved land has also been much modified by human activity: even cliff face vegetation was, until recently, grazed wherever sheep could gain access, and the blanket of Wood-rush on some of the highest Hoy cliffs has increased in thickness within living memory, apparently as a result of sheep being taken off the hills. In the 19th century especially, labour was so plentiful that cattle could be herded all day, and food carried to pigs penned a mile or more from the steading. Heather-dominated moorland, which may seem natural vegetation *par excellence*, is in fact a human creation maintained by man-made fire (although it is now

Fig. 15.
Crofts just above the shore. Many of the more isolated buildings are now deserted and ruined (Photo: *R. S. Moore*).

able to perpetuate itself in Orkney where there are no sources of seed for trees).

Most freshwater habitats have also been modified to a greater or less extent. Small burns, in particular, have been artificially straightened for drainage. Many fens and marshes have been completely drained, and all lowland freshwaters collect farm effluent and fertilisers.

Despite these changes the actual species of wild plants in Orkney are much as they have ever been: the Meadowsweet and Marsh Marigolds in ditches near Kirkwall Airport, the Crowberry growing under the radio-telephone masts on Wideford Hill, all inhabited Orkney before man. Even Bracken was present 6000 years ago. The main changes have been in their abundance and distribution.

Rocks

CHAPTER 3

God, Who in days of old
Created the sea
And the skies – O there behold
What beauties be –
These treeless islands set
Where the wild-goose flies,
Lest men should e'er forget
The sea and the skies.
Robert Rendall.

Orkney is really a piece of the Caithness plateau, scissored from Scotland by the Pentland Firth and the channels between the individual islands. It is best imagined as an undulating plateau tilted to the north and east, with a major central structural depression (Scapa Flow) inland from the residual massif of Hoy. As the land has sunk, a mosaic of islands, firths and straits has been produced.

Fig. 16.
Sandstone cliffs
exposed to the
Atlantic; evidence of
a platform can be
seen at sea-level and
blocks have fallen,
leaving cavities in the
cliff face. (Photo:
Tom Kent Collection,
Orkney Library).

The land of Orkney is not particularly old by Scottish standards. The foundation rocks were folded into the Caledonian mountains 400 million years ago, and have been undergoing erosion ever since. Their debris washed into the seas surrounding the mountains, and formed sediments which compacted to become the Old Red Sandstones of the north and east of Scotland. These basement rocks crop out in the Stromness area between Yesnaby and Graemsay. The largest forms the hill of Brinkies Brae, which used to be quarried for building stone for Stromness. These were once islands; they are bounded by beach deposits, broken from the Old Red Sandstones which form most of modern Orkney.

The Old Red Sandstones were formed about 380 million years ago, when fish first became common. They are often red in colour (as in Devonshire and Herefordshire), but in Orkney the colour can easily be exaggerated. The cliffs of Hoy are magnificently red, as are the stones of St Magnus Cathedral in Kirkwall, but brown, grey and ochre are more usual colours.

Fig. 17.
A mosaic of flagstone, the polygonal desiccation cracks filled with sand, forms terraces at the sea's edge, the result of an intrusion running at right angles to the shore along a fault (Photo: *John Parnell*).

Many of the rocks are flagstones, layers of rock divided into thin and regular beds. Some are so finely divided that the layers can be split off readily for roofing flags; others are thicker and make good paving stones; others again are slab-like, and make easily fashioned building stone. They comprise numerous narrow belts of intensely shattered rock, some of which contain metalliferous minerals.

Orkney rocks are often not very hard. Although grind-stones used to be made from some of them, they were tough enough to grind only bere, primitive barley, which is relatively soft; millstone grit from the Pennines had to be imported to deal with oats.

Orkney geology has become topical as a result of exploration for oil. The offshore equivalents of some of the Orkney rocks may yield oil (see p. 42); although commercial amounts of oil are extremely unlikely to be discovered below Orkney itself, the rocks there serve as convenient models for study by petroleum geologists.

Fig. 18. Flagstones were a traditional roofing material for Orkney crofters' homes (Photo: Tom Kent Collection, Orkney Library).

Detailed Geology

Most of the folds affecting the Orkney sandstones are gentle, with low inclination. The few major folds have a northerly trend, the most important being the Eday and Deerness synclines. The more substantial faults are the North and East Scapa and the Brims-Risa Faults (Fig. 19). The latter two are reversed faults for at least part of their course. Faulting and small-scale folding is particularly prominent on the eastern side of the archipelago in North Ronaldsay, eastern Sanday, Stronsay, eastern Shapinsay, Deerness, and South Ronaldsay. These areas lie to the west of a major zone of faulting which occurs offshore, an extension of the Great Glen Fault of the Scottish mainland.

Much of the basal rock is a pinkish-grey granite with enclaves of gneiss and hornblended-pyroxene and mica-schist, particularly on Graemsay. It has not been radiometrically dated, but resembles rocks of the Moinian succession in the Altnaharra district of Sutherland. Before burial by Old Red Sandstone sediments, the basement inliers formed a range of small, steep-sided hills running north to north-west.

The oldest sedimentary rocks in Orkney are of Lower Old Red Sand-

Fig. 19.
Geological sketch
map of Orkney (from
Mykura, 1976).

stone age which crop out just north and west of the Yesnaby exposure of basement rock. These strata are tilted about 10° to the west, and were extensively eroded before being overlain by the Middle Old Red Sandstone rocks. At Warebeth, a mile west of Stromness a borehole revealed 200 ft (61 m) of purple siltstone, sandstone and breccia below the later flagstones.

There are two major divisions of the Middle Old Red Sandstone: the

Stromness and Rousay Groups of grey and black thinly bedded flagstones, clearly laid down in an extensive freshwater lake whose bed is now partly under the sea, partly exposed; and the Eday Group, composed largely of yellow and red sandstones.

The Stromness Flags contain many fish fossils, particularly in the Sandwick Fish Bed. This is exposed in a number of quarries in the west Mainland. Fossil fish have also been recorded on North Ronaldsay, Westray, Papa Westray, Rousay, Eday, Sanday, Stronsay, Shapinsay, South Ronaldsay and Hoy. The most common species are *Glyptolepis paucidens*, the crossopterygians *Osteolepis macrolepidotus* and *Gyroptychius agassizi*;

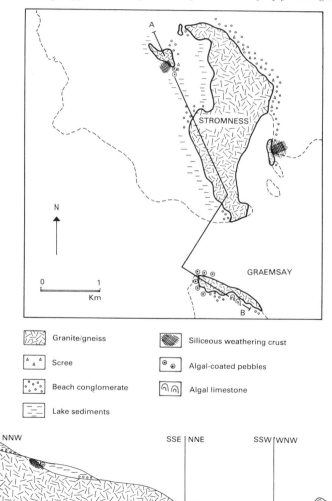

Fig. 20.
Geological section
across the south-west
of Mainland,
showing the different
rock types developed
around the 'islands'
of granitic basement
during early Middle
Red Sandstone times
(prepared by John
Parnell).

the placoderms *Coccosteus cuspidatus*, *Homosteus milleri* and *Pterichthyodes* spp; the acanthodians *Cheiracanthus murchisoni*, *Mescanthus peachi*, *Diplacanthus striatus*, *Rhadinacanthus longispinus* and *Cheirolepis trailli*; and the dipnoan (lung-fish) *Dipterus valenciennesi*; the actual composition and species proportions of the faunas differ somewhat in different deposits.

The profusion of fossil fish around Stromness was known more than a century and a half ago: an extensive collection by Professor Traill (p. 198) was identified by Louis Agassiz, and reported on at one of the early meetings of the British Association. Over 100 fossil fish specimens were exhibited in 1837 in the Stromness Museum. They became widely known through the writings of the Scottish stone-mason, Hugh Miller, whose *Footprints of the Creator* was sub-titled *The Asterolepis of Stromness* (rather ironically, since the fossil that Miller wrote about is not an *Asterolepis!*). Miller's work was part of the background which led Charles Darwin to his theory of evolution by natural selection. In the years when Miller was most active, Darwin was Secretary of the Geological Society.

The fossil-bearing beds are included in a sequence involving four phases which is repeated about 50 times:

Phase 1. A bed of black finely laminated siltstone and mudstone with a high carbonate and carbon content. Carbonate and carbon (organic matter) layers were deposited by the remains of seasonal algal blooms. This bed commonly contains abundant fish remains and appears to have been laid down during a quiescent period when little or no coarse sediment entered the lake and when the water, still shallow, was at its deepest in some cycles. In the Rousay Group, this bed is so carbonate rich as to be petrographically a limestone. Some laminates in the Lower Stromness Flags contain nodules of chert. They are of a type which are forming today in alkaline lakes in arid/sub-arid regions. In most cycles the laminate passes upward into the next phase.

Phase 2. Carbon-rich (bituminous) silty mudstone with thin, irregular laminae of siltstone and sandstone. These beds are characterized by numerous small structures consisting of fine sand or silt which appear to have been injected into finer sediment and then buckled during compaction. Calcareous mats based on blue-green algae (stromatolites) form sheets, mounds or orange-weathering limestones within these beds. During this phase bottom currents became active in the shallowing lake and the influx of fine sediment increased.

Phase 3. The overlying beds in the rhythm are lithologically similar to those of Phase 2, but are characterized by the presence of abundant sand-filled polygonal desiccation cracks. The lake had now become so shallow that the lake bottom was periodically exposed as an extensive mud-flat.

Phase 4. The uppermost beds in the rhythm are usually ripple-laminated, fine-grained sandstones and siltstones with desiccation cracks.

Fish fossils are found in only the first and occasionally the second phase of this cycle. It is possible the fish ran down the rivers to spawn in the Orcadian lake. A small branchiopod crustacean, *Asmussia murchisoniana*, whose living descendants are found in brackish waters, occurs commonly in the Rousay Flags. The thickness of individual rhythms commonly ranges from 10–30 ft (4–10 m), but the Sandwick Fish Bed has a thickness of 180–200 ft (55–60 m), which makes it a good stratigraphical marker. It occurs as two separate tiers at Birsay, showing an oscillation of the lake margin in this part during depositions.

The relationship between the Stromness and Rousay Flags, and the Eday Sandstones is shown in Table 6. The passage is fairly abrupt in Eday and Sanday, but elsewhere there is a transitional series interbedded with red and purple marls. These 'passage flags' are thickest in South Ronaldsay and south-east Mainland. The Eday Flags have a rhythmic sedimentation, but in contrast to the Stromness and Rousay Flags many of the rhythms

Table 6
The Rock Layers of Orkney (thickness in metres.)

STAGE		FISH FAUNA (Caithness, Orkney & Melby)	ORKNEY		
UPPER O.R.S. ?			Top not exposed		
			HOY SANDSTONE **1000+**		
			HOY VOLCANICS	0–90 BASALT	
				0–15 TUFF	
			Gentle folding and some major faults		
MIDDLE OLD RED SANDSTONE	GIVETIAN	*Tristichopterus alatus* *Microbrachius dicki* *Pentlandia macroptera* *Watsonosteus fletti*	EDAY BEDS	UPPER EDAY SST 320+	
				EDAY MARLS 100	
				MIDDLE EDAY SST 100–500	
				EDAY FLAGS ?10–150	LAVAS
				LOWER EDAY SST 220–250	
				PASSAGE BEDS	
		Thursius pholidotus *Millerosteus minor* *'Estheria' membrancea*	**ROUSAY FLAGS** **1500+**		
		Dickosteus threiplandi	**UPPER STROMNESS FLAGS** **330+**		
	COUVINIAN (= EIFELIAN)	*Coccosteus cuspidatus*	*SANDWICK FISH BED*		
			LOWER STROMNESS FLAGS **215+**		
		Thursius macrolepidotus			
			Gentle folding giving rise to angular unconformity of 10°		
? LOWER O.R.S.	? EMSIAN AND SIEGENIAN		WAREBETH RED BED ? FORM	HARRA EBB FORM	YESNABY SST FORM

CO Conglomerate   LST Limestone

contain thick sandstone phases which may be locally pebbly, the in-filled channel of a meandering river. Fish remains are common in some parts here also and form an assemblage particularly similar to those in the John o' Groats beds of Caithness and related to the Exnaboe bed in south-east Shetland.

The sandstones and volcanic rocks of western Hoy are the youngest rocks in Orkney. They rest on eroded Stromness/Rousay Flags which have been faulted and folded before the over-lying rocks were laid down. They have not yielded diagnostic fossils, although the equivalent Dunnet Head Sandstone on the south side of the Pentland Firth contains fish scales typical of the Upper Old Red Sandstone.

In five places in north-west Hoy and at Melsetter on the south coast of the island, lava flows occur. These vary greatly in thickness, up to 300 ft (90 m) in depth (at Hellia on the north coast of Hoy); it is not known if there was originally a single flow of lava over the whole of Hoy, or a number of small local flows. The Old Man of Hoy is a 450 ft (137 m) sea-stack consisting of Hoy Sandstone on a platform of lava.

As early as 1666, John Speed recorded the presence of lead ore in Orkney. Several mineral veins have been worked, but all are small and were rapidly exhausted. Most veins were mined for lead sulphide ore (galena). The two biggest mines, at Warebeth, west of Stromness, and Manse Bay on the north-east coast of South Ronaldsay, were worked in the latter half of the 19th century. Other lead mines were at Selwick in north Hoy, near Hoy Low Light on Graemsay, at North Hill on Sanday, and in south-west Rousay. The lead ores at Selwick and Rousay were notably rich in silver.

Many occurrences of galena in Orkney occur in or adjacent to stromatolite beds (rocks formed from fossilized algae). Metals entered the Orcadian lake in the rivers draining the surrounding hills, and were concentrated during sediment deposition. When the algae died and were degraded, metallo-organic complexes were formed, from which sulphide minerals were deposited.

Copper has been mined on the shore at Wha Taing, Burray, and east of the lead mine on Rousay. Iron ores have been worked at two localities in northern Hoy; fist-sized lumps of haematite are abundant in the Bay of Creedland near the old mine there. Manganese has been exploited in northern Hoy. Uranium occurs in faults and in the basal Old Red Sandstone beds of south-west Mainland, but there is no likelihood of mining in the foreseeable future.

Many of the siltstone horizons (recognizable time-planes in the rocks) in Orkney are carbon-rich, and if deeply buried would produce petroleum. Where such carbon-rich rocks have been intruded by hot igneous intrusions, small quantities of oil have been formed, whose residues can be found in numerous veins. Sandstones through which petroleum has migrated and left a residue can be seen in the vicinity of major faults, particularly the North Scapa and Brima-Risa ones.

The Ice Ages and After

The Pleistocene ice sheets modified Orkney topography in two ways. In many areas they smoothed off and partly obliterated the terrace features formed by the earlier erosion of the flagstones when they were exposed to

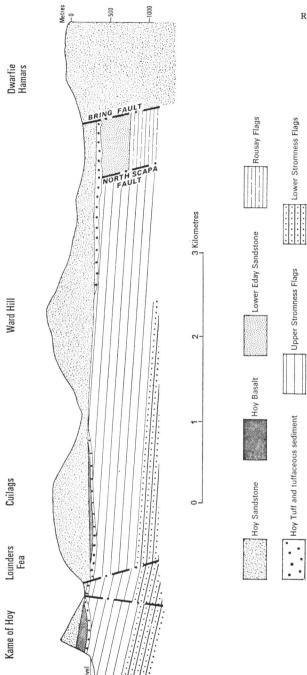

Fig. 21.
Geological section
across north-west
Hoy (from Mykura,
1976).

Rousay Flags

Lower Stromness Flags

Lower Eday Sandstone

Upper Stromness Flags

Hoy Basalt

Hoy Sandstone

Hoy Tuff and tuffaceous sediment

Dwarfie Hamars

BRING FAULT

NORTH SCAPA FAULT

Ward Hill

Cuilags

Lounders Fea

Kame of Hoy

Sea Level

3 Kilometres

Fig. 22.
The Peerie Sea at Kirkwall, an engraving in George Barry's History of the Orkney Islands (1805). The main road to Stromness now runs along the ayre which links the town with the foreground shore.

air, and covered the lower ground with a mantle of debris or till. In contrast, on the steeper flagstone hillsides parallel to the direction of flow, the scouring of the ice has emphasized the terraces by removing the debris that had accumulated at the foot of successive escarpments.

Towards the end of the Pleistocene, small local glaciers remained in the hills of north-west Hoy, and these have given rise to small corries, U-shaped valleys, and small terminal moraines. The finest corries are the Kame of Hoy in the north-western Cuilags (shaped like an arm-chair over-looking Stromness), Quoyawa facing Graemsay, and the Nowt Bield opposite the Dwarfie Stone (or Stane). The two most northerly valleys of Hoy exhibit most of the classical glacial landforms of U-shape, hanging tributaries, and truncated spurs.

When at last the ice melted, it left a deposit of sandy boulder clay over most of Orkney. So complete is this clay-cover that solid rock is rarely seen inland; the steep Hoy hills are the main exceptions. During the melting stage, when the ground was still without vegetation, there seems to have been a long period of very cold climate. It is from this time that the bare rocky 'pavements' on the summits of the Hoy hills originate, as well as the great gashes cut by torrents of meltwater. These precipitous gulleys are called glens in Orkney; oddly enough, large valleys never carry this name.

'Erratic boulders' transported in the ice sheet and then deposited by ice are not common in Orkney. A large erratic of hornblende gneiss near Saville at the north end of Sanday is frequently said to have come from Norway, but it could equally well have come from Scotland. On Flotta, laurdalite, a rock characteristic of Norway but unknown in Britain occurs on a beach with many other foreign rocks, none of which occur in the till at the back of the beach. The most likely explanation is that these were ship's ballast. The huge Cubbie Roo's Stone in the upper Woodwick valley (north Mainland) must have been transported at least from the Head of Holland, about 30 miles (40 kms) away.

The submergence of Orkney since the last major glaciation is responsible for the archipelago's drowned topography, with its partly submerged valleys (straits and voes), its submerged peat beds, and the local occurrence of what appear to be submerged tombolas and bay-mouth bars (ayres) (see p. 74). A classical example of a bay cut off from the sea in this way is the Peerie Sea in Kirkwall, which now has the main road to West Mainland running over it. The old mill (now a warehouse) on the ayre used to be operated by the ebb and flow of tides in the lagoon. Other good examples of ayres are the Long Ayre of Tankerness near Kirkwall Airport, at Finstown, Millsand and Holm on Mainland, Skaill and Fribo on Westray, and Huip on Shapinsay.

The Coast

Modern Orkney has an extensive and varied shoreline. It is approximately 500 miles (800 kms) long, half that of mainland Scotland, and comparable to that of Shetland. Cliffs exceeding 50 ft (15 m) in height comprise just under 20 per cent of the shoreline (50 per cent on Mainland), while sand or

Fig. 23.
The strata of Orkney cliffs rise above a boulder beach (Photo: *John Parnell*).

shingle beaches make up another eleven per cent. In places sand has collected behind the beaches to form dunes and machair areas.

As the land has sunk, much of the coast has become sheltered. The straits and firths between islands are particularly well protected; Scapa Flow, for example, is surrounded by sheltered shores. In contrast, the coasts of Hoy, West Mainland and northern Westray are open to the waves and swell of the open Atlantic. Over large parts of these exposed coasts, deep water extends close inshore, so that the waves break on the coast itself. Exposed shores often consists of a solid rock wave-cut platform, sometimes of great width (and with excellent rock pools), with boulder beaches concentrated in the bays. The west shore of North Ronaldsay, Marwick (West Mainland) and Rackwick (Hoy) are excellent examples of boulder beaches. At the Brough on Stronsay, blocks several tons in weight have thrown up more than 20 ft (7 m), while at the Noup in Westray there is a storm beach 30 yds (27 m) wide and 15 ft (5 m) high on top of a 40 ft (13 m) cliff.

Where folding and fissuring of the rocks occur near the sea, the cliffs are particularly splendid. On the west coast of Mainland from Black Craig (near Stromness) northwards, there is a seemingly endless succession of headlands, bays and geos, together with caves, gloups or blow-holes, arches and sea-stacks in every stage of development and destruction. How-

Fig. 24.
A steep-sided geo in
Orkney (Photo:
Gunnie Moberg)

ever, they pale beside the Hoy cliffs, which are without parallel; a walk along them from Rackwick to the Old Man of Hoy and St John's Head is one of the great walks of Britain.

Within historical times, the sea has encroached on some shores, exploring the weaknesses of the rock structure and making rock arches, on a large scale as in the Bay of Skaill, and on a small scale as in the Old Man of Hoy, which is the remaining leg of a one-time arch. The actual rate of retreat of the coast in these exposed situations is not easy to measure, but the absence of the seaward facing half of the brochs at Borwick, Sandwick and Breckness and the almost total disappearance of that at Stromness Kirkyard suggests that it has been 25–40 ft (8–13 m) in these places. The Old Man of Hoy is not shown on Murdoch Mackenzie's hydrographical map of the 1770's, which suggests it may be a relatively recent result of erosion; it lost a leg early last century.

The opposite effect is found where refraction of waves round an island throws up a loop of storm beach to enclose a small loch. The south end of Copinsay has such a feature, and there is a similar but much longer one in Stronsay. The mysterious Danes Pier in Stronsay may also be a refraction pit. Perhaps the best example of coastal construction is the east end of Sanday. Mackenzie's map of 1750 shows this area as a group of small rocky islets joined by spits, bars and tombolas. The enclosed lagoons have since filled with blown sand, and the whole is now an integral part of the main island. No doubt the almost enclosed Cata Sand, on the eastern side of Sanday, will in due course be assimilated in the same way.

Fig. 25.
Gunnels in the cliffs of Deerness, below the Covenanters' Memorial. The agricultural land extends to the cliff edge (Photo: *Gunnie Moberg*).

CHAPTER 4

Habitats and Vegetation

Since the first list of plants occurring in Orkney was published by Dr James Wallace in 1700, the island flora has received considerable attention from both amateur and professional botanists, and the vascular plant flora is now well known. In recent years, attention has concentrated more on describing individual types of vegetation and some of these are now fully characterized.

The vegetation of Orkney is, in general, more like that of Caithness (described by Crampton as early as 1911) than any other area, but there are also similarities with some of the types occurring in Shetland, especially in the montane zone. The ecological ideas suggested by Professor David Spence (1979) to account for such vegetation types are applicable to Orkney. Normally, any publicity given to Orkney places great emphasis on its rich archaeological and historical heritage and this, together with the economic importance of agriculture, reduces the respect wildlife habitats receive and the treatment they get.

Man has farmed in Orkney for almost 5000 years. Archaeological evidence and written accounts in historical times give some indication of the various changes which have occurred in that period. Although pollen analysis is at present based on comparatively few and localized samples, the discovery of birch wood fragments and hazel nuts from widely scattered localities show that scrub must have been common and that it was capable of some regeneration in those prehistoric periods when human pressure seemed slack. The discovery that blanket peat did not begin to form many centuries after man arrived on Orkney has had an influence on modern attitudes: tree-planting, once thought somewhat eccentric, is now increasing. Studies on natural woodland in Hoy have shown that growth of individual trees compares very favourably with that occurring elsewhere at the same latitude. It seems reasonable to assume that burning was the main agent used to clear heath and scrub and that subsequent heavy stocking with grazing animals prevented regeneration.

Much early farming was carried out on the lighter soils, and the alternation of bere and oats as the only arable crops did little to stabilize such soils; the problem of erosion was recorded as early as 1492 – and much further back if one counts the sand burying that excavations have shown affected the inhabitants of Skara Brae! Draining of wetlands had, and still has, a marked influence on wildlife habitats, as have the various changes of moorland management which have alternated between very heavy pressure from livestock and its almost complete absence in the early part of this century. The dramatic changes that the introduction of wild white clover brought about in improving the land around farms and allowing animals to be taken from the hills to the clover-improved pastures (p. 178) are now being

reversed as the moorlands come under pressure again from farming and other commercial interests.

Since 1949 the arable area has increased by some 25,000 acres (10,000 hectares), almost as much as the total land under cultivation in 1833. Areas classed as rough grazing seem to have declined, although differences in classification make such figures difficult to interpret. In recent years, the total head of cattle has been much greater than that of sheep; this had some influence on the growth of moorland and rough grazing, as has the severity of heather burning which varies, usually according to the wetness of the season. Burning is rarely carried out for grouse management; most burning is mischievous or accidental, or is unnecessarily undertaken for control of heather beetles. Some inland seabird colonies are very large; their manuring has a local effect on the vegetation, but the comparatively recent practice of spreading waste from fish and shellfish factories on moorland and maritime heath has a much greater impact. Some *Primula scotica* colonies have been lost.

There is no doubt that the lack of grazing by herbivores is a very big factor affecting habitats in Orkney today. The Blue Hare is confined to Hoy; numbers of Brown Hares elsewhere are too small to have much influence on vegetation. The decline and subsequent revival of the Rabbit population following myxomatosis certainly had a much greater impact: for example, *Poa alpina* was recorded from the Hoy hills for the first time in 1963, and a few years later it reached astonishing abundance; it is now becoming quite rare again. Although its runs are often conspicuous, the Orkney Vole seems to have a minor effect: There are no wild deer (some Red Deer are farmed but attempts at introducing 'free' deer have been abortive). The breeding sites of the large Grey Seal colonies show negligible erosion and practically no permanent damage to vegetation.

Fig. 26. Westray, looking north from Fitty Hill to Bow Head, with Papa Westray in the distance. Even the North Isles are intensively cultivated. Although population numbers are falling, the Orkney islands still have a high density of human activity (Photo: *Rawdon Goodier*).

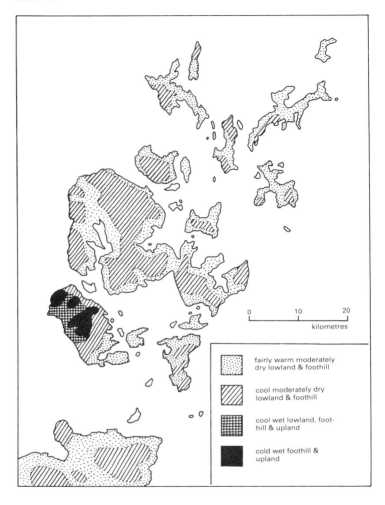

Fig. 27.
Main climatic areas
of Orkney. Only a
small proportion of
the land area is
unsuitable for agri-
culture.

Map legend:

- fairly warm moderately dry lowland & foothill
- cool moderately dry lowland & foothill
- cool wet lowland, foot-hill & upland
- cold wet foothill & upland

0   10   20
kilometres

Man-Made Habitats

Arable land, in spite of modern methods of weed control, still provides *ruithe* (Old Norse *hrooi*) – the small seeds of weeds such as Wild Mustard and Corn Spurrey, which were once used by the very poor to make bread, provide pickings for small mammals and large number of birds. Birds also make good use of improved pasture, especially in winter. Rough pasture is extremely variable in character. It is extensive on the many (mainly small) uninhabited islands in Orkney, most of which carry sheep at the present time. Although reclamation of hill and wetland continues quite rapidly there are some large areas, sometimes even alongside new reclamation schemes, which were once under cultivation but have fallen into disuse or neglect. Dry pasture may revert to grass heath, one-time machair to coarse herbs and the False Oat-grass (*Arrhenatherum elatius*); heavy wet land becomes infested with rushes and eventually poor fen, very tussocky Tufted Hair-grass (*Deschampsia cespitosa*) is not uncommon. In a county where trees and hedgerows are scarce, these rough pastures provide considerable shelter in addition to feed. They are rich in invertebrate life and are frequented by birds of prey and the smaller gulls. Like old peat cuttings which may also become fen but are often colonized by Willow (*Salix* spp.) to become carr, they may develop shrubby patches. These provide Hen Harrier winter roosts.

Water-filled quarries and old mill-dams may be far richer in plant life than natural sources of open water, and presumably their aquatic fauna must also be plentiful. They are diminishing in number as they are often used for rubbish disposal.

Although there are now no areas of natural woodland in the agricultural regions of Orkney, several plantations exist and Sycamore (*Acer pseudoplatanus*) is grown widely around farms and in the towns and settlements. Gardening is a popular hobby, and a variety of shrubs are planted. It is clear that many tree and shrub species can be grown successfully, including Ash (*Fraxinus excelsior*), Beech (*Fagus sylvatica*), Whitebeam (*Sorbus intermedia*), Wych Elm (*Ulmus glabra*), *Alnus* spp. and Gean (*Prunus avium*). Some of these even produce seed. One of the more interesting plantations is at Carrick in Eday where long-established Larch trees (*Larix decidua*) have a most unusual growth form due to exposure. The enormous leaf size of Horse-chestnut (*Aesculus hippocastanum*) in the plantations of Balfour Castle (Shapinsay) certainly casts doubt on the oft-repeated statement that 'trees will not grow in Orkney'. Unfortunately evergreen species suitable for garden or other isolated planting are scarce, but the two most successful conifer plantations in Hoy, after a slow start, are now making apparently normal growth. Alaskan sources of *Pinus contorta* have so far proved the most successful conifer on poor soils. These introduced trees and shrubs add to the range of habitats available naturally. They provide breeding sites for woodland birds which might not otherwise become resident in Orkney, shelter and food for migrants, and probably widen the range of invertebrates, fungi, etc. There is some evidence that tree planting improves the structure and drainage of soils.

Several plants on the Orkney list are known only from roadsides, (e.g. the Bedstraw, *Galium album*, and Greater Stitchwort, *Stellaria holostea*) and often verges are the sole indication of the natural vegetation prior to cultivation. They form a refuge for species normally occurring in grass heath such as Bell Heather (*Erica cinerea*), Birdsfoot Trefoil (*Lotus corniculatus*), Sea Plantain (*Plantago maritima*) and *Carex* spp. Some of the wetter roadsides have relicts of fen conditions in the form of *Lychnis flos-cuculi*, Lady's Smock (*Cardamine pratensis*), Yellow Flag (*Iris pseudacorus*) and Meadowsweet (*Filipendula ulmaria*). The Primrose (*Primula vulgaris*) is particularly abundant, and orchid species delight and surprise visitors later in the season. As in most rural counties, the Islands Council owns a large total acreage of potential wildlife habitat alongside public highways. Present management consists of fairly frequent mechanical cutting, with the cut material being left to rot. This results in a dominance of coarse grasses to the detriment of flowering plants. Cutting starts before most herbs flower and is applied indiscriminately.

The county includes many small islands, varying from rock stacks virtually bare of vascular plants to quite substantial islands still grazed by sheep. Many of the larger islands have been inhabited at some time and almost all except the smallest have had some history of grazing; even on Sule Skerry rabbits were once introduced by lighthouse keepers. Where not over-influenced by past grazing (which has had very specific effects in some cases), the vegetation of these islands is most like that of the nearest larger islands. For instance, the Pentland Firth islands share something of the flora of Caithness or of South Ronaldsay, of grassy heath with a high proportion of *Empetrum-Armeria-Plantago* sward, merging into sedge-dominated pasture, and derelict croft land with an abundance of *Deschampsia cespitosa* tussock. The Copinsay group is similar, although more influenced by blown shell-sand and with no Crowberry (*Empetrum nigrum*). The Scapa Flow islands share *Calluna* heath and some peat bog with Hoy. In the north there is considerable variation. No ericaceous plants occur at all in the *Deschampsia cespitosa-Holcus lanatus* grasslands of the Green Holms and the Holms of Ire, whereas others carry a very mossy grass heath in which *Erica* spp are absent, and *Empetrum* is usually more abundant than *Calluna*; whilst one (Linga Holm), includes Blaeberry (*Vaccinium myrtillus*) in its heath, although this species is absent from adjacent Stronsay. All islands which have been cultivated in the past carry man-made grassland, which often degenerates into marsh as old drains become choked. Where severe modification has taken place over a long period there is an inevitable loss of species. Indeed, there is an increase in the abundance of the more aggressive species, resulting in an additional decline in variety. An interesting example appeared on the Pentland Skerries where the complete absence of both sheep and rabbit grazing for several years produced one large field completely dominated by Cotton-grass (*Eriophorum angustifolium*) and Tormentil (*Potentilla erecta*)! It would be interesting to see how long such places would take to develop any kind of natural vegetation. Large storm beaches and the remains of old clay pits are relatively common on the smaller North Isles, making them botanically important as sites of otherwise locally rare Skull-cap (*Scutellaria galericulata*) and Northern Yellow-cress (*Rorippa islandica*). Islands now too small to carry sheep economically, but sufficiently above high water mark to support vascular plants are usually dominated by an *Atriplex* spp – *Tripleurospermum maritimum* association with Scurvy-grass (*Cochlearia officinalis*). The most striking example of this is on Sule Skerry.

Finally, among man-made habitats, are those which now have their status more or less fixed by designation, as Sites of Special Scientific Interest, as Reserves of various kinds, or as recreation areas laid out by the Local Authority, with increasing emphasis on their educational value. Descriptions of their various vegetation types are given below under appropriate headings.

The Lowland Zone

There is no particular altitude at which a boundary between lowland and upland habitats can be drawn at high latitudes. In theory, a distinction could be made on the basis of land use, the upland zone being that at which cultivation is not possible due to adverse climatic conditions. The problem is that in Orkney this distinction would often apply barely above sea level where very exposed headlands have thin soils. Moreover even such bleak sites may now be expected to carry livestock after the application of fertilizer, particularly fish factory waste, while the altitudinal limit of cultivation is creeping steadily upwards on the more sheltered hills. Underlying the effects, there is a general and well-known northward altitudinal descent of vegetation zones throughout Britain which is closely related to differences in climatic conditions. This means that vegetation types which are restricted to high altitudes in southern Britain occur at successively lower altitudes further north. Good examples are those heath communities including Bearberry (*Arctostaphylos alpinus*) which only occur above 3000 ft (1000 m) in the Scottish Highlands but which descend to around 250 ft (100 m) in Hoy. Indeed, much of the semi-natural vegetation in Orkney has montane characteristics, even at low altitudes, especially in areas which are subject to extreme exposure. To avoid confusion, however, it seems advisable to call those habitats 'lowland' which are strictly maritime or obviously below the 150 ft (50 m) contour even though these must include some extremely exposed sites. Some overlapping is inevitable, especially with heath and peat habitats.

Maritime Habitats

The coast has probably suffered least from man, and there is plenty of it. Orkney's cliffs are famous for their scenery, to rock climbers (especially the off-shore stacks, where the removal of stones to facilitate one climb destroyed a Peregrine's eyrie), and to ornithologists. In the past, some of the cliff-nesting birds were taken for food, but virtually no exploitation now takes place. The bigger seabird cliffs are on the outer coasts, mainly on the Atlantic side. The highest carry little vegetation on their almost vertical faces – nesting birds on almost every ledge inhibits many plants – but the highest cliffs of all, between the Kame of Hoy, St John's Head and Rora Head and those just south of Rackwick, have a thick growth of Woodrush (*Luzula sylvatica*) on some of their upper parts, tall herb in some geos and on the undercliff, and a relatively unexplored vegetation including much *Cochlearia*, on their lowest slopes. The larger Gulls nest among the talus on the lower slopes, while above them Manx Shearwaters burrow in the Woodrush. Puffins, too, seem to prefer some vegetation around their burrow.

The parish of Stromness includes within its boundaries the isolated islands of Sule Skerry and Sule Stack 32 miles (51 kms) to the west, although geologically these have more affinities with Sutherland than with Orkney. Sule Stack rises steeply and is too thoroughly occupied by its Gannet colony to permit the growth of vascular plants. Sule Skerry, low and flat, has a storm-washed belt of lichen covered rocks all round its perimeter with small plants in crevices. Within this the vast Puffin colony burrows under a tangled jungle of Mayweed (*Triplospermum maritimum*) and Orache (*Atriplex* sp).

Most cliffs have a zone dominated by lichens and characterized by *Xanthoria parietina* along their base, just above high water mark. Above this level, crevices and ledges on exposed cliffs have a discontinuous vegetation composed of *Festuca rubra* (sometimes hanging in dripping curtains),

Fig. 28.
Sule Stack, a bird
paradise (Photo:
Gunnie Moberg)

Sea Pink (*Armeria maritima*), *Plantago maritima*, Buck's-horn Plantain
(*P. coronopus*), Sea Campion (*Silene maritima*) and Lovage (*Ligusticum scoticum*), occasionally with Rose-root (*Sedum rosea*) and Sea Aster (*Aster tripolium*). Sea Spleenwort (*Asplenium marinum*) occurs frequently in crevices and caves from near sea level to cliff top even in areas of severe exposure. But there are also many cliffs which are less exposed or which rise too high to experience frequent salt spray; in Hoy vegetation similar to that on the cliff top often extends well down the face of the cliff. In other places the cliffs may have a distinct vegetation showing little maritime in-fluence, particularly when the face is broken by narrow inlets (geos) or protected in some way. A tall herb community on the west coast of Hoy, on a relatively stable boulder-strewn scree slope includes Red Campion (*Silene dioica*), Wild Angelica (*Angelica sylvestris*), Marsh Thistle (*Cirsium palustre*), *Primula vulgaris*, Sorrel (*Rumex acetosa*), Foxglove (*Digitalis purpurea*), Broad Buckler-fern (*Dryopteris dilatata*), Lady Fern (*Athyrium filix-femina*), *Deschampsia cespitosa*, Yorkshire Fog (*Holcus lanatus*), *Calluna vulgaris*, *Empetrum nigrum*, Greater Woodrush (*Luzula sylvatica*), Polypody (*Polypodium vulgare*) and Wilson's Filmy Fern (*Hymenophyllum wilsonii*). Nearby are little grassy flushes with Carnation Sedge (*Carex panicea*), and Grass-of-Parnassus (*Parnassia palustris*) among the herbs. An even more 'woodsy' flora occurs on the high cliffs of Hoy facing Scapa Flow, as at Bring Head where Aspen, wild roses, Honeysuckle and a few Rowan cling to the face of the cliff, Hay-scented Buckler-fern (*Dryopteris aemula*) luxuriates on fine *Agrostis* slopes, and a dense stand of bracken obscures boulders at the cliff's foot. More variety occurs on lower cliffs supporting relict woodland – mainly Aspen and Rowan or *Salix* spp as at The Pinnacles or on the cliffs around Waulkmill Bay, with many herbs and ferns.

An unusual vegetation type is found on the sandstone block cliffs facing Scapa Flow. This consists of a discontinuous cover of *Calluna vulgaris*, *Erica cinerea, Empetrum nigrum* and *Luzula sylvatica* together with ferns, herbs and shrubs including Golden Rod (*Solidago virgaurea*), Wood Sage (*Teucrium scorodonia*), *Dryopteris dilatata, D. aemula, Pteridium aquilinum, Salix repens, S. aurita* and Honeysuckle (*Lonicera periclymenum*). This is usually a drier cliff face than those previously described and the grasses include *Agrostis* spp and Wavy Hair-grass (*Deschampsia flexuosa*). By contrast, earth slopes frequented by seabirds have nitrogen-enriched vegetation, much of it of annuals e.g. Chickweed (*Stellaria media*) and Annual Meadow-grass (*Poa annua*) with *Cochlearia officinalis, Tripleurospermum maritimum, Atriplex* spp and even Knotgrass (*Polygonum aviculare*). Curled Dock (*Rumex crispus*) may be abundant, and in one or two sites there are large beds of Stinging Nettle (*Urtica dioica*). Hemp Agrimony (*Eupatorium cannabinum*), rare in Orkney, is confined to these areas.

Very steep grassy slopes, sometimes rising to a considerable height (as in South Ronaldsay) are particularly interesting as they supply what are probably the only extensive samples of 'natural meadow' in Orkney. In high summer they are very beautiful with taller grasses such as *Arrhenatherum elatius* and Hairy Oat-grass (*Avenula pubescens*). Also dominated by grasses but including many plants usually associated with marsh or fen, are the wetter cliffs cut out of glacial till and deeply gullied – 'gills' in Orkney, such as the Scapa Gills in St Ola. These gills must have a high base status, for Kidney Vetch (*Anthyllis vulneraria*) is very characteristic and they are the main habitat in Orkney of the grass Slender False-brome (*Brachypodium sylvaticum*), usually associated with woodland; at least one Black Bog-rush (*Schoenus nigricans*) flush is well-developed. Orkney lacks the long, narrow voes of Shetland but the arrangement of the islands into groups north and south of Mainland creates two large areas of sheltered waters, which accounts for many of these sheltered cliffs.

In Hoy, parts of Rousay and Westray and a few places elsewhere the vegetation of the hinterland extends to the cliff edge, but usually there is a belt showing maritime influence by the inclusion of Spring Squill (*Scilla verna*) and *Plantago maritima*. In more exposed areas *Plantago-Armeria* sward develops or even a pure sward of *Armeria*, vividly pink in spring. Sometimes small patches of salt-marsh occur, even on high cliff top. *Angelica sylvestris* is a very characteristic cliff-top plant, standing conspicuously above the surrounding vegetation, especially when shelter created by the up-draught of the cliff permits an exceptionally dense stand of heath plants.

Long stretches of the Orkney coastline are intermediate between high cliff and 'soft' coast, and there are a number of wide, almost land-locked bays and 'wicks'. On very sheltered low coasts, farm land extends almost to high water mark. Shores with alternating reefs and small sandy or shingle bays provide a variety of interesting habitats, as do lower cliffs broken by geos with a beach at their foot.

Low rocky shores form over two-thirds of the Orkney coastline. They include rock platforms and zones of periodic accretion together with areas of loose cobbles and boulders mixed with outcrops of solid rock. If the inter-tidal rock platform is nearly flat the accretions tend to be of finer material than when it is steep. These shores carry a sparse flora of *Tri-*

This and the following five tables list the plant species recorded at different sites in the main habitats in Orkney. They have been compiled by Miss E. R. Bullard, and use the nomenclature of *The Excursion Flora of the British Isles* (3rd ed.), as these names are to be used for botanical recording for the foreseeable future.

Table 7   *Cliff face 'sea banks' and 'natural' pasture (No. 7)*
Key to sites
Sites:—1. Banks and cliff face on North side of Waulkmill to Veness. 2. Banks and cliff face on South side of Waulkmill between steps and ridge. 3. Hangaback, Orphir. 4. Long Geo, St Ola. 5. Ward Hill cliffs, South Ronaldsay. 6. Barth Head and north, South Ronaldsay. 7. Ramsdale, Orphir. 8. Scad Head and Brings, Hoy. 9. Scapa.

					Sites				
	1	2	3	4	5	6	7	8	9
Calluna vulgaris	*	*	*	*				*	*
Empetrum nigrum	*	*	*	*	*	*		*	*
Erica cinerea	*	*		*					
Lonicera periclymenum	*	*						*	
Rosa spp		*				*		*	*
Salix aurita	*	*						*	*
S. repens	*	*	*						
Athyrium filix-femina	*	*		*				*	
Blechnum spicant	*	*		*				*	
Dryopteris dilatata	*							*	*
Equisetum palustre	*	*						*	*
Pteridium aquilinum	*	*						*	
Agrostis canina	*	*	*		*			*	
A. stolonifera	*	*	*	*				*	*
A. capillaris	*	*		*	*		*	*	*
Anthoxanthum odoratum	*	*			*	*	*	*	*
Avenula pubescens	*			*				*	
Brachypodium sylvaticum		*		*		*			*
Danthonia decumbens	*	*		*		*			
Deschampsia cespitosa		*			*	*	*		
D. flexuosa	*			*	*			*	
Festuca ovina/tenuifolia		*		*				*	
F. rubra	*	*	*	*	*	*	*	*	*
F. vivipara		*			*			*	
Holcus lanatus	*	*	*	*	*	*		*	*
Poa subcaerulea	*	*	*	*	*		*		*
P. trivialis	*	*			*				
Carex echinata	*	*						*	
C. flacca	*	*		*	*		*		*
C. nigra	*	*		*					
C. panicea	*							*	*
Juncus articulatus	*	*		*				*	*
Luzula sylvatica	*	*				*		*	*
Angelica sylvatica	*	*	*	*	*	*		*	*
Anthyllis vulneraria		*				*			*
Armeria maritima		*	*	*	*	*			*
Bellis perennis				*	*		*	*	*
Cerastium spp.					*			*	*
Cirsium palustre					*	*	*	*	*

	Sites								
	1	2	3	4	5	6	7	8	9
Cochlearia officinalis	*	*	*		*				*
Digitalis purpurea	*	*						*	
Euphrasia spp	*	*		*	*		*	*	*
Filipendula ulmaria	*	*			*	*			*
Galium saxatile					*		*	*	*
G. verum					*		*		*
Hieracium spp	*	*	*					*	
Hypericum pulchrum	*	*		*				*	
Hypochoeris radicata		*	*					*	*
Iris pseudacorus	*	*						*	*
Leontodon autumnalis	*	*					*		*
Lotus corniculatus	*	*	*	*	*			*	*
Plantago coronopus			*					*	*
P. lanceolata	*	*	*	*	*	*	*	*	
P. maritima	*	*	*	*	*	*	*		*
Potentilla erecta	*	*	*		*			*	*
Primula vulgaris	*	*	*		*			*	*
Prunella vulgaris	*	*		*			*	*	
Ranunculus acris	*	*		*	*		*	*	*
Rumex acetosa	*	*	*	*	*	*		*	*
Sagina procumbens	*	*	*						*
Silene dioica					*	*		*	*
Solidago virgaurea	*	*						*	
Succisa pratensis	*	*		*					*
Thymus praecox ssp *arcticus*		*			*		*		
Trifolium repens	*	*		*			*		
Tripleurospermum maritimum	*	*	*		*				
Vicia sepium	*	*	*						
Viola riviniana	*	*		*	*	*	*		

Additional species: *Populus tremula* 2, 8; *Rubus saxatile* 2, 6; *Sorbus aucuparia* 8; *Vaccinium myrtilus* 1; *Asplenium marinum* 6, 9; *Dryopteris aemula* 2, 8; *Equisetum arvense* 5, 9; *Polypodium vulgare* 1, 8; *Selaginella selaginoides* 7; *Arrhenatherum elatum* 5, 8; *Holcus mollis* 1, 9; *Molinia caerulea* 1, 2; *Carex binervis* 1; *C. pilulifera* 7; *C. pulicaris* 2, 4; *Luzula multiflora* 4, 5; *Schoenus nigricans* 6, 9; *Juncus effusus/conglomeratus* 1, 4, 7; *J. squarrosus* 1; *Achillea millefolium* 7; *Ajuga pyramidalis* 2; *A. repens* 5; *Dactylorhiza purpurella* 5, 9; *Equisetum arvense* 5, 9; *Eupatorium cannabinum* 5; *Galium aparine* 2; *Jasione montana* 6; *Lathyrus pratensis* 2, 9; *Linum catharticum* 2, 9; *Menyanthes trifoliata* 1; *Orchis mascula* 9; *Parnassia palustris* 2, 5; *Pedicularis palustris* 1; *P. sylvatica* 1; *Potentilla anserina* 1, 9; *Ranunculus ficaria* 5, 9; *Rhinanthus minor* 5; *Rumex crispus* 1, 2; *Sedum rosea* 8; *Silene maritima* 9; *Sonchus arvensis* 2; *Stellaria media* 1, 2; *Taraxacum* 2, 4; *Teucrium scorodonia* 2; *Trifolium pratense* 0; *Urtica dioica* 5; *Valeriana officinalis* 2; Bryophytes and lichens not fully recorded.

pleurospermum maritimum, *Atriplex* spp., *Rumex crispus* and occasionally *Leymus arenarius*, with Silverweed (*Potentilla anserina*) along the upper shore. A relatively permanent, strongly salt-tolerant vegetation may develop on the reefs and higher parts of the rock platform, contrasting with the rapidly changing areas subject to accretion. These are characterized by annuals or other plants capable of rapid colonization. Where reefs extend the rock platform exposed at low tide, they form favourite sites for Common Seals to haul out, safe from unwanted interference.

Fig. 29.
Although there is not
much tidal altitude in
Orkney, the shallow
sea means that an
extensive area of
flags and kelp are
exposed at low water.
In the background
farmland can be seen
extending virtually
to the high water
mark (Photo:
Gunnie Moberg).

Shingle beaches have a characteristic strandline of *Atriplex* spp and *Tripleurospermum maritimum*, especially where there is a matrix of sand and decayed seaweed. But there may be additional flowering plants: Sea Campion (*Silene maritima*), Corn Sowthistle (*Sonchus arvensis*), Goosegrass (*Galium aparine*), *Ligusticum scoticum* and, more rarely, Oyster Plant (*Mertensia maritima*). Storm beaches composed of sandstone boulders and cobbles (usually impounding a small loch) and the stabilized shingle of spits and bars may have in addition *Festuca rubra*, *Arrhenatherum elatius*, *Urtica dioica*, Forget-me-not (*Myosotis arvensis*), *Armeria maritima*, *Scutellaria galericulata* and a copious development of lichens. Fulmars have adopted some of the higher shingle ridges for nesting sites.

The backshore vegetation of these predominantly stony coasts is strongly influenced by adjacent land use. It may merge into other semi-natural vegetation, as in geos, but is more commonly dominated by coarse grasses such as *Arrhenatherum elatius* and Couch Grass (*Elymus repens*), together with Hogweed (*Heracleum sphondylium*), *Rumex crispus*, Meadow Vetchling (*Lathyrus pratensis*), *Potentilla anserina* and *Galium aparine*. The intertidal zone provides feeding and resting sites for seabirds and waders; several species nest in the shingle.

Soft coast, in the form of dunes, machair and saltmarsh occurs on all the larger islands and in all the Mainland parishes, with the exception of Harray (the only Orkney parish without any coastline at all). Shell fragments are the main component of the sand and in many places the calcium content is very high. Owing to the heavy cost of imported lime, this sand is a very important source of calcium for agricultural use. Stone has been the traditional building material in Orkney but is now largely replaced by concrete, and shell-sand is increasingly used for building purposes despite its high salt content. The heavy extraction now taking place is in some places causing a rapid deterioration of the dunes and their wildlife, and it is not known how far sand replenishment from offshore underwater sources is occurring. Relatively undisturbed dunes and machair ('links' in Orkney) have an interesting and varied flora, support a number of breeding birds and are an important lepidopteran habitat. Some sandy areas are badly infested with rabbits and the outwintering of cattle on dry machair has become popular in recent years. Both these break the fine sward, leading to wind-blow, infestation by weeds, and the deterioration of Marram Grass (*Ammophila arenaria*).

There are no dune systems in Orkney comparable in extent with those of the Scottish mainland; where dunes occur they are usually in the form of a single ridge, although there are extensive areas of dune pasture and machair, especially in the North Isles. Sandy beaches occupy only ten per cent of the total length of the coast; these too are almost all in the North Isles. Although coastal erosion is marked in Orkney, some considerable accretions of sand are taking place through the influence of man-made structures. A striking example is at the southernmost of the Churchill Barriers, where, in a comparatively short time, sand has accumulated on the eastern side so that Burray and South Ronaldsay are now joined by an ever-broadening sandy beach with dunes at each end. Unfortunately its coloniza-

Fig. 30.
Sea and dune
(Photo: *Charles Tait*).

tion by plants was not chronicled. It has afforded a valuable opportunity for the spread of *Mertensia maritima* which is quite abundant there and easily seen; the area is probably the source of this beautiful plant being able to spread within Scapa Flow. There are one or two other sandy bays in Orkney which seem particularly suited to colonization by sea-borne seed.

The commonest drift line community of sandy beaches in Orkney is one dominated by *Atriplex* spp often with Sea Rocket (*Cakile maritima*), and sometimes Sea Sandwort (*Honkenya peploides*). More permanent plants may be *Mertensia maritima*, *Leymus arenarius* and *Sonchus arvensis*. Where farmland lies directly behind the beach there is frequently a narrow zone with the characteristics of machair, including in it *Festuca rubra*, Lady's Bedstraw (*Galium verum*), Hardheads (*Centaurea nigra*), Yellow-rattle (*Rhinanthus minor*), Red Bartsia (*Odontites verna*) and *Euphrasis* spp; *Carex arenaria* and Sand Couch-grass (*Elymus farctus*) usually occur instead if the beach is backed by dunes.

Lyme Grass (*Leymus arenarius*) forms pure stands on a number of fore-dune areas, and, as noted, is a primary colonizer. It is less heavily grazed than *Ammophila arenaria* which dominates the larger areas of grey and yellow dune. In unstabilized dunes, *Ammophila arenaria* may be accompanied by *Sonchus arvensis*, *Carex arenaria*, Ragwort (*Senecio jacobaea*) and *Senecio* hybrids, *Ligusticum scoticum*, *Heracleum sphondylium*, *Elymus farctus*, *Avenula pubescens* and *Arrhenatherum elatius*. The vegetation of grey dunes varies a great deal but *Festuca rubra*, *Ammophila arenaria*, *Lotus corniculatus*, *Trifolium repens* and Lesser Meadow Rue (*Thalictrum minus*) are characteristic species. Some dunes are nearly dominated by Common Violet (*Viola riviniana*) and *Rhytiadelphus triquetrus*, while others have acrocarpous mosses such as *Tortula ruraliformis*.

Dune pasture or machair is much more extensive than true dune. It is generally dominated by *Festuca rubra*, *Carex arenaria* and *C. flacca*, sometimes with a continuous bryophyte layer. Eyebright (*Euphrasia confusa*) can be locally dominant and other associated species are Bulbous Buttercup (*Ranunculus bulbosus*), Meadow Buttercup (*R. acris*), Felwort (*Gentianella amarella* ssp. *druceana*), *Galium verum*, *Lotus corniculatus*, White Clover

Table 8　*Dunes, dune slacks and machair (links)*
Key to sites—
Sites:—1 & 2. Whitemill Bay, Burness, Sanday. 3. Backaskaill, Sanday. 4. Moclett, Papa Westray. 5 & 14. Bu', Burray. 6. Aikerness, Evie. 7. Newark, South Ronaldsay. 8. Rackwick, Hoy. 9. Sty Wick and Bay of Tressness, Sanday. 10. Plain of Fidge, Sanday. 11. Holland, Sanday. 12. Bay of Doomy, Eday. 13. Linklett, North Ronaldsay. 15. Egilsay composite. 16. Ha' Wick, Walls.

	Sites															
	1	2	3	4	5	6	7	8	9	10	11	12	13	14	15	16
Agrostis stolonifera	*	*			*				*						*	*
A. capillaris			*	*	*				*		*		*	*	*	
Ammophila arenaria		*						*	*	*	*	*			*	
Arrhenatherum elatius				*											*	*
Elymus farctus		*					*						*		*	*	*
Festuca rubra	*	*	*	*	*	*		*	*	*	*	*	*	*	*	*
Holcus lanatus				*		*										*
Leymus arenarius	*			*		*	*		*	*	*			*	*	

	Sites															
	1	2	3	4	5	6	7	8	9	10	11	12	13	14	15	16
Poa subcaerulea	*	*	*		*	*		*		*	*		*	*		
Carex arenaria		*		*	*		*	*	*	*	*			*	*	*
C. flacca	*	*	*	*	*				*	*			*	*	*	*
C. maritima		*						*		*			*	*	*	
C. nigra	*	*	*	*	*			*					*	*	*	
Juncus articulatus				*							*	*	*			
Luzula campestris		*						*	*							
Achillea millefolium		*	*		*	*		*	*					*	*	*
Bellis perennis		*		*	*	*	*			*	*	*	*	*	*	*
Cerastium diffusum						*	*			*	*	*		*	*	*
C. fontanum	*	*		*		*				*	*				*	*
Dactylorhiza incarnata				*						*				*	*	
Epilobium parviflorum				*										*	*	
Euphrasia spp	*	*	*	*	*	*		*	*	*	*			*	*	*
Galium sterneri				*						*				*		
G. verum	*	*	*	*		*	*			*	*	*		*	*	*
Gentianella amarella		*	*	*	*	*				*	*	*	*		*	*
Hydrocotyle vulgaris				*					*			*				*
Leontodon autumnalis			*	*												*
Linum catharticum		*		*	*			*		*				*	*	
Lotus corniculatus				*		*	*	*	*	*	*			*	*	*
Parnassia palustris	*	*	*	*				*	*	*	*	*	*	*	*	
Plantago coronopus		*							*				*	*		*
P. maritima			*	*	*			*	*		*			*		*
P. lanceolata		*	*	*		*	*	*	*	*	*			*	*	*
Potentilla anserina	*	*	*					*	*		*	*	*			
Prunella vulgaris			*	*				*		*	*		*	*	*	*
Ranunculus acris	*	*		*				*	*	*			*	*	*	
R. bulbosus				*						*			*	*	*	
Rhinanthus minor	*		*	*				*								
Senecio jacogaea or S. ostenfeldii	*			*			*			*				*	*	
Thymus praecox ssp arcticus				*				*		*	*					*
Trifolium repens	*					*	*			*			*	*	*	*
Viola riviniana									*		*		*			
V. tricolor ssp curtisii		*				*			*	*	*					
Sagina nodosa					*			*				*		*		
S. procumbens					*			*					*	*		

Additional species: *Empetrum nigrum* 8; *Salix repens* 8; *Elymus repens* 8; *Aira caryophyllea* 8; *A. praecox* 6, 8; *Desmazeria marinum* 6; *Avenula pubescens* 11, 15; *Juncus bulbosus* 1, 4; *Anthyllis vulneraria* 6; *Cardamine pratensis* 6, 12; *Centaurea nigra* 2, 15; *Geranium molle* 13, 15; *Hieracium pilosella* 4, 14, 15; *Heracleum sphondilium* 11, 14; *Ligusticum scoticum* 1, 14; *Mertensia maritima* 7; *Primula scotica* 4; *Radiola linoides* 8; *Thalictrum minus* 10, 14; *Ophioglossum vulgatum* 1, 4, 13; *Selaginella selaginoides* 11, 14.

Bryophytes include: *Acrocladium cuspidatum, Barbula convoluta, B. fallax, B. tophacea, B. unguiculata, Brachythecium albicans, B. rutabulum, Bryum pallens, Camptothecium lutescens, Climacium dendroides, Ceratodon purpureus, Cratoneuron commutatum, C. filicinum, Ctenidium molluscum, Ditrichum flexicaule, Drepanocladus aduncus, Eurhynchium praelongum, Hylocomium splendens, Hypnum cupressiforme, Lophocolea bidentata, Pseudoscleropodium purum, Rhytidiadelphus squarrosus, R. triquetrus, Riccardia pinguis, Tortula ruraliformis, Trichostomum brachydontium.*

Fig. 31.
One of the few areas
of sandy dunes in
Orkney (Photo:
R. S. Moore).

(*Trifolium repens*), Heart's Ease Pansy (*Viola tricolor* ssp. *curtisii*), Milfoil (*Achillea millefolium*), Spreading Meadow-grass (*Poa sub-caerulea*), *Luzula campestris*, Purging Flax (*Linum catharticum*), Thyme (*Thymus praecox* ssp. *arcticus*) and *Parnassia palustris*, the last forming huge clumps in the North Isles. A notable feature of this machair is the abundance of Limestone Bedstraw (*Galium sterneri*). A gradual transition to wetter conditions is indicated by *Carex nigra*, *Potentilla anserina* and similarities to calcareous fen which is sometimes associated with machair. Lesser Spearwort (*Ranunculus flammula*), Autumnal Hawkbit (*Leontodon autumnalis*), Common Horsetail (*Equisetum arvense*), Lesser Clubmoss (*Selaginella selaginoides*), Daisy (*Bellis perennis*), Small-flowered Hairy Willowherb (*Epilobium parviflorum*), Knotted Pearlwort (*Sagina nodosa*), Procumbent Pearlwort (*S. procumbens*) and *Carex maritima* are characteristic species although the last may be quite abundant in drier conditions also. The Frog and Early Marsh Orchids (*Coeloglossum viride* and *Dactylorhiza incarnata*) occur in some dune slacks, as do colonies of the Adder's Tongue Fern (*Ophioglossum vulgatum*), but wet slacks dominated by *Salix repens* are comparatively rare. In Hoy, a community of this type merges into an *Empetrum–Carex arenaria* association unknown elsewhere in Orkney.

The larger saltmarshes occur behind bars or 'ayres'. Smaller areas may be found at the head of the more sheltered bays and at the mouths of burns, and they are present on most coasts except where there are long stretches of cliff. Even then the cliff-top vegetation may resemble saltmarsh in certain conditions. The vegetation of sand-flats and mud-flats requires further study: Grass-wrack (*Zostera marina*) occurs locally, with a large bed in St Peter's Pool in the East Mainland; *Ruppia maritima* is frequent in the more sheltered sand-flats, (for example, Otterswick in Sanday, and Herston in South Ronaldsay); Glasswort (*Salicornia*) colonies are never extensively developed, but do occur in the muddy channels of saltmarsh. These flats provide a valuable wildlife habitat. In restricted conditions, stabilized saltmarsh covered by a characteristic northern saltmarsh turf has its seaward margin dominated by a zone of Common Saltmarsh Grass (*Puccinellia maritima*). There is often a transition toward the landward edge through *Juncus gerardii*, *Armeria maritima*, *Plantago maritima*, Sea Milkwort (*Glaux maritima*) and *Festuca rubra*, and its drainage channels may be lined with Sea Arrow-grass (*Triglochin maritima*). More extensive saltmarsh occurs in the shelter of 'ayres' and in these situations the *Puccinellia* zone is generally absent. Other species associated with salt-marsh in Orkney include Narrow Blysmus (*Blysmus rufus*), *Leontodon autumnalis*, One-glumed Spike-rush (*Eleocharis uniglumis*), *Carex extensa* and *C. serotina*. A slightly different association occurs where the substrate contains shingle, characterized by the presence of Sand-spurrey (*Spergularia media*, *S. marina*), *Cochlearia officinalis*, *Euphrasia foulaensis*, and Creeping Bent Grass (*Agrostis stolonifera*), together with the more usual saltmarsh species. A few sites are known where Sea Aster (*Aster tripolium*) is a component of saltmarsh. *Scirpus maritimus* used to be present in the upper part

*Fig. 32.
At the entrance to Loch Stenness the shallow sea of eastern Orkney shades almost imperceptibly into salting and machair.
(Photo: Alan Jones).*

of a small saltmarsh in Westray where it graded into freshwater swamp; it now appears to be extinct.

Although no really large areas of saltmarsh occur in Orkney, vegetation showing close affinities with the higher zones of saltmarsh is widely distributed around the coast especially on rock platforms and exposed reefs or

Table 9   *Saltmarsh*
Sites:—1. Myre Bay, South Walls. 2. Heldale, North Walls. 3. Little Ayre, North Walls. 4. Lyrawa, Hoy. 5. Cumminness, Stenness. 6. Waulkmill, Orphir. 7. Cata Sand, Sanday. 8. Oyce, Finstown. 9. Loch of Swarsquoy, Tankerness. 10. Mill Sand, Tankerness. 11. Otterswick, Sanday. 12. Little Sea, Sanday.

| | | | | | | *Sites* | | | | | | |
	1	2	3	4	5	6	7	8	9	10	11	12
Agrostis stolonifera	*	*			*		*	*	*	*		*
A. capillaris			*	*	*	*						
Festuca rubra			*	*	*		*	*	*	*	*	*
Poa subcaerulea	*					*						
Puccinellia maritima		*	*	*	*		*	*	*	*	*	*
Carex extensa				*		*	*					
Blysmus rufus				*		*			*			
Eleocharis spp.	*			*		*						
Juncus gerardii	*	*	*	*	*	*	*	*	*	*	*	*
Armeria maritima		*	*	*	*	*	*	*	*	*	*	*
Aster tripolium			*		*			*				*
Cochlearia officinalis	*	*	*		*	*	*		*		*	
Glaux maritima	*	*	*	*	*	*	*	*	*	*	*	*
Leontodon autumnalis	*		*			*	*					
Plantago maritima	*	*	*	*	*	*	*		*	*	*	*
Salicornia spp.	*			*	*						*	
Spergularia spp.	*	*	*				*		*	*	*	*
Suaeda maritima							*		*	*	*	*
Triglochin maritimum	*		*			*	*	*	*	*	*	*

Other species occasionally recorded: *Holcus lanatus* 1; *Atriplex* spp. 7; *Euphrasia* spp, *Plantago coronopus* 3; *P. lanceolata* 1, 3; *Potentilla anserina* 7; *Sagina procumbens* 1, 3 and some fresh-water marsh species.

low cliff. Joints and fissures within the sandstones and flagstones are often occupied by a turf of *Puccinellia capillaris* or *Plantago* spp, and rock platforms frequently have 'tables' of saltmarsh vegetation, one or two yards (1–2 m) in width and up to a foot (30 cm) high. These are dominated by *Puccinellia maritima*, together with *Triglochin maritima*, *Juncus gerardii* or *Blysmus rufus*. However, similar formations may just have a turf of *Festuca rubra*.

Lowland Heath Types

Many of the heaths and grass-heaths of the (physically) lowland zone have a floral composition similar to those of obvious upland habitats. Some fragments still remain among predominantly agricultural areas and are locally called 'breck'. Reclamation has tended to encroach heavily on low-land heath but large stretches of species-rich heath are still intact, possibly because the soils are very shallow and the sites exposed. However, as with some of the upland heaths, fertilizing and direct re-seeding have shown that they can be 'improved' for agriculture. At the same time they are being increasingly recognized as important wildlife habitats: on the coast they afford breeding sites for birds – especially terns – and they are the main habitat for the British endemic *Primula scotica*. Since 1965 population studies have been carried out on this species in Orkney, and, among other things, have proved that individual plants are far longer lived than pre-viously believed.

Inland lowland grass heaths may consist of a mixture of grasses, sedges, ericaceous shrubs and herbs. Rarely they may be dominated by shrubs – *Calluna vulgaris*, *Erica cinerea* and *Empetrum nigrum*, with or without Blaeberry (*Vaccinium myrtillus*) and *Salix repens*, and, like the montane heaths, may have abundant bryophytes or lichens or both. In addition to those already mentioned, grassy heaths usually include also *Festuca rubra*, *F. tenuifolia*, *Agrostis capillaris*, *Nardus stricta*, *Holcus lanatus*, *Molinia caerulea*, *Poa sub-caerulea*, *Anthoxanthum odoratum*, *Carex flacca*, *Plantago maritima*, *Potentilla erecta*, *Lotus corniculatus*, *Trifolium repens*, *Hyperi-cum pulchrum* and *Hypochoeris radicata*. They may also have *Lycopodium clavatum*, *Botrychium lunaria*, *Gymnadenia conopsea*, *Pseudorchis albida*, *Rhinanthus minor*, and various species of *Euphrasia*. Over short distances, this type of heath may merge into fen on the one hand, or into acid heath or even peat on the other. Acid heath has more ericaceous shrubs and bryophytes, and usually includes Devil's-bit Scabious (*Succisa pratensis*), Hard Fern (*Blechnum spicant*) and *Deschampsia flexuosa*, with *Festuca vivi-pera* displacing the other fescues. On steep slopes the shrubs are accom-panied by a smaller number of associates, notably *Potentilla erecta*, *Carex nigra*, *C. panicea*, *C. binervis*, *Juncus squarrosus*, *Luzula multiflora*, Cock's Foot (*Dactylorhiza maculata* ssp *ericetorum*) and *Viola riviniana*, although this vegetational composition can also be brought about by certain grazing regimes. It is fairly common on those uninhabited sheep-grazed islands which still retain heath.

By far the most important lowland heath is that classified as Maritime Heath. It is peculiar to northern Scotland in that it is almost entirely con-fined to thin soils overlying Old Red Sandstone, occurring in Caithness and north Sutherland as well as Orkney. Its main characteristic is that it in-cludes both cliff-top and heathland plants. The former are, invariably, *Plantago maritima*, *Scilla verna*, *Carex flacca* and *C. panicea*. The shrubs are *Empetrum nigrum*, *Calluna*, *Salix repens* (more so in Orkney than else-where), Cross-leaved Heath (*Erica tetralix*) (more in Caithness and Suther-land than in Orkney), and sometimes *Erica cinerea*. The basic grasses are fescues – *Festuca rubra*, *F. tenuifolia* and *F. vivipara* in Orkney (*F. ovina* in mainland Scotland), and *Agrostis capillaris*; *Deschampsia cespitosa* is not an uncommon constituent. Maritime Heath tends to occur as a mosaic of species rather than a homogenous sward. It often includes ablation features and flushes, and may grade into lichen heath or into *Plantago/Armeria* sward at the cliff edge. The transition between Maritime Heath and the *Plantago/Armeria* sward is the favourite habitat of *Primula scotica*.

This type of heath has several variants and a total of some 56 vascular plants have been found at various Orkney sites. These include the five shrubs mentioned, nine grass species, six sedges and rushes, and *Selaginella selaginoides*; the remainder are herbs. Frequent among the herbs are Cat's Foot (*Antennaria dioica*), *Bellis perennis Euphrasia* spp, Slender St John's Wort (*Hypericum pulchrum*), *Leontodon autumnalis, Lotus corniculatus, Parnassia palustris*, Ribwort (*Plantago lanceolata*) (in addition to *P. maritima*), *Potentilla erecta, Primula scotica, Prunella vulgaris, Scilla verna, Succisa pratensis, Thymus praecox* ssp *arcticus*, and *Viola riviniana*. Although less conspicuous, 40 species of mosses are found in this heath in Orkney, the most frequent being *Acrocladium cuspidatum, Bryum* sp, *Dicranum scoparium, Drepanocladus uncinatus, Eurhynchium praelongum, Fissidens adianthoides, Hylocomium splendens, Hypnum curessiforme, Isothecium myosuroides, Mnium hornum, Pseudoscleropodium purum* and *Rhytididadelphus squarrosus*. The most frequent of the 16 liverworts recorded are *Calypogeia fissa, Cephalozia bicuspidata, Frullania tamarisci, Lejeunea* sp, *Lophocolea bidentata, Nardia scalaris, Plagiochila asplenioides* and *Riccardia multifida*. Lichens are not abundant, although a total of 16 species occur, but only *Cladonia arbuscula, C. furcata, C. rangiformis* and *Peltigera candina* are at all common. Soil pH varies between 5.1 and 6.4 but mostly falls between 5.4–5.7.

This heath has probably developed as an interaction between exposure, soil type and location, combined with a moderate degree of grazing. As grazing increases and fertilizers are added, Maritime Heath quickly disappears; conversely a complete lack of grazing (by domestic animals and/or rabbits) in more sheltered sites may also bring about changes in composition. Maritime Heath in Orkney is one of the most important habitat types at risk from agricultural pressures. At present the most extensive examples are at Yesnaby in the West Mainland, Brings in Rousay and North Hill in Papa Westray, the last being the largest site of this habitat in Scotland. Smaller areas occur on the west coast of Mainland; there are a few small patches in the East Mainland, South Ronaldsay and Hoy, and in all the other larger islands with the exception of Eday, Sanday and North Ronaldsay. Since 1977 (when a survey was made) a number of sites have disappeared under various forms of reclamation.

The Scottish Primrose *Primula Scotica* (Hook)

Primula scotica merits a fuller account. It is a very special plant in the north of Scotland and has been adopted by the Scottish Wildlife Trust as its symbol. It is one of the very few British endemics and is confined to Caithness, the north coast of Sutherland, and Orkney, appearing nowhere else in the world. At one time it was known from a number of inland sites but is now virtually confined to coastal habitats which have not yet come under cultivation. It survives in three main types of habitat. It is found on shellsand links or machair, the best known site being Dunnet Links in Caithness, but in Orkney now only on the Links of Moclett in Papa Westray, although it was once recorded from Sanday (in Neill's *Tour*). There are a few colonies on the coastal limestones of Durness in Sutherland. Most commonly at present it is found on fine, wind-swept turf on thin soils overlying the Old Red Sandstones in the three counties. It is closely associated with the northern Maritime Heath, often growing where cliff-top *Plantago/Armeria*

Table 10 *Heath, Grass Heath and Maritime Heath, including uninhabited islands.*
Sites:—1. Roadside, Heathery Loan, St Ola. 2. Linga Holm. 3. Hellier Holm. 4. Eynhallow. 5. Hosa. 6. Auskerry. 7. Rysa Little. 8. Switha. 9. North Fara. 10. Gairsay. 11. Holm of Scockness (incomplete). 12. Calf of Eday. 13. Swona. 14. Brings, Rousay. 15. Yesnaby, Sandwick. 16. North Hill, Papa Westray. 17. Burgh Hill, Stronsay. 18. Ward Hill, above cliffs, South Ronaldsay. 19. Rendall. 20. Westray Hills. 21. Greenay Hill, Birsay. 22. Hoy, near Old Man. 23. Hoy, SW of Whitefowl Hill. 24. Hoy, Ward Hill summit. 25. Hoy, Kame/Launders Fea.

	1	2	3	4	5	6	7	8	9	10	11	12	13	14	15	16	17	18	19	20	21	22	23	24	25
Calluna vulgaris	*	*	*	*	*	*	*	*	*	*	*	*	*	*	*	*	*	*	*	*	*	*	*	*	*
Empetrum nigrum		*	*	*	*	*	*	*	*	*	*	*	*	*	*	*	*	*	*	*	*	*	*	*	*
Erica cinerea	*																								
E. tetralix			*		*		*	*	*	*			*	*	*		*	*	*		*	*			*
Arctostaphylos alpinus																						*	*	*	
Salix repens			*			*		*	*		*			*	*	*	*		*	*					
Vaccinium myrtilis			*		*			*	*	*												*		*	
Blechnum spicant						*	*	*											*	*					
Huperzia selago																			*			*		*	
Ophioglossum spp		*				*		*																	
Selaginella selaginoides			*							*			*	*		*	*		*	*			*		
Agrostis canina	*	*	*		*		*	*	*		*		*	*	*		*		*					*	*
A. stolonifera	*	*	*	*	*		*		*	*	*	*	*	*	*										
A. capillaris	*	*	*		*	*	*	*				*	*	*	*		*	*	*	*					
Aira praecox		*	*	*	*	*	*	*					*	*	*										
Anthoxanthum odoratum	*	*	*		*		*	*	*		*	*	*	*	*	*	*								*
Cynosurus cristatus	*		*	*	*			*	*	*															
Deschampsia cespitosa		*	*	*	*	*	*	*	*		*	*	*	*	*		*		*						*
D. flexuosa		*	*	*	*	*		*	*	*						*						*	*	*	*
Festuca tenuifolia		*							*				*	*	*										
F. rubra	*		*	*	*		*	*					*	*			*		*						*
F. vivipera	*								*	*	*		*	*			*		*						
Holcus lanatus			*	*	*	*	*		*		*		*	*	*	*	*								*
Molinia caerulea		*	*		*			*	*				*	*			*			*	*	*	*	*	
Nardus stricta	*	*	*	*	*		*	*	*		*	*	*	*	*	*	*		*					*	*
Poa subcaerulea	*	*	*	*	*	*	*	*	*		*	*	*		*	*	*		*						
Sieglingia decumbens		*	*					*	*			*	*	*	*	*			*						
Carex binervis						*			*										*	*					
C. echinata		*	*		*	*		*											*	*					*
C. flacca	*		*	*		*						*	*	*	*	*			*	*					*
C. nigra		*	*	*	*	*					*	*		*		*	*		*	*				*	*
C. panicea	*		*	*			*	*	*		*		*	*		*	*		*	*		*	*		*
C. pilulifera						*				*			*			*			*	*					
C. pulicaris			*	*	*							*		*	*	*	*		*	*					
Eriophorum angustifolium		*	*			*	*	*	*		*		*						*	*		*	*		*
E. vaginatum						*							*						*	*					
Juncus articulatus			*	*	*			*				*		*	*		*		*						*
C. effusus/conglomeratus	*			*	*	*	*	*	*							*		*			*				
J. squarrosus	*	*	*	*	*	*	*	*									*	*	*		*	*		*	*
Luzula campestris/multiflora	*	*	*	*	*		*	*			*	*	*	*	*	*	*	*	*						*
L. sylvatica									*																
Trichophorum cespitosum													*						*			*	*	*	*
Angelica sylvestris		*				*	*	*			*	*				*	*								*
Antennaria dioica		*													*	*			*	*					
Armeria maritima		*	*			*	*	*	*		*	*	*	*	*	*	*								
Bellis perennis	*	*	*			*	*	*	*		*	*	*	*		*			*	*					*

Table 10 (cont.)

Sites

	1	2	3	4	5	6	7	8	9	10	11	12	13	14	15	16	17	18	19	20	21	22	23	24	25
Cerastium fontanum	*	*	*		*	*		*	*	*	*	*	*	*	*										
Circium palustre	*	*	*		*	*	*		*	*	*	*						*			*		*		*
Dactylorhiza purpurella	*		*						*																
D. maculata ssp ericetorum			*			*		*					*	*	*			*	*						
Euphrasia spp	*	*	*	*	*	*	*	*	*	*		*	*	*	*	*	*	*	*	*	*	*	*		*
Galium saxatile	*	*	*	*	*	*	*		*	*			*	*		*	*		*	*		*	*		*
Hypericum pulchrum														*	*	*	*		*	*		*	*		*
Hypochoeris radicata								*							*			*		*	*				
Leontodon autumnalis	*	*	*	*	*	*	*	*		*	*		*	*	*	*	*		*	*	*		*		*
Linum catharticum			*					*	*				*			*			*						
Lotus corniculatus	*	*	*	*	*	*	*	*		*	*		*	*	*	*	*		*	*			*		
Narthecium ossifragum									*						*	*			*			*		*	
Parnassia palustris													*	*	*	*			*						
Pedicularis sylvatica			*				*	*					*			*			*	*	*				*
Pinguicula vulgaris								*					*			*			*	*	*	*			*
Plantago lanceolata	*	*	*	*	*	*	*	*	*				*	*		*	*		*			*	*		*
P. maritima	*	*	*	*	*	*	*	*	*				*	*		*	*		*			*	*		*
Polygala serpyllifolia					*	*		*					*	*		*			*	*					
Potentilla erecta	*	*	*	*	*	*	*		*	*			*	*	*	*	*	*		*	*		*	*	*
Primula scotica														*	*	*			*						
Prunella vulgaris			*	*	*	*	*	*		*	*		*	*	*	*	*		*						*
Radiola linoides					*			*					*			*			*						
Ranunculus acris		*		*	*	*	*	*	*				*			*	*			*	*				*
Rhinanthus minor	*			*									*			*			*						
Rumex acetosa	*	*	*	*	*	*	*	*	*	*	*	*		*	*	*			*			*			
Sagina procumbens	*	*	*		*	*	*	*	*	*	*	*	*												
Scilla verna	*	*	*	*		*		*					*			*			*						
Solidago vigaurea					*											*			*					*	*
Succisa pratensis			*	*		*	*	*					*	*	*	*	*	*	*	*		*			*
Thalictrum alpinum								*								*			*			*			*
Thymus praecox ssp arcticus				*				*	*	*			*	*	*				*						
Trifolium repens	*	*	*	*	*	*	*	*	*		*	*	*	*		*			*			*			
Veronica officinalis				*				*					*			*			*						
Viola riviniana	*	*	*		*	*	*	*	*	*			*	*	*	*	*			*	*				*

Additional species: *Arctostaphylos uva-ursi* 22, 23; *Vaccinium uliginosum* 23, 24; *Juniperus communis* ssp *nana* 23; *Botrichium lunaria* 20; *Carex demissa* 21; *Coeloglossum viride* 15, 16; *Conopodium majus* 1; *Galium sternerii* 16; *Lathyrus pratensis* 1; *Polygonum viviperum* 16, 20; *Primula vulgaris* 20; *Sagina nodosa* 10, 13; *S. subulata* 15, 20; *Silene acaulis* 20; *Trifolium pratense* 13, 14; *Vicia cracca* 18; *V. sepium* 2, 6.

Bryophytes recorded include: *Acrocladium cuspidatum, Amblystigium* sp, *Barbula fallax, Blindia acuta, Brachythecium albicans, B. mildeanum, B. rutabulum, Bryum* sp, *Camplylium stellatum, Campylopus flexuosus, Ceratodon purpureus, Dicranella heteromalla, Dicranium scoparium, Ditrichum flexicaule, D. heteromallum, Dreponocladus revolens, D. uncinatus, Eurhynchium praelongum, Fissidens adianthoides, F. bryoides, F. cristatus, F. osmudoides, Funaria* sp, *Grimmia maritima, Hylocomium splendens, Hypnum cupressiforme, Isothecium myosuroides, Mnium hornum, Plagiothecium undulatum, Pleurozium schreberi, Polytrichum juniperum, P. urnigerum, Pottia truncata, Pseudoscleropodium purum, Rhacomitrium canescens, R. lanuginosum, Rhytididadelphus loreus, R. squarrosus, R. triquetrus, Sphagnum* ssp, *Thuidium tamariscinum, Trichostomum brachydontium, Ulota phyllantha, Calypogia fissa, C. muellerana, C. trichomanis, Cephalozia bicuspidata, Diplophyllum albicans, Frullania tamarisci, Lochocolea bidentata, Marsupella emarginata, Nardia scalaris, Pellia endiviifolia, Plagiochila aspelflioides, Riccardia multifida, R. pinguis, Scapania gracilis, Scapania undulata*. **Lichens recorded include:** *Cetraria islandica, Cladonia arbuscula, C. coffifera, C. furcata, C. gracilis, C. rangiformis, C. subservicornis, C. uncialis, Cornicularia aculeata, Hypogymflia physodes, Parmelea omphalodes, P. sulcata, Peltigera canina, P. polydactyla, Ramilina subfarinacea.*

Fig. 33.
The Scottish
Primrose (Primula
scotica) (Photo:
Gunnie Moberg).

Fig. 34.
The Scottish
Primrose (Photo:
Gunnie Moberg).

sward merges into the heath. The Scottish Primrose's most frequent associates are *Plantago maritima*, *P. lanceolata*, *Armeria maritima*, *Lotus corniculatus*, *Bellis perennis*, *Prunella vulgaris*, *Carex flacca* and *Carex panicea*, *Festuca rubra* and *Agrostis capillaris*, with scattered *Calluna* or *Empetrum* or even *Salix repens*, but there can be many others. The lists given (p. 67) for Maritime Heath should be consulted.

Primula scotica is much smaller than the Common Primrose. Our life-size photograph (fig. 33) shows a barely discernible plant; to see detail it must be blown up out of proportion. On the other hand, artistic portraits usually fail to convey the very sturdy stance of this plant which has to survive in the teeth of severe gales. To complicate matters, published descriptions are rarely accurate. In most seasons the flowering scape would not exceed a couple of inches (5 cms) – much less in a dry year.

It is a miniature polyanthus or auricula with 2–8 upright 'pips' fairly tightly clustered at the end of a stiff stem although – again in dry seasons – the scape may not develop at all, leaving the 'pips' sitting directly in contact with the rosette of leaves. Each individual 'pip' or flower is typical primrose shape, but with a colour which varies according to weather and age and can be described as amethyst, or a pinkish or even blueish violet. Reports of white-flowered forms in cultivation seem to refer to another species. There is a yellow throat or eye; the calyx is campanulate and it and the slightly swollen bracts are slightly mealy. The leaves are more or less spoon-shaped with a winged but barely noticeable petiole, and usually forming a flat, compact rosette, not unlike that of the common daisy in a well-mown lawn. However, in *Primula scotica* they are densely covered with white or creamy-white farina and this helps to distinguish the rosettes from those of daisies and ribwort with which they are often found. Such a small plant may grow in colonies of considerable density so that it is difficult to describe its status as 'rare'. Nevertheless it is necessary to say very emphatically that its *colonies* are rare and becoming increasingly so.

Among the many misconceptions which have surrounded this plant since its 'recognition' in 1819 is that it is a form of Bird's-eye Primrose or that it is a form of, or even identical with the Norwegian *Primula scandinavica*. It is quite distinct cytologically: the diploid chromosome number in *P. farinosa* is 18, in *P. scotica* it is 54 and in *P. scandinavica* 72. It is always reported to be a short-lived species; it certainly hates cultivation and will show its resentment by flowering quickly and dying, but in its natural habitat individual plants are known to have lived at least 20 years. It may not flower until 10 years old, and then not necessarily every year, let alone twice a year as some books state. Admittedly, some plants do, very occasionally, produce two scapes in one year but it is the colony as a whole which has two distinct flowering periods – an early flush in May and the main flush from July onwards. In the wild, plants hardly ever produce a secondary rosette although in cultivation they are known to do so, producing a rather ugly 'cabbagey' appearance.

In the last century 30 separate sites of the species were recorded in Orkney. Its 'discovery' excited a lot of interest and it was quickly sought out and recorded. By the end of the 19th century, however, it seems to have been reduced to 27 sites, neither of the sites mentioned in Neill's *Tour* having been known to later botanists although both are now definitely under cultivation. Up to the end of 1939 some 23 sites were still known –

one of which was later buried under war-time constructions. In 1984, only 15 sites remained. Several of the losses have been within the last 20 years, and all to cultivation; several of the survivor colonies are very small and under threat. The direct use of slag or shell-fish waste as fertilizer quickly eliminates a colony. Unfortunately *P. scotica* seems long since to have occupied all habitats suitable for it; new colonies are very rare and in the whole north of Scotland only one is known to have survived more than ten years. A few plants may spring up in hitherto unknown situations but they fail to reproduce themselves. It is notoriously resistant to cultivation and although known introductions in Orkney have survived a remarkably long time they have always failed to establish a self-perpetuating colony.

In 1965, at the instigation of the late Rev. N. Dennis, the Orkney Field Club undertook a detailed study of *Primula scotica* in Orkney. Until then, few long-term studies had been carried out on individual plants of any species *in situ*, and the project has stimulated interest in similar long-term studies elsewhere on other species. The *P. scotica* study concentrated on 'life histories' of more than 400 individual plants. By 1984 it had shown that some individuals can live for at least 20 years. But of five original 1m² plots, two have been lost to cultivation and one to severe winter storms (affecting the actual plot but not the whole colony).

Natural Woodland and 'Tree-less Woodland' Habitats

Islands in lochs are often reservoirs of natural vegetation, but lochs in Orkney have few islands, and the lochs themselves are too shallow to completely protect the vegetation on these islands from grazing. Such relict woodland of which they still show trace does not differ from that still present elsewhere, usually *Salix* and *Rosa* spp. Natural woodland, apart from *Salix* carr, occurs only as remnants on the sea cliffs facing Scapa Flow and in the ravines of some of the Hoy burns, especially Berriedale. The small wood in Berriedale, the most northerly 'natural' woodland in Britain, is strikingly similar to the woods of the Dunbeath strath in Caithness, with the same composition of Birch, Rowan, Willow, Aspen and Hazel, an underlayer of *Rosa* spp and Honeysuckle, and a ground flora of ferns, *Luzula sylvatica*, *Vaccinium myrtillus*, *Brachypodium sylvaticum* and tall herbs. It is probably identical with the scrub which must have been widespread in Orkney before the arrival of Neolithic man, although with less Hazel and the possible loss of such species as Bird Cherry (*Prunus padus*) (which has been recorded in archaeological investigations). The absence of grazing by domestic animals and freedom from fire for nearly 20 years has allowed a fair degree of regeneration in the vicinity of the Berriedale site and in the Burn of Quoys, although the latter was severely damaged by fire in 1984. In Berriedale there are about a hundred mainly multiple-stemmed Birch (*Betula pubescens* ssp *odorata*) and these have been shown to make normal growth and regularly produce viable seed. It is, however, a species which seems unable to regenerate except under very favourable conditions, such as where spates have deposited gritty material on the banks of burns.

Rowan (*Sorbus aucuparia*) is widespread, large specimens occurring on the Hoy cliffs facing Scapa Flow and in the ravines and gullies in the hills. A solitary specimen in the Red Glen of the Ward Hill has a trunk a foot (30 cm) in diameter. Smaller, gnarled plants grow in the crevices of many rock outcrops and seedlings may be found almost anywhere. Hazel (*Corylus avellena*) appears to be represented by only two individuals, a third, in Berriedale, having apparently died. One of the two still alive is, however, large and thriving. Also in Berriedale are two stands of Aspen (*Populus tremula*); this is the only native tree species which still occurs in Orkney outside Hoy. It is fairly frequent as scrub on cliffs but forms well-grown trees in a few localities, including Pegal where it is practically on the shore. Curiously, no seed has ever been recorded; although catkins appear on plants grown in Rackwick from Berriedale stock, they are all male. *Salix* scrub is frequent in Hoy and occurs in many places in Orkney (as already noted). On peaty soils it is usually *Salix aurita* and is especially pretty in spring when the yellow male and silver female catkins adorn the short compact bushes. Also common are *S. phylicifolia*, *S. cinerea* ssp *oleifolia* and many hybrids, some including *S. repens*, itself a very variable species. *Salix myrsinites* has the distinction of being Orkney's rarest 'tree', one clump, all female, perching precariously on rock outcrops in the Glen of Greer. There are no records of male plants of this species in Orkney. *Salix cinerea* ssp. *oleifolia* can form very large bushes and some carrs formed of this species are miniature woods. There are no osiers native to Orkney but they are frequently planted. In areas where the native tree canopy merits such a description, its undercover is similar to that described for Berriedale.

Allied to the Berriedale woodland, for they almost certainly did carry very similar vegetation, are the 'dales' – valleys of burns draining moorland hills. These are most frequent in the West Mainland at the present time. They are a particularly important habitat in Orkney and nearly unique. Only in Caithness does a similar configuration of the Old Red Sandstone permit similar shallow valleys, and there all traces of the 'tree-less woodland' have been grazed or cultivated out of existence (as, indeed, has happened in some parts of Orkney). Further south and west in Scotland such sites under semi-natural conditions still carry trees. Like Berriedale, the dales have ferns, tall herb and a *Luzula sylvatica – Vaccinium myrtillus* vegetation, sometimes with rushes and *Schoenus nigricans*. The main growing period of this vegetation coincides with the time of nest building of the Hen Harrier; it is by far the most-used breeding habitat of that species. Fairly closely allied to dale vegetation are the montane tall herb and fern communities of the gullies of the Hoy hills, which are specially noted for their abundance of *Saussurea alpina* and their Holly Fern colonies. An apparently local and specialized fern community occurs in some of the more open Hoy gullies and in almost all the Mainland dales and in Rousay. All stands have *Dryopteris dilatata*, *Blechnum spicant*, *Vaccinium myrtillus*, *Calluna vulgaris*, *Empetrum nigrum*, *Luzula sylvatica*, *Deschampsia flexuosa* and *Potentilla erecta*; the Northern Buckler-fern, *Dryopteris expansa* is virtually confined to it.

It seems probable that these dale and gully habitats have attained their present conditions since the reduction of hill grazing following the introduction of wild white clover; the gullies in Quoyawa in particular only achieved their present botanical distinction some time after 1926. The Berriedale and other woodlands and the dales are at particular risk from fire and all these habitats would deteriorate under the resumption of heavy grazing.

Wetland and Open Water Habitats

There are no true rivers in Orkney but some of the deeper artificially straightened burns may have a river flora of *Sparganium erectum*, *Myriophyllum alterniflorum*, *Potamogeton filiformis*, *P. natans*, *Callitriche hamulata*, and *Ranunculus* (*Batrachium*) species. Where effluent is discharged, the submergent plants may be hidden by algal growth.

Lochs within the agricultural area are markedly eutrophic (rich in organic and mineral nutrients). Their catchments include hills carrying little or no blanket peat, but often layers of calcareous till. They commonly receive farmyard and silage effluent. Most have free trout fishing and artificial stocking is carried out (Chapter 7). The Lochs of Stenness and Harray have a complete range from salt through brackish to eutrophic freshwater conditions; they are a Grade 1 Site of Special Scientific Interest. Both are internationally important for wintering wildfowl. At least one *Prymesium parvum* 'bloom' has occurred on the Loch of Harray and in an attempt to prevent further incidents the Islands Council has installed sluices to limit the inflow of salt water into the loch, although the present effect of this is not great (see p. 114). The local Angling Association have been alerted to the importance of the wildlife of these lochs and are sympathetic; they are aware that effluent is a contributory factor to the problem. The rare *Ruppia cirrhosa* grows in the Loch of Stenness. Complete vegetational studies of the various pond-weeds have not been made, but in addition to the two *Ruppia* species and *Zannichellia palustris*, 15 species or hybrids of *Potamogeton* have been reliably recorded in Orkney. Of these, *Potamogeton polygonifolius* is more often a bog species and *P. lucens* and *P.* × *zizii* are confined to the hill lochs; and of the remainder, *P. natans*, *P. gramineus*, *P. perfoliatus*, *P. filiformis* and *P. pectinatus* are common, *P. crispus* fairly frequent and the small species *P. friesii*, *P. pusillus* and *P. berchtoldii* not uncommon, although tending to favour small pools rather than the larger lochs. Past drainage has led to *P. obtusifolius* becoming lost to the County, whilst *P. praelongus*, known reliably from only one loch, seems to have become extremely scarce, perhaps extinct, in recent years. Other common submerged species are Spiked Water Milfoil (*Myriophyllum spicatum*), Autumnal Starwort (*Callitriche hermaphroditica*) and Shoreweed (*Litorella uniflora*), also emergent. The distribution of the bladderworts (*Utricularia* spp) is less well-known; flowering in Orkney has never been recorded but they are sometimes abundant in small pools. Other emergent species which are frequent are Mare's-tail (*Hippuris vulgaris*), Amphibious Bistort (*Polygonum amphibium*), Water Horsetail (*Equisetum fluviatile*) and *Ranunculus* (*Batrachium*) spp. The moss, *Fontinalis antipyretica*, can be conspicuous on stony substrates, especially where there is water movement. Common Spike-rush (*Eleocharis palustris*) is by far the commonest marginal species of open freshwater. Some good Reed (*Phragmites australis*) beds occur but Bulrush (*Schoenoplectus lacustris*) is becoming scarce as the bigger beds were in lochs which have been partially drained. Bogbean (*Menyanthes trifoliata*) is a very common emergent species and has probably contributed to changes from open water to marsh or fen. At the present time, however, the majority of the large, shallow lochs have a stony shore rather bare of vegetation except for *Ranunculus flammula*, *Myosotis* spp, *Potentilla anserina*, *Caltha palustris*,

Euphrasia spp and bryophytes. Huge clumps of *Festuca arundinacea* grow on such a shore at the head of the Loch of Harray. Parts of larger, and sometimes the whole margin of the smaller lochs merge into swamp or fen. Some quite startling contrasts may be seen, such as a rock platform forming part of the shore on the east side of the Loch of Swannay supporting tangled growth of the basicole, *Rubus saxatilis*; while at the south end of the loch, where water drains off peat moorland, the stones are thickly covered with mosses supporting Butterwort (*Pinguicula vulgaris*) and Bog Pimpernel (*Anagallis tenella*).

Many small areas of open water in Orkney occur as impounded lochs, separated from the sea by a ridge, originally of shingle but often well overgrown and sometimes even supporting a public road. These are the 'Ouse' and 'Ayre' systems. They most commonly arise as a result of the gradual submergence of the land – a small valley running down to the sea becomes drowned and forms a loch, but they can also result from changes in coastal currents producing a sandbank joining the two headlands of a small bay, as is at present happening at No. 4 Churchill Barrier. On the other hand, what were freshwater lochs or even fens may now be sea, as at Skaill in Sandwick where the outer bar or sandbank has long since gone (and erosion is still taking place). Many are far less brackish than would be expected, although species tolerant of brackish conditions are usually found in them (e.g. Horned Pondweed, *Zannichellia palustris*, and Water Crowfoot, *Ranunculus baudotii*). They are probably among the richest and most diverse of the smaller open water habitats in Orkney, as their surroundings vary from machair, through saltmarsh, fen, farmland and peat bog according to their situation. Glaucous Bulrush (*Schoenoplectus tabernaemontani*) is confined to such lochs in Orkney; it is sometimes heavily grazed when the water level is low. Many are frequented by waterfowl and otters.

There are several areas in Orkney which were once shallow eutrophic lochs with a history of open water going back to the end of the last Ice Age, and which have had a more recent history of either encroachment by peat and subsequent peat cutting, or unsuccessful attempts at drainage, or both. Changes from eutrophic to oligotrophic (poor in nutrients, rich in oxygen), and even conditions where pools dry out, occur over very small distances with equally rapid and fascinating changes in plant life. They have a status difficult to describe as either open water or fen, but are of great importance in a wildlife, particularly an ornithological, context. The two best known are the Loons in Birsay, part of which is now an RSPB Reserve, and the Loch of Banks in Twatt. The former has had its ancient open-water status modified by peat formation, the latter by a series of drainage attempts, but they have much bird and plant life in common today.

Both areas carry reed (*Phragmites*) beds which in Banks includes *Salix* spp. There are patches of flood-tolerant vegetation including *Juncus articulatus*, Marsh Cinquefoil (*Potentilla palustris*), Marsh Marigold (*Caltha palustris*), Meadowsweet (*Filipendula ulmaria*), *Eleocharis palustris*, *Equisetum* spp and *Carex rostrata*. Where the calcareous ground water is impeded, or where clumps or banks of vegetation rise above it, a typical ombrogenous bog association develops with *Calluna vulgaris*, *Erica tetralix*, *Succisa pratensis*, and mosses such as *Pleurozium schreberi* and *Hylocomnium splendens*. This may be confined to quite small tussocks based on a clump of *Schoenus nigricans* (or, in non-calcareous sites, *Eriophorum vaginatum*). In this type of habitat there can be such unlikely companions as *Triglochin palustris* and *T. maritima*, *Iris pseudacorus* and *Anagallis tenella*, *Thalictrum alpinum* and *Menyanthes trifoliata*, *Acrocladium giganteum* and *Polytrichum commune* within a very small compass. Other very rich fens have developed away from open water, although the presence of marl beneath sedge peat and silty detritus indicates that open water was once present. One such area in a valley has archaeological remains indicating that at some time in its history it had been sufficiently dry for human use but insufficient studies have been carried out on this type of fen to indicate to what extent it is man-made. These fens have similar species to the two partially open-water sites described with the addition of an abundance and variety of *Carex* spp (including *C. diandra* and *C. paniculata*), Knotted Pearlwort (*Sagina nodosa*), *Lychnis flos-cuculi*, *Parnassia palustris* and orchids of the *Dactylorhiza* genus, and of such bryophytes as *Ctenidium molluscum*, *Cratoneuron filicinum* and *Trichocolea tomentella*. One of the best examples of this type of fen lies alongside the Hillside Burn in the West mainland; it has been designated a Site of Special Scientific Interest.

The pale grey-green foliage of patches of *Schoenus nigricans* appear almost throughout Orkney (the species has not been recorded from Eday, the north-east of Sanday nor from North Ronaldsay). It is a good indicator of calcareous drainage but the flushes it dominates may also be influenced by the nearness of the sea and can form in the vicinity of saltmarsh, on sea banks and in fens influenced by water from dune and machair, although not in actual dune slacks. They are a frequent part of fens and, as described above, may allow a mosaic of vegetation to develop, with the edges of the *Schoenus*-based hummocks supporting *Parnassia palustris*, Butterwort (*Pinguicula vulgaris*) and *Sagina nodosa*, their bases carpeted with *Campylium stellatum*, *Crateneuron commutatum*, *Bryum pallens*, together with *Riccardia latifrons* and various leafy liverworts. In open flushes there is a sparse growth which may include *Eleocharis quinquiflora*, *Carex demissa*, *C. panicea*, *C. dioica*, *Juncus articulatus*, *Equisetum palustre* and *Cratoneuron commutatum*. Other species often associated with *Schoenus* in Orkney are *Thalictrum alpinum*, *Viola riviniana*, *Carex pulicaris*, *Festuca rubra*, *Molinia caerulea* and a number of bryophytes. In Hoy, *Schoenus* flushes are well-developed, especially in the valley of the new Rackwick Road where they include Yellow Mountain Saxifrage (*Saxifraga aizoides*). They also form a part of the mosaic of Maritime Heath, sometimes apparently as a colonization of an ablation feature but more frequently in the vicinity of small springs (e.g. at Brings in Rousay, Burgh Hill on Stronsay, and North Hill in Papa Westray). *Schoenus nigricans* appears to be preferentially grazed if cattle are overwintered on such heaths.

In non-calcareous soils within the 'lowland' area, the fen – or marsh – community is dominated by *Iris pseudacorus* and Reed Canary-grass (*Phalaris arundinacea*), sometimes to the exclusion of all other species except *Poa trivialis* and *Agrostis stolonifera*. However, it may include *Filipendula ulmaria*, *Deschampsia cespitosa* (often showing a strong tendency to form tussocks or 'burrowy too'ers'), *Veronica anagallis-aquatica* or *V. beccabunga*, and grade into swamp community of *Juncus conglomeratus*, *Potentilla palustris*, *Mentha aquatica*, *Caltha palustris*, *Equisetum* spp, *Cirsium palustre* and *Senecio aquaticus*. Although botanically unexciting at first glance one such swamp community was found recently to include the rare Holy Grass, *Hierochloë odorata*. It is also worth noting that two frequent and otherwise undistinguished members of wetland communities in Orkney – Shore-weed (*Littorella uniflora*) and Pennywort (*Hydrocotyle vulgaris*) – are becoming increasingly scarce in Europe as a whole as wetlands are lost.

Montane and Upland Habitats

Due mainly to geological differences, Orkney has a less highly specialized vegetation than Shetland on its highest hill-tops. Nevertheless there are large areas of fellfield and erosion (ablation) surfaces, mainly in Hoy but also on Rousay and Westray, with minor traces in parts of the West Mainland. Compared with the Scottish Highlands, rock outcrops are less conspicuous, especially on Mainland, but the sharply terraced hills of Rousay and Westray have a number of 'hammars'. Most of these tend to be rather dry, with the tougher ferns, including *Asplenium trichomanes* and *A. adiantum-nigrum*; they have few obviously alpine plants, but rather those of adjacent moorland. Their higher base status may be indicated by the presence of *Rubus saxatilis*. They are now much colonized by nesting Fulmars, and where they carry cover are a favourite site for Hooded Crows and Kestrels. Fuchsia (*Fuchsia magellanica*) has become naturalized on some of the lower hammars. There is one area of very wet rock outcrop in Westray which does have distinct alpine characteristics.

It is in Hoy that Orkney's only corries occur, and they and the long stretches of hammars linking them provide the biggest area of more or less vertical rock in an inland situation. Fulmars are now prospecting these cliffs. Much of the Hoy rock is wet with a high base status. It supports a good montane flora and the steep slopes between the rock outcrops are rich

Fig. 35.
Agriculture and tundra merge in Orkney in an almost unique way. Here the Hoy Hills rise above the rich agricultural land of the east side of Hoy and the Mainland under its winter covering of snow. The entrance to Scapa Flow can hardly be seen between the islands (Photo: *Charles Tait*)

ın bryophytes. Ravens, Peregrine Falcons, and occasionally Buzzards and Eagles have bred on the more inaccessible cliffs, also Ring Ouzels and Manx Shearwaters. Ptarmigan have not been known to breed in Hoy recently, but did so more than 100 years ago.

Vegetation closely related to or probably identical with the Tall Herb assemblage (or nodum) described by McVean and Ratcliffe in their definitive account (*Plant Communities of the Scottish Highlands*, 1962) occurs in many gullies and on ledges. It has six constants: *Deschampsia cespitosa, Luzula sylvatica, Angelica sylvestris, Geum rivale, Sedum rosea* and *Hylocomium splendens*. Between 50 and 60 of the 121 plants listed by Mc-Vean and Ratcliffe have been recorded in Orkney, 50 of these from one stand, but several plants not listed by them occur in Orkney, e.g. *Plantago maritima, Asplenium trichomanes,* Lesser Twayblade (*Listera cordata*), Northern Bedstraw (*Galium sterneri*), *Hymenophyllum wilsonii* and *Primula vulgaris*. The most notable absentees from Orkney are Alpine Lady's mantle (*Alchemilla alpina*), Wood Cranesbill (*Geranium sylvaticum*) and Globe Flower (*Trollius europaeus*). Twenty-four of the vascular plants in the Orkney lists are recognized calcicoles, and the bryophytes often indicate calcareous conditions. The absence of *Alchemilla alpina* and *Sibbaldia procumbens* makes it impossible to assign the vegetation of the more open ledges, screes and steep silty slopes to the recognized Dwarf Herb nodum, although Orkney has 62 of the 101 vascular plants listed by McVean and Ratcliffe for this nodum. In Orkney, in addition to Lesser Clubmoss (*Selaginella selaginoides*), *Agrostis capillaris, Deschampsia cespitosa, Festuca ovina* (as *F. vivipera* and *F. tenuifolium*), *Silene acaulis* and *Thymus praecox* ssp *arcticus*, it seems probable that *Thalictrum alpinum, Saxifraga oppositifolia* and *Saussurea alpina* are constants in suitable habitats on the Ward Hill of Hoy. On other hills and in Rousay and Westray, *Saxifraga oppositifolia* is absent.

The vegetation of the upland areas of Orkney includes a range of open communities from sub-arctic fellfield developed on the higher parts of Hoy, through heath communities strongly affected by exposure and with pronounced ablation features, to closed grass-heath communities. They are found almost to sea level where they become difficult to distinguish from strictly maritime communities. As a wildlife habitat they carry bird and mammal species – the Blue Hare in Hoy and, as hill walkers are often painfully aware, the summer nesting sites of Great and Arctic Skuas.

In 1973 the hill vegetation of the Ward Hill of Hoy and the Cuilags was studied in some detail. Other studies have been made in connection with land use and conservation, and they have made interesting and sometimes surprising additions to the understanding of upland vegetation in Orkney. For example, it used to be accepted that snow rarely lies for any length of time in Orkney, even on the higher hills, but vegetational studies found *Nardus* snow-beds, later confirmed by aerial survey. They had escaped notice previously through discoloration by wind-blown soil and fragments.

Ablation surfaces and fellfield occur on the highest parts of the Cuilags, the Ward Hill ridges and spurs, the Knap of Trowieglen and several other hills as far south as Bakingstone Hill in Hoy, parts of the coastal hills in the West Mainland north of the Black Craig, small areas on the tops of the Rousay hills, and on some of the Westray and Eday hills (although these last may be partly due to removal of peat or excessive burning or both).

Table 11 *Rock outcrops, rocky gullies and 'hammars', sites 1–6; 'dales' and tall herb, sites 7–12*
These habitats are impossible to delineate precisely and the lists are not complete.

Sites:—1. Gullies and rock outcrops, Ward Hill, Hoy. 2. Berriedale, Hoy. 3. Kame of Hoy and Enegars. 4. Rock outcrops, Fitty and Skea Hills, Westray. 5. Stours Kinora, Hoy. 6. Rock outcrops, Rousay Hills. 7. Dale of Cottescarth, Rendall. 8. Woodwick, Evie. 9. Muckle Eskadale, Firth. 10. Burn of Swartabreck, Orphir. 11. Wideford Burn, St Ola. 12. 'Dales' off Ward Hill, Orphir.

	Sites											
	1	2	3	4	5	6	7	8	9	10	11	12
Calluna vulgaris	*	*	*	*	*	*	*	*		*	*	*
Empetrum nigrum	*	*	*	*	*	*		*		*	*	*
Erica cinerea	*	*		*		*	*					*
Lonicera periclymenum		*				*	*					
Rubus saxatilis	*	*	*			*	*					*
Salix spp	*	*		*		*	*	*	*	*	*	*
Vaccinium myrtillus	*	*	*			*	*			*	*	*
Asplenium adiantum-nigrum	*			*		*						
A. trichomanes			*	*		*						
Athyrium felix-femina	*	*	*	*	*	*	*		*	*	*	*
Blechnum spicant	*	*	*			*	*			*	*	*
Cystopteris fragilis	*			*		*						
Dryopteris dilatata	*	*	*	*	*	*	*	*	*	*		*
D. filix-mas s.l.	*	*	*	*		*	*					*
Equisetum palustre	*	*	*	*		*						*
E. sylvaticum						*	*				*	*
Hymenophyllum wilsonii	*	*	*		*							
Polypodium vulgare	*		*	*		*						*
Selaginella selaginoides	*	*				*			*			*
Agrostis canina	*					*	*	*		*	*	*
A. capillaris	*	*				*	*				*	*
Anthoxanthum odoratum	*	*	*	*		*	*	*		*	*	*
Deschampsia cespitosa	*	*	*	*	*	*	*	*		*	*	*
D. flexuosa	*	*				*				*	*	*
Festuca rubra	*			*	*	*					*	*
F. vivipara	*	*	*	*							*	*
Holcus lanatus		*	*			*	*	*	*		*	*
Poa trivialis	*								*		*	*
Juncus conglomeratus/effusus							*	*	*	*	*	
Luzula sylvatica	*	*	*		*	*	*	*		*	*	
Angelica sylvestris	*	*			*	*	*	*		*	*	*
Cardamine spp							*			*	*	*
Cerastium fontanum	*	*				*				*	*	*
Chrysosplenium oppositifolium								*		*		*
Cirsium palustre	*	*				*	*			*	*	*
Digitalis purpurea					*		*				*	
Draba incana	*			*		*						
Epilobium spp	*	*						*		*	*	*
Filipendula ulmaria							*		*	*	*	*
Galium saxatile	*					*				*	*	*
G. sterneri	*					*						*
Geum rivale	*	*						*	*	*	*	
Hieracium spp inc. *Pilosella*	*	*	*	*		*					*	*

	Sites											
	1	2	3	4	5	6	7	8	9	10	11	12
Hypericum pulchrum	*		*	*	*	*	*	*		*	*	*
Iris pseudacorus							*			*	*	*
Leontodon autumnalis	*			*						*		*
Listera cordata	*		*				*					*
Lotus corniculatus										*	*	*
Pinguicula vulgaris	*	*	*			*					*	*
Plantago maritima	*		*	*		*	*			*	*	*
Polygonum viviparum	*			*		*			*			
Potentilla erecta	*	*	*	*		*				*	*	*
Primula vulgaris	*	*	*		*	*	*	*	*	*	*	*
Ranunculus acris	*	*		*		*	*			*	*	*
Rumex acetosa	*	*	*	*	*	*	*	*		*	*	*
Sedum rosea	*		*		*							
Silene dioica	*					*					*	*
Solidago virgaurea	*		*		*							
Succisa pratensis	*	*	*	*	*	*	*		*	*	*	*
Taraxacum spp	*		*				*			*	*	*
Thalictrum alpinum	*		*	*		*	*		*			*
Thymus praecox spp arcticus	*	*	*	*		*						
Valeriana officinalis						*	*	*	*	*		*
Veronica officinalis	*	*				*				*	*	*
Viola riviniana	*	*	*	*		*	*			*	*	*

Some additional species recorded: *Betula pubescens* 2; *Populus tremula* 2; *Sorbus aucuparia* 2; *Asplenium marinum* 4, 6; *A. ruta-muraria* 4, 6; *Phyllitis scolopendrium* 6; *Polystichum lonchitis* 1; *Brachypodium sylvaticum* 2, 6; *Avenula pubescens* 6; *Poa alpina* 1; *Ajuga pyramidalis* 2, 12; *A. reptans* 7; *Antennaria dioica* 1, 6; *Oxyria digyna* 1; *Saussurea alpina* 1, 6; *Saxifraga azoides* 1, 3; *S. oppositifolia* 1; *Silene acaulis* 1, 4; *Teucrium scorodonia* 6; *Urtica dioica* 1, 11, 12.

Mosses and hepatics recorded in these habitats include: *Acrocladium cuspidatum, Aulacomnium palustre, Bazzania tricrenata, B. trilobata, Breutelia chrysochroma, Calypogeia muellerana, Camptothecium sericeum, Campylopus flexuosus, Ctenidium molluscum, Dicranium majus, D. scoparium, Diplophyllum albicans, Ditrichum flexicaule, Eurhynchium striatum, Fissidens adianthoides, Hylocomium splendens, Hypnum callichroum, H. cuppressiforme* var. *tectorum, Hamesoniella carringtonii, Lepidozia pinnata, Lophocolea bidentata, Mnium hornum, Nardia scalaris, Orthothecium intricatum, O. rufescens, Pellia endiviifolia, Plagiochila asplenioides, P. spinulosa, Plagiothecium undulatum, Pleurozia purpurea, Pleurozium schreberi, Polytrichum commune, P. formosum, P. juniperinum, Radula lindbergiana, Rhytidiadelphus loreus, Scapania gracilis, Thuidium tamariscinum.*

Paring, which was once a common agricultural practice, has also produced an ablation effect in some areas. On the level parts of the Hoy tops there is a true fellfield community composed of stone pavement which affords little roothold for vascular plants apart from *Salix herbacea* and the occasional tufts of *Deschampsia flexuosa*. The well-drained areas of ablation terracing are also usually bare on the outer strip of each terrace, with a dwarf shrub heath of *Calluna, Rhacomitrium* or lichen on the inner strip. The vegetation of these strips varies however and may include *Erica cinerea, Solidago virgaurea, Thymus praecox* ssp *arcticus*, Cat's-foot (*Antennaria dioica*), *Plantago maritima, Carex pilulifera* and *C. flacca*. Less pronounced terracing occurs in wetter conditions on some saddles. In Westray, *Silene acaulis*

Fig. 36.
Wind furrows on the
side of Ward Hill,
Hoy (Photo:
Rawdon Goodier)

occurs on wet terracing; in Hoy it is more a plant of rock outcrops with strips of species-rich heath between. Ablation on coastal hills in the West Mainland, Eday and elsewhere forms a less regular pattern, islands of heath standing in stony flushes often completely bare of vegetation or with scattered plants of *Plantago maritima* and *P. coronopus*.

A more or less unbroken cover of dwarf shrub heath occurs over large areas on thin peat or mineral soils. On poorer soils this may consist largely of *Calluna*, with or without *Rhacomitrium* or other mosses. *Empetrum nigrum* is almost always present, and on more exposed slopes its cover may be greater than that of *Calluna*. *Empetrum hermaphroditum* does not occur in Orkney; its place is taken by *E. nigrum*. *Erica cinerea* may be present, together with *Potentilla erecta*, whilst *Juncus squarrosus* or *Nardus stricta* may be locally abundant. Sedges are often present, in particular *Carex binervis*, *C. panicea*, *C. pilulifera*, *C. nigra* and *C. bigelowii*. The slightest shelter, in hollows or the lea of local irregularities, allows the intrusion of *Luzula sylvatica*. On the north and west clifftop areas of Hoy, this quickly becomes dominant. *Erica cinerea* achieves co-dominance with *Calluna* on the drier, east-facing slopes of the Hoy hills south of the Knap of Trowieglen and on some of the strips of heath separating scree shoots and gullies on the Ward Hill. In unburned areas this heath becomes very deep and locally includes *Vaccinium myrtillus* and the Eared Sallow (*Salix aurita*). It compares strikingly with old photographs showing much visible stone. Much of this deep heath on the Ward Hill was lost in a major fire in 1984.

Prostrate Juniper scrub, though never well developed, is widely distributed, even occurring in the predominantly low-level heaths of headlands in Rousay and North Ronaldsay (although it may now have disappeared from the latter). It is normally associated with *Calluna vulgaris*, *Empetrum nigrum*, *Deschampsia flexuosa*, *Trichophorum cespitosum*, *Hypnum cupressiforme*, *Rhacomitrium* and other mosses or lichens, and on partially ablated shoulders of the higher hills in Hoy with *Arctostaphylos uva-ursi* and *Arctous alpinus*. It also occurs sparingly in thicker *Calluna* with *Molinia* on their lower slopes. It is particularly susceptible to fire.

Of the other ericaceous shrubs, *Arctostaphylos alpinus* is of particular interest as it occurs at much lower elevations in Orkney than in the Scottish Highlands, and its autumn colouring adds a touch of brilliance to the hills when other plants are fading. It is a component of dwarf shrub heath on the flat or gently sloping summits of the Hoy hills, and also occurs as a crevice plant in pavement. With *Calluna vulgaris*, *Empetrum nigrum* and *Loisleuria procumbens* it forms a prostrate mat in the most exposed situations. More commonly it is part of a more open summit heath with *Calluna vulgaris*, *Empetrum nigrum*, *Carex binervis*, *C. pilulifera*, *Rhacomitrium* and lichens. Small species-rich variations of this heath occur, both near the highest parts of the Ward Hill and on lower slopes, e.g. Moor Fea, with the addition of other species such as *Arctostaphylos uva-ursi*, *Vaccinium uliginosum*, *V. myrtillus*, *Erica cinerea*, *Lotus corniculatus*, *Succisa pratensis*, *Potentilla erecta*, *Dactylorhiza maculata* spp *ericetorum*, *Luzula multiflora*, and *Nardus stricta*. However it is not totally absent from bog, on *Eriophorum vaginatum* hummocks, with *Empetrum*, *Calluna*, *Molinia* and *Sphagnum* spp, and, in Rousay, *Orthilia secunda*. In a wet heath below 250 ft (80 m) near the Green Heads, Hoy, it forms a closed community with *Arctostaphylos uva-ursi* and bushy *Empetrum nigrum*. *Arctostaphylos uva-ursi* itself is characteristic of block screes and on a few of the very stony slopes beneath the shoulders of the higher Hoy hills where it normally occurs with *Calluna*. A few of these sites have a fairly rich bryophyte flora. The distribution of *Vaccinium myrtillus* in Orkney is rather puzzling. In the montane zone it is almost invariably accompanied by *Luzula sylvatica* in a bryophyte-rich heath with *Calluna* and *Empetrum*. There are some communities where *Salix repens*, *S. herbacea* and *Carex bigelowii* occur. Ferns may be present, including *Dryopteris dilatata*, *D. expansa*, *Blechnum spicant* and *Hymenophyllum wilsonii*. This latter community occurs in some gullies in Hoy and elsewhere, and with increasing base status, may include *Rubus saxatilis* in which case it has close affinities with McVean and Ratcliffe's '*V. myrtillus–Luzula sylvatica* treeless facies' of their Betulo–Adenostyletea. *Vaccinium myrtillus* is also known to occur in very mossy grass-heaths predominantly lowland in character.

Montane grass heaths are poorly developed in Orkney, ablation surfaces and screes forming the upper altitudinal limit to dwarf shrub heath. The remarkable dominance of *Luzula sylvatica* along the top of cliffs between the Old Man of Hoy and St Johns's Head is not unlike McVean and Ratcliffe's '*Luzula sylvatica* grassland nodum' but has far fewer species. *Festuca*, *Agrostis* and *Deschampsia* species occur in many lists of the montane vegetation but only *Molinia* and *Nardus* achieve a conspicuous cover. In addition to *Luzula sylvatica*, grass-like plants such as sedges, *Eriophorum* and *Trichophorum cespitosum* may also dominate small areas of grass-heath but where *Molinia* is dominant it has more affinity with oligo-trophic mires. It occurs sparingly throughout the well-drained but damp bryophyte heath of the sheltered hillslopes and its dead foliage can be a fire hazard. *Nardus*, however, is more frequently associated with lichen heaths, as is *Trichophorum cespitosum*. Transitions between lichen heath and other vegetation types in Hoy are complex. *Juncus squarrosus* is locally abundant in montane or sub-montane situations in Orkney. The top of Fitty Hill in Westray has also *Erica cinerea*, *Calluna*, *Empetrum nigrum*, *Potentilla erecta*, *Luzula sylvatica*, *L. multiflora*, *Agrostis* spp, *Rhacomitrium lanuginosum*, *Hypnum cupressiforme* and *Cladonia* spp; no doubt similar communities occur elsewhere although adequate data are not available.

Areas which are frequently flushed on these thin peat or mineral soils within the montane zone vary according to the base content of the water. They may be dominated by *Carex nigra* and *C. echinata* with a large number of herbs and bryophytes, or by *Carex panicea* with herbs and bryo-phytes including *Campylium stellatum*, and these may be associated with a nearby gravel flush community characterized by *Carex panicea*, *C. demissa* and *Saxifraga azoides*. The last also occurs in *Schoenus* flushes. On the Enegars in Hoy, base-poor flushes include, sparingly, *Saxifraga stellaris*; bryophytes such as *Mnium hornum*, *Diplophyllum albicans* and *Anthelia julacea* are locally abundant. Hoy in particular has a rich hepatic flora. The saxifrages are confined to Hoy but otherwise similar flushes occur in most upland areas, often in the upper parts of valleys.

Although blanket peat is of relatively recent origin in Orkney it was formerly more widespread compared with its present distribution. It still covers much of the West Mainland hills, where it is often thick and severely

Fig. 37.
Peat cutting at Rendall. Deep peat covers much of the west and north of Orkney and provides fuel for many islanders (Photo: *William Paton*).

hagged on the summits; the East Mainland ridge, where it is less thick and where much land has been substantially reclaimed in recent years; much of Rousay and Eday; and on Rothiesholm in Stronsay. It is scarce or absent in the other North Isles. Some peat occurs also on some of the South Isles, including the small Scapa Flow islands. It is thinner on the steeper sides of the hills but in several places thick peat extends over large areas of low-lying land where it may cover the far older fen peats; basin formations are relatively few. There are indications that fen peat is buried under some agricultural land and it can also be seen in inter-tidal zones, showing that the land area of Orkney has shrunk since it was formed. In parts of Glims Moss the mean depth of peat is about 10 ft (3 m).

Frequent burning has left large areas of blanket peat with no botanical interest; *Eriophorum angustifolium* is very common, especially in the Mainland and Rousay. Gull colonies, some of them extremely large (e.g. the Greater Black-backed Gull colony in the valley of the Forse in Hoy) modify the vegetation locally. Peat mires and unbroken areas of bog occur mainly in Hoy but they are found also in the West Mainland and Rousay, where they provide a habitat for colonies of the beautiful Larger Wintergreen (*Pyrola rotundifolia*). Unburned heather on the drier peats may reach a height of 3 ft (1 m) without collapsing; it provides good breeding sites for ground-nesting raptors. As noted elsewhere, there has been a long tradition of peat cutting for household and for distillery fuel, but until recently this has been by hand and entirely for local use.

Blanket bog is most extensive in Hoy, on the gentle slopes of the hills south of Rackwick valley. On the north of that valley it merges into the dwarf shrub heaths already described, and is less continuous. The vegetation of these upland blanket bogs is similar to the Calluneto–Eriophoretum of the Scottish Highlands but is distinguished by an abundance of *Nardus stricta*, *Juncus squarrosus*, *Carex binervis*, *C. nigra*, *Trichophorum cespitosum* and *Rhacomitrium lanuginosum*, thus showing considerable affinity with the blanket bog vegetation of Shetland. Some areas of blanket bog close to St John's Head have a lichen-dominated vegetation in which *Cladonia impexa* is the dominant species whilst other areas have a dwarf-shrub vegetation in which *Calluna vulgaris*, *Empetrum nigrum* and several mosses are dominant. Much of the blanket bog in Hoy shows little evidence of burning and has a luxuriant vegetation in which dwarf shrubs and lichens are particularly well developed, the lichens often covering a bryophyte layer. Bryophytes include *Plagiothecium undulatum*, *Hylocomium splendens*, *Rhytidiadelphus loreus*, *Sphagnum rubellum* and *S. papillosum*. Some of the characteristic plants of Calluneto–Eriophoretum such as Cloudberry (*Rubus chamaemorus*) and *Listera cordata* occur locally. Blanket bog on the flatter parts of the Hoy hills has well-developed pool systems. In such areas *Sphagnum papillosum* and *S. rubellum* are common, together with dense stands of *Narthecium ossifragum* and *Eriophorum angustifolium*. In more exposed situations, where the blanket bog thins and grades into areas of ablation surface, islands of peat stand above the surrounding mineral detritus: *Calluna vulgaris*, *Erica cinerea*, *Empetrum nigrum* and *Carex binervis* occur on the peat, whilst the mineral ground is colonized by *Juncus squarrosus* and *Nardus stricta*.

Many of the bog areas on Hoy and the Mainland are eroding to some extent but there are some areas of actively growing bog such as the Moss of the Whitestanes in the Rackwick valley, which is a good example of a pool and hummock bog developed in a hollow and enclosed by moraines. This bog has a *Sphagnum*-dominated surface with numerous pools and hollows. The dominant species are *Sphagnum papillosum*, *S. magellanicum*, *S. rubellum* and *S. tenellum*, but other species also occur including *S. cuspidatum*, *S. recurvum*, *S. plumulosum*, *S. subsecundum* var *auriculatum* and *S. compactum*. Other bryophytes which are particularly abundant are *Pleurozia purpurea*, *Campylopus atrovirens* and *Rhacomitrium lanuginosum*. The vegetation is similar to western Scottish blanket bog vegetation dominated

Table 12   *Fens, Flushes and Loch Sides*
Sites:—1. Langamay, Sanday. 2. Russadale, Stenness. 3. Loch of Banks, Harray. 4. Syradale. 5. Banks, South Ronaldsay. 6. Dee of Dirkadale, Birsay. 7. The Loons, Birsay. 8. Cruland (Yesnaby) Sandwick. 9. Graemshall, Holm. 10. Burgh Hill, Stronsay. 11. Whitemill Bay, Sanday. 12. Bea Loch, Sanday.

| | | | | | *Sites* | | | | | | | |
	1	2	3	4	5	6	7	8	9	10	11	12
Calluna vulgaris			*		*							
Empetrum nigrum		*			*	*			*			
Erica tetralix			*		*				*			
Salix repens			*		*	*	*	*				
Equisetum arvense				*		*	*		*			
E. fluviatile	*	*				*	*	*			*	*
E. palustre	*	*	*		*	*		*				*
Agrostis stolonifera	*	*	*		*	*	*	*			*	*
A. capillaris		*		*		*	*					
Anthoxanthum odoratum		*			*	*	*		*			
Deschampsia cespitosa		*				*	*	*				
Festuca rubra	*	*	*		*	*	*					
Holcus lanatus		*			*	*	*					
Molinia caerulea		*	*	*	*	*	*	*		*		
Nardus stricta		*			*	*	*	*				
Phalaris arundinacea						*			*			*
Phragmites australis			*			*	*	*	*		*	*
Poa trivialis	*					*			*			*
Carex demissa				*		*	*					
C. dioica		*		*	*	*	*	*		*		
C. echinata			*	*		*	*					
C. flacca	*	*	*		*	*	*		*			
C. hostiana		*		*	*							
C. lepidocarpa		*		*		*	*	*		*		
C. nigra	*		*		*	*	*	*			*	
C. panicea		*	*		*	*	*			*		
C. pulicaris		*	*	*		*	*					
C. rostrata						*	*		*			*
Eleocharis palustris	*		*		*	*	*		*		*	*
E. quinqueflora		*	*	*	*	*				*		
Eriophorum angustifolium		*	*	*	*	*	*					
Juncus articulatus	*	*		*	*	*	*	*		*		
J. bulbosus		*				*	*	*			*	
Luzula multiflora		*	*		*	*						
Schoenus nigricans			*	*	*	*	*	*		*		

	Sites											
	1	2	3	4	5	6	7	8	9	10	11	12
Anagallis tenella			*	*	*	*	*					
Angelica sylvatica			*		*	*	*	*	*	*		
Bellis perennis		*			*	*	*					
Caltha palustris	*					*			*		*	*
Cardamine pratensis	*			*	*	*	*	*				*
Cirsium palustre		*				*	*	*				
Dactylorhiza purpurella			*			*	*	*				
D. incarnata	*		*			*	*					
Epilobium palustre	*					*	*					
Euphrasia spp	*	*			*	*						
Filipendula ulmararia			*			*	*	*	*			
Galium palustre	*					*	*	*	*	*		*
Hippuris vulgaris						*		*	*		*	*
Hydrocotyle vulgaris	*		*		*	*	*	*	*		*	
Iris pseudacorus			*			*	*	*	*		*	*
Leontodon autumnalis	*			*	*				*			*
Littorella uniflora				*						*	*	
Lotus corniculatus			*			*	*					
Lychnis flos-cuculi	*					*	*	*		*		
Mentha aquatica	*				*	*	*	*			*	*
Menyanthes trifoliata			*			*	*	*			*	*
Myosotis spp	*		*			*	*	*	*		*	*
Parnassia palustris	*		*		*	*	*					
Pedicularis palustris	*		*	*	*	*	*	*				
Pinguicula vulgaris		*		*	*	*	*			*		
Plantago lanceolata		*			*	*	*			*		
P. maritima	*	*			*	*	*			*		
Potentilla palustris			*			*	*	*				
Prunella vulgaris		*		*	*	*				*		
Ranunculus acris	*	*			*	*	*					
R. flammula	*	*	*		*	*	*	*	*	*		
R. repens	*						*	*		*		
Rhinanthus minor	*						*	*		*		
Sagina nodosa	*		*		*		*	*				
Senecio aquaticus (s.l.)	*		*		*	*	*		*		*	
Succisa pratensis			*		*	*	*			*		
Thalictrum alpinum		*		*			*	*				
Triglochin maritima			*		*	*	*		*			
T. palustris	*	*	*	*	*	*	*	*	*		*	

Additional species: *Salix phyllicifolia* 6; *Ophioglossum vulgatum* 1; *Selaginella selaginoides* 2, 4; *Arrhenatherum elatius* 9; *Festuca vivipara* 3, 6; *Avenula pubescens* 6; *Carex diandra* 6; *C. limosa* 6; *C. paniculata* 6; *Juncus bufonis* 11; *Gymnadenia conopsea* 4; *Hypericum pulchrum* 6, 7; *Lathyrus pratensis* 3; *Narthecium ossifragum* 7, 10; *Polygonum amphibium* 11, 12; *Potentilla anserina* 1, 8; *P. erecta* 3, 6; *Rumex acetosa* 7, 9; *Stellaria alsine* 9, 11; *Sparganium erectum* 3, 9; *Taraxacum* spp. 7; *Veronica anagallis-aquatica* 11, 12; *Viola palustris* 8; *V. riviniana* 2, 3.

Bryophytes recorded include: *Acrocladium cordifolium*, *A. cuspidatum*, *A. giganteum*; *Brachythecium rutabulum*, *Bryum pseudotriquetrum*, *Cratoneuron filicinum*, *C. communtatum*, *C. commutatum* var. *falcatum*, *Climacium dendroides*, *Campylium stellatum*, *Drepanocladus fluitans*, *D. revolvens*, *Eurhynchium praelongum*, *Fissidens adianthoides*, *Mnium punctatum*, *M. pseudopunctatum*, *Philonotis fontana*, *Trichocolea tomentella*.

by *Trichophorum cespitosum* and *Eriophorum angustifolium*. Both *Erica tetralix* and Bog Asphodel (*Narthecium ossifragum*) are abundant whilst *Eleocharis multicaulis* and the Great Sundew (*Drosera anglica*) occur in shallow pools.

Mires, in which there is a distinct water movement, occur throughout the upland blanket bog. On thin peat in the upper parts of the hills they are usually dominated by *Narthecium ossifragum* and/or *Carex panicea*; in certain conditions (such as in the upper parts of gullies) they may occur on extremely steep surfaces with or without *Sphagnum*, *Pinguicula vulgaris* and *Carex nigra* and are often slimy with gelatinous algae. Where there is deep peat in steep valleys without erosion, *Sphagnum*-dominated springs may occur, or, with stronger flushes, *Juncus bulbosus* and *Carex panicea*. The sheltered slopes of the Rousay hills above the Muckle Water have grassy flushes with *Juncus* spp, *Epilobium palustre*, *Primula vulgaris*, *Equisetum palustre*, *E. sylvaticum* and *E. pratense*. These grass and Primrose flushes also occur elsewhere, especially at the base of detritus fans in Hoy, albeit without *Equisetum pratense*. Tall solitary plants of *Cirsium palustre* are often conspicuous in them; these are heavily grazed by rabbits.

The only large areas of open water in the montane zone are Heldale Water, Hoglinn's Water and Sands Water in Hoy, and the Muckle and Peerie Waters in Rousay. Heldale and Hoglinn's Waters act as reservoirs and their outflows have been re-directed. As none of these lochs receive drainage water from farm land, they are far less eutrophic than lowland ones, even though their base status is uncertain. They are all rather shallow with stony bottoms, in many cases resembling the blockfields of the higher hills, although deep pockets of peaty sediments occur. As their names imply, both Sands Water and the Sandy Loch have sandy sediments.

The two large Hoy lochs lie in moderately steep-sided valleys. Their margins are slightly undercut in places and (when unburned) are overhung with thick heath, ferns and *Luzula sylvatica*. By contrast, the two Rousay lochs have very wide stony margins. Emergent marginal vegetation is rare. Small beds of *Eleocharis* and scattered *Equisetum fluviatile–Potamogeton polygonifolius* occur in Hoy, *P. lucens*, *P.* × *zizii* and *P. perfoliatus* in Rousay. *Isoetes lacustris* grows in the Muckle and Peerie Waters; it has been recorded from Heldale and probably occurs in Hoglinn's Water also. *Lobelia dortmanna* and *Sparganium angustifolium* can be found in all four, but *Littorella* and *Elodea canadensis* occur only in Rousay.

Small groups of pools occur in the blanket peat on the saddles and spurs of the Hoy and Rousay hills; elsewhere (on the Mainland and Rothiesholm in Rousay) they are usually solitary. Many afford nesting habitats for Red-throated Divers; some of these lochs are called 'Loomashun'. A few have peaty bottoms but most are either muddy or stony. They are all irregular, shallow and steep-sided, with a thin and species-poor vegetation. This may include *Sparganium angustifolium*, *Juncus bulbosus* var. *fluitans*, *Potamogeton polygonifolius* and *Callitriche hamulata*. *Sphagnum cuspidatum* and *S. subsecundum* may also grow in the water, partially submerged. A few pools have a dense growth of *Menyanthes trifoliata* and are probably in the process of drying out. Marginal vegetation is usually sparse with only the semi-submerged species as above, with perhaps *Juncus effusus*, *Deschampsia flexuosa*, *Glyceria fluitans*, *Molinia*, *Sphagnum recurvum* or luxuriant *Polytrichum commune*.

Sea and Shore

'The sea was the great mother: she gave them, sometimes lavishly, sometimes stingily, from her stores of fish, whale, salt, tangle, driftwood. Winter after winter she hurled freighted ships on the rocks and crags; while the cargoes of rum or wheat or apples lasted, life in this island and that was a long winter festival. But the sea did not give for nothing; another of her names was 'the widow-maker'. From time to time the sea took a single life to herself, or at a stroke a whole ship's crew. And this was her due.'

George Mackay Brown (1981)

The sea is less important to Orkney than to many island groups. That may seem a ridiculous statement, since the sea has formed, protected, provided, and isolated Orkney for thousands of years. But we must remember that Orkney is first and foremost a farming community; the sea may help with fertilizer or building material or saleable harvest, but few people in Orkney depend on the sea in the same way as they do in Shetland or, even more, in barren, basaltic Faroe. Yet the sea holds enormous interest for the natural historian; faunally and florally the waters around Orkney are among the most diverse in the United Kingdom. Despite this, the shores are compara-

Fig. 38.
Atlantic westerlies
pound the west coast
of Orkney (Photo:
Charles Tait).

tively poorly known, although the coming of the oil industry to Orkney has stimulated concern and research for her surrounds and, as knowledge increases, so may interest grow.

Tide and weather determine life on the shore. Like the air temperature, which varies comparatively little between summer and winter, extremes being rare, the sea temperatures around Orkney range only from 5°C (41°F) in February to 13°C (57°F) in July. Since littoral organisms are sensitive to heat, light and desiccation, the Orkney climate can be regarded as kind to them, and hence likely to favour the development of diverse communities. Probably the worst enemy is the drying effect of the wind.

Orkney has complicated tides. It is affected by two independent systems, that of the North Atlantic and that of the North Sea. The two tides reach the Orkney coast with similar strengths, but from different directions and with different timings, the Atlantic peak arriving two to three hours before the southward travelling North Sea wave. This produces a net flow of water from west to east, and complex tidal interactions among the island sounds and in Scapa Flow. Some areas such as Hoy Sound and the Pentland Firth are subject to considerable tidal streams as a result (up to nine knots in the Pentland Firth). Another consequence, particularly important for shore life, is the effect of all this on the rise and fall of the tide: crests or troughs of the progression may be flattened, and irregular gradients may result from uneven acceleration of the mid-tide water level. These modifications may alter the usual vertical zonation of littoral organisms due to changes in the immersion period at some beach levels.

The mean tidal range for Stromness is 9 ft (3 m) at spring tides, and 4 ft (1.2 m) at neap tides. Low water of spring tides occurs during the early morning or late afternoon. Since the air temperature at these times is cooler than at mid-day, this favours the development of a diverse littoral fringe.

Orkney is to some extent influenced by the current of the North Atlantic Drift which carries water north and east through the Faroe–Shetland Channel to the Norwegian coast. A branch of this stream enters the North Sea round the north of Shetland, but its strength varies annually. Another stream, which may comprise Atlantic or more coastal water, passes between Orkney and Fair Isle, and runs southward close to the Orkney coast. The current continues on into the Moray Firth, but only rarely enters the North Sea proper. Finally a sub-surface flow from the Mediterranean moves up the west coast of Britain, becoming less marked as it moves north. This current may be sufficiently strong in some years to mix with coastal water on the continental shelf to the west of Orkney, and then passes through the Orkney–Fair Isle passage into the Moray Firth area. Thus, the west coast of Orkney is dominated with northward-flowing oceanic water from the North Atlantic Drift or from the Mediterranean current; whilst the north and east coasts are likely to be influenced by mixed water from the Orkney–Fair Isle passage. Evidence from salinity patterns and from drift bottles indicate that the net flow through the Pentland Firth is westwards. The consequence is that Orkney is roughly encircled by a clockwise set of tidal streams.

The Orkney shore often falls rapidly to deep water (25–50 fathoms; 12–25 m), particularly on the west coast, while the firths, sounds and Scapa Flow are rarely deeper than 18 fathoms (9 m). Large parts of the coastline

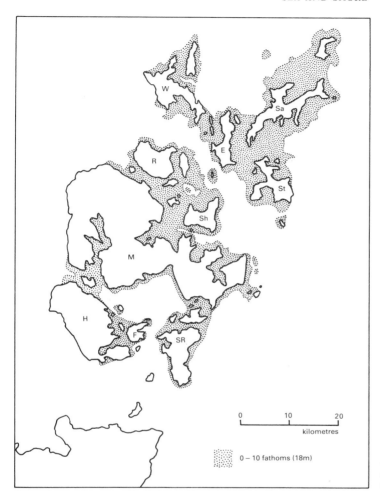

Fig. 39.
Sea depths around
Orkney.

have a shallow extensive shelf of rock favouring extensive *Laminaria*
forests and good lobster fishing. The floor of Scapa Flow is fairly flat with
a variety of bottoms from mud to rock; the tidally-scoured sounds have
bottoms of sand, shell-gravel or rock; the more sheltered firths have some
localized mud deposits, but mud is fairly uncommon in Orkney.

The littoral is largely bedrock or boulder shores, although there are well-
developed sandy areas in many bays. The grade of sand varies with the
amount of wave action or tidal scour to which the beach is subject, fine
sands being found in the more sheltered bays and firths only. The flagstone
and sandstone of the bedrock erodes fairly easily with the development of
microhabitats for many invertebrates.

Studies of the plankton in Orkney waters clearly demonstrates the significant influence of the warmer western currents, although the extent of

Fig. 40.
Point of Nevin,
Sanday, where land,
sand and sea meet
(Photo: *Gunnie*
Moberg).

this varies from year to year, and can be virtually undetectable. Scapa Flow is rich in planktonic life, much of which must enter through Hoy Sound. It is an area particularly rich in meroplankton in the spring and summer months.

Shore Biology

The supra-littoral fringe is particularly well-developed on rocky shores throughout Orkney, with a very diverse and abundant lichen flora. The damp conditions also permit the development of a conspicuous belt of Myxophyceae (blue-green algae).

The inter-tidal zone communities vary with the amount of exposure to wave action, the topography and substrate, the slope, and numerous other physical, chemical and biological variables. Only generalizations can be made. Very exposed coasts are usually dominated by the barnacle *Balanus balanoides* and/or the mussel *Mytilus edulis*. Populations of the latter are particularly well-developed where the rock slope is fairly gentle. The barnacle *Chthamalus stellatus*, a western and southern form, reaches its northern limit in Orkney, and only a few individuals are found on the very exposed rocks of Hoy and West Mainland. Other flora and fauna associated with these barnacle- and mussel-dominated shores are particularly well represented in Orkney, especially the Red Seaweeds, the Rhodophyceae. Slightly less-exposed shores frequently have a zone of the Brown Seaweed

Himanthalia elongata in the lower shore, with *B. balanoides* on the mid-shore. Dog-whelks (*Nucella lapillus*) in Orkney are almost completely unbanded, in contrast to Shetland where a large number of banded forms exist. Sheltered shores dominated by fucoid algae are common among the North Isles and in Scapa Flow, where they are the most frequent type of shore. The typical algal sequence from top to bottom of the shore is *Pelvetia canaliculata*, *Fucus spiralis*, *F. vesiculosus* and/or *Ascophyllum nodosum*, and *F. serratus*. Cover is often complete. The most sheltered shores are marked by substantial growths of *A. nodosum* and, where stable boulders are present beneath the algae, very diverse populations of other littoral organisms are often present.

The fauna of sandy areas varies with the physical and chemical conditions on each shore. Most sandy shores subject to considerable wave action or tidal scour are of a coarse nature and support relatively larger species. Sand on sheltered shores tends to have fine grains, and contains high densities of annelids, crustaceans, and molluscs – important foods for many bird species. A pronounced black anaerobic layer is commonly present in fine sands in Scapa Flow. This indicates a restricted circulation of water in the sand and a high organic content of the sediment. A giant race of the common cockle, *Cardium edule*, has been recorded in Scapa Flow.

Muddy areas are usually associated with freshwater inflows or with urban development, as at the Bridge of Waithe and Stromness Harbour. Like sand, mud often contains abundant invertebrates which may form locally-important food reserves for birds.

The shallow sub-littoral is well-developed throughout Orkney, but particularly in the North Isles and in Scapa Flow and its approaches. The dominant species are the large oarweeds or kelp, *Laminaria digitata* in the sub-littoral fringe, *L. hyperborea* in deeper water and regions of water movement, and *L. saccharina* in still-water areas and adjacent to sand. *Alaria esculenta* replaces *Laminaria* spp in areas of extreme wave action, and *Saccorhiza polyschides* is common in strong tidal currents such as Hoy Sound. The brown alga *Chorda filum* forms dense beds in many areas where tidal currents are weak (as in Scapa Flow), and here plants may grow 15 ft (5 m) or more in length.

The fauna of this zone is typical of laminarian forests in general with many molluscan, crustacean, annelid and echinoderm species represented. The dominant forms in Scapa Flow tend to be the common sea urchin *Echinus esculentus*, and the top-shell *Gibbula cineraria*. *G. cineraria* seems to be an important grazing organism in many areas, and may be locally abundant on *L. hyperborea* just below low water. Encrusting species are common on the laminarian holdfasts. Crabs and lobsters (*Portunus puber*, *Carcinus maenas*, *Cancer pagurus* and *Homarus vulgaris*) are frequent where broken rock forms the substrate.

The sub-littoral fauna in sandy areas varies with the physico-chemical conditions, but frequent components are dense beds of razor shells *Ensis ensis* and/or *E. siliqua*, together with cockles, *Echinocardium cordatum*. The extensive collections of the Orkney naturalist Robert Rendall suggest that very diverse molluscan populations may be present round Orkney, but many of his records are for shell material only, and the location and abundance of many sub-littoral species remains unknown.

There is very little known about the level-bottom communities in Orkney. There are considerable populations of scallops (*Pecten maximus*) and queens (*Chlamys opercularis*) scattered around the sounds, firths, and in Scapa Flow. The benthos in Scapa Flow varies considerably from place to place, depending on depth and the nature of the sediment. The large tunicate *Ascidia mentula* is abundant where shells and other solid debris occur; a red alga *Callophyllis* sp is common where the tidal stream is negligible, as in Scapa Bay; ophiuroids (*Ophiocomina nigra* and *Ophiura albida*) are the dominant forms where the bottom is largely sandy and tidal streams are pronounced, as in Burra Sound.

Otters, Seals and Whales CHAPTER **6**

The sea mammals are among the most attractive and spectacular wild-life of Orkney. They are also among the most publicized – otters (which are effectively sea mammals in north Scotland and the islands) for their shyness and vulnerability; whales for their rarity; and seals, ironically, because of their commonness and the periodic controversies about culling them.

Fig. 41.
Otter with prey
(Photo: *William Paton*).

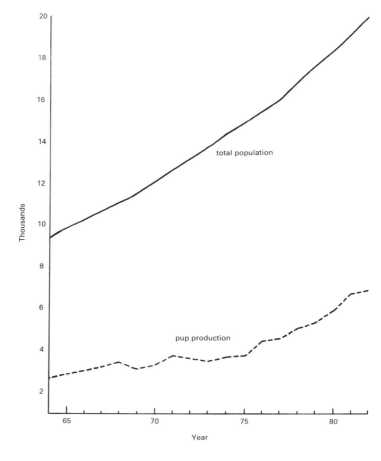

Fig. 42.
The increase in Grey
Seal numbers is
shown by estimates of
the total population
of all Grey Seals
alive which were
born on Orkney and
of Orkney Grey Seal
pup production.

Seals

Both of the resident British seals live and breed around Orkney: about
3500 Common (or Harbour) Seals (*Phoca vitulina*) (17% of the British
population, 4% of the world population) and about 20,000 of the larger
Grey Seals (*Halichoerus grypus*) (25% of the British population and 15%
of the world total). Common Seal numbers seem to have remained constant
in recent years; Grey Seal numbers more than doubled between 1964 and
1982 (Fig. 42).

Seals have long been an important resource for Orcadians, and are
almost as close to everyday life as a farm animal. Folklore (which Orkney
shares with both Shetland and the Hebrides) has it that seals ('selkies')
possess magical powers and are able to cast off their skins and come ashore
as beautiful (and seductive) people. Many an islander is said to have fallen
in love with a selkie and gone to sea:

I am a man upo' the land
I am a selchie in the sea
And when I' far frae every strand
My home is on Sule Skerry.

A rather more mundane approach is represented by the stories linked with seal hunting. The Barrel of Butter skerry in the middle of Scapa Flow is said to have got its name from payments made by seal hunters to the owner of the skerry. The *Old Statistical Account* refers to an annual sealing expedition to Sule Skerry; Pitcairn, writing a *Retrospective View of the Scotch Fisheries* (1787) describes between 500 and 1000 seals being killed there in a couple of days. This expedition ceased after 1786, when the ship was swept away northwards and all but three of the crew of 30 or 40 lost. Netting was a common method of catching seals on the skerries off Hoy, Walls, North Ronaldsay, Eday, Westray, Wyre and the Pentland Skerries. Nets were set up while the tide was rising, with the upper edge at such a height that the seals could swim over. When the tide fell sufficiently and enough of the net was clear, the seals were scared off the skerry and into the net. They were killed by clubbing or shooting.

Seal-skins were exported from at least the 17th century. With the hair on the outside they were used to make shoes, and covers for saddles and trunks. Oil was used in lamps, for feeding to cattle, and for dressing leather. A good-sized seal would yield about 8 gallons (25 litres). The meat was eaten, usually after being salted and hung in the chimney to be smoked. Low commented in the *Fauna Orcadensis* that seals (he did not distinguish between the Common and Grey)

'are with us very numerous: they lie off-shore in the desert isles and sea rocks: they swim with vast rapidity: they are yearly caught about our coasts with net and shot for the sake of the skins and oil, though in North Ronaldsha they take them for eating: they say they make a good ham.'

In the mid-16th century the Swedish Church regarded seal-meat as fish, but it was later forbidden on saint days in Norway. The comparatively small amount of modern hunting has been almost entirely for skins.

Grey Seals

The Grey Seal can be found from the Baltic to Iceland and on the eastern coast of Canada. It is larger than the Common Seal, an adult male weighing up to 9 cwt (300 kg), compared with just over 2 cwt (120 kg) for a male Common Seal. Its old Orkney name is 'haaf-fish', from the Old Norse *haf*, for ocean, presumably referring to its habit of frequenting off-shore skerries. The Common Seal used to be known as the 'tang' (or sea-weed) fish.

There are two main groups of breeding Grey Seals on Orkney, the larger one being centred around Rousay, Wyre and the Westray Firth, and a smaller one around the southern approaches to Scapa Flow. There are a number of sites used almost entirely by non-breeding animals, including Pentland Skerries, Auskerry and Seal Skerry near North Ronaldsay. Breeding females come ashore from late September and throughout October, giving birth to a single white-coated pup, weighing about 25 lb (12 kg).

Fig. 43. (*top*)
Grey Seal cow hauled out on the beach to enjoy the winter sunshine (Photo: *William Paton*).

Fig. 44. (*bottom*)
Grey Seal suckling its calf. Note the tag on the calf's tail – part of the research necessary to measure life span and individual movement (Photo: *William Paton*).

Three to four weeks later it has been weaned, moulted into its adult coat, and goes to sea. The females mate on land (with one or more males), and all the adults then disperse to feed.

Fig. 45.
A month-old Grey
Seal pup; most of its
white coat has been
moulted (Photo:
William Paton).

Grey seals become sexually mature at around six to seven years of age. Females may breed at this time, but males do not achieve sufficient social status to mate until ten years of age. In Orkney the peak numbers of pups are found ashore during the last week in October, and at this time they can be counted on aerial photographs, and thus censussed without being disturbed. Each island is photographed three or four times in order to obtain the maximum number of pups. In 1977, an intensive study of breeding was carried out on Auskerry. Repeated counts on the ground showed that total pup production could be measured by multiplying the maximum pup count by 1.5. This multiplication factor is now used to estimate the productivity of all the Orkney colonies.

Since 1951, 3000 seal pups have been tagged at breeding sites in Orkney. About 250 of these have been subsequently recovered, all but 27 within nine months of tagging. The recoveries show that Orkney seals may disperse as far south as Holland, north up to Norway and the Faroes, and west to the west coast of Ireland. Pups tagged in the Hebrides and the Farne Islands have been found in Orkney waters. What is not known is the likelihood of a seal returning to its birth-place to breed, and how much interchange there is between different breeding groups. There is a small amount of genetic divergence between seals from Orkney and the Hebrides, which suggests that the groups are isolated to some extent, but the available data are very limited. Grey seals are present throughout the year around Orkney, but most of the breeding islands are deserted during the summer months. Adults are mostly frequently seen hauled out in February and March, when they undergo their annual moult.

Productivity of all the Orkney seal breeding sites increased during the 1960s and 1970s, except for Muckle and Little Green Holm, where the 1964 figure (650 pups) was three times that of 1982. This decrease can probably be attributed to the large hunting effort there in the 1960s, but it represents emigration of breeding females, not their loss: pup productions on the islets of Spurness Sound between Stronsay and Sanday to the east of the Green Holms rose thirteen-fold (to 3000 pups per year) over the same period, whilst in the Westray Firth productivity only increased three and a half times (to 1600 per year). All the Spurness Sound colonies have expanded in the last 20 years, and at least seven new ones have been established since then. From 1978 no licences for hunting have been issued for the Green Holms, but still there has been no increase in pups born there.

Ironically, the nadir of breeding on the Green Holms (and the year of most human disturbance) was in 1978, when protesters against seal hunting

Fig. 46.
Counts of Grey Seals can be made from aerial photographs. This picture shows part of the Holm of Spurness on 23rd October 1984. The Sea Mammal Research Unit used this shot and others to estimate the number of pups born on the entire island to be 271 (Photo: *Sea Mammal Research Unit* (*NERC*)).

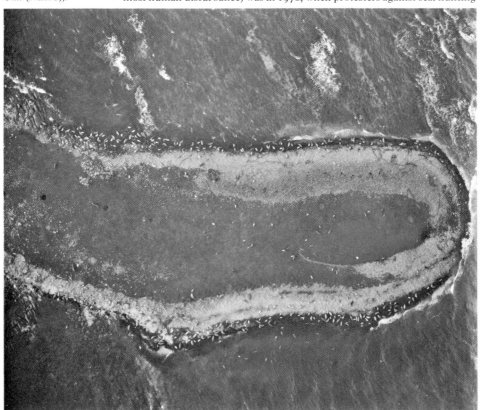

camped there for several weeks. A vivid account of this episode is given in a book *Let the Seals Live!* by Sue Flint (1979).

The rapid recent increase in the Orkney seal population is well documented. In the past there have been times when they have been rare. Low recorded that on occasion seals (of uncertain species) had a 'murrain' (illness) which 'caused them to cough much, make a sort of plaintive noise, and when they died and drove ashore were much swelled, and appeared as if very fat, but when cut up were nothing but skin and bone.' This would have been around 1770. Apparently similar epidemics occurred in 1836 and in 1869 and 1870, 'since which time certain bays have been quite deserted by seals.' Whether it was disease or human predation that controlled numbers in past centuries we may never know. The first Grey Seal Protection Act was passed in 1914 prohibiting the 'killing, wounding or taking of any grey seals between 1st October and 15th November' (extended in 1932 to cover the period 1st September to 31st October). When it was before Parliament it was asserted that Grey Seal stocks around the whole of Britain had been reduced by over-killing to as few as 500. However, although there are no hard data, there are anecdotes which suggest that seals were already increasing at the end of the 19th century.

During the 1950s, increase in seals in Scottish waters led to concern among both the commercial and salmon fishing communities about depredation and damage to fish, and about the apparently rising incidence of a worm (*Porrocaecum dicipiens*) parasitic in Cod and other fish, whose intermediate host is the Grey Seal. (Cod worm infestations increased in the 1960s, giving rise to the idea that they were dependent on seal densities. However, they remained relatively constant in the 1970s despite the continued growth in seal numbers.) This concern led in 1959 to the formation of a Consultative Committee on Grey Seals and Fisheries. One of the recommendations of this committee was that there should be an annual cull of Grey Seals in Orkney, in order to reduce the population by a quarter. From 1962 to 1982 an average of 834 pups were taken every year by local hunters, but this policy failed to stop the population increase. In 1976, the Department of Agriculture and Fisheries for Scotland and the Nature Conservancy Council proposed that the Scottish Grey Seal stock should be reduced to the mid-1960s level (around 35,000). The Natural Environment Research Council, who had the responsibility of giving scientific advice to the Government, recommended that the safest way of achieving this was to remove 900 cows and 4000 pups every year for six years. Bad weather interfered with this programme in the Hebrides in 1977, and the focus was turned on Orkney in 1978, where it was proposed that 1000 moulted pups and 450 adult cows plus their pups should be removed. The protests and obstructions that followed led to the Secretary of State abandoning the cull. Eventually just over 1000 Grey Seal pups were taken in Orkney during that and subsequent years (until 1983, when no licences were issued).

In his statement cancelling the 1978 cull, the Secretary of State for Scotland stated

'Research has been undertaken over many years into seal behaviour, diet, etc. and there is no doubt that they are consuming considerable quantities of fish which has been put at a value of some £12m per annum. The simple facts of the matter are that seals eat fish as their main diet, mostly fish suitable for human consumption, and the more seals there are, the greater the damage done to fish stocks.'

He went on to commission the Sea Mammal Research Unit to check and quantify the diet of Grey Seals. Their report on the *Interactions between Grey Seals and UK Fisheries* was published in 1984. They found that the proportion of seal-damaged salmon around salmon nets did not indicate a change in the number of seals attacking salmon over the period of 1959 to 1982. It was not possible to determine the actual number of salmon eaten by seals, but certainly there was no increase in the fish attacked but not killed. More direct investigations of seal diets were carried out by analysing the fish remains in seal faeces collected at various places round Britain. These showed that Sand Eels were by far the most important prey species, making up 60% of the faeces by weight. Next in order of importance were Ling and Tusk (12%), followed by various *Trispoterus* species such as Poor Cod and Pout Whiting (7%), Whiting (6%), Haddock, Saithe and Pollack (5%), and Cod (3%). No Salmon remains were found, but if Salmon comprised only one or two per cent of the diet, their remains might well be undetected. If the mix of species represented by these analyses reflect the seals' diet, then in 1981 the seals were eating the equivalent to 11 lb (5 kg) of fish per day per seal. There was little seasonal variation in faecal contents, suggesting that the prey species were more or less the same at different stages of the life-cycle of the seals. Making apparently reasonable assumptions, seal consumption as a proportion of the commercial fisheries catch is highest for Tusk and Ling (45%), followed by Sand Eels (11%) and Whiting (5%). For all other species, the seals are catching less than 5% of the amount caught by commercial fishing.

These data do not support the contention that seals are direct and important competitors with commercial fishermen, or even salmon netters. However, there are still many imponderables, and the large consumption of Sand Eels raises questions about the effects of further increases in exploitation of this important prey of sea-birds (see p. 147).

Common Seals

Common Seals are smaller than Grey Seals, up to about 6 ft (1.9 m) long and weighing 2 cwt (120 kg). The sexes are approximately equal in size. Pups are born in June and July. Unlike Grey Seals, they are born in their adult grey-brown coat; the white coat is moulted in the uterus, the occasional one which survives birth being shed within a day or two. At the high tide following their birth, the pups are capable of swimming off the pupping beach with their mothers. This makes it difficult to catch and tag Common Seal pups and little is known about their dispersal. Pups may suckle up to six weeks, either on land or in the water. The relationship of the pups to their mother is closer than in the Grey Seal, with the pups following their mother closely, even, it is said, after weaning. The adults moult after the pups are weaned, and mate (usually) after the moult. They are around the islands for the whole year, and it is assumed that most of their feeding is done closer to the shore than Grey Seals. Even the estimated numbers of Common Seals are unlikely to be as accurate as for the Common Seal, because the haul-outs of the latter are much more scattered and counting individuals is more difficult.

The Common Seal was totally unprotected until the Conservation of Seals Act of 1970. In the years before this, there were drastic declines of the

Figs. 47–48 (opposite page) Common Seals (Photo: Sea Mammal Research Unit (NERC)).

species in a number of areas, including Shetland, through over-hunting. Killing is now only permitted following the granting of a licence from the Department of Agriculture and Fisheries.

The seal situation in Orkney is very different from that in Shetland. In the latter islands, the Grey Seal breeding beaches are almost all very exposed to wave action, many of them in caves, and a large proportion of pups starve or are drowned each year. In contrast to every other part of the country, Grey Seal numbers in Shetland have remained fairly constant in recent years. As a result, Common Seals were hunted much more intensively than Greys in Shetland. Between 1972 and 1976 an annual average of 140 Common Seal pups were shot in Orkney, but only eight between 1977 and 1982. During the 1960s an average of 700 pups a year were taken in Shetland; by 1970 it was thought that about 90% of the pups born each year were being taken by hunters. From 1972 no licences have been issued for shooting in Shetland.

As far as Orkney is concerned, Common Seal numbers have remained approximately constant for several decades, although actual counts have only been made since 1972. Oil-related developments do not seem to have affected them: there have been changes in the distribution of seals around Flotta and the western fringes of Scapa Flow, but the total numbers have remained constant. When the Egilsay pier was rebuilt in 1972, the animals normally resident on the nearby Holm of Scockness deserted their regular beach for a less disturbed part of Egilsay. Once the construction work was finished, the seals moved back to their regular site.

Other Seal Species

Vagrant seals of other species from the Arctic appear in Orkney from time to time, but they are very rare. Most reports are of the Walrus (*Odobenus rosmarus*), but some of these in former years were transported in ships, for it is said that Arctic whalers used on occasion to bring back young Walrus. There is a story of a Walrus at Longhope which annoyed people crossing the bay on the way to church, by putting its tusks over the gunwale of the boat . . . History does not relate the end of the story.

Whales

It is not uncommon to see whales from Orkney, and 18 different species have been recorded. Pilot or Caain' Whale (*Globicephala melaena*) is the most common, but the schools in Orkney seem to be smaller than in Shetland, where the largest recorded was of 1540 whales which came into Quendale Bay, south Mainland on 22nd September 1845. Orcadians and Shetlanders have traditionally used only the blubber from stranded whales, unlike the Faroese who eat whale meat regularly. In Orkney, the blubber was boiled and turned into oil, while the carcasses were left to rot.

The earliest mention of whales being driven ashore in Orkney was of 114 grounded near Kairston, Mainland in 1691. There are a number of accounts from the 19th century: a shoal of 50 whales ran aground at Rothiesholm in Stronsay in November, 1834, and yielded about £100 of oil; early in 1841, 287 whales came ashore on the west side of Eday and yielded a return of £398. In Sanday, whale hunting was regarded as the most exciting form of fishing. An eye-witness wrote in the mid-19th century:

'Shoals ranging from 50 to 500 in number get occasionally embayed; and upon this happening, all boats are launched, all hands active, every tool which can be converted into a weapon of offence to the strangers, from the roasting-spit of the principal tenant, to the ware (seaweed) fork of the cottar, is put into requisition. The shoal is surrounded, driven like a flock of timid sheep to shallow water on a sandy shore, and then the attack is made in earnest. The boats push in, stabbing and wounding in all directions. The tails of the wounded fish lash the sea, which is dyed red with their blood, sometimes dashing a boat to pieces. The whales in dying emit shrill and plaintive cries, accompanied with loud snorting and a humming noise easily mistaken at a distance for fifes and drums.'

This description is reminiscent of the Faroe Islands, where the whole operation of driving the whales to recognized beaches, and of killing them and dividing the produce, is highly organized. John Buchan captured well the lust of a Faroese whale hunt in the *Island of Sheep*.

Whale hunting was still taking place in Orkney in the 1860s. It was noted then that they always swam upwind if they could, and if the leader was once ashore, the rest followed easily. They could be easily killed by a rifle bullet in the throat. A visitor to Stronsay described a school driven into Mill Bay in the old *Orkney Book*. Men and women from far and near assembled to kill them with harpoons, three-pronged graips and hayforks. The boat crews beat pitchers, rattled rowlocks, and shouted, as they surrounded the school in a crescent formation. A skiff that put out from the shore in front of the whales disturbed them so that they turned, but the boats followed them and eventually got them ashore at Rothesholm Bay, which the Stronsay minister described as 'the best whale-trap I know in Orkney.' On that occasion 170 whales were killed. At Sourin Bay, Rousay, 60 were slain and sold for £260. In the 1870s 300 were caught in Linga Strand, Stronsay. A dyke at Grainbank Farm, Wideford Hill, was built of the skulls of Caain' Whales driven into Kirkwall Bay.

At that time a whale chase added welcome excitement and a valued addition to an islander's income. A Westray farmer, about to make a coffin for his newly-dead wife, when he heard the call 'Whales in the bay', set off immediately leaving two of his men working on the coffin, since this meant two less to share the produce. The laird who was to divide the catch was surprised to see him at such a time. The farmer's explanation was, 'I could na afford to lose baith wife and whales on the same day.'

Caain' Whales may be seen at any time of the year around Orkney, but are most often seen between November and January. Other whale species are occasionally recorded in Orkney waters. The baleen whales tend to migrate southwards along the continental shelf edge in late summer and autumn, and the proximity of the shelf to Orkney, together with the rich upwelling areas to the south and west of Orkney, make the region important for cetaceans. There are whale bones in Neolithic middens at Skara Brae, showing that 5000 years ago man was using whales for house building and kitchen utensils, as well as (presumably) for food. At the turn of the century there were approximately 20 whaling stations in Iceland and Faroe. In North Norway, whaling was banned as a result of disputes with the Cod fishermen, and, as the Greenland whaling began to collapse, Norwegian

Fig. 49.
*A Pilot Whale
stranding* (Photo:
*Tom Kent Collection,
Orkney Library*).

whalers set up three stations in Shetland (at Ronas Voe, Olnafirth and Collafirth), as well as in the Hebrides and the west of Ireland. The Shetland stations were always the most important of these, and over 3400 Fin and 1800 Right Whales (together with other species) were caught before the stations closed in 1929. Before the 1914–18 war there was no evidence of over-exploitation, but afterwards it became obvious that the stocks of whales passing through the waters around Orkney and Shetland, particularly the Blue, Humpback and Right Whales were not enough to withstand the hunting pressure.

There have been no recent sightings of Sei (*Balaenoptora borealis*) or Blue Whales (*B. musculus*) off Orkney but Fin Whales (*B. physalus*) are sometimes seen, usually in autumn to the west of Orkney, while its smaller relative the Minke Whale (*B. acutorostrata*) seems to be not uncommon in the vicinity of upwelling areas around headlands, small islands or shallow banks. These baleen whales are usually seen singly or in pairs, and there is some evidence from studies elsewhere that they return year after year to the same areas to feed and defend a home range from which other whales are excluded.

Comparable in size with some of the larger baleen whales, is the Sperm Whale (*Physeter catodon*). This species occurs in deep water off the edge of the continental shelf where it feeds on large squid. Lone males are the most commonly recorded in British and Irish waters, females and their calves tending to remain in equatorial waters throughout the year. In recent years there have been a number of sightings of Sperm Whales in

Orkney waters, particularly in Scapa Flow between September and January. Included amongst these was a pod of six or seven individuals, juveniles probably accompanied by females, seen in October 1976.

During the 19th century one of the beaked whales, the Northern Bottlenose Whale (*Hyperoodon ampullatus*) was thought to be common in Orkney waters, although its specific identity cannot be confirmed. However, it has since been recorded in the seas west of Orkney, usually in late summer. In the North-east Atlantic concentrations occur in the Norwegian Sea, from which it migrates south in late summer and early autumn. Other beaked whales are rare visitors to British waters, occurring generally further south in warm temperate seas. Two species, Cuvier's Whale (*Ziphius cavirostri*) and Sowerby's Whale (*Mesoplodon bidens*) have been recorded stranded on Orkney coasts in summer, though only very rarely (the former stranded at Rackwick, Hoy in January and again in September 1963, and on the East Mainland, October 1920; and the latter at Burwick, South Ronaldsay in July 1933, North Ronaldsay, April 1954, and two females on Birsay in June 1961).

Orkney also receives visitors from colder waters. Two Arctic species, the White Whale (*Delphinapterus leucas*) and Narwhal (*Monodon monoceros*), have both occurred in summer or autumn in Orkney waters. The White Whale has been the most frequently observed with strandings of single animals in October 1845, August 1964 and a probable one in October 1981, and a single individual seen in October 1960. There is only one record of a Narwhal in Orkney, when two were seen off Gairsay in June 1949. In recent years White Whales have been seen relatively frequently in sub-Arctic waters off the Norwegian coast.

The Killer Whale (*Orcinus orca*) is often confused with the adult Risso's Dolphin (*Grampus griseus*) since the latter is larger than most people expect and has a relatively tall dorsal fin. The term 'grampus' has been commonly applied to both species, and past descriptions of their abundance in Orkney waters may confuse the two. Small herds of the former (usually 3–6 individuals) may be seen most years, usually between July and September although it has also been recorded in Orkney waters in midwinter. Most sightings come from north-west and west Orkney, or to the south from Scapa Flow and the Pentland Firth. It is possible that the species is preying at this time upon seal pups in inshore waters.

Other Cetaceans

The Harbour Porpoise (*Phocoena phocoena*) is the most commonly observed small cetacean in Orkney waters, albeit in relatively small numbers. It occurs mainly in sheltered voes where it is probably feeding on small shoaling fish such as Sand Eels (*Ammodytes* spp) and sprats (*Clupea sprattus*). It may be seen at any time, although most sightings occur in July–September and very few are recorded from winter months when it is possible that much of the population moves offshore. Young individuals have been seen in late summer, and breeding probably takes place around May–June not far from Orkney.

The White-beaked Dolphin (*Lagenorhynchus albirostris*) is probably the most abundant dolphin in Orkney waters during the summer and autumn, occurring in herds of between five and twenty individuals. Sightings peak in the August to October period, at the same time as large numbers are regularly seen off the North Sutherland coast, in the north Minches and off the east coast of Shetland. Most herds in Orkney appear to occur off the west coast and near Sule Skerry, although this may be because Sule Skerry is visited fairly often by naturalists, and occurrences are more likely to be sighted and reported.

The White-sided Dolphin (*L. acutus*) is a more pelagic species than the White-beaked Dolphin. It is also observed mainly west of Orkney and in the vicinity of North Rona, Sule Skerry and Sule Stack. Herd size, though commonly between five and twenty individuals, may sometimes be up to one hundred, particularly during apparent long-distance movements. Sightings also peak between August and October. White-beaked Dolphins give birth in late summer and autumn, whereas the young of White-sided Dolphins are born slightly earlier, around mid-summer. Their occurrence in the vicinity of Orkney at this time may indicate that they both breed not far from the islands.

The overall situation is of large whales passing through Orkney waters during summer and autumn on their way south to more equatorial regions, while the dolphin species (such as White-beaked and White-sided Dolphins and the Harbour Porpoise) appear to be more resident in Orkney waters although offshore movements may occur at particular times of the year. This also seems to be the case for Risso's Dolphin, which is very rarely seen during winter or spring in Orkney waters.

Risso's Dolphin is frequently observed, in numbers ranging from 4–15 individuals, between July and October west of Orkney, and often seen in the vicinity of Sule Skerry.

Two dolphin species, though not uncommon elsewhere in Britain, are rarely observed in Orkney waters. There is only one record of the Bottlenosed Dolphin (*Tursiops truncatus*), which occurs primarily in coastal waters, shallow bays and estuaries of the British mainland, and the Common Dolphin (*Delphinus delphis*) is rare in Orkney too, though commonly seen offshore of southwest Britain and Ireland. Stranding records over the last half century suggest that these species were formerly amongst the commonest of dolphin species in UK waters. However, the former has almost certainly declined in recent years and the latter rarely occurs in coastal waters as far north as Orkney.

Before leaving whales, mention must be made of Orcadian involvement in polar whaling, which used to be an important source of hard cash to many families. Whalers heading from Greenland and the Davis Straits used to call in to Orkney and Shetland for crews. In 1816, 34 whaling ships were recorded at Stromness, of which 25 came from Hull. Fifty men from Stromness alone were at the Straits in 1821. Stromness merchants acted as agents for shipowners elsewhere. Arctic whaling came to an end a few years before the 1914–18 war, and (apart from the East Atlantic whaling mentioned earlier), attention shifted to the Antarctic with the establishment of bases at Grytviken in South Georgia in 1904 and in the Falkland Islands in 1908. Many men from the North Isles were involved in this whaling, but it was proportionately much less important to Orkney than the Arctic phase had been.

Otters

The *Orkneyinga Saga* says of Orkney otters that they 'often lay among the rocks,' and describes otter-hunting a thousand years ago on Rousay: 'The Earl had risen early, and he and nineteen men had gone to the south end of the island to hunt the otters that lay on the rocks under the headland.' This persecution extended down the centuries, and the export of otter skins from Orkney is on record from the 17th century onwards. They were rarely shot, but knocked down with sticks. The skin of a winter-killed otter with plenty of fur was worth about ten shillings in the early 1880s.

Otters (*Lutra lutra*) were commonly caught in stone traps known as otter-houses. Traces of these can still be found in some parts, more commonly in Shetland than Orkney. They were built across the tracks of otters, and roofed with heavy flat stones, with a sliding door which slipped into place when the otter displaced a stone inside.

Otters are fairly general carnivores. They will raid hen houses in winter, and in the summer take breeding duck and Black Guillemots. However, their main diet in the islands is fish. Analysis of faeces collected in Fetlar, Shetland showed that 10% of the identifiable contents were of crabs, the rest were fish (half being 'long fish' such as Blennies, Butterfish and Eels).

It is very difficult to make accurate counts of Otter numbers. It has been estimated that there is at least one Otter every three-quarters of a mile on the more remote Shetland coasts; they are probably rather less common in Orkney. The Orkney Otter Group surveyed the entire coastline of Scapa

Fig. 50.
A characteristic view of an Otter. At dawn or dusk it is often possible to glimpse these shy and enchanting creatures (Photo: *William Paton*).

Flow in spring and summer 1980 and found that 96 of the 167 kilometre squares (57%) had spraints in them. Elsewhere around the coast of the Mainland 36/46 (78%) sites were found to contain spraints. The average number of spraints per site was 3.9. This is significantly less than the mean figure of 6.7 spraints per site for the Highland Region, Western Isles and Shetland, and supports the subjective estimate that Otters are not as numerous in Orkney as in Shetland.

There is no way of knowing how the Otter population compares with,

Table 13   *Occurrence of Sea Mammals in Orkney.*

	Otter	Grey Seal	Common Seal
Mainland	*	*	*
Shapinsay	*		*
Gairsay	*	*	
Wyre	*	*	*
Egilsay	*	*	*
Rousay	*		*
Eynhallow	*	*	*
North Faray		*	
Westray	*		*
Papa Westray	*	*	*
Eday	*		
Stronsay	*	*	*
Sanday	*	*	*
North Ronaldsay	*	*	
Burray			*
Glims Holm	*		
South Ronaldsay	*	*	*
Hoy	*		*
Longhope	*		*
Graemsay	*		
Flotta	*		*
Cava	*		*
Copinsay	*		*
Swona		*	*
Switha	*	*	*
South Faray	*		*
Holm of Aikerness			*
Auskerry		*	
Linga Holm		*	
Muckle Green Holm		*	
Little Green Holm		*	
Holm of Faray		*	
Wart Holm		*	
Rusk Holm		*	
Sweyn Holm		*	
Holm of Boray		*	
Grass Holm		*	
Little Skerry		*	

say, a century ago, when Buckley & Harvie-Brown could say in their *Vertebrate Fauna* that 'Otters are yet abundant in most of the islands.' There is a suspicion that the population has declined in the past decade or two. However, it is not particularly difficult to catch a glimpse of an Otter particularly at dawn or dusk, and many Orcadians have anecdotes about meeting them unexpectedly (including the one which walked up Stromness Pier on New Year's Day 1964, and went to sleep in the Harbourmaster's Office), or of people who have reared orphan pups. In view of the virtual extinction of the species in southern England, it is encouraging to find that Otters, although very susceptible to oil pollution (at least ten Otters were killed in a notorious incident at Sullom Voe), can tolerate a surprising amount of disturbance. Recently an Otter family was raised in a holt below one of the main jetties at the Sullom Voe oil terminal. Although hunting and pollution must be elements in the decline of the Otter in England, a major factor is the availability of suitable breeding sites which have been removed in the south as river banks have been tidied and straightened. At least this last is not a problem for Orkney Otters.

CHAPTER **7 Freshwater Habitats**

'They have no Rivers, no place of the Land being above 2 or 3 miles distant from the Sea, therefore they draw water out of wells for their Cattel, or drive them to Lochs or Lakes, some whereof they have, or to some small brooks which run from these Lochs: Which Lochs likewise cause their Mills to go.'

Thus Reverend John Brand wrote of Orkney in 1701. He says nothing about the abundant sea and loch trout of the lochs and streams which provide excellent eating. They were an important food source, in particular for the people of Harray, which is the only parish in Orkney with no sea-coast, and was traditionally, therefore, a poor one. However, he does write of the abundance of sea fish which . . .

'is pleasant to the taste, and also they say very wholesome, which seems to be confirmed by this that in the years of great scarcity, the poorer People lived upon them, almost as their only food, they often not enjoying a crum of Bread for many Weeks. So our good God, on the shutting of one door, opened another in his holy and wise Providence for the relief of the poor.'

Fig. 51.
Hill Lochan
(Photo: *Charles Tait*).

Orkney is not unlike Shetland in having no rivers and few streams, but the Orkney waters are less diverse than the Shetland ones, because of the nature of the underlying rocks; Shetland geology is much more varied than that of Orkney. Consequently, in the past there's been little interest in Orkney lochs and streams (except among fishermen). In recent years this neglect has been recognized and an overdue interest is now developing. Certainly the importance of the local waters within the natural Orkney environment has been underestimated in the past. There are now some limited surveys of Orkney fresh waters, which supplement the few small studies of the past; a full list of publications pertaining to Orkney fresh waters is to be found on page 225.

Table 14 shows the paucity in numbers of Orkney waters in comparison with Shetland, the Western Isles and Caithness. Orkney possesses few streams of any note, though locally they are important as spawning and nursery grounds for trout, growth areas for eels and, as Brand pointed out, in former years for milling. However, whilst the standing-water body (loch) count is also comparatively low, the few that exist in the county are large; this is due largely to the underlying geology (see Chapter 3).

Freshwater Bodies of the North of Scotland.   Table 14

	Orkney	Shetland	Western Isles	Caithness
Number of streams	131	298	287	120
Number of standing water bodies	48	195	1094	73
Number of standing water bodies of area greater than $\frac{1}{4}$ km²	17	28	176	25
Mean area of standing water bodies (km²)	0.78	0.17	no figure available	0.33

Water chemistry data are comparatively scarce, the Orkney Islands Council being the only regular analyser of water – and that limited to drinking sources. The sandstone rock of which Orkney is composed results in little chemical variation in analyses from loch water. The proximity of the sea is an obvious factor influencing the sodium and chloride content of the fresh waters, but recent analyses show that gross salinity (measured as 'chlorinity') varies surprisingly little from loch to loch; recorded values range from only 0.15 $^o/_{oo}$ (= parts per thousand) to 0.5$^o/_{oo}$, the average being 0.26$^o/_{oo}$. Typical results of recent analyses are shown in Table 15, together with some salinity values. Extreme high values are shown in italics in the Table and merit comment: $CaCO_3$ levels are high in South Ronaldsay and Sanday where the rock has influence (blown sand in Sanday); the lowest pH value was 5.1 from Hoy, otherwise the remaining figures are all within the range of 6.1–8.7. Perhaps the most significant information is the bio-chemical 'oxygen-demand' figure; this gives an indirect measure of the amount of organic matter in water and as this uses up oxygen, so the oxygen disappears from the water sample. A wide variation exists here: Kirbister Loch in Orphir, Mainland is particularly rich, with two Westray samples showing high values as well.

Table 15 *Analyses of Island Water Sources (Orkney Islands Council Figures 1974–1980)*

Water Source	Total dissolved solids ppm	Chloride	NaCl	Total hardness (as $CaCO_3$)	pH	NO_3	Oxygen absorbed in 4 hours
Borehole 2, Eday	420	87	144	220	7.2	—	0.16
Meikle Loch, Stronsay	332	112	185	98	7.8	—	5.1
Kirbister, Orphir	230	42	69	58	6.1	0.4	13.2
Boardhouse, Birsay	268	70	115	126	8.5	—	3.0
Saintair, Westray	407	93	153	200	7.4	0.9	36.7
Hoglinns, Hoy	138	64	105	24	5.1	—	2.7
Heldale, Hoy	141	59	97	32	7.0	—	2.6
Pool of Cletts, S. Ron.	490	80	132	364	7.8	1.0	0.3
Rue, N. Ronaldsay	670	164	270	346	7.2	3.6	2.8
Ancum Well, S. Ron.	690	157	259	342	7.2	4.0	3.9
Borehole 2, Shapinsay	n.d.	76	125	246	7.1	—	1.2
Borehole 3, Shapinsay	n.d.	68	112	112	6.4	3.4	5.5
Borehole 4, Shapinsay	425	77	127	246	7.3	—	0.5
Fea Hill Spring, Sanday	n.d.	86	140	380	8.1	2.0	0.6
Bealoch, Sanday	n.d.	85	140	138	8.7	—	2.4
Burness, Westray	n.d.	76	125	230	7.9	—	6.5

It is a pity that analyses have not been carried out elsewhere, for the sources listed cover only a small proportion of the water bodies in Orkney. Moreover freshwater biologists are interested in a greater range of chemicals, and at present this information is simply lacking. The only analyses carried out in recent years for freshwater study purposes were on two streams, Swartaback Burn (which runs into the loch of Kirbister at GR 373072) and the Toab Burn (entering the sea at 516046). Data for these two are shown in Table 16 together with data on four other Orkney fresh waters. All these data are within the ranges found in other parts of Britain.

How the lochs and streams and pools fit into the Orcadian scene depend on one's point of view. The West Mainland, with most of the lochs and (because of the hills) most of the streams can present an extremely pleasant water-farmland patchwork from Ward Hill in Orphir to the Evie hills in

Table 16 *Chemical Analyses on Six Orkney Freshwaters (after Heppleston 1984).*

m mol/l	Toab Burn	Swartaback Burn	Binscarth Stream	Echnaloch	Loch of Tankerness	Peat Pool
Sodium	2.20	1.80	2.20	3.00	2.20	2.20
Potassium	0.17	0.05	0.10	0.16	0.11	0.06
Calcium	1.13	0.32	0.89	0.77	0.72	0.38
Magnesium	0.63	0.40	0.45	0.40	0.40	no data
Chloride	0.33	0.67	3.00	1.30	1.30	0.60
Phosphate	0.04	0.04	0.02	0.04	0.01	no data

the north and to the high ridge of the Rendall–Firth hills in the east. These are the lochs of the fishermen and the ornithologist.

Little attention has been given to the East Mainland or to the outer isles; in both areas there are very few water bodies of note, although lochs of moderate size occur in Sanday, Stronsay, Westray and Papa Westray. Hoy moorland possesses two notable lochs set in narrow valleys; they are the deepest lochs in Orkney (Hoglinns is 57 ft (17.4 m) deep and Heldale is similar). The latter supports the only known population of Char (*Salvelinus alpinus*) on Orkney. Its present status is unknown. Rousay is similarly hilly and has two 'highland' lochs – Peerie Water and Muckle Water (each 20 ft (6 m) deep). Other outer-isles freshwaters are few and their nature poorly understood save for those that provide water supplies to the islanders; these have been analysed by the local water authority.

Streams are not common, but are attractive sights, whether they are rushing down the gulleys of West Mainland hills in spate or running through the flatter East Mainland farmland. Marsh and bog are common in all peat-land areas, rich in plant and bird-life, but among some of the most threatened habitats in the islands. In the hills (and occasionally in old peat workings) are dark brown pools – frequented by Red-throated Divers (and hence called 'loomashuns'). Close to the shore, particularly in the eastern part of mainland Orkney, are lagoons – impounded pools at the edge of the sea.

All these habitats are to be found within only a short distance of Orkney's capital, Kirkwall, and offer a wide range of freshwater habitats which need only a brief visit to encompass them all.

Lochs Harray and Stenness

These two lochs deserve separate treatment: together they form an important conservation site (SSSI), popular with anglers and birdwatchers, and are the two largest lochs in Orkney with about 60 sq miles (160 sq km) of drainage area. Although shallow by mainland Scotland standards (because of the flat sedimentary rock and glacial drift underlying them), they are nevertheless amongst the six deepest lochs in the islands. It is for these reasons that they have received particular attention over the past half-century. Their significance emerges when the history of their 'exploration' is considered.

Prior to 1936 the lochs were considered something of a speciality by ecologists of the day. Harray Loch drains a shallow basin in the centre of the West Mainland and pours its contents out into Loch Stenness through a narrow channel at Brodgar, across which there now passes a major county road. Ducts under the roadway allow the flow of fresh water into the second loch (Stenness), which in turn opens to the sea at the much wider channel at Waithe. Stenness has therefore always been a salt-water loch which receives at its eastern end a great volume of fresh water from Harray (2.5 sq miles (6.5 sq km) in area). But when the tide flows in at the Bridge of Waithe, Stenness fills up with saline water to such an extent that the direction of water flow at Brodgar is reversed and brackish water moves back into Harray.

For years it was believed that these two lochs formed a salinity continuum from Waithe to the north end of Harray. As such it seemed to be a brackish-water ecosystem unique to Britain, even without the vast numbers of wildfowl that gather there. An early study was based on salinity differences at a few sites. In 1936, however, Edith Nicol carried out a thorough analysis of the lochs, their water, and flora and fauna; she found that Stenness water had a fairly uniform salinity (about half to threequarters that of seawater), and that Harray water was very low in salt.

The next development came some 25 years later when local anglers became concerned about algal blooms of *Prymnesium* which occurred on Harray. They associated these with saline influence from Stenness and in 1968, one-way sluice valves were inserted in the channel ducts under the Brodgar road, permitting fresh water to flow out of Harray, but preventing salt-water entering Harray from Stenness. These halved the salinity of Harray water (north end) from around $0.19-0.72\%_{00}$ to $0.08-0.35\%_{00}$. Since that time there appears to have been little in the way of algal blooms and certainly no significant effect on local fish.

In 1978 workers from Kirkwall Grammar School carried out a project to see how the two lochs had changed since Nicol's study of the 1930s. They took water samples at the 1930 sites and made invertebrate collections to see how far salinity differences affected the animals living in the lochs. Over the 42 years between the surveys the salinities had changed little: Stenness had increased from $15\%_{00}$ to $18\%_{00}$ on average and Harray decreased from $1.3\%_{00}$ to $0.7\%_{00}$. The sluice is now not as efficient as it was supposed to be: some salty water moves from Stenness into Harray at high tide, but the influence in Harray is restricted to the area close to the sluices; elsewhere in the loch the salinities of the water are fairly uniform (around $0.5\%_{00}$), very close to that for fresh stream water in Orkney.

The animals were similar in the two surveys. *Gammarus duebeni* (brackish water shrimp) was abundant in both lochs; it was found in Harray at salinities as low as $0.33\%_{00}$. Jenkins' Pond-snail (*Potamopyrgus jenkinsi*) was locally very abundant and seems to thrive equally well in brackish and fresh water. This snail has spread its range and habitat tolerance dramatically over the last 50 years and in Orkney is found in lochs, streams, brackish lagoons and ditches. However, Stenness Loch was evidently too saline for it and laboratory experiments with Orcadian specimens confirmed that they do not survive for long in water that is more than 50% seawater. Another mollusc of note is *Theodoxus fluviatile* found locally abundant in Harray, perhaps the only Scottish locality for this calcium-loving animal. The invertebrate variety of these lochs seems to be typical of similar freshwater bodies elsewhere, each loch possessing about 35 known kinds of bottom-dwelling invertebrates.

There is other evidence to suggest that Harray (and Stenness) are remarkable lochs, unique in many ways. In Harray the green alga *Cladophora* (*Aegagrophila*) *sauteri* occurs, forming small balls on the loch bottom; it is only known in Britain from two other localities. Chemical analyses highlight the high nutrient status of Harray and Stenness – most brackish lochs have low alkalinity with a high nutrient level, but in these two, alkalinity is high. Furthermore they retain oligotrophic shore-lines despite eutrophic water. There is some evidence that Harray vegetation is characteristic of eutrophic waters.

Other Lochs

In comparison with lochs and lakes in other parts of Britain, most of Orkney's other lochs support a comparatively narrow variety of animal and plant species. In broad terms this feature suggests that the lochs are less rich than many, but in fact water analyses and plant records indicate that in some respects, Orkney lochs exhibit features that are found in southern lochs/lakes of considerable richness. The pattern is of great complexity, and the degree to which one can properly assign a water body to 'oligo-trophic' or 'eutrophic' categories is limited; in some ways the distinction is arbitrary and artificial, but comparison with other localities does provide certain pointers; the vegetation chapter (Chapter 4) should be consulted to ascertain the extent to which this classification system is appropriate in the case of Orkney lochs.

Swannay is the deepest mainland loch, 16 ft (5 m) deep, whilst at the other extreme Isbister and Sabiston Lochs, 3 ft (1 m), are shallow enough for the growth of rooted plants in the middle. The shallow edges of many lochs support good growths of rooted vegetation (see Chapter 4), but otherwise shore vegetation is rather sparse.

Many observers have noted that the flat stones bordering the Orkney lochs (and extending well into the middle) tend to be comparatively clean and free from silt. Peat fragments and silt are not scarce in Orkney and the explanation of this observation is that the frequent autumn and winter gales agitate the whole water mass of these shallow lochs and prevent the

Fig. 52.
Shallow lochan
(Photo: *R. S. Moore*).

Fig. 53.
Lowland loch fringed
by Bogbean (Photo:
William Paton).

deposition of silt on the bottom; spates of water then sweep away the suspended particles. The likelihood is that lochs deeper than about 20 ft (6 m) will have silt-free stones only around the very perimeter with the remainder of the substrate being buried under a dense and accumulating mass of tiny particles washed in by streams. However, most of Orkney's lochs have unclogged stones, available as a habitat for invertebrates.

A number of lochs receive run-off from the rich farmland which borders their shores; even so they resist these potentially eutrophic effects and remain partially oligotrophic. Surveys have shown that there is little variation between lochs as far as their invertebrate fauna is concerned. Commonest species include the freshwater shrimp *Gammarus lacustris*, water boatmen (various species), the wandering Pond-snail (*Lymnaea pereger*), and sticklebacks. Jenkins' Pond-snail is common in Orkney. Other species found frequently include leeches and Caddis-fly larvae; a number of case-building species of the latter are very common in certain lochs such as Tankerness, Brockan and Echnaloch, where there is plenty of vegetation available for manufacturing cases.

The base of the food chain is, of course, green plants in the form of algal plankton, rooted vegetation or attached algae. Plankton surveys have not been a priority for Orkney limnologists; one survey in Kirbister Loch found a poor selection of species – fewer in number than comparable samples from Shetland. Rooted plants are found in few Orkney lochs; they are a major element of the flora in perhaps only a quarter of the islands' lochs. An interesting exception is Graemeshall Loch which supports an extensive bed of reeds (*Phagmites australis*). Algae seem to be the most abundant group of primary producers in the lochs, often covering the surface of flat rocks and stones, making it difficult to pick them up. The most comprehensive survey of these algae and others living on mud and other plants was conducted at the beginning of this century. It showed that Orkney and Shetland had many species in common, although some species occurred in only one or the other of the island groups.

In general the lochs with the richest flora also have the richest fauna. Echnaloch has a particularly varied spectrum of animal species and is an example of a loch with considerable shore vegetation and a good faunal community associated with it.

Angling

Orkney lochs have great attractions for wildfowl and ornithologists, but perhaps most of all they are a mecca for anglers. Fishing is free in Orkney's lochs; it provides a rich hunting-ground for fishermen from all over Britain for Brown Trout (*Salmo trutta*). The natural stocks are augmented each year by introductions from local eggs hatched in a small hatchery near Kirkwall, under the auspices of the Orkney Trout Fishing Association. Of the major lochs, Harray is considered to offer the best fishing. The trout here form a self-sustaining population which requires no stocking. The loch has a very long, indented shore-line and a large area of off-shore shallows, factors which combine to produce large populations of trout and excellent fishing. The annual catch from Harray is reckoned in hundreds of thousands, mainly caught from boats rather than by shore wading. The sister loch to Harray – Stenness – is much more saline and there is less good fishing; the variety of species caught is, however, greater and includes Sea Trout.

Every loch has its devotees, but perhaps Swannay can be singled out as being rather special for the angler. Deepest of all the mainland lochs, it has a shallow southern half, but with skerries and troughs, which provides the best (boat) fishing; shore wading conditions are notoriously treacherous and have caused many an upset. Swannay has a reputation for fickleness, but its trout are said to be wild and strong, considered by some to be amongst the best quality wild Brown Trout in the country.

It is inappropriate here to discuss the best fly to use in which loch at what season and under which circumstances. Suffice it to say that local anglers have adapted well-tried flies to suit local conditions and it is remarkable how close to the natural invertebrate prey a fly fisherman can get when constructing a fly. For example there are many who fish with shrimp-like flies and sedges (caddis mimics); analysis of stomach contents of Orkney Brown Trout show that these two invertebrates are the most abundant prey – at least during the summer months.

Streams

Orkney's geology is responsible for its comparative lack of streams. Those that are present can be classified as either moorland streams or farmland streams. Until the coming of the Vikings, most of Orkney was probably moorland, so one can consider the few truly moorland streams today as being the original type of Orkney stream, relatively unaffected by man. But

Fig. 54.
Stream and mill
(Photo: *Charles
Tait*).

farming has changed the landscape and in modern times has had effects on streams through inputs of fertilizer run-off, farm effluent and, very occasionally, sewage. Studies on Orkney streams affected by farming operations show that (as in other parts of the UK) the deprivation of oxygen due to the growth of bacteria (which thrive on the materials entering the water) has had the greatest effect. Only those species which can tolerate low oxygen concentrations are able to survive, such as chironomid (midge) larvae (bloodworms), etc. The enrichment effect which must presumably exist where phosphate and nitrate fertilizers drain into the streams has not yet been adequately studied, but there are no major effects. In general the farming community is very aware of the problems, and legislation to control, for example, silage run-off prevents severe pollution.

The natural stream environment exists not only in moorland streams but (perhaps surprisingly) also in many of those running through farmland; this confirms the comparative lack of any acute, widespread farming influence on stream organisms. The most abundant animals are those typical of hill streams elsewhere – stonefly and mayfly nymphs, cased caddis and caseless caddis larvae; the river limpet *Ancylus fluviatile* is also found, especially in faster-flowing regions. Shrimps are scarce, but noteworthy is the presence of *Gammarus pulex* in Swartaback Burn; this species has only recently been discovered in Orkney, although it is a common freshwater stream shrimp further south in Britain.

Most of Orkney's main hill streams have a particular charm: from the point where they emerge from peat seepage into a recognizable flow, they pass their brown peat-stained burden through some most attractive scenery with, in Spring, Primroses along the banks, pond-skaters darting over the pools, and Curlew and Lapwing calling around. The fast flow of such reaches was harnessed as millstreams in days gone by. In many parts mill-houses still remain, with recognizable mill-races and often millwheels too. When they were functioning, water flow was ensured throughout the year by the construction of a mill-dam with sluice-type controls which allowed the required water to pass along the mill-race when grinding needed to be done. There are a host of places in Orkney today with names like Milldam and Millhouse.

The wheels are now still and the dams empty, but the streams continue. They provide local trout fishers with annual tasks when spawn is collected each autumn from adult fish. This spawn is transferred to the hatchery where the young are reared until they are about three months old and just over an inch (3 cm) long; the fry are then released into the lochs.

Reclamation and improvement of Orkney's land has resulted in fewer hill-type streams than in the past. About three-quarters feed lochs, the others flowing direct into the sea, forming mini-estuary conditions and some salt-marshes (notably at Toab, East Mainland). But the outward, physical appearance of most of the streams has not altered appreciably this century.

Peat Pools

Peat working is still a common activity in Orkney and has been a feature of island life for centuries. The presence of abandoned peat-workings gives rise to pools of still, dark water under the banks. In addition there are pools high in the moorland hill landscape even where no peat is dug.

Both sorts of pools are similar: the water is a rich brown colour with pH 4–5 (i.e. fairly acid); the oxygen content of the water is low and the substrate almost always a muddy peat deposit; vegetation includes rushes and a variety of surface plants.

The main problem faced by animals in such pools is the lack of oxygen. For that reason pool dwellers have special adaptations. For example, bloodworms (chironomid larvae) have haemoglobin in their body fluids. Water beetles are common, including a species of the Great Diving Beetle (*Dytiscus*) which come to the water surface to obtain oxygen in the form of air bubbles which are taken down and used as an oxygen supply; when the oxygen is used up, the beetle returns to the surface to replenish the supply. Other water insects such as Pond-skaters and Whirligig beetles avoid the problem by living on the water surface. The food supply for animals like these is not as poor as one might think, since most surface insects eat terrestrial insects blown on to the water, and there is an abundance of water fleas and planktonic organisms of various kinds, particularly in summer. Carnivorous phantom midge larva (*Chaoborus*) are also found in these interesting, wild and lonely habitats.

Lagoons

Water bodies which actually border onto the shore – the lagoons, or as some people call them in the north, 'oyces'. Typical lagoons are shown in Fig. 55, the average area being five to ten acres (two to four hectares). Table 17 gives salinity figures for eight Orkney lagoons.

Clearly, all these lagoons are more salty than the truly freshwater lochs, but their salinity is not as high as one might expect bearing in mind their

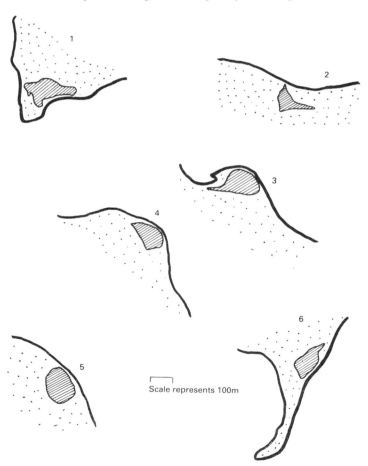

Fig. 55.
Coastal lagoons in
Orkney: 1 Brae-
buster, Deerness:
2 Mirkady, Deerness;
3 Messigate, Tanker-
ness; 4 Vastray,
Evie; 5 Yinstay,
Tankerness; 6 Lake-
quoy, Tankerness.

Scale represents 100m

Table 17   *Salinity of Eight Orkney Lagoons.*

Lagoon	Salinity ($^0/_{00}$)
St Mary's Loch, Holm	7.05
Yinstay, Tankerness	3.50
Lakequoy, Tankerness	2.00
Messigate, Tankerness	14.10
Braebuster, Deerness	0.80
Mirkady, Deerness	3.90
Carness, St Ola	5.40
Loch of Vastray, Evie	0.60
(seawater	35.40)

proximity to the sea, even allowing for the variation in the figures. All the oyces are similar in structure: they have narrow short channels – about 18 inches (45 cms) wide – which often look as if they were man-made and which allow the entry of seawater at high spring tides, particularly during gales. But the water flow in and out of these lagoons fluctuates. It would be useful to collect water samples throughout the year to establish salinity patterns more accurately.

All the lagoons have muddy bottoms, with occasional stones embedded

*Fig. 56.
Ayre and lagoon,
Shapinsay* (Photo: *Gunnie Moberg*).

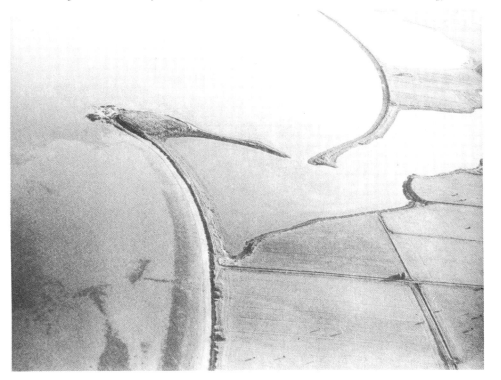

in them. Vegetation quantity is very variable; Vastray, Yinstay and Mirkady have abundant bottom-rooted rushes (*Eleocharis* sp) providing food and shelter for a wider variety of invertebrates than in other lagoons. Apart from *Eleocharis*, most lagoons are characterized by a lack of plants with emergent leafy and flowering shoots. Even floating-leaved plants are uncommon, being replaced by pondweeds (*Potamogeton* spp) with wholly submerged leaves, some of them grass-like. The reason for this may be connected with the relatively high salinity of the lagoons which dehydrates cellular material, especially if large surface areas of leaf are exposed. Typical brackish-water species have been recorded in at least four of the seven sampled: Jenkins' Pond-snail, brackish-water shrimp, mysid shrimp, Sea-slater; but typical freshwater species are also present: cased-caddis larvae are particularly abundant in vegetation, Water-boatmen (corixids) are common, together with sticklebacks and pond-snails, such as *Lymnaea pereger*. Other species recorded are lake shrimps *Gammarus lacustris*, diving beetles and midge larvae. Many of the lagoons have large populations of planktonic organisms.

These lagoons have received little attention in the past. A recent survey of lagoons by R. S. K. Barnes suggests that Orcadian lagoons are fairly typical as regards salinity and fauna; his book is worth consulting.

Vegetation Note. Complete vegetational surveys of Orkney lochs have not yet been made. Well over 30 freshwater species have so far been identified, some rarer than others; Spike-rush (*Eleocharis* sp) is the most common species of loch margin areas, providing micro-habitats for many invertebrates. Whilst the extent of our knowledge is generally matched by the relative scarcity of Orkney loch-vegetation, there are some localities where the abundance of plant growth is such that marsh or fen conditions may develop (see Chapter 4). Under these circumstances mud particles and decaying vegetation are trapped, leading to a plant succession, which may even turn into firm ground (over a period of years) with associated terrestrial vegetation. More permanent marsh habitats can arise where seepage or flushes emerge from the ground. These permanent damp patches are often good breeding grounds for the mud snail *Lymnaea truncatula* which is a host of the sheep liver-fluke parasite during part of its life cycle. In damp summers liver-fluke disease reaches significant levels in Orkney, sufficient for there to have been control programmes carried out in an attempt to eradicate the disease by killing the snails in damp, boggy patches and ditches.

Amphibians

Toads and frogs are generally associated with freshwater habitats, but there is little sign of them becoming naturally established in Orkney, though casual introductions have been attempted. Their status is at present in some doubt, but old records suggest that things were very different in the last century; records of Barry (1805) and Low (1813) both claim the Common Frog (*Rana temporaria*) and the Common Toad (*Bufo bufo*) as present, the latter being sometimes found in gardens in the evening. Frogs were patchy in distribution. Buckley & Harvie-Brown (1891) however, only mention the Toad ('common'); frogs had presumably been wiped out by the end of the nineteenth century, although both tadpoles and adult frogs are said to have been released on a number of occasions in more recent years.

Change

The most severe threat to Orkney wetlands is through drainage. In recent years a number of lochs throughout the islands have been drained and there are likely to be other marshy areas (and perhaps shallow lochs) considered for reclamation in the foreseeable future. It is difficult to predict what will happen in the farming/conservation conflict, but it is essential that each and every drainage application should be examined most carefully; wetlands are part of Orkney's most precious heritage and their destruction or alteration in any way would detract from the islands considerably, to say nothing of the moral responsibility which Orcadians have to accept for their own habitats.

CHAPTER 8 Terrestrial Animals

The land animals of Orkneys are not, in general, well known. There are few mammals, of which the Orkney Vole and the seaweed-eating sheep of North Ronaldsay are the most distinct. The Lepidoptera have been studied in some detail, largely due to the labours of a London business man, Ian Lorimer, who married an Orcadian, spent many holidays in the islands, and then retired there. The Mollusca were lovingly collected for many years by Robert Rendall, poet, theologian, and local business man; his labours have been continued by Alan Skene of Stromness and Mrs Nora McMillan of the Merseyside Museum. All other groups are very patchily known.

Fig. 57.
Orkney Vole (Photo: *Gunnie Moberg*).

Mammals

Orkney Vole

Arguments over the origin of the Orkney Vole have already been presented (Chapter 2). It was first recognized as distinct from the Common Vole (*Microtus agrestis*) of mainland Britain by Millais in 1904. The original specimens came from Stenness. Their discovery caused great excitement, and Millais was stimulated to collect voles from other islands. A year after his original description, Millais added a subspecies from Sanday, *Microtus orcadensis sandayensis*, on the grounds of a lighter colour than the Mainland form ('hair-brown rather than mummy-brown' above; cream-buff ventrally) and a shallow 'first outer re-entrant angle of the first molar'. In the next few years further subspecies were added from Westray, Rousay and South Ronaldsay. The Westray voles were said to be slighter, smaller and darker than the Sanday ones; the other two races could not be distinguished from the Mainland form on external appearances but were differentiated on trivial cranial measurements.

It was pointed out as early as 1905 that the Orkney Vole was very similar to the widespread continental vole, *Microtus arvalis*. In the 1950s, it was shown that *arvalis* and *orcadensis* had apparently identical chromosomes, and could in fact hybridize freely and produce fertile young. Consequently the various Orkney races are now regarded as subspecies of *M. arvalis*. It is doubtful if the inter-island distinctions are worth even subspecific recognition. The Westray animals are the most distinct.

Some years ago, Fred Rose, biology teacher at Kirkwall Grammar School, and I carried out a detailed examination of the relationships of the different Orkney races to each other, and to different continental populations. We were led to do this by a remark of Dr Gordon Corbet of the British Museum (Natural History), that Orkney Voles seemed to be more like *M. arvalis* from southern Europe than from Germany. My flippant response to this was that it suggested voles were originally introduced to Orkney from ships of the Spanish Armada which were wrecked on the islands. Mr Rose and I then set out to determine the relationships between as many population samples as we could obtain. We used the frequency of non-metrical skull traits in our work. (These are characters such as extra bones in sutures, missing foramina, etc.) These traits are known to be inherited, and their incidences in different populations can be used as a measure of the genetic difference between the populations in question. When a large number of such measures are combined, a single multivariate statistic is obtained which can be treated as a measure of genetic distinctiveness or distance: the larger the distance, the less closely are the populations related.

It was clear from our work that the Orkney races were markedly different from all other populations to which they were compared; most of the continental samples were apparently closely related to each other. The only place where *Microtus arvalis* occurs in the British Isles, outside Orkney, is in Guernsey. The Guernsey Voles were very similar to north German animals on the characters we used (Fig. 58).

Now if the Orkney Voles are a relict of a previously widespread northwest European population, they should resemble most closely their geographical neighbours. Most differences would be assumed to have arisen

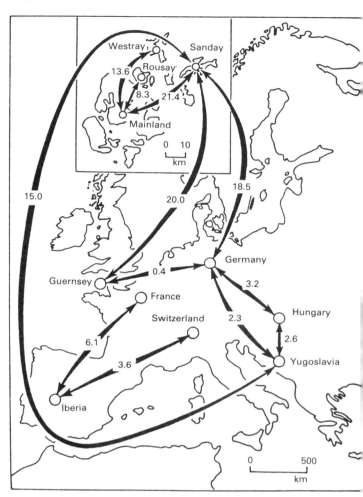

Fig. 58.
Measures of genetic distance based on non-metrical skull characters between samples from Microtus arvalis *populations. The closest relatives of the Orkney Voles (inset at top) are in Yugoslavia; the Continental forms are much more homogenous than the introduced Orkney races; and the four Orkney races can be most easily derived from an original colonization on Sanday, thence to Mainland and from there independently to Westray and Rousay (based on Berry and Rose, 1975).*

following isolation. If, on the other hand, the voles colonized Orkney after the islands were cut off from mainland Scotland, they might be expected to show much greater differences: although their closest affinities will obviously be with the population from which they came, the alleles fortuitously carried by the founding animals will mean that the 'genetic distance' between the two may be quite large from the start, never mind any subsequent adaptation as they establish themselves in their new habitat. Consequently, the existence of large and apparently random differences between geographically close (but isolated) populations indicate that the populations have been founded by introduction rather than surviving as relicts. On these criteria, Orkney Voles are clearly not relicts.

Voles have been in the islands 4000 years or more, since their remains have been found in the lower layers of excavations of buildings at Skara

Brae. It seems reasonable to assume that they were introduced by some of the first human colonists to the islands, presumably inadvertently. It is possible that these colonizers came from the eastern Mediterranean, where the Orkney Voles have their apparent closest relatives, but that is rather a long way to stretch the argument.

The Sanday Voles are the ones most like any continental sample, followed by Mainland, Rousay, and Westray, in that order. From comparisons with other populations, it is likely that the Rousay population was founded from the Mainland and this makes geographical sense.

The Mainland population could have been an off-shoot of the Sanday race, or may have been a completely different introduction; the Westray population is rather nearer Mainland than Sanday, but the Westray and Sanday voles are now regarded as indistinguishable in traditional taxonomic traits (despite their separation by early workers). Hence it seems reasonable to suggest that the Westray race originated from Sanday. There is no case for arguing that the sandy colour of the Sanday voles is a cryptic adaptation to the widespread exposed sand on that island, since Westray is topographically very different to Sanday and not at all sandy – but on average the voles are the same colour. Voles on the South Isles (South Ronaldsay and Burray; there are no voles on Hoy) are probably indistinguishable from Mainland ones. There are now no voles on Shapinsay; they were last recorded there in 1906.

A number of colour forms have been reported; in his book, Groundwater notes black, white, russet, and grey. Most of these are probably recent mutants. However black animals occur not infrequently in (particularly) the Stenness area. Although some of these may be true melanics, others are 'slow moulters' which lose their black coloration after several weeks. This is a phenomenon which needs more investigation.

The Orkney Vole occupies a wide range of habitats, including marsh, heather, grass, and growing crops. It is found up to about 700 ft (200 m) in the hills. Unlike the continental form it does not seem to inhabit short pasture or arable land. It makes long runways, with, if the ground permits, subterranean nests. The runways extend up to 20 ft (6 m) from the nest. In captivity, the animals are docile, and readily live in groups as long as only one mature male is present. They are the main prey of Hen Harriers and Short-eared Owls.

North Ronaldsay Sheep

The North Ronaldsay sheep are small and short-tailed, related to the Soay sheep of St Kilda, and the primitive sheep of Shetland and Iceland. They were formerly found on Flotta, as well as on North Ronaldsay, but they are now confined almost entirely to the latter island (plus Linga Holm off Stronsay, where the Rare Breeds Survival Trust established a flock in 1974 to ensure their survival if anything happened to the animals on North Ronaldsay).

On North Ronaldsay, the sheep are kept away from the cultivated land by a 6 ft (2 m) high, 12 mile (19 km) long wall, which runs right round the island. Since there is little grass outside the wall, the sheep feed almost entirely on seaweed.

The date of the wall is unknown; its earliest mention is in the *New Statistical Account* of 1832. It was associated with strip cultivation and

Fig. 59.
Seaweed-eating
North Ronaldsay
sheep with lamb
(Photo: *Gunnie*
Moberg).

corresponded to the boundary wall of common hill grazing, to which the shore on North Ronaldsay is equivalent. Strip cultivation was abolished on the island in the 1880s, but the communal sheep husbandry continued apparently unchanged, regulated by an island Court of twelve elected 'sheep men' acting on regulations laid down by the landlord. The regulations state that the tenants of each of 71 holdings were allowed to keep between 10 and 60 sheep on the shore, with the sheep men being permitted an extra 10 sheep for their trouble. From the earliest records in 1790 until comparatively recently there were about 2000 sheep on the island; there are now at least twice as many, largely because of inadequate manpower to organize effective management. Each tenant was responsible for the repair of a length of the perimeter wall, so that it remained 'above leaping height'. The decline in the island human population means that the wall is not now kept in as good repair as it should be, and it is not infrequently breached.

Although the sheep are free to wander over all the shore, they behave like hill sheep and keep to their own area or *clowgang*, a term that is elsewhere given to the sheep pasture of a crofting township. The only time the sheep come within the wall is after lambing, when the ewes are tethered on grass.

The North Ronaldsay sheep are small, the carcass weight of a mature ewe being only about 30 lb (13.5 kg). The lambs are also small at birth, around three to four pounds (1.4 to 1.8 kg); lambing takes place in late April–early May. Traditional management involves one lamb of any twin pair being killed, so that each ewe has a single lamb to feed. On average, one in four ewes and their lambs are returned to the shore in August. One ram lamb to every 20 ewes is left uncastrated. This is a high proportion of rams, even by mediaeval standards. This may be to allow for deaths on the shore; despite their adaptation to exposed conditions, mortality is relatively high.

The original North Atlantic sheep were very variable in colour. Iceland and Shetland sheep still contain many brown and black individuals. In 1730 on Sanday, there were 57% white, 24% black, 18% grey, and 1% 'tanay'. However, the North Ronaldsay crofters select lighter coloured rams for breeding: some use grey animals in the belief that they are the most vigorous, others preferring white males because white wool fetches the highest prices. The commonest colour nowadays is grey, often with a black line along the backbone.

As in Soay sheep, there is a hairy and a woolly type of coat. Both black and white fleeces can be hairy, but because hairy fibres tend to be dark, black and grey fleeces are usually more hairy than white ones. In fact, grey fleeces are the hairiest, because they consist of mainly white wool mixed with black hairs. White hairs are typically woolly, and as fine as the best Shetland wool. In his *Tour*, Low described the annual 'rooing' or plucking of fleece in midsummer, which enabled the wool to be obtained unmixed

Fig. 60.
Sheep on a stone
fort at Skeny, south
of Ruskholm, built to
provide refuge for
sheep cut off by high
tides when grazing
seaweed along the
shore (Photo:
Gunnie Moberg).

Fig. 61.
Bundles of tangles set out to dry on the beach of North Ronaldsay, with the sheep wall lining the agricultural land (Photo: Gunnie Moberg).

with hair. 'Rooing' still takes place, although more often in Shetland than Orkney.

Well-meaning animal lovers have sometimes been offended at the rather scruffy appearance of North Ronaldsay sheep, and taken animals away to good pasture. Invariably many animals die if this is done. This used to be thought to be because they in some way needed seaweed in their diet. It is now known that the deaths are due to copper poisoning: there is only a small amount of available copper in seaweed and Orkney sheep have an inherited ability for high efficiency in absorbing copper; when they feed on grass containing more copper than they are used to, they absorb it in often toxic quantities.

Other Mammals

The other land mammals of Orkney are largely unremarkable. There are only a few species present, and many of them reflect nothing more than the interests and endeavours of past generations of naturalists. The best evidence of this is the Hedgehog (*Erinaceus europaeus*). Writing in 1848,

Baikie and Heddle do not list the Hedgehog as being present in Orkney. Buckley and Harvie-Brown (whose book was published in 1891) state that a few hedgehogs brought from Dirleton, near Edinburgh, were released around 1870. However, they were not abundant on mainland Orkney until the 1950s. The known later introductions are:

1930s	The cargo boats *Cormorant* and *Busy Bee* came each summer to Orkney with fencing stabs from Loch Eriboll. The crews gave out hedgehogs to small boys who played about the pier at Kirkwall.
1946	Four hedgehogs from Shetland were released at Holm in the mainland. In exchange, a box of Cabbage White butterflies was taken from Orkney and released in Shetland.
late 1940s	Hedgehogs from Netherbutton, Holm were released in Westray.
1949	Twelve hedgehogs from Stroma were released in Hoy.
1950s	Hedgehogs from Mainland Orkney were released in Egilsay.
1965	Hedgehogs from Mainland Orkney were released at Melsetter in Longhope.
1965	Hedgehogs from Egilsay were released in Wyre.
1969	Hedgehogs from Shetland were released in north Hoy.

Another species whose history is known is the Brown Hare (*Lepus capensis*), which was introduced into both Orkney and Shetland about 1830 by the then Member of Parliament, Samuel Laing. A number of individuals were released on the Mainland, near Kirkwall. Writing in 1891, Buckley and Harvie-Brown record that hares were present in good numbers on Hoy, Eday, Rousay, Shapinsay and South Ronaldsay, and that they had been taken to Papa Westray by the Traill family. However after the Traills left, the hares were rapidly exterminated by the local tenants. Nowadays they are found only on the Mainland and Rousay. The Mountain Hare (*Lepus timidus*) occurs on Hoy and nowhere else. John Bellenden recorded as long ago as 1529 that 'white hares' were on Hoy. Buckley and Harvie-Brown say that they were introduced into Gairsay in 1875, but they have not survived there.

Rabbits are abundant on the larger islands, and are mentioned by all the early naturalists. Myxomatosis spread rapidly in the 1960s and reduced populations for a time. Outbreaks still occur, but many individuals do not show symptoms and others recover; rabbits seem more abundant than ever in some places.

Among rodents, the Orkney Vole has been discussed. No other voles occur. The Long-tailed Field Mouse (it is meaningless to call it by its English and Continental name of 'wood mouse' since in Northern Scotland it is much more an animal of the hills and moors) (*Apodemus sylvaticus*) was described by Low in the 1770s. It is probably under-recorded (Table 18); as recently as 1984 it was reported from Sanday for the first time (although it may, of course, be a new introduction there). Shetland and Hebridean Field Mice are more closely related to the Norwegian population than to that of the Scottish mainland; they were probably brought to the islands as commensals by the Vikings. Nothing is known about the relationships of the Orkney animals.

House Mice (*Mus domesticus*) were recorded by Baikie and Heddle as being common everywhere except on a few of the smaller isles; Buckley and Harvie-Brown note they were abundant everywhere 'including Stronsay'. Numbers have decreased in recent years as the main reservoir of the species in winter stacks of corn has declined, and with it the availability of secure refuge habitats. In the 1770s, Low stated that the Black (or Ship) Rat (*Rattus rattus*) was 'still present in South Ronaldsay where there were no Brown Rats,' but numbers appeared to be declining on other islands as Brown Rats (*Rattus norvegicus*) increased. However, Black Rats persisted on South Ronaldsay at least until the 1930s when it was recorded on three separate occasions. The only Black Rats in Orkney now are in Westray. They came from a German grain boat which ran aground in 1939 below the farm of Skaill at the south end of the island. Rats spread rapidly over the southern half of the island, but then apparently retreated again to the south end. The *Old Statistical Account* of 1795–98 recorded both Black and Brown Rats in Kirkwall and St Ola, but no rats of either species on Eynhallow, Rousay or Egilsay. Buckley and Harvie-Brown reported Brown Rats on Stronsay in 1868 and Sanday in 1888. Among the

Table 18   *Occurrence of Terrestrial Mammals in Orkney.*

	Brown Hare	Mountain Hare	Hedgehog	House Mouse	L-t Field Mouse	Rabbit	Black Rat	Brown Rat	Pygmy Shrew	Water Shrew	Orkney Vole
Mainland	*		*	*	*	*		*	*		*
Shapinsay			*	*	*	*		*	*		
Gairsay						*					
Wyre			*	*		*		*			
Egilsay			*	*		*		*			
Rousay	*			*		*		*	*		
Eynhallow											
North Faray				*							
Westray			*	*		*	*	*	*		*
Papa Westray				*		*					
Eday				*		*					
Stronsay				*		*		*	*		
Sanday				*	*	*		*			*
North Ronaldsay			*	*	*	*					
Burray			*	*		*					
Lamb Holm											
Glims Holm											
South Ronaldsay			*	*		*		*	*		*
Hoy		*	*	*		*		*	*	*	
Longhope			*	*		*		*	*		
Graemsay			*	*	*	*		*	*		
Flotta			*	*		*		*	*		
Cava											
Copinsay				*	*	*			*		
Swona											
Holm of Grimbister				*				*	*		
Linga Holm					*						

larger islands they are still absent from Eday, Westray, Papa Westray and North Ronaldsay.

In common with many of the other Scottish islands, the only shrew is the Pygmy Shrew (*Sorex minutus*). Low stated it to be rare in the 1770s. It is recorded from Birsay in the *Old Statistical Account*. Water Shrews (*Neomys fodiens*) are said to occur on Hoy.

Bats only reach Orkney as occasional vagrants. Baikie and Heddle refer to Pipistrelles (*Pipistrellus pipistrellus*) in the 19th century around St Magnus Cathedral and in an old church in South Walls. They are sometimes seen in Stromness at dusk, although the only certain recent record was one found drowned in Kirkwall on Boxing Day 1979. A female Noctule (*Nyctalus noctula*) was caught at North Ronaldsay lighthouse in June 1976, only the third Scottish record for the species (the two previous being in Morayshire in 1909 and Perthshire in 1904). There were strong southerly winds in the week preceding its discovery, and it seems most likely that the bat originated from England. The *Orcadian* reported a Long-eared Bat (*Plecotus auritus*) in Sanday in 1931 and in Holm (South Mainland) in 1948.

There are no native deer in Orkney although bones of red deer (*Cervus elaphus*) have been found in peat, notably on Hoy and Westray. A Westray farmer experimented with Red Deer farming in the early 1980s.

Invertebrates

Although many people have collected or incidentally recorded invertebrates in Orkney, the only fairly well known group is the Lepidoptera, largely as the result of the work of Ian Lorimer of Orphir, who has summarized his own and other people's records in the *Lepidoptera of the Orkney Islands*. Other groups with more than fortuitous records are listed in the Appendix (pp 266–275). Orkney is no better or worse off than other British islands in invertebrate knowledge as can be seen by comparing the publication lists for different groups in Ken and Vera Smith's *Bibliography of the Entomology of the Smaller British Offshore Islands*.

As far as Lepidoptera are concerned, 375 species have been recorded, almost half of them since the early 1960s. This list is apparently very slight when compared with the 2515 species for Great Britain as a whole. Notwithstanding, and recognizing that species will continue to be added to the Orkney total, it probably represents fairly the depauperate nature of the fauna of a north temperate, windswept archipelago. It is difficult to compare the Orkney list with those for Caithness or Shetland, because of the neglect of microlepidoptera in those counties (only partial as far as Shetland is concerned). However, there is no doubt that the Orkney Lepidoptera are much more closely related to Caithness than Shetland, because of the proximity of the former and the fact that insect flight virtually ceases in northerly winds. With the possible exception of *Entepheria falvicinctata*, Orkney has no resident species which are absent from Caithness. In contrast, most of the endemic Shetland forms (e.g. *Eupithecia venosata*, *Xanthorhoe munitata*, *Perizoma albulata*, etc.) are absent, and in the few cases where a similar local form exists in Orkney and Shetland, it extends also into Caithness (e.g. *Chloroclysta citrata* and *Paradiarsia* (*Amathes*) *glareosa*). In a few cases (mostly robust and fast-flying noctuids, such as *Diarsia mendica* and *Hadena confusa*), an Orkney series bridges the gap between Caithness and Shetland specimens; among the more fragile and less mobile geomtrids (e.g. *Perizoma albulata*), there is a great difference from the Shetland form.

The Orkney Lepidoptera can be regarded as being divided into 'natives', immigrants, colonists, and imported. This is a rather arbitrary classification, because it is often impossible to know where a particular species should belong, and in particular when a colonist becomes a 'native'. However, there are 31 species (including five with wingless females) which are found only in the sheltered Berriedale to Burn of Segal area of Hoy, which are likely to have been resident for a very long time, perhaps from the times at the end of the Pleistocene when a land connection with Caithness may have still existed (see pp 28–31).

Comparison of the species recorded in the 19th century and those currently present show that some species that are now so common and conspicuous that they could not be missed by competent observers are missing from the earlier lists. It seems likely that *Scotopteryx chenopodiata*, *Diachrysia chrysitis* and *Hypena proboscidalis* come into this category; there is good evidence that *Pieris napi* first appeared in Orkney in the mid-1930s. To 'natural' colonists must be added some species introduced inadvertently on food plants. Such species are found particularly around Binscarth on the Mainland. *Hofmannophila pseudospretella* was recorded in Orkney (on Hoy) only 45 years after the probable date of its first introduction into the United Kingdom from South America.

Finally, immigrant species have been recorded from 1869 onwards, in every season when lepidopterists have been active. They can be divided into immigrants from the south and south-west (from the UK, but also butterflies and moths from south Europe and the Mediterranean Basin), usually associated with depressions moving around high pressure areas well to the south of Orkney; and those from the east and south east following sustained high pressure over the Low Countries and southern Scandinavia, most commonly in early August when there is a light on-shore breeze.

Probably some hazel-feeding species still common in Caithness (e.g. *Colocasia coryli*, *Electrophaes corylata*) became extinct in Orkney centuries ago (although *Epinotia tenerama* survives locally, presumably having changed its food plant). Nevertheless, the general picture is of a gradually increasing lepidopteran fauna. The only breeding species whose future seems in doubt (and which should therefore not be collected until more information about it is available) is *Entephria flavicinctata*, which has probably been over-collected; it is distinct, being recognizably brighter than the mainland Scottish form. However, the devastation of the sand-dunes on Burray and the continuing reclamation of moorlands could put other species at risk. The opposite problem – over-abundance causing damage to plants – is rare in Orkney; only *Plutella xylostella* has ever been a serious agricultural pest, *Pieris brassicae* is a minor nuisance, and there is no record of *Cerapteryx graminis* ever destroying upland pasture as it may do elsewhere. *Operophtera brumata* has shown an increase in recent years, sometimes defoliating large areas of heather in midsummer. In southern England it is a pest of orchards and forest trees. Flocks of up to 400 Common and Lesser Black-backed Gulls may be seen feeding on the species. The only other major gull predation in Orkney is on tipulids and the cocoons of *Phragmatobia fuliginosa*.

Weather affects moths in Orkney very little, the main exception being northerly winds which almost completely inhibit flying. On the other hand, butterflies are very vulnerable to rain and lack of sun. Wet summers in 1978 and 1979 produced a drastic collapse in butterfly populations, especially *Maniola jurtina*, *Argynnis aglaja* and *Polyommatus icarus*. Early flying species were less affected.

Early spring moths emerge in late April, four or so weeks later than the same species in England, while late autumn species appear relatively even earlier. The total period of breeding activity is thus reduced by about a quarter. Individual species have adapted in different ways. For example, *Thera juniperata* on Hoy flies in high summer rather than early winter; *Aglais urticae*, the only Orkney butterfly which hibernates as an imago, goes into hibernation almost immediately on emerging in mid-August, although over most of Britain it feeds for 6–8 weeks before hibernating.

Mite Allergy

An interesting interaction between invertebrates and man has emerged from an investigation into the causes of asthma and rhinitis (hay fever) among the farming population of Orkney. One of the principal factors in these conditions is the high level of mite infestation of stored hay and grain. These so-called 'stored product' or 'storage' mites feed on the fungi that grow in stored feedstuffs, and are therefore particularly numerous in the damp and humid climate of Orkney, being particularly prevalent after a wet summer when the hay has been baled and stacked before being adequately dry. Although individuals are barely visible to the naked eye, very large numbers can often be seen as a coating of pinkish dust on the floor of the barn in which the hay is stacked. The numbers of these mites are greatest in October soon after stacking, when the fungal content is high and they have adequate food available.

In the winter of 1977–8, samples from a number of Orkney farms showed an average of over 1000 mites per gram of stored hay in October, falling to 350 in November and eventually averaging out at about 500 mites per gram (which represents over 12 million mites in a half hundredweight bale).

There are a wide variety of 'storage' mite species present in the hay but those found most frequently and in the greatest numbers in Orkney hay are *Acarus farris*, *Tyrophagus longior*, and *Calvolia* sp *hypopi*. *Glycyphagus destructor* is also found but to a lesser extent, although it appears to be one of the principal causes of allergic symptoms. These species are also important in producing allergic respiratory diseases on the Scottish mainland but the numbers are there less than in Orkney.

The house dust mite (*Dermatophagoides pteronyssinus*) and other pyroglyphid species, which are among the commonest causes of allergic asthma generally, are as prevalent in Orkney houses as in houses elsewhere, but are not found in stored hay or grain.

CHAPTER **9 Birds**

Ornithologists have tendency to by-pass Orkney on their way to Shetland, lured by Fair Isle and its rarities, the Gannets on Herma Ness, the Snowy Owl and Red-necked Phalaropes on Fetlar, the highest cliffs in the British Isles on Foula, and so on. Orkney is thought of primarily for its numerous Hen Harriers, and more sombrely, as the place where the last Great Auk in Britain was killed (on Papa Westray in 1813). This neglect is unfair. Orkney has 29 regular breeders not found in Shetland, and there are only six species which breed regularly in Shetland but not in Orkney (Common Scoter, Black-tailed Godwit, Red-necked Phalarope, House Martin, Fieldfare, and dubiously now, Snowy Owl). Moreover, the sea-cliffs of Hoy, Mainland and Westray are amongst the finest in Britain. The importance of Orkney for birds is recognized by the fact that the RSPB is the

Fig. 62.
Kittiwakes (Photo:
William Paton).

biggest single landowner in the islands owning or renting eight major reserves:

1. A huge area of hill and moorland, fringed by cliffs in North Hoy – 9700 acres (3925 hectares);

2. A large area of largely ungrazed and unburnt moorland and saltmarsh at Hobbister, five miles from Kirkwall – 1875 acres (759 hectares);

3. A basin mire supporting a high density of breeding ducks and waders, at the Loons in North-west Mainland – 139 acres (56 hectares);

4. A mile of cliffs in the north Mainland, including the Kitchener Memorial, in memory of Lord Kitchener of Khartoum who was killed when the ship in which he was travelling, *HMS Hampshire*, was sunk nearby in 1916 – 46 acres (19 hectares);

5. A third moorland reserve, more varied than those of Hoy and Hobbister, in the parish of Birsay, north Mainland – 4719 acres (1910 hectares);

6. A small group of islands centred in Copinsay, $2\frac{1}{2}$ miles (4 km) off the East Mainland, bought as a memorial to the noted ornithologist and author, James Fisher – 375 acres (152 hectares);

7. Two miles of cliffs at the Noup, Westray – 35 acres (14 hectares);

8. The largest continuous area of maritime heath in Britain, with the largest colony of Arctic Terns, at North Hill, Papa Westray – 510 acres (206 hectares).

The flavour of these sites can be judged by a 1979 census at Marwick Head, where 35,035 Guillemots, 718 Razorbills and 1062 Fulmars were counted, together with 9710 apparently occupied Kittiwake nests.

Some of the birds which breed in Orkney are at the edge of their world range, especially such southern forms as the Little Grebe, Coot, Sandwich

Fig. 63.
Razorbill (Photo:
William Paton).

Tern and Stonechat. Indeed, there are 37 species which breed in northern Scotland, which have not established themselves in Orkney. Half of these are associated with trees, although the Kestrel and Wood-pigeon have scorned this problem and nest on the ground in Orkney. Most of the other missing species would have apparently suitable habitat in Orkney, and their absence must be attributed to isolation or some subtle environmental deficiencies. Shetland lacks a third of Orkney breeding species, and the Faroes nearly half (see Table 19). The absence in these more northern

Table 19

a. *Birds breeding regularly in Caithness and Sutherland but not Orkney*

Black-throated Diver	Little Tern	Redwing
Slavonian Grebe	Tawny Owl	Whinchat
Common Scoter	Swift	Redstart
Goosander	Great Spotted Woodpecker	Grasshopper Warbler
Greylag Goose	House Martin	Whitethroat
Sparrowhawk	Sand Martin	Wood Warbler
Ptarmigan	Magpie	Tree Pipit
Black Grouse	Great Tit	Grey Wagtail
Partridge	Blue Tit	Siskin
Dotterel	Coal Tit	Redpoll
Woodcock	Long-tailed Tit	Bullfinch
Wood Sandpiper	Treecreeper	Greenshank

b. *Birds breeding regularly in Orkney but not Caithness or Sutherland*

Manx Shearwater	(Leach's Petrel?)	Gannet

c. *Birds breeding regularly in Orkney but not Shetland*

Little Grebe	Water Rail	Willow Warbler
Heron	Moorhen	Goldcrest
Wigeon	Coot	Spotted Flycatcher
Pintail	Sandwich Tern	Dunnock
Shoveler	Short-eared Owl	Greenfinch
Mute Swan	Song Thrush	Linnet
Golden Eagle	Ring Ouzel	Chaffinch
Buzzard	Stonechat	Yellow Bunting
Hen Harrier	Robin	Dipper
Kestrel	Sedge Warbler	

d. *Birds breeding regularly in Shetland but not Orkney*

Common Scoter	Red-necked Phalarope	(Snowy Owl)
Black-tailed Godwit	House Martin	Fieldfare

e. *Birds breeding regularly in Shetland but not Faroe*

Wigeon	Black-tailed Godwit	Skylark
Tufted Duck	Common Tern	Blackbird
Common Scoter	Woodpigeon	Corn Bunting
Peregrine	Collared Dove	Reed Bunting
Corncrake	(Snowy Owl)	Jackdaw
Curlew	Long-eared Owl	Rook

f. *Birds breeding regularly in Faroe but not Shetland*

Greylag Goose	Ptarmigan	White Wagtail
Mute Swan	Purple Sandpiper	Redwing

(The status of a good many of these birds in the different archipelagoes fluctuates and the information for the Faroes in particular is incomplete and probably not up to date).

groups of such small mammal predators as Kestrel, Hen Harrier, and Short-eared Owl (all of which are quite numerous in Orkney) is presumably due to the non-occurrence of voles in Shetland and Faroe.

Changes in Status Table 20 summarizes changes in status of Orkney birds during this century. The most important influence has undoubtedly been human activity, directly through predation and indirectly through

---

Table 20
Changes in
status of
Orkney birds

a. *Former breeding birds not now breeding*
Common Scoter (1953), Whooper Swan (*c.* 1800), Sparrowhawk (*c.* 1940), White-tailed Eagle (*c.* 1870), Ptarmigan (*c.* 1830), Red-necked Phalarope (*c.* 1970), Great Auk (*c.* 1810), Sand Martin (? *c.* 1900).

b. *Regular breeding species which have decreased in this century*
Manx Shearwater, Heron, Eider, Red-breasted Merganser, Peregrine, Merlin, Red Grouse, Water Rail, Corncrake, Coot, Lapwing, Ringed Plover, Golden Plover, Common Sandpiper, Dunlin, Skylark, Greenfinch, Yellow Bunting, Corn Bunting.

c. *Species which were lost but returned again*
The Golden Eagle ceased to breed about 1840 and the Dipper about 1940 but both are now breeding again.

d. *Regular breeding species which have increased this century*
Red-throated Diver, Mallard, Shoveler, Hen Harrier, Oystercatcher, Curlew, Arctic Skua, Great Black-backed Gull, Kittiwake, Stonechat, Reed Bunting.

e. *Species recorded breeding for the first time since 1800 and now regular*
Fulmar (1900), Wigeon (*c.* 1870), Pintail (1908), Mute Swan (*c.* 1890), Buzzard (1961), Great Skua (1915), Woodpigeon (*c.* 1940), Collared Dove (1962), Rook (after 1850), Goldcrest (? *c.* 1830), Tree Sparrow (1961–*c.* 1977).

f. *Species which have bred occasionally this century*
Gadwall, Scaup, Pochard, Long-tailed Duck, Quail, Whimbrel, Black-tailed Godwit, Greenshank, House Martin, Mistle Thrush, Fieldfare, Whinchat, Black Redstart, Blackcap, Garden Warbler, Whitethroat, Wood Warbler, Grey Wagtail.

---

changing habitats. Archaeological evidence from Neolithic and Bronze Age sites shows the occurrence of the following birds in ancient times: Great Northern Diver, Grebe sp, Shearwater (probably Manx), Gannet, Cormorant, Shag, Duck sp, Pink-footed Goose, Whooper Swan, Golden and White-tailed Eagles, Buzzard sp, Falcon sp, Martin sp, Curlew, Skua (probably Arctic), Greater Black-backed, Herring and Common Gulls, Great Auk, Guillemot, and Crow. In addition a Bittern has been recorded, suggesting that some, at least, of the changes in avifauna may possibly be attributed to cooling of the climate.

The major surveys of Orkney birds have been those of Buckley & Harvie-Brown, in their *Vertebrate Fauna of the Orkney Islands*, 1891; David Lack in 1942, with the first definitive 'List of breeding birds of Orkney'; E. Balfour with an Orkney printed *Status and Guide* (1972); and the most recent study by Booth, Cuthbert and Reynolds (1985). Species noted as showing a 'noticeable decrease' are the Manx Shearwater, Corncrake, Coot, Lapwing, Common Sandpiper, Red-necked Phalarope,

Fig. 64.
Lesser Black-backed
Gull with eggs
(Photo: *William*
Paton).

Lesser Black-backed Gull, Mistle Thrush, Corn Bunting, Peregrine, Merlin, Red Grouse, Dipper and Common Scoter. A suggestion that Arctic Terns are declining, based on a decrease of 17,700 pairs on Westray and Papa Westray is unproven; other colonies in Orkney and Shetland have shown a net increase of 26,000 pairs. Probably their numbers are fairly stable. Corncrakes have declined in Orkney as everywhere else, but in 1979 there were 27 breeding pairs (18% of the Scottish population), slightly less than in the Outer Hebrides (31 pairs), but many more than Shetland (2 pairs). Dippers have become only very occasional breeders (on Hoy), while the Common Scoter is now regarded as a scarce visitor. The Red-necked Phalarope was first recorded as a British breeding bird on Sanday and North Ronaldsay, but they were heavily persecuted. For example, Buckley & Harvie-Brown record that they 'seem to have been pretty common on Sanday about 25 years ago. At that time a party landed from a ship and destroyed the greater part of them. None was seen at the locality for ten years afterwards.' However, seven or eight pairs were nesting in 1927, and Lack noted several pairs in the 1940s, especially on North Ronaldsay. By 1968, Balfour could only write 'the bird has not bred on North Ronaldsay for many years past, and at present is holding its own on only one other island, where only one or two pairs have lately been nesting.' It is now only seen as an uncommon passage migrant.

Other species which have been lost are the Whooper Swan, Greylag

Goose, Golden and White-tailed Eagles. Increased interest and protection has reversed the trend of decrease, and at least one pair of Golden Eagles is now usually resident. The species returned in 1966 after an absence of over a century. There has also been an influx of species associated with human activities especially those linked with agriculture. Large flocks of Curlews in particular are now a common sight on agricultural land near the coast.

Coastal Breeders

Where the cliffs around Orkney are flag-stones, they commonly erode to give ledges on otherwise vertical faces which are attractive to breeding seabirds. When this is coupled with the high productivity of the seas round Orkney, where the rich plankton attracts many small shoaling fish upon

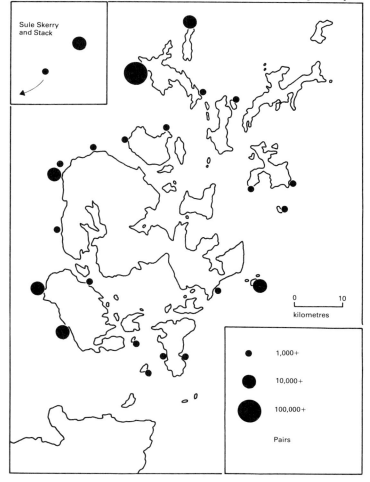

Fig. 65.
Main sea bird
colonies of Orkney.

which seabirds prey, the result is that Orkney provides one of the main breeding sites for seabirds in the whole temperate North Atlantic. The largest colonies are found at Marwick Head and Noup Head on Westray, while there are substantial ones on the west of Hoy, east of Copinsay and south of South Ronaldsay. Marwick Head equals in size the largest colonies on the Scottish mainland such as Handa (50,000 pairs) and Fowlsheugh (70,000 pairs), whilst the west side of Westray holds the largest single assembly of cliff-breeding seabirds in the British Isles with the possible exception of St. Kilda, several times larger than that on Marwick Head. The total number of seabirds breeding in Orkney is greater than that in Shetland and nearly as many as that in the Outer Hebrides (including St. Kilda) (Table 21). The only rider that one has to make to that statement is that the Orkney Gannets all occur on Sule Stack, traditionally a part of the country, but way to the west of the main group of islands, 32 miles (51 km) into the Atlantic. Orkney has particularly large numbers of Guillemots, Kittiwakes and Arctic Terns, whereas the Outer Hebrides have more Gannets and Puffins, and Shetland more Fulmars and Great Skuas (both species which have significantly increased in recent years). At least one fifth of the United Kingdom Arctic Skuas, Greater Black-backed Gulls,

Table 21   *Number of Pairs and Proportion of the British Total of Seabirds reported breeding in the Outer Hebrides, Orkney and Shetland during Operation Seafarer, 1968-1970.*

Species	Outer Hebrides		Orkneys		Shetland		British Total
Fulmar	60,000	21%	47,000	16%	117,000	41%	285,000
Manx Shearwater		?		?		?	
Storm Petrel		?		?		?	
Leach's Storm Petrel		98%		1%		1%	
Gannet	60,000	53%	4,000	3%	10,000	9%	114,000
Cormorant	380	6%	600	10%	460	7%	6,200
Shag	2,800	10%	3,600	13%	8,600	30%	28,500
Great Skua	18	½%	90	3%	3,000	97%	3,200
Arctic Skua	40	4%	230	21%	770	70%	1,100
Great Black-backed Gull	2,600	14%	6,000	32%	2,500	13%	19,000
Lesser Black-backed Gull	500	(1%)	800	(2%)	570	(1%)	(45,000)
Herring Gull	3,600	(1%)	7,800	(3%)	10,150	(4%)	(278,000)
Common Gull	640	(5%)	4,850	(39%)	1,400	(11%)	(11,600)
Black-headed Gull	800	(1%)	4,500	(6%)	530	(1%)	(72,000)
Kittiwake	25,000	6%	128,000	30%	43,000	10%	427,000
Common Tern	76	1%	200	2%	390	3%	11,200
Arctic Tern	1,200	4%	12,300	41%	7,650	26%	30,000
Sandwich Tern	—		390	4%	—		9,700
Razorbill	22,000	23%	8,500	9%	8,900	9%	96,000
Guillemot	65,000	13%	129,000	26%	77,000	15%	498,000
Black Guillemot	530	7%	2,240	29%	2,300	30%	7,600
Puffin	186,000	37%	66,000?	13%	50,000	10%?	500,000
Totals	430,000	17%	426,000	17%	344,000	14%	2,500,000

National totals and proportions in parentheses refer to species where substantial numbers breeding inland were not counted. Some three quarters of the Hebridean total breed on St Kilda, including very roughly 173,000 pairs of Puffins, 52,000 pairs of Gannets and 37,000 pairs of Fulmars. There were also 66 pairs of Little Terns breeding in the Outer Hebrides, and three pairs of Roseate Terns in Orkney.

Orkney: Main Seabird Breeding Population.   Table 22

Species	Number	% British and Irish Population
Guillemot	160,000 individuals	22%
Razorbill	9000 individuals	6%
Black Guillemot	1176 individuals (incomplete survey)	?
Puffin	55,000 pairs	8%
Kittiwake	128,680 pairs	30%
Fulmar	47,304 apparently occupied sites	16%
Arctic Tern	33,000 pairs	43%
Arctic Skua	1034 pairs	42%
Great Skua	1652 pairs	28%
Shag	3600 pairs	13%
Cormorant	600 pairs	10%
Gannet	4000 pairs	3%

Fig. 66.
Shag (Photo:
William Paton).

Fig. 67.
Cormorants on the
Calf of Eday (Photo:
William Paton).

Kittiwakes, Arctic Terns, Common and Black Guillemots breed in Orkney, as do more than 10% of the Fulmars, Shags, Cormorants and Puffins (Table 22). Many of these species have a large part of their European population breeding in Britain. To take one example, 79% of the British and Irish Arctic Terns are found in Orkney and Shetland together, with 33,000 pairs in Orkney and 32,000 pairs in Shetland (1980 figures). A quarter of the Orkney population may be found on Papa Westray alone, although in some years this colony is rivalled or even exceeded in size by others, such as those on the Pentland Skerries or Swona.

Five of the common seabirds (Fulmar, Shag, Kittiwake, Razorbill and Guillemot) are primarily cliff nesters. In some areas Shags and Razorbills nest also among boulders with Black Guillemots. Gannets are fast growing in numbers and it would not be surprising if new colonies were founded. They began nesting on Fair Isle recently, and Copinsay appears a possible site for another colony. The comparatively few Cormorant colonies are of national importance; although they are usually on small holms or cliff tops, part of the Calf of Eday colony is sometimes about 300 yards (275 m) inland from the cliff edge.

Where the ground is suitable, Herring Gulls nest on the cliffs, and together with Lesser Black-backed and Common Gulls, skuas and terns nest also on many of the smaller holms, and the maritime and inland heaths. It is hard to estimate numbers because the birds naturally seek the less visited sites; the terns in particular tend to move around.

Apart from a huge colony on Sule Skerry, Puffins tend to have a scattered distribution, occurring in comparatively small numbers where the slope of a cliff allows the development of grassland with sufficient depth of soil for burrowing, or in crevices and burrows near the cliff edge. Black Guillemots nest mainly among boulders close to the shore, occasionally using rabbit burrows; they appear to be most common on the smaller, more remote islands, although a few pairs breed amongst the large concrete blocks used to build the Churchill Barriers along the east side of Scapa Flow. The 120 pairs on the Holm of Papa Westray constitute one of the largest colonies in the United Kingdom. The final pair of Great Auks probably nested on a rock slope on the sheltered north-west side of the Holm of Papa Westray. A review of the fate of this last pair is given in Buckley & Harvie-Brown's *Vertebrate Fauna*; the last bird took refuge on the main island of Papa Westray after its mate was killed (see p. 197).

Little is known about the distribution of Manx Shearwaters or Storm and Leach's Petrels. Shearwaters were formerly persecuted as a food and egg source. Wallace, writing in the 1670s notes

'They roast it with the guts on a spit, that it may cut the pleasanter (for it has something of a fishie taste), and they sprinkle it with ginger and vinegar . . . (It is) very fat and delicious.'

Only two small colonies are known at present, both on Hoy. However, quite large rafts occur off Rackwick on the west coast of Hoy, and they have also been reported off Rousay further north, so there may be other colonies, although the rafts may be formed of non-breeding birds, or even commuters from the great colonies of the Inner Hebrides.

Storm Petrels have been proved to breed at ten sites (Sule Skerry, Pentland Skerries, Switha, Auskerry, the Green Holms, and the Holms of Papay, Faray, Rusk, Wart and Skea of Westray), nesting among boulders and on cliff faces, and also in holes in the peat, where the spaces tend to get overlooked. It is probably much under-recorded, though its numbers are

Fig. 68.
Puffin (Photo:
William Paton).

certainly not as large as they are further south-west. The Head Lighthouse-keeper on Sule Skerry claimed to have found a nest of Leach's Petrel in 1933, and there are five eggs of the species in the Stromness Museum labelled 'Sule Skerry, 1934'. Birds with brood patches have been caught on Sule Skerry, and it seems likely that it does breed there.

The Peregrine, Raven and Jackdaw nest mainly in the cliffs, together with Hooded Crows, Rock Doves and Wrens. Wallace listed 25 places where Peregrines nested in Orkney, and also recorded that the 'king's falconer comes every year and takes the young, and a hen or dog out of every house in the countrey,' an ancient right by which the king claimed a hen (or, presumably a dog) for feeding his hawks from every house with a fireplace. In 1919, there were only half a dozen occupied eyries in Orkney, but this had increased to 25 in 1945. In 1971, 14 sites were occupied, eggs were laid in at least nine, and large young were seen in six. Hoy also used to support up to three pairs of White-tailed Eagles until they were wiped out in the middle of the 19th century. A report in Buckley & Harvie-Brown's book that there used to be 10 or 12 pairs probably refers to gatherings of young birds which may still reach up to 50 individuals around seabird colonies in North Norway.

Observations at sea around Orkney have shown that the area is fre-quented by large numbers of seabirds throughout the year. Even the auks travel west to the edge of the continental shelf in summer; it is difficult to get information for this extremely exposed area in winter. Local concen-trations are also found off the east coast of Orkney as they are all down the east coast of Scotland, although not on such a scale as off the east coast of Shetland. Numbers of birds also scatter north and east over the North Sea inflow current, but the distribution tends to be rather patchy.

Concentrated movements through the sounds, and around projecting headlands appear to be less marked than in Shetland, presumably due to the local topography. Most birds seem to disperse straight out to sea from colonies facing their feeding grounds. The main concentrations which have attracted attention have been round Duncansby Head in Caithness to the south-east, round the north end of North Ronaldsay in the north, and along to the north coast of Sutherland to the south-west. Some of these birds may be going to feed, but often they appear to be taking part in migratory or weather movements. Throughout the year a regular move-ment of unknown significance takes place up the east coast of Scotland, turning west into the Atlantic round North Ronaldsay. There is also a clear migratory movement in the autumn westwards along the north coast of Sutherland. Comparatively few birds seem to pass through the Pentland Firth, although there has been relatively little sea-watching here, in con-trast to North Ronaldsay, Mull Head on Papa Westray and the Brough of Birsay.

In calm weather, the more pelagic seabirds can often be seen feeding socially over shoals of fish, apparently taking small gadoids, clupeids and sand-eels, and, in the case of Gannets, larger Mackerel and Herring. The big gulls, Kittiwakes, Fulmars and sometimes Gannets also feed round trawlers by day or night. The Auks do not follow trawlers but feed by deep diving, while Fulmars, Kittiwakes, and small Petrels may also feed on plankton coming to the surface at night. The Skuas appear to feed to a large extent at sea, occasional birds visiting fish shoals or trawlers, although

Fig. 69.
*Kittiwake alighting
at nest* (Photo:
William Paton).

comparatively few join the mixed flocks of other species feeding there. It
is uncertain to what extent they rob other species when they are fully fed
and leave the flocks. Shags travel up to five miles out to sea to feed on small
shoaling fish, especially sand-eels, but Cormorants feed mainly in the more
sheltered sounds where they take flat-fish. Black Guillemots feed largely
on the bottom, where they concentrate on a range of crustaceans, although
they also bring small fish (particularly butterfish) to their young.

Calculations that the sea feeding birds may take between 6% and 48%
of the North Sea fish production are probably gross over-estimates; the
fishery statistics suggesting that they remove only 0.25%–4% are probably much nearer the mark. The ecological calculations are based on the
amount of food needed to sustain the observed numbers of birds. In fact,
they do not take full account of the nutritious Atlantic inflow to the North
Sea, or the trophic level at which the birds feed. It seems likely that the

Fig. 70.
Eider drake in
breeding plumage
(Photo: William
Paton).

offal discarded by fishermen is more important to the birds than the fish
which they (the birds) catch for themselves. A crucial test will come if 'in-
dustrial fishing' for food species directly important to birds (such as
sand-eels) continues to increase.

Some birds of most of the larger species are present through the year,
but the nocturnal petrels, skuas, Lesser Black-backed Gull, terns, and
most Puffins migrate south in the winter. They are replaced from the north
by more individuals of the larger species, and by variable numbers of Little
Auks. The birds leave the breeding colonies when the young fledge, which
is in July and August for most species. They then moult, gathering along
or just off the shore. The auks, divers and sea ducks become flightless on
the water, although only Eiders and Red-breasted Mergansers are commonly seen near the shore. By October Fulmars and Guillemots return to
the colonies in good weather; most other species wait until the spring:
Razorbills and Kittiwakes begin to return in January and February, others
in March and April, while some long-distance migrants do not return until
May. The Red-throated Divers feed almost entirely at sea, returning to
their breeding lochs in March or April.

With a large area of shallow, sheltered water round its coast, Orkney is
a much more important wintering area than Shetland for coastal species.
Considerable numbers of Shags, Black Guillemots, Eider and Red-
breasted Mergansers are present throughout the year, although they leave
their nesting sites in winter. They are joined after the breeding season by
Great Northern Divers, Velvet Scoters and a few thousand Long-tailed
Ducks – one of the largest concentrations in Britain.

The inter-tidal zone is exploited by large numbers of waders and gulls
which also feed on adjacent farmland. The availability of shoreline feeding
may be of particular importance to certain species during hard weather.

Survey work carried out by the Tay and Orkney Ringing Groups during the winters of 1982–83 and 1983–84 have revealed a total shore wader population of some 60,000 birds, a figure which, in a national context, is exceeded only by six other British estuaries – Morecambe Bay, the Wash, the Ribble, the Solway, the Dee and the Severn. The Orkney shore is of international importance for seven species of waders and nationally important for eleven (with more than 1% of the European and British wintering totals respectively).

The species for which Orkney is of international importance are Ringed Plover, Turnstone, Purple Sandpiper, Sanderling, Redshank, Bar-tailed Godwit and Curlew, while the additional four of national significance are the Oystercatcher, Golden Plover, Lapwing and Dunlin. Of this impressive array, the three birds which really stand out are the Purple Sandpiper (with some 28% of the British and 12% of European) and the Curlew (25% of British and 8% of European). If one can brave the Orkney shoreline on a winter day spectacular bird-watching is to be had!

Fulmars on Eynhallow

One of the longest-running intensive studies of an individual bird population anywhere in the world was begun in 1950 on the small (300 acres (125 hectares)) uninhabited island of Eynhallow, which lies between the Mainland and Rousay, by James Fisher, Robert Carrick and George Dunnet, and has continued since 1958 under Professor Dunnet, helped by students and Orkney Field Club members. Over 8,000 Fulmar nestlings have been ringed, and their subsequent breeding success and fate monitored.

Fulmars first bred in Orkney at Noup Head, Westray, in 1901, and gradually extended their range southwards. On Eynhallow, as around every Fulmar colony, there are many non-breeding birds. The original

Fig. 71.
Fulmar (Photo: *Ann Jackson*).

research was to find out whether these birds were adolescents, or whether breeding did not take place every year. Ringing studies showed that the birds breed for the first time at any time between 6 and 19 years of age, with most males beginning at 8 years and most females at 12. Once they start, they are remarkably faithful to both mate and nest site. Breeding success (i.e. the production of a fledged young) is strongly correlated with age and breeding experience over the first 8–10 years of breeding. Breeding success is maintained at over 35% throughout the reproductive span of the birds, which is often more than 30 years. In other words, a Fulmar pair are likely to fledge more than 20 young during their life. The survival rate of an adult from one year to the next is 96%; mortality is very low.

The Eynhallow colony has grown at just under 5% per annum, although the number of breeders in any year may vary by up to a half. The changes seem to be the result of inexperienced breeders failing to breed every year, rather than mortality or emigration. Why this should should be so is unknown.

Inland Habitats

The sea birds of Orkney are important by almost any measure that one likes to use: numbers, international significance, place in the ecosystem, and so on. During the 1970s, they received a great deal of attention because they were perceived to be at risk from the development of the oil industry. However, the inland habitats are no less important in the national context, particularly the moorlands.

The Moorlands

Orkney moors present a complex variety of habitats dominated by heather; most areas fall into the category of 'wet heath'. This habitat holds an exceptionally rich bird community, especially on the Mainland and Rousay where the rich invertebrate fauna supports large numbers of birds. The moors of Hoy are not so rich and, together with the island's lack of Orkney Voles, this creates a different community with somewhat less diversity of species.

The Mainland and Rousay moors are undoubtedly best known for their breeding Hen Harriers. The research carried out on them by Eddie Balfour and, later, Nick Picozzi, is dealt with later (pp. 159–162). Suffice it to say here, that these moors remain the national stronghold of the species, holding some 15% of the known British nests. The Orkney Vole is an important food item for the Hen Harrier but it probably forms an even higher proportion of the diet of two other birds of prey which nest on the moors, the Kestrel and the Short-eared Owl. Balfour noted an increase in Kestrel numbers during the 1940s and it was apparently at that time that some birds became adapted to nesting on the ground among long heather. This habit continues to the present day, doubtless aided by the lack of ground predators such as Stoats, Weasels and Foxes, which cause the failure of so many ground-nesting species in mainland Britain. The Orkney Kestrel population now appears to be declining, for reasons which are not clear. Short-eared Owls in mainland Britain are subject to marked fluctuations in numbers coinciding with the population cycles of their main prey the

Common Vole (*Microtus agrestis*). In Orkney owl numbers are more stable, recent estimates suggesting that perhaps 50–60 pairs may attempt to breed each year. Their dependence on the Orkney Vole is perhaps the greatest of all; it is rare for a pellet to be examined which does not contain the remains of at least one of these small mammals.

Fig. 72.
Merlin and young
(Photo: *Ben Garth*).

Until recently the moorlands were also nationally known for their breeding Merlins. Balfour estimated the population of this dashing, bird-eating falcon at 25 pairs in the late 1950s and even in 1974 a survey of the West Mainland recorded 13 occupied territories. However, a marked decline has taken place in the 1980s so that in 1984 only six pairs were present. Four of these were in the West Mainland, but all failed to rear young. A worrying observation is that many pairs appear to be laying thin-shelled eggs which break during incubation. Such egg-breakage is often a symptom of contamination by DDT, a toxic agricultural chemical still sometimes used in Orkney.

Spring on the moors is dominated by the sound of the Curlew. Enormous numbers of Curlews nest, almost 100 pairs being found during a 1980 survey of the 1875 acres (759 hectares) of the RSPB's Hobbister Reserve alone. Other waders include Snipe and Redshank in some of the damper areas, small numbers of Dunlin, usually around the hill-top lochans, and Golden Plover on the high tops and ridges. Whimbrels nest only on Eday where six to eight pairs have become established. Of the ducks, Mallard, Teal and Wigeon can all be found amongst the heather, as can small

Fig. 73.
Red-throated Diver
(Photo: *William*
Paton).

numbers of Eiders and even Shelduck, while the well-hidden nests of the Red-breasted Merganser occur along the courses of burns. Several of these species take their newly-hatched young on to nearby lochans, but these small pools are particularly renowned for their Red-throated Divers. More than half of the Orkney diver population of some 70–80 pairs (about 10% of the British total) is to be found on Hoy, the rest being distributed between the Mainland, Rousay, Eday and Stronsay. As the Diver nests on the lochan shore and flights to feed in neighbouring areas of sea, its wild call is a common and evocative sound of the Orkney Moors in spring and summer.

Hoy also has the largest colonies in Orkney of Skuas, both Great and Arctic. The Great Skua (or Bonxie), was shown in a 1982 survey to have a population of 1652 pairs in the islands, Hoy with 1573 pairs holding 96% of the total. This is the second largest Bonxie colony in Britain after Foula in Shetland. The Bonxie has been the subject of much criticism because it is locally very common and an alleged hazard to lambs: there have been calls to remove it from the list of protected species. However, it must be remembered that it is a rare species on a world scale, Orkney and Shetland holding the majority of the world population. Moreover the Bonxie obtains some 80% of its food by splash-diving for fish; the killing of other sea-birds and their young provides a relatively minor part of the diet. This level of predation has no effect whatsoever on the population of the prey. The Arctic Skua, a less controversial species, was shown in 1982 to have a population of 1034 pairs. It was pleasing to note that this overall total represented a 44% increase since 1974 of this, Britain's rarest breeding sea-bird. Hoy, with 407 pairs, held 38% of the Orkney total while other important colonies were on Eday, Papa Westray, Rousay, the Mainland, Westray and Stronsay. The colonies on Westray, Papa Westray, Rousay and at least some of those on the Mainland, are found on that almost unique brand of 'moorland' known as maritime heath. It is this threatened habitat which holds, as well as Arctic Skuas, the majority of Orkney's Arctic Terns and good populations of waders, especially Oystercatchers.

Considerable colonies of gulls nest on the moors. Orkney supports between 20–30% of the British populations of both Great Black-backed and Common Gulls. The Wood Pigeon and the Starling, like the Kestrel, have adapted themselves to ground-nesting, a habit, of course, universal among most moorland birds, of which the Skylark and the Meadow Pipit are the most numerous. The Wren, Stonechat, Wheatear, Hooded Crow, Twite and, in damper areas, especially those with willow scrub, the Sedge Warbler and Reed Bunting, complete the bird community of these unique moors.

Many of the species which nest on the moors also feed there but some, including to a certain extent the birds of prey and waders, feed on the surrounding farmland. There can be no doubt that the proximity of this rich arable land to the moorland contributes to the well-being of the moorland nesting species. Reclamation of the moors and their conversion to arable land, coupled with excessive burning and, more recently, overgrazing, is believed to be currently tipping the scales against the moorland bird community. It is this conflict of interest which is the cause of much of the controversy over conservation today.

Fig. 74.
Great Skuas (Photo: *Ann Jackson*).

Fig. 75.
The Starling, which
normally nests in
trees, has adapted to
ground-nesting in
Orkney (Photo: *Ben
Garth*).

Marshes and Lochs

Fresh water lochs are numerous in the islands but marshland is a habitat
in decline as agricultural drainage progresses.

The breeding birds of the loch margins and the remaining marshes are
naturally dominated by wildfowl and waders. No fewer than ten species
of ducks breed regularly in Orkney. Of these, several have relatively small
populations or restricted distributions in Britain; the twenty breeding
pairs of Pintail is perhaps half the national total. The Mute Swan is a
conspicuous component of the wetland community. The 67 pairs recorded
in the 1983 census are the most northerly in Britain, this being one of the
species totally absent as a breeder from Shetland.

Oystercatchers, Ringed Plover, Lapwing, Dunlin, Snipe, Curlew, Red-

*Fig. 76.
Oystercatcher nesting
(note the eggs in the
foreground) (Photo:
William Paton).*

*Fig. 77.
Lapwing (Photo:
Anne Jackson).*

shank and Common Sandpiper are the waders nesting in these habitats. Some, notably the Oystercatcher and the Lapwing, have shown the ability to utilize arable land as well, but others, particularly Snipe and Redshank, require such wet conditions for feeding that only the dampest ground can support them. Black-tailed Godwits have bred occasionally, but at present do not, and another species which unfortunately has been lost is the Red-necked Phalarope. Last known to nest on Sanday, it is now some 15 years since this delightful species, which has been contracting its range northwards, last graced Orkney's marshes.

The lochs attract large numbers of passage and wintering wildfowl. The Loch of Harray in particular is of national importance for its flocks of Pochard and Tufted Duck. At times this loch can hold in excess of 7000 wildfowl in mid-winter; and there is no finer sight than the enormous compact gathering which occurs at the junction of the Harray and Stenness Lochs, which a strong current keeps ice-free when the main lochs are frozen. Whooper Swans often form part of this congregation although their peak numbers tend to occur earlier in the winter, in November and December, when the islands may hold up to 600 birds; many of these eventually make their way further south.

Birds of prey frequently hunt the high densities of small birds found on the marshes and loch-shores. In addition the marshes are important in providing several communal winter roost sites for Hen Harriers. These roosts are usually in beds of reeds (*Phragmites communis*); the two largest are at the Lochs of Banks and Durkadale.

Woodland

Woodland is rare in the islands. The only remaining natural woodland is found at Berriedale on Hoy, where there are also four experimental Forestry Commission plantations. The Mainland has a few plantations dominated by Sycamores, the most extensive being Binscarth (Finstown) and Berstane (Kirkwall). Similar woods exist at Balfour (Shapinsay) and at Trumland and Westness (Rousay). At Carrick (Eday) there is a virtually impenetrable Larch (*Larix* sp) plantation on the sheltered slope of Vinquoy Hill.

These woods provide a welcome diversity of habitat and are perhaps in need of active management. All the deciduous plantations are of similar age (about 100 years) and are showing signs of deterioration. Some 14 species (15% of all the regular breeders) nest almost wholly within this habitat and its demise would be unfortunate. Orkney's only Chaffinches, Goldcrests and Willow Warblers are found here, as are most of its Robins, Blackbirds and Song Thrushes; the woods are the only localities where Orcadians can listen to their five songs. The woods, too, provide the only possible nest sites for the Rook which, with a 1982 population of 1347 pairs, is perhaps more common than one would expect in these exposed islands. The larch plantation on Eday at one time supported Orkney's only Tree Sparrow colony but the species has not been seen there for several years and occurs now only as a rare migrant.

Woods and gardens with trees are havens for other migrants too, and it is to these localities that bird-watchers turn their attention in spring and autumn when small passerine birds are on the move. The systematic

Fig. 78.
Sonagrams of three Chaffinch songs from Orkney. These diagrams are plots of frequency against time, the trace being where there is sound at a particular point. Songs are around two seconds long and the top scale runs from

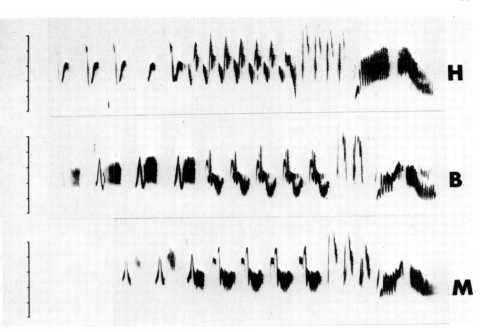

check-list (pp. 284–303) show the variety of migrants which may occur in the islands, especially when easterly winds drift birds across the North Sea from the Continent.

The lack of woodlands in Orkney has been turned to positive use in an ingenious study of song in chaffinches carried out in 1976–78 by Peter Slater, then at the University of Sussex. Most of the chaffinches in Orkney nest in the three main woods at Trumland on Rousay, Balfour on Shapinsay and Binscarth in Finstown. There are also one or two pairs in other woods such as those at Berstane, Woodwick and Gyre, but the total population in the islands is probably only around 50 breeding pairs.

Earlier work on chaffinches had shown that song varies from place to place following a system of dialects rather like those in human speech. With isolated woods separated by long stretches of unsuitable habitat, Orkney was an ideal place in which to examine this phemonenon in detail. The development of the sound spectrograph, a machine which plots out the characteristics of sound on paper, made it possible to examine the songs in much more detail than was previously possible.

The result turned out to be complicated, with no simple dialect structure. Individual chaffinches have between one and six song types, and each of them is produced very precisely every time it is sung. Birds in the same wood tend to share a song type because young birds learn their songs from singing adults and usually copy them very exactly. But the copying is not always accurate and, as a result, each wood contains a spectrum of different song types. Some of these are similar to each other, and have probably arisen by a young bird failing to copy accurately, while others are much more distinct and are likely to have been introduced from woods elsewhere.

1–6 kHz. Although similar, each song is distinct enough to be labelled as a different song type. The distinction can be very subtle: the main difference between B and M is that there is a single rather different note between the first and second phrases of M (the third node on the sonagram shown) which has no equivalent in B. But this is a reliable difference which must be detected by the birds since a bird at Woodwick was recorded to sing both these different types; it must have learned them separately (Photo: P. J. B. Slater).

The total number of song types Slater recorded in Orkney was 16, though many of these were only sung by a single bird. The commonest song type (labelled type B) was sung by several birds at Binscarth, Balfour and Trumland. Other types were more or less restricted to one of the woods: types W and J to Binscarth, types H and G to Balfour, and types F and M to Trumland. One bird in Finstown village sang both H and G and so had, almost certainly, learnt its songs on Shapinsay before moving to the Mainland to set up its territory.

This study of chaffinch song showed that there are no simple dialects, but that some songs are widespread while others are more restricted in their distribution. It also yielded results on several other facets of their singing, such as how birds use their song in communicating with one another, the way in which song changes with time through cultural evolution, and the extent to which neighbours share songs with one another.

Farmland

Permanent pasture (the 'arable' of local usage) geared to the rearing of beef cattle has increasingly become the most extensive land use on all the major islands with the exception of Hoy. Such land provides rich feeding for such waders as Curlew, Lapwing and Golden Plovers, especially outside the breeding season. Large numbers of gulls, particularly Common and Black-headed, find rich pickings in such situations. However, among the waders only the Lapwing, Oystercatcher and, to a certain extent the Curlew, have adapted to nesting on this habitat and even they are at their highest densities in pasture which has been neglected and reverted to *Juncus*. The extremely poor breeding success of Lapwings in dry summers is chiefly the result of improved land drainage which has caused the disappearance of the damp holes and corners of the fields, which were previously a refuge in dry years.

Fig. 79.
Curlew (Photo:
Anne Jackson).

The large numbers of birds present on farmland outside the breeding season is a great attraction for birds of prey, and Hen Harriers, Peregrines and Merlins may often be seen quartering, stooping or dashing after their quarry. Rock Doves and Starlings, in addition to those species already mentioned, find abundant feeding opportunities.

The change from oats to barley as a source of winter fodder is felt by many in the farming community to be the cause of a reduction in the numbers of certain passerine birds on farmland. This may well be true, for example, in the case of the Yellowhammer, which has not bred in the islands for ten years, or of the Corn Bunting, which is now reduced to fewer than 20 pairs concentrated on Sanday and Stronsay. The major source of winter fodder is now silage, the cutting of which has steadily replaced hay-making in recent years. The main species which this change seems to have affected is the Corncrake; its stronghold now is in the North Isles, especially Papa Westray and North Ronaldsay where modern, intensive farming is not so prevalent.

The evolution of modern farming in Orkney has thus had its pluses and minuses as far as birds are concerned. Rich feeding habitat has been provided for a limited range of species but only a few species have been able to adapt to breeding in such an environment.

Orkney Hen Harriers

The Hen Harrier is unique among British birds of prey. It has been increasing at a time when virtually all other species have been decreasing; it has an extraordinary breeding biology; and the detailed information on behaviour and population dynamics collected in Orkney over a 40-year period by Eddie Balfour, for many years RSPB representative in Orkney, is unrivalled for any other raptor in Britain and perhaps anywhere else in the world.

The Hen Harrier was common in Orkney during the 19th century, but it became rare after the turn of the century through human persecution. Protection produced a recovery during the 1930s and numbers increased greatly in the 1940s. The present population is around 70–80 females and about half that number of males. Most of these are on the Mainland, nesting in tall vegetation in damp sites on upland moors, with small numbers on Hoy and Rousay, and occasional breeding on Eday. There are perhaps 250 pairs on mainland Scotland, north of the Tay, 100 pairs elsewhere in Britain, and 50 pairs in Ireland.

Hen Harriers seldom fly very high above the ground, and if they are seen flying high, they are not hunting. They very often inhabit windy uplands, where they can glide against the wind maintaining a low ground speed, which helps them to locate small prey in dense low cover. On still days they are obliged to hunt by steady flapping flight, but on windy days they glide with an occasional wingflap, the wings being held well above the horizontal. In a strong wind a harrier looks as if it is being blown about, but in fact it retains close control of its movements, and can remain poised in a gale above possible prey until it finally locates the quarry. It then drops quietly into the vegetation and either catches the prey or fails. Harriers can catch some birds in flight, but normally take nearly all their prey on the ground in this manner. The hunting methods of the Hen Harrier thus do not differ

Fig. 80.
Hen Harrier at nest
(Photo: *William Paton*).

from those of other British harriers in open country, or of other species of harriers elsewhere in the world. However, the Hen Harrier is a rather larger and more powerful species than Montagu's and it may take rather larger prey.

Very little is recorded outside Orkney of what a Hen Harrier actually eats. Small mammals and birds are probably the most important item throughout. Part of the reason for the success of the Orkney population may have been the Orkney Vole, which, unlike most voles, does not appear to suffer violent fluctuations of population, so that it provides a steady reliable source of food for the breeding harriers. Hedgehogs, rats, and fair-sized young Rabbits are also taken and, if such mammalian prey are too large to carry entire, they are dismembered and parts carried away. Large numbers of moorland birds are also eaten, including young waders such as Curlews and Lapwings, Meadow Pipits and other small passerines, notably Starlings. Young gulls, which are often commonest on northern moorlands, especially the young of Common Gulls which nest on open short heather or moorland, do not often seem to be taken, an indication that gulls are generally distasteful to birds of prey sharing their habitat.

The male Hen Harrier is polygynous. This was first recognized by Desmond Nethersole-Thompson in 1931 in Orkney, and has since been described elsewhere in Scotland and in the United States; it occurs also in the Marsh Harrier. The sex ratio among breeding birds is about two females to each male, but each year there are a few males with up to six females, usually simultaneously. It is the older males who tend to associate with more females. Presumably because these males are more experienced, the overall breeding success is not significantly depressed, even though the females must be stressed during the incubation and early nesting periods when the female normally relies on the male to supply the food. Indeed, males with three or more females raise more young than those that are monogynous, although fewer young per nest are raised in situations involving 2, 3 or 4 females than in monogynous ones. Clearly a female is at a disadvantage in a polygynous situation; on the other hand, it may be that it is the only chance for her of occupying a territory where breeding is possible (Table 23).

Only a third of the young survive to breed at the end of their first year, although the survival rate in subsequent years is 70%. Of birds ringed in Orkney, 16 out of 26 found dead outside the islands were shot, trapped or

Performance of individual Hen Harriers in breeding groups of different sizes in Scotland. Table 23
In the males the trend from 1–6 is statistically significant, as is the difference between monogamous and polygynous females mated to older males (Calculated from details in Balfour and Cadbury, 1979; after Newton 1979).

	One female mated to yearling male	Number of females mated to older males					
		1	2	3	4	5	6
No. of nests	27	28	92	84	36	13	6
No. (%) of nests successful	17(63)	23(82)	60(65)	45(54)	14(39)	5(38)	3(50)
Young produced per male	1.6	2.3	3.0	3.9	4.0	6.5	—
Young produced per female	1.6	2.3	1.5	1.3	1.0	1.3	—

Fig. 81.
Hen Harrier with young (Photo: *Anne Jackson*).

poisoned, compared with none of the 10 recovered in Orkney; harrier persecution is obviously still widespread.

Breeding pairs or groups of several females with one male are found in the breeding grounds from March onwards. At that time the male displays with or to one or more females. The display is largely aerial, and in the later stages, extremely spectacular. At first the pair soar together, the male diving often at the female, who sometimes turns over and presents her claws to his. As courtship progresses the male performs undulating flights of increasing vigour, alone. Finally, in April, the most spectacular display is performed, in which the male hurls himself earthwards from a hundred feet or more above the ground, twisting or spinning in flight with threshing wings. The display is not only visible but audible at some distance, and is accompanied by 'chedk-ek-ek-ek' calls not unlike alarm notes. Although the male appears out of control he checks within a few feet of the ground and then rises again to his former pitch, repeating the performance up to twenty of so times, and rarely even over a hundred times. Normally this spectacular diving display, which is similar to that of other harriers, is performed immediately above a nesting station; but displaying males may range over half a mile or so.

Females normally take no part in this spectacular display but remain perched on the ground. When the male eventually alights a female may fly to join him, and this is perhaps part of the process of nest selection. Some females, however, also perform this swift diving display, especially in sites where females outnumber males. This may be how individual females ensure separation of their own nest site from those of other females attached to the same male. The actual nest sites of the several females mated to one male are usually rather regularly spaced. Diving displays by the female continue into the late fledgling period, which would tend to support the view that each female holds her own territory within the male's wider home range.

Present and Future

The number of bird species breeding regularly in Orkney is almost identical with that recorded in 1941 by David Lack, and the number of occasional breeders is much larger. At least part of the reason for the latter fact is that more and more people are taking an interest in bird-life, and are less inclined to persecute birds or their eggs. It would, however, be dangerous to become complacent. Although the record of the Oil Terminal on Flotta for preventing oil spills is good, a single bad spill could have devastating effects, particularly if it occurred in winter.

We need to know more about the unusually rich moorland bird communities of Orkney, and how birds survive on the heaths and adjoining farm land, when so many apparently comparable areas further south have lost many of their birds. Agricultural improvement and the reclamation of moors and marshes is a continuing process in Orkney; agriculture is the islands' most important industry. There must be a limit to the amount of breeding habitat the birds can afford to lose. As man has evolved in Orkney, he has helped to produce a county of great beauty and serenity, with a rich and diverse scenery and wildlife. Both human life and bird populations will continue to change. Our responsibility is to make sure that the rate of change is not so great that either suffers.

Orkney Man

First the aborigines
That houked Skara Brae from the sand.
Then the Picts,
Those small dark cunning men
Who scrawled their history in stone . . .
And then the tigers from east over sea,
The blond butchering Vikings,
Whose last worry on sea or land
Was purity of race, as they staggered couchwards
After a fill of ale.
Finally, to make the mixture thick and slab,
The off-scourings of Scotland,
The lowest sleaziest pimps from Lothian and the Mearns
Fawning in the train of Black Pat,
And robbing and raping ad lib.
But that's not all.
For many a hundred ships have ripped their flanks
On Rora Head, or the Noup,
And Basque sailor lads and bearded skippers from Brittany
Left off their briny ways to cleave a furrow
Through Orkney crofts and lasses.

Not to speak of two world wars
And hordes of English and Yanks and Italians and Poles
Who took up their stations here:
By day the guns, by night the ancestral box-bed.
Only this morning I delivered a bairn
At Maggie O'Corsland's
With a subtle silk-selling Krishna smile.

A fine mixter-maxter!
George Mackay Brown *What is an Orcadian*

Orkney lies at a cross-road of sea-ways, and sea-farers have called in at the islands briefly or permanently for as long as they have had boats able to cross the North Sea or the Pentland Firth. There have been suggestions that there were Mesolithic settlers in Orkney, based on flint tools found in various places. However, the most northerly good evidence of Mesolithic activity known to British archaeologists is at Freswick Bay in Caithness and the first certain human occupants of Orkney were Neolithic farmers. The earliest radiocarbon dates from human dwellings and pollen from peat cores show that food-producing communities were well established in the islands by about 3500 BC. The earliest settlements that have been excavated are Skara Brae on Orkney Mainland, Rinyo on Rousay, Links of Noltland on Westray, and Knap of Howar on Papa Westray. These are sites of established farming communities; it seems unlikely that they include the

Fig. 82.
Wildfowling on the
cliffs of Orkney in
the early 1900's.
Seabirds, especially
Auks, were an
important source of
food in Orkney in
earlier times. Note
the figure on the
centre ledge near the
bottom (Photo: *Tom*
Kent Collection,
Orkney Library).

homes of the first pioneering colonists. We know effectively nothing about the first Orcadians.

Two different sorts of pots have been found in the four well-known Neolithic sites. The inhabitants of Knap of Howar had 'Unstan ware', while the other three villages used 'Grooved ware'. There are other differences in the artefacts and house-plans between the villages, showing that there were at least two cultural traditions present in Orkney, characterized by the different pottery types. The later radiocarbon dates from Knap of Howar are contemporary with the earlier ones from Skara Brae; these two cultures persisted alongside each other. It has been suggested that Grooved ware is a development of Unstan ware; this is uncertain. We have to admit that we do not know if the two cultures were ethnically the same or whether they derived from different areas in Britain or even continental Europe.

A large tomb at Isbister on South Ronaldsay (the 'Tomb of the Eagles')
dated at around 3000 BC contained skeletons of people physically very
similar albeit slightly shorter than modern Orcadians. A sobering reflection is that very few adults among the 340 individuals excavated had
survived beyond their twenties.

The Neolithic villagers brought with them cattle, sheep, goats, pigs,
dogs and seed corn. They lived in compact villages, and built complex
chambered tombs. Skara Brae is the best known of the early settlements.
Radiocarbon dates have shown that it was inhabited from a little before
3100 BC to around 2500 BC.

Most of the houses we can see today belong to the later phase of occupation and then, as now, they would have appeared subterranean; they were
built into previous midden deposits, and then had more rubbish piled
round them. The dwelling rooms are all remarkably similar in size and
shape. They have a central fireplace, up to four stone box beds, sometimes
a dresser, small stone boxes in the floor, and cupboards in the wall. Each

Fig. 83.
Main archaeological
sites on Orkney.

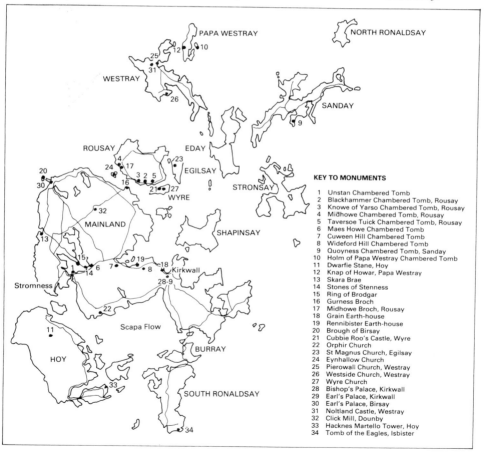

KEY TO MONUMENTS

1 Unstan Chambered Tomb
2 Blackhammer Chambered Tomb, Rousay
3 Knowe of Yarso Chambered Tomb, Rousay
4 Midhowe Chambered Tomb, Rousay
5 Taversoe Tuick Chambered Tomb, Rousay
6 Maes Howe Chambered Tomb
7 Cuween Hill Chambered Tomb
8 Wideford Hill Chambered Tomb
9 Quoyness Chambered Tomb, Sanday
10 Holm of Papa Westray Chambered Tomb
11 Dwarfie Stane, Hoy
12 Knap of Howar, Papa Westray
13 Skara Brae
14 Stones of Stenness
15 Ring of Brodgar
16 Gurness Broch
17 Midhowe Broch, Rousay
18 Grain Earth-house
19 Rennibister Earth-house
20 Brough of Birsay
21 Cubbie Roo's Castle, Wyre
22 Orphir Church
23 St Magnus Church, Egilsay
24 Eynhallow Church
25 Pierowall Church, Westray
26 Westside Church, Westray
27 Wyre Church
28 Bishop's Palace, Kirkwall
29 Earl's Palace, Kirkwall
30 Earl's Palace, Birsay
31 Noltland Castle, Westray
32 Click Mill, Dounby
33 Hacknes Martello Tower, Hoy
34 Tomb of the Eagles, Isbister

Fig. 84.
The Ring of Brodgar,
on Mainland,
probably dates from
the latter part of the
Neolithic period
(Photo: *Gunnie*
Moberg).

building would house a family; probably half-a-dozen houses would have
been in occupation at any one time.

Contemporary with the Neolithic villages are chambered tombs, of
which there are two main types: 'Maes Howe' (Maeshowe itself; Quoyness;
Cuween Hill, Firth; Wideford Hill and Quanterness, Kirkwall), and
'stalled' (Isbister in South Ronaldsay; Unstan in Stenness; Midhowe on
Rousay); pottery from them suggests that the former was linked with the
Grooved ware culture, and the latter with the Unstan ware. The Maes
Howe chambers are entered by a relatively long, low passage which opens
into a central room with several smaller side cells. The passage in stalled
tombs leads into an elongated chamber which is partially divided by shelves
at the end. Apparently the dead were first reduced to skeletons (perhaps by
being left exposed to the elements), and then a selection of bones was
taken into the chamber, together with food offerings, broken burnt pottery,
bone pins and flints.

The Ring of Brodgar and the Stones of Stenness are ceremonial complexes apparently belonging to the latter part of the Neolithic period.

'Burnt mounds' at Beaquoy, Harray, and Liddle, South Ronaldsay, are
Bronze Age remains, formed largely from rubbish piled round a building.
In contrast to the preceding Neolithic, the Bronze Age buildings were

alongside small streams and not confined to the coast. No classical crouched burials which typify the Beaker folk, have been found in Orkney, although Beaker sherds occur at Rinyo in Rousay.

Picts and Brochs

The most spectacular archaeological remains in Orkney (and in north Britain generally) are isolated round towers, built without mortar and 40–80 ft (10–25 m) in diameter. There are 102 known in Orkney alone. These are brochs. There have been many theories about their inhabitants and purpose, but their real nature has been shown from Orkney excavations. Traditionally, they were dated to the 1st and 2nd centuries AD by Roman artefacts. However, similar structures occurring much earlier than this are now dated from the Iron Age. A number of brochs in Orkney were still sufficiently recognizable when the Vikings arrived in the late first millenium for them to be called *borgs* (defences), transformed later into the word 'broch' by which they are known today. It is now almost certain that they were a development from round houses, which appeared in Orkney at the beginning of the Iron Age, as early as 700 BC. The possibility of making these into defensive keeps was recognized, and brochs are found contemporaneous with surrounding buildings, ramparts and ditches (as at Gurness in Evie, and Midhowe on Rousay). The internal layout of both

Fig. 85. The best preserved broch in Orkney is at Aikerness, on the west Mainland. The abruptness of the marine erosion on the east can here be clearly seen (Photo: *Gunnie Moberg*).

roundhouses and brochs is very similar, with a central hearth and perhaps a cooking box, surrounded by a service area which had several large storage cupboards and a series of interconnecting rooms. This plan differs from that in non-round houses of the early Iron Age (and from the previous Neolithic and Bronze Age structures) and, to a lesser extent, from that in buildings around the later brochs.

The brochs were inhabited by Picts. The 12th century *Historia Norvegiae* placed these shadowy people firmly in legend:

'they little exceeded pigmies in stature; they did marvels in the morning and the evening in building towns, but at midday they entirely lost their strength, and lurked through fear in little underground houses . . . Whence they came there we are entirely ignorant.'

There has long been mystery about the Picts. Orkney was described as Pictish in AD 46, in a 4th century document which was known to Bede. Their kingdom came to an end when it was united with that of the Scots under Kenneth Mac Alpin in AD 843. There is limited place name evidence about the Picts in Orkney (for example, the Pentland or Pightland Firth), there are carved symbol stones and instriptions using the Ogam (Pictish) alphabet, and a few pieces of metalwork, most dateable to the 7th and 8th centuries. Perhaps the best way of thinking about the Picts is to regard anything and anywhere in Orkney and northern Scotland as Pictish from early Iron Age to Viking times.

Christianity was brought to Orkney in the 7th century; there was said to be an Early Christian monastery on the Brough of Birsay. During the pagan Pictish period there is some evidence that the dead were cremated and put in short cists. The introduction of Christianity led to simple burial in cemeteries, probably in long cists; there is an example on the Brough of Birsay.

The Vikings

The saga accounts imply that the Viking settlement of Orkney began only a little before the reign of King Harald Fairhair (*d.* 945), but in fact it must have been much earlier. The years 790–800 saw the beginning of Viking raids not only in the Hebrides and Ireland, but also on the east and south coasts of England. Clearly such a flood could not have bypassed Orkney which lay on the main route to the west and south.

There is a well-entrenched tradition that the Vikings came to a virtually empty land when they crossed the North Sea at the end of the 8th century. The old *Orkney Book* which formed the educational background to generations of Orcadians had no doubts:

'If there had been a native population, and if these had been expelled or exterminated by the invaders, we should surely have been told of it by the Saga writers, who would have delighted in telling such a tale. It has accordingly been supposed that at the time of the Norse settlement the islands were uninhabited save by the hermits of the Culdee Church. When or how the former Pictish inhabitants disappeared, it is impossible to say.

Possibly some early Viking raids, of which no history remains, had resulted in the slaughter of many and the flight of the rest of the less exposed lands south of the Pictland or Pentland Firth. Whatever the reason may be, the chapter of [Orkney] history which opens with the Norse settlement is in no way a continuation of anything which goes before, but begins a new story.'

This was in no way atypical. The Shetlander, Goudie, writing at much the same time, believed that the Picts 'and their Christianity alike' appear to have vanished before the arrival of the Scandinavians. A generation later another writer claimed that 'the Pictish inhabitants, numerous as they must have been, had been wiped cleanly off the page of history in some unexplained fashion . . . an entire people disappears in silence.'

The fullest exposition of this point of view is in a book by Professor A. W. Brøgger, published in 1929:

'The Norsemen did not destroy a numerous Celtic population in the Shetlands and Orkneys. They did not wage a war of extermination against such a population or drive it into the sea and seize its possessions, its farms, and its civilization. It seems clear that a race which possessed the great brochs for defence and real fleets of ships, would not have allowed itself to be destroyed by the Norsemen even if the craftmanship of the latter in the shaping of weapons was superior and their art in shipbuilding of a very high order. Perhaps the broch-people, small in numbers, a warlike aristocracy, had gradually drifted away from the islands into the Scottish mainland, leaving the poorer classes of Celts in possession. The Norse settlers came sailing to a land in which there were few people. On all sides they saw traces of old houses and farms, ruins and foundations of houses and outhouses. The greatest impression they received was that created by the sight of old brochs. All their imagination was fired. Did they not step ashore into a veritable museum?'

Fig. 86.
Early Viking
remains on the
Brough of Birsay.
The Vikings
established themselves
here before venturing
onto Mainland
Orkney (Photo:
Gunnie Moberg).

Not all agreed with this. The 'traditional understanding' that modern Orkney was founded by a pure Viking race rested upon a debateable lack of evidence (of place-names). For example, Jakob Jakobsen, the doyen of place-name researchers, began by believing that no pre-Scandinavian place-names had survived in Orkney or Shetland, but then changed his mind and produced a list of over 40 Celtic place-name elements in Shetland; while the Orcadian Hugh Marwick strengthened the argument by listing nearly 30 Celtic elements in Orkney place-names.

If we add the positive evidence of Pictish symbol stones and Ogam inscriptions which can be dated confidently to Viking times in the islands, and the continuity of Christian traditions in places like Birsay, Deerness, Papa Westray, and probably Eynhallow, we are forced to the conclusion that the pre-Viking inhabitants of Orkney were, in Hugh Marwick's words, not so much exterminated as expropriated, or as John Hedges has put it, the 'archaeological record indicates integration rather than continued violent conflict.'

The best description of the state of Orkney in the first millenium AD is given by the late F. T. Wainwright in a collection of essays he edited under the title *The Northern Isles* (1962). He summarizes the arguments of Brøgger and others, then goes on:

'During the historic Pictish period (AD 300–850) the inhabitants of Orkney and Shetland became part of the historical Pictish kingdom and were included within the all-embracing collective name Picti. Long before the Scandinavians arrived they were being subjected to intrusive Scottish influence from the Gaelic west, represented most clearly in missionary activity and Ogam inscriptions and commemorated in the Papae of history and place-names. It is not surprising that the sagas do not mention the Picts. The sagas are concerned chiefly with the deeds of great men and the feuds of great families, and they were composed at a time when, in England at least, the Picts were less than a memory and no more than a fable. There is no reason why the Picts should appear in the sagas, and their failure to do so certainly cannot be used as evidence that they did not exist or were too few to merit notice. The Scandinavian settlement was the result of a mass-migration, and its impact on the Picts must have been overwhelming.'

The Scandinavian settlement of Orkney was a major event, perhaps the most important event in the human history of the islands after they were first colonized. But it was not a hiatus; it did not represent a complete end to the old order, followed by a brand new beginning. Despite the changes that must have taken place, there was a continuity of occupation and at least some traditions, from Pictish to Viking times.

There are at least three lines of positive evidence for continuity, apart from the traditional arguments about the survival of Pictish place-name elements and the emerging conclusions form archaeology. Firstly the Vikings did not suddenly appear and take over around AD 800. For at least two centuries before this, trading contacts had existed between people on both sides of the North Sea.

Secondly, it seems highly probable that the Pictish land-units (*davochs*) were directly taken over as the early Norse *uresland*, which formed the basis of the taxation system. [This was suggested by Captain Thomas as long ago as 1884; the idea was developed by Storer Clouston in his classical *History of Orkney* (1932) and later by Hugh Marwick in his *Orkney* (1951)].

Thirdly, place-names, burials, and inscribed stones all suggest that

Christianity (traditionally brought to Orkney in the 6th century by followers of Kentigern) survived the Viking settlement, and fairly rapidly drew the incomers into its embrace (almost certainly much earlier than the threat recorded in the *Orkneyinga Saga* of Olaf Tryggvason to kill Sigurd the Stout and devastate his followers unless they all accepted the true faith).

The continuity of Orkney life from Pictish to Viking times needs emphasizing because almost all histories divide the occupation of the islands into three or four periods: the early settlers, often linking these with the Picts (up to about AD 800); the Viking period; and the period of Scottish influence, beginning in 1471 when James III 'annexed and united the earldom of Orkney and the lordship of Shetland to the Crown, not to be given away in times to come to any person or persons except to one of the king's sons got of lawful bed.' The coming of the Vikings is then described in great detail, usually relying on the doubtful historicity of the saga accounts. (It is worth recalling that the *Orkneyinga Saga* is not equivalent to the Icelandic *Landnamobok*; it is an Earls' saga treating of individual people and their relationships in life or death with little concern for history or geography). The effect is that each phase of history is treated as a separate unit, with a beginning and an end. Although it is clearly necessary to identify the dominant influences of different eras, too often the giving of names to a period isolates it from the ongoing interactions of history, and thus distorts our understanding of the whole process. This distortion tends to be magnified by the attention that is given to the Pict–Viking divide.

Orkney history is a continuum. We know that now. It is an ongoing story with high and low points, triumphs and tragedies, incomers and out-migrants, but with no absolute interruptions. Despite Goudie, Brøgger, and the like, it is wrong to think of Orkney being occupied at different times by different peoples. A present-day Orcadian is a person moulded by something like 6000 years of life in the islands, although we can distinguish five major immigration episodes:

Episode 1. The original two groups of Neolithic incomers (the 'aborigines', of George Mackay Brown), who were largely contemporary with each other and had more in common than they had differences.

Episode 2. Around 700 BC, the Bronze Age came to Orkney. Archaeologically, it is often difficult to distinguish overt invasion from imported influence, but the fairly sudden appearance together of metal artefacts, horses, rotary querns, round houses and long-headed combs implies a new wave of immigrants. These are the people we call the Picts. Perhaps in time the archaeologists and anthropologists will be able to tell us more about them. Pictish times are still very mysterious. They may be nothing more than a simple evolution of the 'aboriginal' culture through an intensification of contacts which were taking place all the time.

Episode 3. Beginning in the early 7th century, Scandinavians began to make their presence felt, culminating in a massive population movement into Orkney at the end of the 8th century, when they 'arrived in numbers sufficient to overwhelm the earlier inhabitants politically, socially, culturally and linguistically'.

Episode 4. During mediaeval times there was a considerable influx of Lowland Scots, originally merchants and bureaucrats, but increasingly followers of the land-owners. However, we have virtually no idea of the numbers who contributed genetically to the population.

Episode 5. Finally, we have recent immigration – soldiers and sailors in two world wars, but even more recently a massive influx of (mainly) English people who have halted and reversed the population decline which had been continuous in Orkney for more than a century.

Life in Ancient Orkney

It has been said that Orkney stayed in the Stone Age until the 17th or 18th centuries. This is clearly a gross exaggeration, but for long time technological developments had less impact in Orkney than elsewhere. There were no cultural differences to enable archaeologists to date artefacts and this caused major problems in distinguishing one period from another until the introduction of radiocarbon and other methods of independent dating. The dietary staple in Orkney must always have been grain, albeit mixed with weed seeds. In Neolithic times, mortars and pestles seem to have been a favoured means of reducing this to flour, but in the Bronze Age saddle querns appear; these are long stones, with a central shallow trough along which a 'rubbing' stone was pushed backwards and forwards. At some time in the Iron Age, rotary querns made an appearance. They consisted of an upper circular stone, rotated on a similar lower one while grain was fed down a central hole. This principle is still used to a limited extent in Orkney, although it is now mechanized. Quernstones need to have their grinding faces periodically roughened and this could well be the function of some of the beach pebbles found in the sites of all periods. Other pebbles could have been grinders and pounders used with different sorts of devices designed to reduce hard foodstuffs to powder; mortars, for instance, continued in use and there were 'trough querns' in the Iron Age.

In the Neolithic, most meat came from sheep and cattle, which were kept in almost equal numbers. Both were smaller than Neolithic ones elsewhere, and the sheep were rather like the modern North Ronaldsay animals. Pigs were kept, but were few in number. Most animals were killed when young, presumably because of the difficulty of providing food for them in winter. The meat would have had to be skinned and jointed, and up to the Iron Age this was probably accomplished with tools of flint and chert or split stone. Thereafter iron knives were probably used.

Large saithe, cod and similar fish were eaten, as well as inshore fish, suggesting that catches were made several miles off shore. Seal and whale-bone found in excavations may have been carrion, but show that early Orkney man exploited his environment to the full. Crabs were found at Isbister. Hens appear by late Pictish times; domestic geese, oats and flax occur by Viking times. Red deer were eaten during Neolithic times (notably at Noltland); it is unknown whether they were farmed or were wild.

Neither the potter's wheel nor the kiln seem to have been significant in Orkney and during two periods, the Bronze Age and the Viking, the art of potting was neglected. There are other materials from which vessels can be made and there are alternative methods of cooking. Judging from the amount of debris found, the most popular means in the Bronze Age was to drop hot stones into a trough of water; this may have been a local equivalent to the cauldrons used elsewhere. This method remained popular into the Iron Age, although by Pictish times it seems to have fallen out of favour. In the Viking period the main vessels used were of steatite (soapstone); this does not occur in Orkney and must have been imported from Shetland or Scandinavia. From the high period of the brochs throughout the Pictish period socket holes are commonly found on either side of hearths; these probably housed a superstructure from which pots were suspended.

Bones (and wood) can be split and shaped with stone blades, as can pumice (grooved pieces of which are known for all periods), but bone items from the Iron Age have been found in Orkney which could only have been made with the use of saws, gravers, and even some sort of auger. The main implement for shaping stone implements and furnishings was probably a hammerstone, which can be picked up on most beaches in every shape and size. Metalwork, both bronze and iron, was introduced slowly and in only limited roles. Since the moulds found are made of steatite, it may be that visiting itinerant metalworkers, rather than the resident population, were responsible for casting Bronze Age objects.

It is very difficult to detect the manufacture of perishable items such as leather, woodwork and textiles but one large group of implements which are probably relevant are the numerous bone 'awls', 'gouges' etc. These decrease in number with time, being comparatively rare by later Pictish and Viking times when iron was fully integrated into use. Although finds of spindle whorls and needles only start in Orkney with the Iron Age there is a good probability that people spun (and wore clothes of textiles) at least by the Bronze Age.

Necklaces seem to have been in vogue in the Neolithic. In his account of the excavations at Skara Brae, Gordon Childe painted an imaginative picture of a woman losing her beads as she ran along a passageway being inundated by sand. Similar beads of bone, shell and antler were found (together with a polished dog's tooth) in the tomb at Isbister.

There have been many finds of Bronze Age jewellery in the British Isles particularly from the earlier part of the period: gold and copper neckrings or diadems, lunulae, torcs, bracelets, rings and pins as well as necklaces of amber and jet, and toggles and buttons of jet and bone. Such articles do not seem to have been at all common in Orkney but a cist in one of the Knowes of Trotty, Harray, which contained a cremation, yielded an amber spacer-plate necklace and four gold discs (of unknown use).

Mediaeval and Modern Orkney

Historians have tended to regard Viking times as a Golden Age in Orkney, and later events as indicative of decadence. The islands came under the Scottish crown in 1468, but this was only one stage in a process which had been continuing for centuries. From the days when Earl Thorfinn, one of the major figures of the *Orkneyinga Saga*, held nine earldoms in Scotland, and when St Magnus (of the Cathedral) was intruded on Orkney as a Scottish-backed candidate for a divided earldom, links with Scotland were both frequent and important. Until 1375, and briefly from 1455 to 1468, the Earls of Orkney owed allegiance to Norway, but they were also Earls of Caithness owing allegiance to Scotland. Ties of kinship extended into the

Fig. 87.
Most traditional
settlement in Orkney
is around the sea.
The Earl's Palace,
lying at the northwest
corner of the Main-
land, is not far from
the original Viking
Settlement on the
tidally-protected
Brough of Birsay.
Thr area is now a
flourishing farm
district (Photo:
Gunnie Moberg).

Celtic frontier lands of Sutherland, to the Hebrides, the Isle of Man and Ireland, as well as throughout Orkney. From the 12th century onwards, marriages of earls were more likely to be made in Scotland than in Norway. In the last century of Scandinavian rule, the names of those in the earls' entourage are predominantly Scots.

Despite these indications of considerable Scottish influence in the upper strata of society at a time when Orkney was still politically part of Scandinavia, it is impossible to be sure what degree of immigration it implied, or to what extent such influence spread downwards into Orkney society as a whole. The last official document written in Norse is dated 1425, 43 years before the transfer of sovereignty to Scotland, but Orkney Norn, the local language, was still being spoken at the end of the 17th century.

The Reformation period and the end of the Stewart earldom in 1615 was undoubtedly a period of major Scottish immigration. Nevertheless 'continuity' is a word which can be appropriately applied to Orkney history. Genetic comparisons between the present-day Orkney population and other North Atlantic populations, based on blood groups and other inherited traits, show that the biological affinities of the Orcadians are not particularly clear-cut. They are more or less equally related to the Scots and Irish on the one hand, and Scandinavian and Scandinavian-derived populations (Iceland, Faroe, etc) on the other. Despite being at the crossroads of sea-ways for over a thousand years, there is still such a person as a real Orcadian. At the 1981 census there were 19,056 people in Orkney, 611 of them visitors. Of the 18,425 residents, 16,638 are recorded as having been born in Scotland, most of course, within Orkney itself.

Life in Recent Centuries

Life has almost always been a battle in Orkney, with sometimes the humans, sometimes the elements in the ascendancy. It is only in the past few years that modern technology has given weapons and protection to enable the people to win more often than not. Although the climate is never really cold, the wind and damp mean that adequate supplies of fuel are essential. For most of this century, imported coal, and now electricity or oil, have been available for heating, but in earlier centuries, the population depended on the availability of peat.

Most people had access to peat from neighbouring mosses, but in places where there was little peat, or where the banks were exhausted, alternative sources had to be sought. As a result, there was quite a movement and trade in peat throughout the islands. Horses with 'mezzies' (straw baskets) transported peats throughout the Mainland. After the roads were im-

Fig. 88.
Peat was gathered
and transported in a
basket carried on the
back (Photo: *Tom*
Kent Collection,
Orkney Library).

Fig. 89.
Old fuel and new.
Old peat cuttings
extend right up to the
oil terminal on Flotta
(Photo: Occidental).

proved, this movement was greatly facilitated; up to 40 or 50 oxcarts at a time made a dramatic sight as they moved loads of peat from the moorlands of Birsay and Harray to parishes less fortunate in their fuel resources.

Some of the islands were extremely badly placed in relation to adequate winter fuel supplies. South Ronaldsay had virtually no peat and had to ship in fuel from Burray; Graemsay had to import from Hoy and Walls; Sanday and North Ronaldsay had to send boats to Eday. Some of the larger Sanday farms needed up to 80 tons of peat every year, for which the proprietor had to be paid, while the poorer folk dried tangles (*Laminaria* spp) and cow-dung as cheaper sources. By the end of the 18th century, those who could afford it were burning imported coal, although increasing fuel costs and the development of commercial peat extraction are once again making peat-burning a worthwhile economic practice.

The moorland commons had other uses besides livestock grazing and peat cutting. Heather was gathered for thatching, and the tough wiry stems of crowberry (*Empetrum nigrum*) provided material for thatching ropes. Tethers and bridle reins for livestock were made out of long moorland grasses. The fish-oil cruisie lamps had wicks made from the pithy stems of rushes. In Firth Parish this was done at Lammastime, and by the light of a full moon.

The state of unimproved Orkney was described by Murdoch Mackenzie in 1750:

'The soil of the Islands is various, and not unfertile if rightly improved; but the Inhabitants have not yet acquired a competent knowledge of Agriculture. Bear (*sic*) (a small species of Barley) and Oats are the only Grain they produce; of which, however, they have a Deal more than supplies their own Necessities. Cabbages, Garden-greens, and most Kinds of Kitchin-roots, grow to as great Perfection as in other Parts of Scotland; which, with Geese, Fowls, and other Provisions they afford, are a great Refreshment to Shipping that pass this way.'

Agricultural Improvements

The agricultural improvements of the early 19th century brought sweeping changes to the human landscape of Orkney. Although grass and clover seeds and turnips were introduced about 1770, the big change in agricultural practice came with the enclosures of the commons and the abolition of run-rig strip cultivation soon after 1830. The division of common land brought particular problems for squatters who had carved out small-holdings for themselves beyond the hill dykes. They had no legal right to the land they farmed. In practice, holdings broken in for 40 or more years were held to belong to those who had improved them.

By 1845 extensive drainage programmes were being discussed, partly to employ fishermen and whalers during the winter months, with an additional bonus that the sub-soil from the drains was valued as manure. The use of artificial manures was introduced and although the practice of flaying or paring was stopped, the impact of agriculture on the environment quickly increased. Far more stock could be carried as increased yields meant that more winter feed became available, although these animals were still herded on the 'hill' during the summer months, except for a few tethered milk cows and perhaps ewes with lambs. The impact of large numbers of animals on the uncultivated countryside must have been considerable. One writer describes a population of about 5800 pigs in the 1870s, when 'one was liable to encounter droves of angular, black, hairy apparitions among the peat bogs'. Reclamation was accelerated. There was an increase from 25,000 acres (10,000 hectares) under cultivation in 1833, to 70,000 (30,000 hectares) by 1870, and another increase of a further 19,483 acres (8120 hectares) between 1872 and 1936. Much of this reclamation was of 'brecks' – mineral soils or thin peat which carries a more or less natural vegetation of grass-heath rich in herbs.

A major step in reclamation of hill land came in 1848 when the Government allotted a first grant of £20,000 to Orkney. This was principally spent by the large landowners, major grants going to S. Balfour of Trenabie (£6000), J. G. Heddle of Melsetter (£3000), G. W. Traill of Wyre (£3000), the Earl of Zetland (£2000) and A. Fortescue of Swanbister (£1000). These five owned about 56% of the total agricultural area; their tenants were very poor. *A Guide to the Highlands and Islands of Scotland*, 1850 (G. & P. Anderson) recorded,

'Their cottages are, in general, miserable looking abodes, with peat stacks in front, and the intervening space sadly cut up by the feet of the cattle. The door, which is in many cases common to the cot and the cow-house, is sometimes less than five feet high – the cows turning into one end of the building and the people to the other; and often a favourite or delicate cow, or a few calves, are kept in the fore-house or but, along with the family.'

Agricultural Practice

By the mid-19th century, the previously ubiquitous run-rig was being replaced by a five-shift rotation:

1. Oats after ley land.
2. Turnips, potatoes, and a few marigolds.
3. Bere and oats with grass.
4. Grass cut for hay.
5. Grass pastured by cattle.

Farmers who had an abundance of seaweed for manure often increased this to a six-shift rotation, growing oats for two years. The intensification of cereal production was marked by increased mechanization. Between 1869 and 1872, 300 threshing machines were imported.

Some time in the early part of the 20th century another substantial transformation in agricultural practice took place which seems to have had almost as much effect as the earlier destruction of trees and shrubs. Today it seems difficult to appreciate the importance of this and why the low-growing, perennial variety of *Trifolium repens* introduced then was so vitally 'better' than the old White Dutch clover, or the modern leafier and more upright strains. However a chat with any Orcadian farmer of 60 or over, or reference to the debates of the Orkney Agricultural Discussion Society around the mid-twenties will show that the introduction of Wild White Clover in grass seeds mixtures was indeed a major milestone in Orkney's agricultural history. Its effect on the natural environment was

Fig. 90.
Many crofts are now deserted and ruined
(Photo: *R. S. Moore*).

extremely rapid. Within a few years, the use of heathland for summer pasture ended; herding and tethering were no longer necessary; and inby land (i.e., that near the farm buildings) could, with increased fertility, support all the stock carried on most farms.

The post-improvement mainstay of Orkney's farming economy has varied between poultry, pigs, dairying and beef cattle. Grain requires a drier and sunnier climate than exists in the north in most years, but the conditions for grass growth are almost ideal. Barley is also now widely grown, and harvested for silage while still green. An essential factor has been access to markets; efficient communications were vital before cash agriculture could flourish.

Fig. 91. Agricultural practices in Orkney have changed rapidly in recent years, but corn is still cut by binder and stacked – although horses are now rarely seen (Photo: Charles Tait).

Improved Communications

The steam service from Stromness to Scrabster commenced on 3rd April, 1856, and the first steamship to the North Isles nine years later. This stimulated the export of livestock and surplus cereals. Farm income changed very rapidly from that coming from primitive goods such as hides to more advanced and perishable products such as eggs. The Orkney Road Act of 1857 was another landmark in the development of the islands.

Writing in 1936, W. S. Tait of Birsay tells of problems in previous days:

'My father, who was a Caithness man, used to tell stories about crossing to Orkney with his father to buy cattle. The cattle were collected on places like the Point of Carness and herded there for a week. On one occasion they had 18 sail-boats hired to take about 200 cattle across the Pentland Firth. When halfway across the Pentland Firth the wind changed, and it became so stormy they all returned to Longhope (on Hoy). The cattle were landed, and they all remained there for a week waiting for better weather. When the weather improved they set out again on a fine morning, but had not gone far till it became bad again. The first nine boats managed to get across all right, but the other nine had to put back and they lay at Longhope for another week before they could venture to cross to Caithness.'

By the late 1860s about 10,000 head of cattle a year were being shipped out of Orkney and by 1900 there were 28,000 cattle on the islands. This number remained fairly constant until the 1950s, when it doubled, and continued to increase, so that there are now about 90,000 beef cattle and 5000 dairy cows. The former were mainly Aberdeen Angus, increasingly crossed with Herefords, Charolais, Simmentals, and Friesians. The old Orkney cattle are rarely seen: they produced tough meat and little milk; their chief virtue was their ability to survive on poor pasture.

Proposals to enforce the extinction of 'wild sheep' were made at about the same time as those for the abolition of run-rig in the 1850s. Modern breeds of sheep are now kept almost entirely on improved pasture. Their numbers declined between 1939 and 1949 from 88,000 to 61,000. There are now about 30,000 breeding ewes on the islands, plus another 4000 North Ronaldsay sheep. The comparatively few areas of peat-covered hill which are still grazed are very lightly stocked, and in some cases only used for a few months every year; in others, mixed sheep and cattle grazing is practised. There are even areas of heathland on peat or mineral soils which are virtually unstocked.

Orkney had 789,330 hens in 1950, and exported 80 million eggs annually. With the ever increasing price of imported feed, the abolition of the Egg Marketing Board and its subsidies, and large-scale egg production in the south, the number of hens has now declined to 19,000. The cost of food has also brought about a decrease in pig numbers from a peak of 13,500 in the mid 1950s to under 1000 in 1979. Associated with these falls, the acreage of land devoted to grain has been more than halved from 3200 in 1970 to 1500 in 1980. In 1977 the area of barley overtook that of oats, and the swing towards barley and silage production continues. Grain yields are around 11 tons per acre. Bere is still grown by a few farmers for grinding into meal for making bere bannocks. In 1923, 3500 acres were grown, but less than 100 acres is currently under bere, and only one meal mill is still in operation.

Considerable reclamation of hill land has taken place since the 1939–45 war, but the rate of this is now decreasing, although the concern of conservationists remains. Nevertheless, substantial areas of semi-natural vegetation still remain: within the agricultural landscape there are numerous patches of wetland which owe their survival to problems of drainage; and along the coast there are many areas which are unsuitable for agricultural use, and the total area of semi-natural vegetation in coastal habitats must be considerable in view of the length of the coastline. However, a significant loss of wet-lands is still taking place; their area has been almost halved in the last ten years.

Fig. 92.
A ploughing match,
showing the rich
agricultural land of
much of the islands
(Photo: *R. S.*
Moore).

Man and the Sea

Agriculture has always been the main occupation in Orkney, but the sea has been a permanent standby. All the Neolithic sites in the county are by the sea; fish and molluscs formed a substantial part of the diet. Flagstones for building were easily collected from the shore. This dependence continued through the centuries. In 1774, Low recorded vast quantities of cockles being gathered with rakes at Longhope, and noted that the shells were much in demand for lime for whitewashing houses, once the contents were eaten. In time of crop failure, the value of this natural food resource was greatly enhanced. At the time the Orkney ministers were sending descriptions of their parishes to Sir John Sinclair for the *Old Statistical Account*, there were a series of harvest failures due to cool and rainy summers; the Sanday minister noted

'the grey fish called cuths afforded some supply in 1782 and 1783; as also a cockle-sand, where it was usual to see from 50 to 80 people gathering cockles in the months of April, May and June.'

Commercial fishing in Orkney has a shorter history than in Shetland, with the exception of the South Isles lobster fishing which in *Old Statistical Account* times had been organized 'for many years past' by London companies. About 60 small open boats with two man crews were employed in Scapa Flow and among the South Isles, and a fleet of 15 smacks carried

Fig. 93.
Sea, land and
mortality (Photo:
Charles Tait).

their catch to the London market. In the early 19th century, an estimated 120,000 lobsters were exported annually.

Shetland fishing was long dominated by line fishing for ling and cod from open boats. Indeed, the Shetland economy was distorted by this fishery in the same way that kelp later came to dominate the Orkney economy (p. 184). The line (or haaf) fishing was very labour intensive, and the land-owners who controlled the marketing of the fish exercised sanctions against their tenants (notably payment in kind rather than money) to discourage them leaving. As a result Shetland became over-populated in the early part of the 19th century. The power of the lairds was finally broken by the Truck Acts of the 1870s and the Crofters' Act of 1886 which guaranteed tenure and fair rents. The Orkney equivalent of this thrall to land-owners was the kelp boom of 1780 to 1830 (see below), but it was never so extreme as in Shetland.

What long-line fishing there was in Orkney was originally centred on Walls at the south end of Hoy; the Pentland Firth was fished mainly for cod. In a good year, between 50,000 and 70,000 cod were cured. The few families living on Swona and Switha at the southern entrance to Scapa Flow (both islands now uninhabited) were virtually entirely dependent on saithe and dogfish. They built small houses with open drystone through which the wind could blow freely, and thus preserve the fish, in like manner to the *cleitean* of St Kilda. The fish oil used in lamps was traded from these South Isles among surrounding communities, while places in the north received fish oil from the skiffs which were rowed across from Fair Isle. In the case of North Ronaldsay, fish oil from Fair Isle was traded for seed oats which were often in short supply after poor harvests in the latter's difficult environment and small cultivated area.

Some of the Dutch boats which regularly visited Shetland for herring fishing, used also to fish in Orkney waters. In addition Fife boats began to visit Orkney in the early 1800s. Then in 1815 an Orkney-based industry was begun when a fishing station was established on Stronsay. The original station was at Huip in the north of the island, but it soon moved to White-hall on Papa Sound, where the proprietor (Lang of Papdale, now the site of Kirkwall Grammar School) built a pier and houses for the fisherfolk, and established cooperages and airing yards. The settlement itself had a population derived from several places, including Caithness and the over-populated Fair Isle. Despite the setting up of other stations on the Mainland and South Isles, the Stronsay station retained its pre-eminence not only among the North Isles, but in the whole of Orkney. In 1848, about 600 boats were fishing for herring each year, 240 of them out of Stronsay.

At the same time, efforts were made to exploit cod and ling. Eday and Westray were the main centres for this, using both line and drift-net. However fishing began to lose its importance by the 1860s, allegedly due to increased remuneration due to improvements in agriculture. Nevertheless, in 1872, 1317 vessels were fishing out of Kirkwall (although many of them were travelling to the Faroe and Iceland grounds). In 1913, Kirkwall was the eighth busiest fishing port in Scotland, with 340,194 cwt (17.3 million kg) landed, but much of this was caught by boats owned outside Orkney.

Fishing (both white and shell fish) still plays an important part in the economy of Orkney, particularly in that of the North Isles, but in general

Fig. 94.
The herring fleet returning to Stromness around 1900 (Photo: *Tom Kent Collection, Orkney Library*).

Fig. 95.
Kirkwall harbour
(Photo: *William*
Paton).

it is much less important than agriculture. The Stronsay herring station closed in 1936. The last herring drifter (the *Beezaleel* from Burray) stopped fishing in the same year. There now seem to be far fewer fish in Orkney waters than there were 50 years ago. A crab-processing factory on Rousay has recently turned to canning rabbits.

The Kelp Industry

Seaweed has long been important in Orkney. Winter gales cast huge quantities ashore, and it has been traditionally used widely as fertilizer. In past days, some of the North Isles kept work horses well in excess of those needed for ploughing in order to haul the weed from the shore. Seaweed also provides food for sheep, particularly in winter when normal pasture is short. This has been capitalized on particularly by the farmers of North Ronaldsay, whose seaweed-eating sheep are widely known. But for 50 years seaweed was the mainstay of the Orkney economy.

Kelp making (as opposed to seaweed gathering) was first introduced to Orkney in 1722 by James Fea of Stronsay. It involved the burning of dried seaweed, and collecting the ash ('kelp') formed. The initial reaction of the islanders was antagonistic, and led to the so-called 'Kelp Riot' of 1762. At the ensuing court case the instigators pleaded that:

'It is the common opinion . . . that the burning of tang in this county has not only been the cause of bad crops these three years, but also that the same has been prejudicial to their persons and their cattle when in a sickly condition, and some of the cattle dyed of the smoke thereof, and the lampods growing upon the rocks . . . the poor people were derived of part of their food'.

However, the potential was recognized by Fea's more enterprising neighbours, and the practice spread rapidly. In truth, it suited the way of life of both landlord and tenant. Small tenant farmers were in need of ancillary employment; they were traditionally accustomed to gathering large quantities of seaweed for manure, and they were bound by obligations of service to the principal tenant.

Remoteness meant that a good deal of compulsion could be exercised by 18th century lairds. Later, when the Reform Bill had introduced dangerous ideas of equality, Captain William Balfour could look back with regret to the days when the laird's word was law:

'Lazy kelp burners have no longer any fear of my pouncing on them at 3 or 4 o'clock in the morning and if I could they would be far indeed from dreading my anger as in days of yore.'

But in the 1790s revolutionary ideas had made little progress on the islands, and the labour force was docile and easily subjected to that degree of compulsion which kelp-making required.

Kelp-making was labour intensive. It involved cutting the *Laminaria* stipes from the rocks (drift-weed was less valuable). The weed was spread out to dry, and then burned in simple beach kilns, circular depressions lined with stones. It was said that 'to the eye of the passing mariner the smoke from the kilns distinguished Stronsay from the other islands, and gave it the appearance of an active volcano.' The resulting slabs of ash, much adulterated with sand, stones and partly-incinerated seaweed, were much valued for their alkali content. It was shipped south in Orkney vessels and commanded good prices from glass manufacturers and soap makers particularly in the Newcastle area, but also those on the Forth and in Dumbarton, Liverpool, Hull, London and Bristol. During the period from 1780 to 1830, the Orkney economy was totally dominated by kelp-making. Wars and protective tariffs excluded foreign sources of alkali, particularly the much-prized Spanish barilla. The price of kelp was high, and production soared in response. The *Old Statistical Account* records the early years of the great kelp boom when Orkney production reached 2000 to 3000 tons a year at a price approaching £10 a ton and occasionally much more. Profits from kelp were twice as great as income from rents and about six times greater than the total value of agricultural exports.

The great rise in the value of kelp induced many to purchase land, and estates came to be valued more in terms of their shoreline than for the potential of their farmland. Orkney farming in the second half of the 18th century was barely profitable, so that an emphasis on the harvest of the shore rather than of farmland is understandable. Furthermore, the tenants involved in kelp-burning had an assured contribution towards paying off their rents, instead of having to rely absolutely on a grain crop which might suffer badly in a poor season.

In the North Isles, where vast quantities of kelp were produced, families

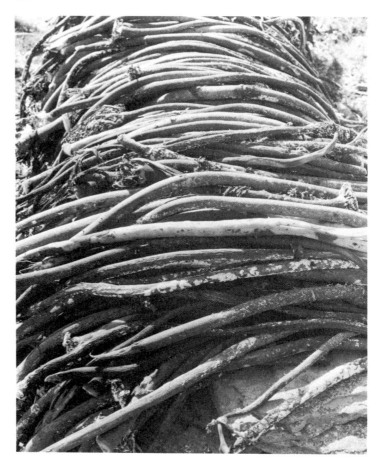

Fig. 96.
*Kelp is still a
valuable addition to
Orkney's economy*
(Photo: *Gunnie
Moberg*).

such as the Traills, who owned whole islands had most to gain. Every bit of shore that could produce kelp became involved in an activity which, at the time, offered a sure reward. Small offshore holms were inhabited, and the remains of the kelpers' hut can often still be seen. On Damsay and the Holm of Grimbister in Firth, the kelpers were supplied with food and peats, and their kelp shipped over to Eday and Kirkwall respectively. In the 1780s, many lairds would undoubtedly have gone bankrupt were it not for their kelp shores.

The poor state of much of Orkney agriculture at the time of the kelp boom both explained the dependence on kelp revenue, and came to be explained by it. Similarly, the preoccupation with kelp went far towards accounting for the poorly-developed state of commercial fishing in the islands. The kelp industry did not completely disappear after its boom years of the early 19th century, but never again attained the status that it had then.

Orkney Future

Can true Orcadians survive? For the past 20 years, migrants have been moving into Orkney who have had no previous links or interests in the islands. Egilsay had only one native-born Orcadian in 1983 in a population numbering 24, and a number of the other islands (especially the North Isles) now have as many incomers as native Orcadians. A sociological study of the effect of this has been carried out in one of the islands, disguised under the name Stormay (*Urban–Rural Migration, Change and Conflict in an Orkney Island Community*, Diana Forsythe (1982)).

'Stormay' had a population in 1981 of 186, of which 77 (41%) were incomers, all except nine of these from outside Orkney. This produced a degree of distancing between members of the community which did not exist previously:

'Despite the incomers' expressed desire to preserve the Stormay way of life, their very presence is helping to destroy it. Although individually the incomers are generally pleasant and well meaning additions to the island's community, they are also contributing to a cultural evolution in which ethnic, regional and national differences are being eroded away, to be replaced by a more standardized and homogeneous way of life. In 1981, incomers were still a minority on Stormay, albeit a vocal and powerful minority. But the receiving population on Stormay is relatively old, whilst continuing in-migration from Scotland and England brings in a steady stream of young adults in their prime child-bearing years. In the face of this in-migration, its influence augmented by national radio, television and standardized education, the number of people who actually use and identify with Stormay speech and customs will inevitably diminish. There is tragedy in this situation for both islanders and incomers. The Stormay folk have welcomed the migrants as bringing new life and new ideas to their depopulated and ageing community, but they already have reason to regret their generosity. The energy the incomers bring to the island is committed to a vision of the future in which local people have no active part. They have sought to attain this vision by moving to a remote island to partake of the mystique of country life. But these migrants are not countrymen, nor do they really wish to become so; instead they seek a stage on which to act out an urban conception of what rural life should be like. The coming of urban refugees may revitalize the community in a demographic sense, but it will also transform it beyond recognition, for most incomers have little understanding of the distinctiveness and value of Orkney's cultural heritage as different from their own. In the long run, the conflicts that have accompanied the incomers' move to the island probably will be resolved through the submergence of the way of life of the receiving community – a high price to pay for the personal fulfilment of a few.'

It is difficult not to be depressed by this analysis, or to disagree with Forsythe's conclusion:

'Through history the Orcadian way of life has continually changed and developed. Successive waves of in-migrants have helped to shape the course of island life, contributing to the mixture of Pictish, Norse, Scottish and English elements that make up the heritage of Orcadians today. Over time, Orkney has managed to retain an identity related to but consciously separate from those of Norway and mainland Britain. Now, once again, outsiders are coming into the archipelago, not as conquerors this time but as refugees from the cities of the south. Like those of earlier eras, this latest wave of migration will lead to a new cultural synthesis. However because of the nature of this particular in-migration, it is doubtful that the new synthesis will retain very much that is distinctively Orcadian.'

Nonetheless 'Orkney-ness' still survives strongly. Westray has hardly any incomers. Douglas Sutherland has written an enchanting account of returning to his roots in Stronsay (*Against the Wind*). The land shapes those who live in Orkney with a distinctive genius. It contributes to the 'mixter-maxter' of George Mackay Brown's poem at the head of this chapter. Robert Rendall called it 'necromancy':

I sing the virtue of country living
Of long days spent without misgiving
In calm fulfilment of rustic labours
Among good friends and kindly neighbours.

I sing of Nature's necromancy,
The beauty and wonder that wake the fancy,
When after winter's cheerless rigour
Gay summer flowers the earth transfigure.

I sing of sea-swept burial places,
Shore-graves where native legend traces Time's finger
and glimpses as in vision
Our ancient Orkney sea tradition.

Orkney Naturalists

It is impossible to live in a place like Orkney and be unaware of its animals and plants, its moods and seasons. Rain is foretold by the especially loud calling of the Loon (or Red-throated Diver); children are warned away from burns because of the lurking otters, which 'never let go once they bite you'; sea urchins are 'scaadman's heids' (the heads of drowned men); and so on. Children populate imaginary farms with shells chosen for their similarities to farm animals: a scallop shell becomes a sheep, and is called a 'gimmer'; 'cattie buckies' are farm cats; and gaper shells are like the snout of a pig, or a 'grice'. The names are old, probably dating back to Viking times; parallels are recorded in games played by children in Nor-

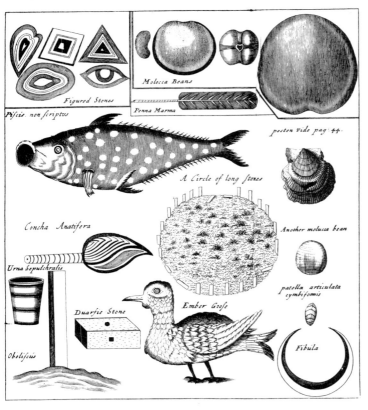

Fig. 97.
Illustration from
James Wallace's
Account of the
Islands of Orkney
(*1700*) *shows archaeo-
logical features,
an Ember Goose,
various shells . . .*

way. One of the earliest accounts of Orkney (*Descriptio Insularum Orcha-dearum*) was compiled by Jo Ben around 1529. He wrote of Sanday that

'a great monster, called Troiccis, often associates with women living there. When I resided there, a beautiful woman that was married to an able-bodied farmer was much tormented by a great spirit, and both were soon against the farmer's will lying on one bed. The woman became emaciated with sorry. I advised that she might get freedom by prayer, almsgiving and fasting. The description of the monster is this: he was covered with seaweed over his whole body and resembled a dark horse with wrinkled skin, with limbs like a horse.'

In his *Herbal* of 1597, John Gerard gave Orkney as one of the localities for the fabulous Barnacle Tree:

'They are found in the north parts of Scotland and the Islands adjacent called Orchades, certain trees whereon do grow certain shells of a white colour tending to russet, wherein are contained little living creatures, which falling into the water do become fowles, which we call Barnacles (Geese).'

The first serious work of natural history was compiled by the Rev. James Wallace, minister of Sanday, and then from 1672 to 1688 of St Magnus Cathedral, who gathered material on Orkney at the request of Robert Sibbald, Scottish Geographer Royal to Charles II. Wallace's observations were published by his son, also called James, in 1693 after his father's death. Sibbald's own account of Orkney (1711) is not very informative, and was obviously based on second-hand knowledge. In contrast, Wallace's book seems to have been a reasonable success, because James Wallace junior brought out a revised edition in 1700 in which the anecdotal

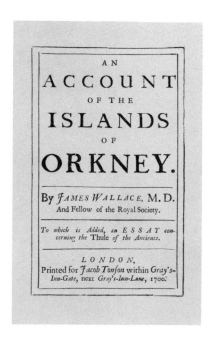

Fig. 98.
Title page of
Wallace's book.

descriptions of the original version were supplemented by systematically arranged lists of marine molluscs and land plants. These were the first records of Orkney plants and animals. There is also a nice record of a Hoopoe:

'Sometimes they find exotick fowls driven in by the wind in time of a storm: myself saw one that had a long Beak, a large tuft on the head in the fasion of a crown, with speckled feathers, pleasant to behold: which I believe is the Upupa.'

In 1700, the General Assembly of the Church of Scotland sent seven ministers and one ruling elder 'to settle the ecclesiastical affairs of the islands on a presbyterian basis'. One of the ministers was John Brand, who published *A Brief Description of Orkney, Zetland, Pightland Firth and Caithness* in 1701. He was a wondermonger who is well worth reading. His description of the Arctic Skua (Scuti-allan in the North Isles) is far more entertaining than modern ornithological literary asceticism:

'There is a fowl called the Scutiallan, of a black colour and as big as a Wild Duck, which doth live upon the Vomit and Excrements of other Fowls whom they pursue and having apprehended them, they cause them to Vomit up what they have lately taken and not yet digested: the Lord's Work both of Nature and Grace are wonderful, all speaking forth His Glorious Goodness, Wisdom and Power.'

Wallace and Brand were isolated figures; the real beginning of Orkney natural history took place at the end of the 18th century, and its father was undoubtedly the Reverend George Low. Low arrived in Orkney in August 1768, a 21-year-old student of divinity and philosophy from Edzell in Forfarshire, appointed as tutor to the family of Mr Robert Graham of Breckness, Stromness. By the time of his death in 1795 he had achieved an enduring contribution to Orkney scholarship.

Fig. 99.
Light and dark phases of the Arctic Skua (Photo: *Anne Jackson*).

Plate 1. Orkney in winter: sea and solitude (*Photo*: Gunnie Moberg).

Fig. 100. Copinsay. The cliffs below the lighthouse provide sites for thousands of seabirds, the land sloping steeply down to the low spit that connects the other end of the island. Far left can be seen a lagoon, added to the island by the creation of an ayre (see p. 47). The Orkney Mainland is in the middle distance; the Churchill Barrier can also be seen; mainland Scotland is in the far distance (Photo: Aerofilms).

Orkney suited him. Ingenious enough to construct his own microscope, he quickly developed a talent for patient and meticulous observation which he expressed in accurate and beautiful drawings. He met Sir Joseph Banks, President of the Royal Society, when the latter visited Orkney on his way home from Iceland, and Banks introduced him to Thomas Pennant, a wealthy Welsh landowner and the influential author of *British Zoology*. Pennant, an indefatigible instigator and prestigious patron of naturalists, encouraged Low to embark on a tour of Orkney and Shetland. With some financial help from Pennant, Low set out on 4th May, 1774. He visited most of the South isles of Orkney and the parishes of the East Mainland before returning to Kirkwall for a passage to Lerwick, arriving there on 19th June, 1774. His description of Copinsay is a good example of his prosaic, but never dull literary style:

'Mony., May 30th. – Visited Copinsha, about a mile long, towards the mainland low, and a small part of it cultivated, the habitation of two families; the sea side of the island there are altogether tremendous rocks about 50 fathoms high, the resort of millions of wildfowl, with which every shelf is so covered that it is impossible to figure a greater quantity. Observed Auks in 1000s., Skouts in like numbers, Cormorants, Shags, Taistes, Gulls of various kinds, and a single pair of a large specis of Hawk which people told me built in one spot of rock and have done so in past memory of man. This kind is much valued and saught after by the falconer, who gives the people 5sh. for the nest, which they procure by letting one another over the precipice.

1. △

2. ▽

3. △

4. △

3. Loch of Bosquoy in Harray partially drained, with Bulrush (*Photo*: E. R. Bullard).

4. Corn Holm off Copinsay, with Oyster Plant and Silverweed (*Photo*: E. R. Bullard).

5. A burn with Marsh Marigolds, Watercress, Iris and Bur-reed (*Photo*: E. R. Bullard).

6. A rare example of an untouched fen on North Hill, Papa Westray, with Water Crowfoot (*Photo*: E. R. Bullard).

Opposite page
7. Natural deciduous woodland on Hoy (Berriedale) (*Photo*: I. Lorimer).

8. Roadside flowers at the Hall of Rendall, Orkney Mainland (*Photo*: E. R. Bullard).

5. △   6. ▽

16. △

17. △

18. ▽

19. △   20. ▽

The old hawks kept at such a distance that it was impossible to know them with any certainty, the people told me that they have a white band round their neck, by their appearance, I imagined them to be *Falco peregrinus niger* . . .'.

Plate 20. Sites regularly monitored for changes that might be caused by oil pollution (*Photo*: A. Simpson).

In September, Low returned to Orkney. Marriage and appointment as minister of the Mainland joint parishes of Birsay and Harray quickly followed. Birsay is one of the most beautiful of all the Orkney parishes: a rich mosaic of brown moorland, interspersed with silver lochs and fertile green farmland with the clear blue of the North Atlantic stretching to the western horizon. Low's manse was situated at its heart.

For a short period after his marriage Low was happy, but, tragically, Helen Low died on 2nd September 1776 – a blow from which her husband never really recovered. Pennant, meanwhile, was procrastinating over the publication of the manuscripts Low had so assiduously prepared, while, at the same time liberally plagiarizing them in his own works, particularly in his monumental *Arctic Zoology*. Low was in despair. He wrote to a mutual friend, '. . . But stay, what is to be published? Is it not all published already. One has taken a leg, another an arm, some a toe, some a finger and, MR PENNANT THE VERY HEART'S BLOOD OUT OF IT.'

By 1790, Low's eyesight had deteriorated to such an extent that he was compelled to give up fieldwork. He died a disappointed man on 13th March, 1795, aged 49.

Low wrote two books, his well known *Tour of Orkney and Shetland* (which remained unpublished until 1879), and a *Fauna Orcadensis*, or the *History of the Quadrupeds, Birds, Reptiles and Fishes of Orkney and Shetland*. This was published some time after his death in 1803. The book was arranged according to the classification scheme devised by John Ray. In the foreword, Low wrote:

'I hope what follows will encourage everyman of curiosity in these isles to throw in his mite to bring the natural history of the Orkneys as near perfection as possible.'

Low's death created a vacuum, although his flora, the manuscript of which disappeared shortly after his death, resurfaced without acknowledgement, in the Rev. George Barry's formidable *History of Orkney*, published in 1805. Barry was minister of Shapinsay. He and Low provided two of the fuller accounts of Orkney parishes in response to Sir John Sinclair's 166 questions, sent to every parish minister, and published as *The Statistical Account of Scotland* between 1791 and 1799. (This is known as the 'Old Account' to distinguish it from the 'New Account' which appeared in 1845). Barry's natural history is suspect but always colourful, and he was the first person to apply the word 'vole' to a small mammal. Here is his description of the Sea Eagle:

'. . . frequently seen in the hills, is of a large size, distinguished from the rest by a band of white encompassing the root of the tail, and the legs being covered with feathers down to the very feet; and it is such prodigious strength that it is said to have carried from a considerable distance to its eyry not only foulis, but lambs, pigs and in some instances young children . . .'

At the time Barry was writing his book, the scholarly Dr Patrick Neill (1776–1851), Secretary of Edinburgh Natural History Society, was touring the northern isles. The results of his tour were published in 1806. Neill interspersed his natural history with perceptive comments on the social

Fig. 101.
Title page, George
Barry's History of
Orkney, *1805.*

THE

HISTORY

OF THE

ORKNEY ISLANDS:

IN WHICH IS COMPREHENDED AN

ACCOUNT OF THEIR PRESENT

AS WELL AS

THEIR ANCIENT STATE;

TOGETHER WITH

THE ADVANTAGES THEY POSSESS FOR SEVERAL
BRANCHES OF INDUSTRY,

AND THE

MEANS BY WHICH THEY MAY BE IMPROVED.

ILLUSTRATED

With an ACCURATE and EXTENSIVE MAP of the WHOLE ISLANDS,

AND

With PLATES of some of the most INTERESTING OBJECTS
they contain.

By THE REV. GEORGE BARRY, D. D.
Minister of Shapinshay.

EDINBURGH:
Printed for the Author by D. Willison, Craig's Close, and Sold by
ARCHIBALD CONSTABLE AND COMPANY, EDINBURGH;
AND LONGMAN HURST REES & ORME,
LONDON.
1805.

Fig. 102.
A view of Stromness,
Graemsay and Hoy
from Barry's
History.

conditions of the Orkney people, especially the poor. He added 100 flowering plants and ferns, and 50 mosses to the Orkney list, raising it to a new total of 462 species. Conchology was another of his specialities and he recorded a number of previously unrecognized species.

By 1830, Orkney was well established on the itinerary of serious travellers. Charles Clouston, minister of Sandwick, contributed a comprehensive summary of what might be seen by the intrepid explorer, in Anderson's *Guide* (1834). Clouston was a man very much in the mould of Low. His West Mainland parish of Sandwick was a large one; Clouston served his parishioners as both minister and doctor, but also found time to pursue an astonishing wide range of interests – archaeology, geology, meteorology, ornithology and botany. Although he wrote and lectured on all these subjects, his chief interest lay in the study of marine algae and he is commemorated by having a kelp species, *Laminaria cloustonii*, named after him; he is also credited with adding *Chara aspersa* to the British list. Clouston was a dominant figure in Orkney natural history circles until well after the mid-decade of the 19th century. With professional biologists and collectors coming to the islands each year in ever increasing numbers (a reflection of the national interest in natural history) and the steady increase in the numbers of local enthusiasts, it was an exciting period. It was perhaps inevitable that this should be institutionalized in some way; in December 1837, the Orkney Natural History Society was inaugurated. Clouston, the doyen of local naturalists, became its first President; membership in the first year reached 150. The first Annual Report of the Society declared that the Society:

'. . . was instituted for the two-fold object of investigating the natural history and antiquities of the County, and stimulating the inhabitants of these Islands to the study of the Almighty's works.'

The Report noted proudly that the Herbarium could boast a collection of over 600 specimens and, that a 'truly excellent collection' of algae had been presented by the President and others. There was also great optimism for the future:

'. . . what holds out the highest prospect of success, there are not wanting among the members some eminently, zealous cultivators of the natural sciences.'

The Society and its Museum in Stromness, still flourish today.

Some six years later another organization, the Antiquarian and Natural History Society of Orkney was established in Kirkwall. Its first Annual Report is a minor masterpiece of Victorian verbosity:

'. . . the study of natural history is both interesting and instructive . . . is eminently calculated to improve the taste, enlighten the mind, and lead the contemplative student to recognise, in the delicacy of structure and adaptation of parts to the purpose intended, the finger of a being possessed of unerring wisdom, and infinite power.'

Natural history was thought to be particularly suited to the young: '. . . as it is based directly on facts not abstract theorising.' A small museum was created in the home of the first secretary, and the Society was keen to obtain: 'natural and antiquarian specimens of all kinds,' particularly 'whale remains, rare fish and marine animals.' Prominent on the list of desiderata were plans to 'open tumuli' and compile a comprehensive flora and fauna of the islands. However, continual problems over housing the ever growing museum collection and the departure from Orkney of two of the Society's most enthusiastic founding members, William Baikie and Robert Heddle, led to its demise after little more than ten years. The contents of the Museum were dispersed at public auction.

The insatiable appetite at this time for specimens representative of the British fauna had its darker side. It was the age of the professional collector; men whose stock-in-trade ranged from Wrens to Peregrines and Golden Eagles. Eggs and skins were equally in demand. One such man was Robert Dunn, a Hull taxidermist, who established himself in Stromness in the 1830s. Styling himself 'naturalist', he offered convivial lodgings: 'at reasonable rates for tourists and gentlemen collectors' and as part of an inclusive 'package deal', lessons in skinning, shot and cartridges might be included. His comprehensive catalogue of specimens makes interesting but, to the modern eye, somewhat alarming, reading. Dunn was able to offer Golden Eagle eggs at 23/– (115p, but allow for a century and a half's inflation) each. The skin of the same species was offered at 40/– (200p),

Fig. 103.
The Great Auk, from
an old engraving.

but for the skin of the majestic Great Northern Diver (in winter plumage) the price dropped sharply to 8/– (40p), and the same price was asked for the skins of Red-throated Divers (in summer plumage). The eggs of this last species were listed at 1/6 (7½p), a comparatively low price suggesting that they were relatively common in Orkney then as a breeding species, or more probably, that the eggs could be collected without too much effort. In 1837, Dunn in his small book *The Ornithologist's Guide to the Orkneys and Shetland* (mostly reminiscences of his shooting exploits), lists 87 species of birds.

At the end of the first decade of the 19th century, the proprietor of the London Museum, W. Bullock, was directly responsible for the destruction of the last pair of Great Auks to nest in Orkney. The birds, approximately the size of a Gentoo Penguin, were completely flightless and very clumsy on land. However, away from their breeding sites and dependence on land they were supremely adapted to water. Once common over the whole of their North Atlantic range, they were, through the ease with which they could be caught at their breeding sites, becoming increasingly rare by the end of the 18th century. The appearance of the species at its Orkney breeding site on Papa Westray was very sporadic. The female was stoned to death in 1812. Bullock tried to obtain the male as well, but the bird managed to escape, only to be shot the following year by a local man named William Foulis, the skin being sold to Bullock. A local tradition survived on Papa Westray that the birds were: 'the King and Queen of "a' the acks" '. Both birds are now in the Natural History Museum in London.

The relative remoteness of the Orkney archipelago was not without attraction for naturalist/collectors. A typical book of the period, Crichton's *Ramble to the Orcades*, 1866, enthuses:

'It is very pleasant to wander forth in the exhilarating morning air with no slaughtering Cockneys with their rusty artillery harrassing every inoffending bird . . . On rounding a point of rock I saw and shot a female wheatear.'

Despite the depredations of such people as Dunn, Bullock and Crichton, the serious study of Orkney natural history took hold. Apart from the patriachal influence of Clouston, much of the credit for this resurgence of interest must be given to two young Orcadians, William Balfour Baikie (1825–1864) and Robert Heddle (1827–1860). Robert Heddle was the son of an influential Orkney Laird, Heddle of Melsetter and Hoy, and the son-in-law of the highly respected doctor and botanist A. R. Duguid. He was educated at Edinburgh University. His main interests lay in botany and ornithology. William Baikie was a ship's surgeon and keen philologist. After leaving Orkney he earned international recognition for his exploration of the River Niger. Baikie seems to have been particularly adept at encouraging other naturalists to tackle difficult or under-recorded faunal groups (although he did undertake some dredging on his own account) and helping them prepare their results for publication. Together with Heddle, he sensed that the time was appropriate for descriptive work on the natural history of Orkney, and in 1848, the first part of their *Historia Naturalis Orcadensis* was published. This book rapidly established itself as *the* book on the birds and mammals of Orkney and it was not superceded until T. E. Buckley and J. A. Harvie-Brown published their *Vertebrate Fauna* towards the end of the century.

Subsequent volumes on the flora and on the invertebrates were planned. However, five years after the publication of the first part of their history, nothing else had appeared, although Baikie, when presenting a catalogue of the 'Echinodermata of Orkney' in the *Zoologist* could still write optimistically:

'My friend, Mr. R. Heddle and myself, being prevented by numerous pressing avocations from continuing at present, in a separate form, an account of the Natural History of Orkney, are nevertheless anxious to have one or two of our lists of species published in order to show what has hitherto been done in that locality, and also to preserve our claim to priority of publication.'

The *Historia*, although sadly never completed, was a very 'modern' work with great attention paid to accurate description and nomenclature. The width of Baikie's scholarship can be seen in the time it took for his extensive library to be sold after his death. A great many of the books were on natural history, and the sale lasted for five days. Robert Heddle emigrated to America in 1856, but returned home to Orkney after only a year. He died in 1860.

Meanwhile, geologists were studying the rocks of Orkney. The beginning of this research can be attributed to Robert Jameson, a Shetlander by descent. His natural history interests led his father to apprentice him to an Edinburgh surgeon. Whilst at university, he attended lectures given by the Professor of Natural History, John Walker, a noted geologist. He became fascinated with geology and in 1794 at the age of 20 gave up his medical career, and spent three summer months studying geology and natural history in Shetland. In 1799 he made a six week survey in Orkney, declaring it the most interesting journey he ever made; an account of it appears in his *Outline of the Mineralogy of Scottish Isles* (1800).

In 1804, Jameson became Professor of Natural History at Edinburgh, and remained in this post until his death 50 years later. He was a poor lecturer, but students were attracted by his subject matter, his field excursions, his genial nature, and his ability to befriend them. His most famous student was Charles Darwin, who declared that Jameson's lectures were so dull that they made him determined never to read a book on geology.

One of Jameson's earliest students was an Orcadian, T. S. Traill, who went on to have an eminent career in medicine, becoming Professor of Medical Jurisprudence in Edinburgh. He had a lifelong interest in mineralogy, and made an important collection of fossil fish from Orkney (which were identified by Louis Aggasiz, who used them to establish the correlation of the Caithness and Orkney flagstones). Traill's account of Orkney geology was published in Neill's *Tour through some of the Islands of Orkney and Shetland* (1806).

Another of Jameson's Orcadian students was W. F. Heddle. He was a medical student, qualifying in 1851. As a child he was already a fanatical collector but, when a prize-winning herbarium of his was dropped into a stream by a fellow student, he resolved to collect only indestructible objects, and became a mineral collector. He spent some of his undergraduate years in Germany studying mineralology and chemistry, and his graduation thesis was entirely mineralogical. He taught at St Andrew's University for 20 years. He was one of the most dedicated, ruthless and successful mineral collectors who ever lived. He attacked rocks with 28 lb hammers, wedges and explosives, and when possible, travelled by boat to save time. His description of *The County Geognosy and Mineralogy of Scotland, Orkney and Shetland* (1878) remained unimproved for about 80 years. His collection of Scottish minerals grew to be the greatest collection of any single country made by one man. But he was much more than a collector, analysing his minerals both chemically and crystallographically, describing them in detail and publishing the results.

The first comprehensive account of Orkney geology was prepared by two career geologists, B. N. Peach and J. Horne; it appeared in 1880. Peach's father was a customs officer and keen amateur geologist, who recognized the effect of glaciation in Shetland during a cruise on a ship belonging to the Commissioners of Northern Lights. Horne and the junior Peach used to spend their holidays surveying together, and they established the major effects of the ice sheets in the Highlands and Islands, as well as confirming Heddle's conclusions.

Other important Orcadian naturalists of the mid-19th century included the Rev. J. H. Polexfen (1813–1899) marine algae specialist, Alexander Russel Duguid (1798–1869), joint author with Robert Heddle of an important although unpublished flora of Orkney, William Layman Cowan (1824–1916), who contributed valuable records of Orkney marine fishes to the Natural History Museum in London, John Guthrie Iverach (1836–1897), who studied marine invertebrates, George William Traill (1836–1875) who produced the definitive 19th-century list of Orkney's marine algae, and his brother William Traill of Woodwick, noted local botanist and conchologist. The flora of Heddle and Duguid provided the basis for the studies of an Orphir farmer, A. R. Fortesque of Swanbister, who published a comprehensive list of Orkney vascular plants in the *Scottish Naturalist* during the early 1880s.

The *Scottish Naturalist* provides a direct link with the indefatigable J. A. Harvie-Brown who founded and co-edited the *Scottish Naturalist*'s precursor the *Annals of Scottish Natural History*. His book, *A Vertebrate History of the Orkney Islands*, written jointly with T. E. Buckley, an Englishman, has become the classic work on Orkney birds and mammals. Harvie-Brown was, by any standards, a remarkable man. The son of a wealthy Stirlingshire landowner, with obsessive singlemindedness he pursued a quest to know everything there was to know about Scottish natural history. He was a great innovator and one of the first naturalists to use questionnaires as a standard means of soliciting facts from landowners, gamekeepers and lighthouse-keepers. Information and records poured into his home at Dunipace from all over Scotland. In 1887, he launched the Fraserburgh-built yacht *Shiantelle* to explore the Scottish Islands. Eminent fellow scientists such as Professor Heddle, by then at St Andrew's University, and the ornithologist W. Eagle Clark accompanied the Harvie-Brown entourage on their cruises around the islands. The need for a new fauna of Orkney was urgent:

'Considering the number of local faunas already issued, it seems not a little curious that Orkney should have been left so long to take care of itself, there having been no attempt made to write a fauna of the whole group, since Baikie and Heddle's work appeared in 1848.'

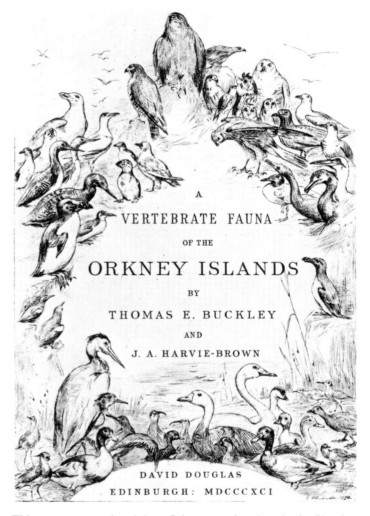

Fig. 104.
Title page from the
Vertebrate Fauna.

This was not mere chauvinism; Orkney was changing. As the *Vertebrate Fauna* points out:

'A great impetus was given to Orcadian agriculture about 1832, when kelp burning became unremunerative and steam communication with the South commenced. Since then the reclamation of the wasteland has gone on to the present time, and now the advance guard of fields may be seen well up some of the lower hills, the surrounding walls showing by their whiteness their new appearing. And the Grouse, Golden Plover, Short Eared Owls, and other birds, interesting alike to sportsman and naturalist, are gradually getting crowded out. The draining of the moors drives out the snipe, once so extremely numerous, while the unnumbered, so called Shepherds' dogs – most happy misnomer, together with cats, are sadly reducing the breeding stocks of such birds as Lapwings, Ring Dotterels, etc., which once swarmed.'

All Harvie-Brown's regional faunas followed a similar pattern: a general chapter on topography and geology, followed by descriptions of all but the smallest islands. The species accounts, which comprised the greater part, were considerably bulked out by local information and anecdotes supplied by local 'gentlemen'. In the Orkney volume, Mr Moodie-Heddle of Hoy, is one of the best. Writing of the disappearance of the Sea Eagles from Hoy he says:

'There has only occasionally been a nest here for the last 25 years. I remember when there used to be seven or eight breeding places. My father and grandfather used to keep a pair tame. I believe they have really been exterminated by people offering rewards for eggs, since I never knew of anyone shooting or trapping an eagle in Orkney in living memory.'

Harvie-Brown devoted a considerable amount of space to the local extinction of the Sea Eagle. He made no apology for this, stressing that:

'the Sea Eagle is rapidly disappearing all through Scotland, so it behoves naturalists to try and make their memorials accurate and full, seeing that, in the Orkneys at least, this is all that is left to us.'

The increasing interest then being shown in the new study of bird migration is reflected by the inclusion of a long chapter analysing migration records submitted by the lighthouse keepers on the isolated Pentland Skerries.

The *Vertebrate Fauna of the Orkney Islands* is one of the better known volumes of a slightly uneven regional series. It raised the county bird list to 223 species. In Orkney it has rightly attained the status of a minor classic, and commands a high price whenever it is offered for sale. The book was illustrated in part by J. G. Millais (son of the pre-Raphaelite painter, Sir John Millais) who visited Orkney on several occasions. It was Millais who was to make an exciting discovery. One evening in 1886 on returning from an evening's fishing on the Loch of Stenness he 'noticed what looked like a water vole running swiftly along the sheeptrack in front of me.' Millais's water vole turned out to be a previously undescribed species of British vole, which he named *Microtus orcadensis*. Oldfield Thomas hailed the discovery as one of the most 'interesting and unexpected finds ever made in British mammalogy,' while Eagle Clark asserted 'that from a scientific standpoint this little mammal is one of the most interesting and important of existing British vertebrates.'

Previous writers, Low, Barry, Baikie and Heddle, and Buckley and Harvie-Brown had all assumed the Orkney Vole to be a variety of *Microtus agrestis*, the common British Vole. Despite this, Low gives a good description of the animal's runways:

'It is found very common in the mossy and fogay heaths, where it makes itself tracks of several miles along over the whole heath. These tracks are about 3″ broad, much worn by continual treading and warped through a thousand directions. Where the fog (grass) is short they are open, but where this is long, by it arched above.'

Local scholarship and expertise continued to flourish in Orkney after the turn of the century, despite an increasing number of visiting professionals. In 1905, a slim volume was published entitled *Orcadian Papers*

Fig. 105. J. G. Millais'
illustrations of the
Orkney Vole from the
second volume of his The
Mammals of Great
Britain and Ireland.

which included a diverse range of subjects such as the trap dykes of Orkney, the glacial history of the islands, the flora and fauna of an Orkney
lagoon (oyce), and two papers on the birds of Sule Skerry.

Some of the more isolated islands of the archipelago were beginning to
attract ornithologists. In 1913, one of Harvie-Brown's collaborators, W. E.

Clark, best known for his pioneering researches into bird migration, endured the miseries of a tempestuous Orkney Autumn for five weeks on the island of Auskerry. Notable among the list of rarities he recorded were Scarlet Grosbeak, Barred Warbler, Red-throated Pipit and Black Tern. Although he had received valuable records from the lightkeepers, he firmly believed that fellow ornithologists had not yet appreciated the potential of the islands as places to study migration.

At the turn of the 19th century Orkney botany was in the hands of a Deerness schoolmaster, Magnus Spence. Essentially kind, he could also be cantankerous and obstinate. 'He was in the real sense symbolic of a type now passing "the village dominie",' said Robert Rendall, who vividly recalled his first encounter with him:

'First of all he took me through his entire herbarium (now preserved in Stromness museum) and I gained my first insight into scientific methods of handling and arranging specimens. I observed his extreme caution when offering opinions and his deliberate care in his examination of particular plants, all this being in marked contrast to my own precipitate boyish enthusiasm; it was my first lesson in scientific discipline.'

Spence's years of patient fieldwork culminated in 1914 with the publication of his *Flora Orcadensis*. It was much more than simple flora, for it contained chapters on geology, climate, natural selection (Spence quotes Darwin with approval, and he was obviously aware of the importance of islands as natural laboratories for testing the theories of evolution; he tentatively compared the floras of Orkney, Caithness and Shetland within a Darwinian framework), and the 'new' science of ecology.

Ecology was then in its infancy as a science, but a young Orcadian research student, George Scarth (1881–1951) wrote a seminal paper 'Ecology of Orkney vegetation in relation to different classes of soil' in 1911. Scarth was to become Professor of Botany at McGill University in Canada but he always maintained a close interest in the natural history of his native islands.

A distinguished contemporary of Spence's was another botanist, Colonel H. Halcro-Johnstone. An army doctor, Halcro-Johnstone was, during his period of active service, able to visit Orkney only for short spells. His army career meant long tours of duty abroad, and this interrupted his real passion – the study of native Orkney plants. It was not until he retired that he could concentrate on his interest from his home in Orphir. His main period of collecting in Orkney covered the years 1923–1939, during which he created a herbarium of over 4000 specimens and an irreplaceable archive of field notes and observations.

Robert Rendall was fascinated, if not a little intimidated by the sheer magnitude of Halcro-Johnstone's achievement; after asking to be shown *Primula scotica* in the herbarium, he recalled:

'the herbarium contained numerous specimens of this one species, gathered from different localities and during different seasonal periods of development. Behind the collected specimens was a wealth of recorded fact, stored in a series of exercise books somewhat illegible to anyone unaccustomed to the Colonel's handwriting. These notebooks left me dazed, for they not only recorded the normal data of scientific collecting, but a series of systematic arrangements, each illustrating some particular aspect of plant study; data over a period of years showing the seasonal variation in the annual dates of flowering and seed formation, the difference in flowering times in different stations in one year; the flora of each separate island and holm, to give but three examples . . . when it is considered that the rest of these trays in these six cupboards were left unexamined, something can be realised of the thoroughness with which the great Orkney botanist pursued his formidable task.'

When Col Halcro-Johnstone died, his herbarium was transferred to the Royal Botanic Gardens, Edinburgh. His field notebooks and diaries are still in Orkney. It is perhaps, invidious to compare Spence and Halcro-Johnstone: Spence is remembered for his marvellous book; Halcro-Johnstone was undoubtedly the better botanist. Most of his results and records were published in specialist botanical journals.

A protegé of Colonel Halcro-Johnstone's, James Sinclair (1913–1968), a farmer's son from Hoy, was to become, after the death of Johnstone, a kind of leading Orkney botanist in exile. That he successfully made the transition from gifted amateur to respected professional must be due, in part, to Halcro-Johnstone's influence. Incredibly, although we have Halcro-Johnstone's testimony for this, Sinclair had, by the age of twenty-three, amassed a collection of 522 species and 89 varieties of flowering plants and ferns; almost 80% of the then accepted total of 653 species.

After completing his university education at Edinburgh he spent two years teaching on the island of Stronsay until he was called up for military service. During his spell on Stronsay he took an intense interest in the marine algae of the island, supplementing the earlier work of G. W. Traill with many additional records. The Second World War took Sinclair to India and Pakistan, beginning a romance with the East that was to last for the remainder of his life. In 1946 he was appointed to the staff of the Royal Botanic Gardens, Edinburgh. During his time in Edinburgh he arranged the transfer of Colonel Halcro-Johnstone's herbarium from Stromness to Edinburgh in order that it might be properly conserved. After the Colonel's death, Sinclair was generally regarded as the authority on Orkney botany, a reputation he sustained despite being appointed as Curator of the Herbarium of the Singapore Botanic Gardens in 1948. Although his personal knowledge of the Orkney flora was great, most of his published writing was devoted to his work on the flora of Malaysia. He did, however, contribute a chapter on the Orkney flora to the *New Orkney Book*.

Perhaps the best known, loved and respected of all Orcadian naturalists was Robert Rendall. He devoted his life to the study of Orkney shore life, especially the mollusca, but he was also a poet (*Country Sonnets, Orkney Variants, Shore Poems, The Hidden Land*), theologian, archaeologist and folklorist. Rendall was born in Glasgow on 24th January 1898, the elder son of Orcadian parents. The family returned to Orkney in 1905. At the tender age of thirteen the young Rendall left Kirkwall Grammar School to become an apprentice draper, embarking on what was to be a long and successful career in commerce. He read widely and voraciously and was almost entirely self-taught. As a boy he delighted in the freedom offered by the Orkney countryside:

'Gradually, I became accustomed to this new freedom, and my acquaintance with flowers grew. I came to know the scalies and the curly doddies, the sea pinks, the cocks and hens, the wild white clover (sucking this for its sweetness), the seggies in the Crantit meadows, golden dandylions run to seed, meadowsweet in the gullies of the cliffs at Scapa and Berstane, wiry 'sodgers' to slash in mimic battles. Insects, too, of all sorts laid a spell upon me: burnished beetles scuttling in the sun, cabbage butterflies in the garden, small blue ones by the roadside ditches, bumble bees in their ceremonial splendour of colour and many a thing besides.'

Marine life in general and shells in particular fascinated him; he knew his Orkney beaches intimately and maintained an articulate and enquiring correspondence with all the leading conchologists of his day. Mrs N. McMillan wrote of his work:

'The non-marine species Rendall did not much care for, but he dredged and shore collected marine species with the utmost assiduity . . . His work was careful and thorough and his *Mollusca Orcadensia* will long be the standard list for these northern Isles.'

Mollusca Orcadensia was published in 1958 by the Royal Society of Edinburgh, listing approximately three hundred species with data on habitat and abundance.

Rendall also wrote a beautiful book, the *Orkney Shore* (1960), an evocative interweaving of autobiography with biography, reminiscence with natural history. Light and colour spill from its pages and in its own way it is a simple testament to the beauty of the Orkney landscape and the people who inhabit it:

'It was the end of the season, and the day's fishing was over. We landed on one of the small islands before making homeward. It was the last lingering hour of the day. Sitting on big lichened stones at the edge of the water we silently ate our "Pieces" and drank our thermos tea. There the three of us were, old James, Dave and myself. Casting out the dregs of the tea from our flasks we rose and prospected the little islet, one of the chain-like group at the lower end of the loch. James picked up a few wing feathers (he had a use for these), and with a boylike simplicity strange to see in an old man gathered a posy of water mint. I did likewise and added to them single specimens of a few wild flowers found in late bloom. They stood all winter in an Italian majollca vase; when next spring came they had become dull and colourless, with leaves shrivelled and dry, their fragrance gone. James, too, had gone, and lay buried beneath the turf. The last day of the season remains like a faded flower, preserving in thought moments and motions that never will return.'

Robert Rendall died on 8th June 1967, not long after being awarded a Civil List pension for his services to literature and science. His collection of shells is now in Stromness Museum.

Orkney has attracted a good many competent birdwatchers into its midst, while Alfred Wood, James Omand, George Arthur, Duncan J. Robertson and William Groundwater, all Orcadians, have each added significantly to our knowledge of birds. Omand's *How to know the Orkney Birds* (1925) raised the total Orkney list to 264 species.

In 1923, a solicitor and keen naturalist from Kirkwall, Duncan J. Robertson, purchased the lovely island of Eynhallow. Set in the violent tide rips of Rousay Sound, Eynhallow, or Holy Island, with its ruined Cistercian monastery, is one of the most attractive and haunting of all the Orkney islands. Under Robertson's ownership it became, unofficially, Orkney's first bird reserve. Robertson knew his Eynhallow birds well, especially the Eider ducks and the Fulmars and his patient studies of them resulted in a fine behavioural and ecological study, *Notes from a Bird Sanctuary* (1934). He wrote of the Fulmar, with genuine affection:

'it is amazing how the whiteness of the snow is dimmed by contrast. In one way the Fulmar excels in beauty above any of the gulls. Its large and liquid eye gives it an appearance of gentleness which is unequalled in any bird I know.'

Edward Balfour of Rendall was, unquestionably, the finest ornithologist Orkney has produced. His early interest in birds was encouraged by Alfred Wood of Finstown, and strengthened by collaboration with Kirkwall baker and expert ornithologist, George Arthur, who introduced him to the varied bird community of Orkney's moorlands, which became Balfour's main love. Balfour's long association with the Royal Society for the Protection of Birds began in 1937 when the Society appointed him honorary watcher in Orkney. In 1954 he became a paid employee and a year later the RSPB's first full-time Orkney officer, a position he held until his death in 1974. He published valuable studies on Orkney Cormorants and Kestrels and contributed a plethora of shorter papers to the leading ornithological journals, as well as writing many popular bird articles. One bird came to dominate his life, the majestic raptor of the Orkney moors, the Hen Harrier, on which Eddie Balfour was rightly acknowledged the world authority. His study of the Orkney population of Hen Harriers lasted 43 years, the longest study of any raptor anywhere in the world. His last major paper on the species was published posthumously in collaboration with Dr J. Cadbury in 1979.

Eddie Balfour was a passionate advocate of conservation, but his arguments were always carefully tempered by realism. The rate at which good natural history sites in Orkney were disappearing under plough and bulldozer in the late 1960s and early 1970s saddened him greatly. In 1959, Eddie Balfour and others were the moving spirits behind the formation of an Orkney Field Club. The aims of the Club were straight-forward: 'to promote the study and the conservation of the natural and cultural heritage of the County of Orkney.' The Club was well served by its early chairmen – John Scott and Eddie Balfour (Balfour's commitment was astonishing: in 15 years involvement he only missed three full committee meetings and one Annual General Meeting), and by acting as a forum for naturalists, it was able to play a significant and influential role in a variety of natural history and conservation issues (seals, mink, uranium, etc) which have been such a feature of Orkney life in recent years.

Conservation, Development and the Future

The statutory Structure Plan of the Orkney Islands Council, dated 1975 and revised in 1978, states that

> 'whilst proposals to increase the industrial development and housing supply of Orkney are acceptable from a social and economic viewpoint, there is also a need to protect the physical environment from undue pressures resulting from these developments. The physical environment is a combination of cultivated farmland and moorland, cliffs and sandy beaches, inland lochs and areas of sea. The natural vegetation and the bird, animal and marine life it supports must be protected against pollution and destruction.'

Part of the background to this assessment of the non-human environment of Orkney was the Nature Conservancy Council's identification of 'features of national and international importance':

The vast seabird stations, particularly of Marwick Head and Westray.

The over-wintering wildfowl: Orkney supports a significant proportion of wintering marine and freshwater wildfowl (Table 24).

Fig. 106.
The stones of Stenness, a plate from Barry's History. Both wildlife and archaeology need careful conservation in Orkney.

The seal populations: 25% of the British and 15% of the world population of the Grey Seal, and 20% and 5% respectively of the Common Seal.

The Orkney moorland in addition to their botanical interest, contributes significantly to the British population of birds of prey, especially the Hen Harrier.

The particular scientific interest of the Lochs of Harray and Stenness and the North Hoy 'site of special scientific interest' make them of national importance.

Table 24   *Wintering Seafowl, Orkney (data of David Lea).*

Species	Scapa Flow 1974–78 (including Loch of Stenness)	Sounds round Wyre (Max. no. recorded 1974–75, 1975–76)	Orkney (estimated wintering population
Great Northern Diver	*c.* 200	44	*c.* 500
Long Tailed Duck	*c.* 2400	1090	*c.* 6000
Eider	*c.* 2000	570	*c.* 6000
Red-breasted Merganser	350	Present	?
Black Guillemot	*c.* 1000	53	?
Shag	*c.* 4000	Present	?
Slavonian Grebe	up to 60		?
Velvet Scoter	up to 100	15	?
Goldeneye	*c.* 270	Present	?

In order to protect the environment the Structure Plan noted:

'1. It is the intention of the Islands Council to conserve the unique character of the land, sea, and skyscape of Orkney and its wildlife. Apart from the National Scenic Area of Hoy and West Mainland, and areas classed as of outstanding natural beauty, there are, throughout all the Islands, areas of special value and viewpoints from which wide outlooks over land and sea can be appreciated. These areas and scenes cannot be placed in categories in order of merit and the natural environment must be considered as a whole and will be protected from undue pressures from development and from pollution.

2. Buildings are clearly visible and it is not possible to screen them in the open landscape. The siting and design of new buildings in Orkney will be carefully controlled by the Islands Council.

3. On the basis of environmental and tidal studies carried out for Orkney Islands Council by Dundee University and advice from the Nature Conservancy Council, a scheme for dealing with oil pollution on the coasts of the Orkney Islands has been drawn up by Orkney Island Council and will be reviewed on a regular basis.

4. Sites of Special Scientific Interest notified by the Nature Conservancy Council will be protected from excessive public access and from pollution. Explanatory notices, shelters, and direction posts should be put up at some of these sites, so that the public can know and appreciate all of these special sites in Orkney. There will be a general presumption against development which is likely to have an adverse effect on the scientific interest of Sites of Special Scientific Interest.

5. The Nature Conservancy Council have recommended policies to the Islands Council to protect the natural environment of Orkney.'

The NCC proposals included the establishment of nature conservation zones arrived at by consultation with the Planning Authority, the extension of environmental monitoring programmes, requirement for developers to analyse the environmental impact of any projects, and suggestions for consultation and coordination (rather than confrontation) in environmental matters. The Islands Council undertook to 'consider these policies as the need arises'.

It might reasonably be thought that these expressions of concord between the elected authority of the islands and the statutory guardian of the environment would have led to progressive conservation policies being adopted in Orkney, but in fact conservation arguments have been as heated in Orkney as anywhere in the country, and possibly more bitter because personalities tend to intrude more in the small island community than in larger groupings elsewhere. There are four environmental issues which have caused conflict in Orkney: oil-based developments; reclamation of hill and wet-land; seal culling; and uranium mining and the disposal of radioactive wastes. Two others could cause problems: fish-farming and mechanical kelp harvesting.

Oil

In the 1960s there were widespread forecasts of the damage that the nascent North Sea oil industry would do the human and biological communities of Orkney and Shetland. To general relief, these prophecies have not been fulfilled, at least not yet. There are two reasons for this: marine oil pollution is far less damaging to animal life than once seemed likely (although it can be extremely destructive in certain restricted circumstances); and, despite common cynicism about their operations, the oil companies in general have worked hard with both local authorities and conservation organizations to minimize the impact of their operations.

Oil was discovered in the North Sea about 130 miles (200 kms) south east of Orkney in 1973 by a consortium of four oil companies, led by Dr Armand Hammer's Occidental Oil. Rather than load the oil directly into tankers in the middle of the North Sea, it was decided to build a pipeline to bring it ashore for processing and storage, and in January 1977 oil began flowing along a 30 inch (85 cm) wide 135 mile (220 km) long pipe to a terminal built on the small island of Flotta in Scapa Flow. One of the reasons for choosing Flotta was that its human population was rapidly declining (it had fallen from 425 in 1881 to an ageing 73 in 1971), and had been recognized as a development area by the Islands Council. Ferries now bring workers to the terminal every day from Hoy and the Mainland.

The key sensitive factors in designing the terminal were integrating it visually into the low-lying Flotta and protecting the marine environment. One of the surprising discoveries was the ignorance that existed about water movements in Scapa Flow, despite its major use as a naval base in two world wars. The oil companies commissioned a series of measurements of winds, tides and currents so as to establish the likely effects of oil pollution. These led to the treated ballast water outfall being sited outside the

Fig. 107.
The old and the new:
the oil terminal on
Flotta surrounded by
the depopulating
southern isles of
Orkney (Photo:
Charles Tait).

Flow, and an effluent water treatment monitoring system being installed, which recycles treated water if its quality falls below a set standard.

A biological monitoring programme was set up in 1974 by the Biological Sciences Department of Dundee University on behalf of the Orkney Islands Council. This monitors a series of sites around (and outside) the Flow, to detect any changes in the shore and planktonic animals and plants which might be attributable to pollution (Fig. 108). The wisdom of such an extensive programme has been vindicated by the large changes which have been found on some shores which have nothing to do with oil pollution, but might have been attributed to it if comparable sites had not been available.

In addition the Nature Conservancy Council in 1976 established a seabird monitoring programme, based on sample counts at five Mainland colonies in June each year. Counts are made of individual Guillemots, Razorbills, Kittiwakes and Fulmars, and apparently occupied nests of Kittiwakes and Fulmars. The chief problem with this programme is the variability of the counts, which in turn influences the level at which statistically significant changes can be detected. The sensitivity varies so that for Kittiwake nests a decrease of more than 3% a year can be detected, for Guillemots a decrease of 13% is necessary before a change can be detected, and for Razorbills a decrease of 22%. In the first five years of operation, there were 19 oil pollution incidents around Flotta, most of them minor and due to human error during the loading of tankers; they appear to have had no lasting effects.

Ironically, most oil pollution in Orkney has not been associated with the Flotta terminal, but has arisen from the disposal of ballast and tank-water from ships outside Scapa Flow. However, analysis of oil samples on Orkney shores showed that the proportion which came from tank-washing fell from almost a half in 1979 to less than a quarter in 1981. The proportion of bird corpses on Orkney shores which are oiled also declined over the same period, from 23% of the total to 5%. Clearly the situation has improved, probably as a result of increased tanker surveillance around Orkney and Shetland following considerable adverse publicity, and the completion of ballast water treatment facilities at Sullom Voe (the Shetland oil terminal) in spring 1979.

Fig. 108.
Scapa Flow, showing
the main pollution
monitoring sites.

Although the Flotta terminal has been commendably 'clean', obviously there is always the risk of a major pollution incident. The environmental consequences of such an occurrence could be serious, particularly if it took place during the winter, when the Flow is harbouring large numbers of water fowl. The Flotta authorities, the Harbours Department, and the Marine Biology Unit have contingency plans for dealing with spillages of all sizes, but it has to be accepted that all that would be possible in the face of a major spill, would be to document the environmental damage. This is a case where precaution is all; 'cleaning-up' would be little more than a public relations exercise.

The large seabird breeding colonies are all outside the Flow, but they too would be vulnerable to large slicks in their vicinity. Exploration licences have already been allocated for blocks to the west of Orkney and Shetland. Oil leaking from wells to the west of Orkney would be blown inshore by the prevailing winds, to threaten the enormous bird colonies on the westward facing cliffs. Rafts of six or seven thousand Guillemots are frequently on the sea below the Marwick Head colony during the breeding season, with even greater concentrations in the vicinity of the west Westray cliffs.

Reclamation

As worries about oil pollution have become less acute, so concern about agricultural reclamation in Orkney has increased. It is difficult to get this into perspective because the whole history of Orkney over the last five millennia has been a battle to tame the land for agriculture. The toughness of the battle is reflected in the time it has gone on, with neither wilderness nor human order clearly having the upper hand. The farmers have a love-hate relationship with the land: loving its openness and wild-life, but hating its recalcitrance to grow enough to provide sufficient winter feed or to increase their stock numbers. More and more land is being broken into agriculture, albeit at a declining rate (Table 25); is there any real cause to think that Orkney is being permanently harmed?

Conservationists argue that significant environmental damage to Orkney is very near, as areas of 'natural' habitat contract and become fragmented. Some areas have completely lost their wildlife interest. One of the main reasons why Orkney is archaeologically so rich is that up to now large areas

Table 25   *Amount of Land used for Agriculture in Orkney (including rough grazing).*

Year	Area hectares	% of total land area
1833	10,110	10.4
1870	28,300	29.1
1900	34,000	35.0
1923	37,600	38.7
1936	36,213	37.3
1952	71,600	73.7
1960	74,700	76.9
1981	77,974	80.9

of the county have been little worked compared to southern parts of Britain, and buried records of human activity have therefore been preserved.

Among birds, Starlings and House Sparrows, for example, seem to be able to adapt totally to modern agricultural systems. The majority of the characteristic Orkney species are moorland breeders and frequently of wet moorland at that. Thus, Curlew, Golden Plover, Hen Harrier, Short-eared Owl, Merlin, Kestrel and Red-throated Diver all require moorland for their breeding, even if some partly feed in agricultural areas. Lapwings frequently nest in areas of rough pasture, often damp in nature. Remove breeding or feeding habitats, and you remove an essential requirement, and the species concerned will inevitably decline. About 15% of British Hen Harrier nests are on Orkney moors, together with significant numbers of Short-eared Owls, Merlins, and ground-nesting Kestrels. About 10% of the British breeding Red-throated Divers are found in Orkney. The wetlands are frequented by nationally important concentrations of wintering birds (particularly wildfowl), and Otters use such areas for both breeding and feeding. Harvie-Brown expressed his concern over the extent and rate of reclamation in Orkney nearly a century ago (p. 200); Eddie Balfour, probably Orkney's greatest naturalist and a true lover of his native country, put up very similar warning signals in 1972:

'Everywhere, even in Orkney, bits of natural habitat are being despoiled . . . Now is the time to stop the eroding away of our natural heritage, our fauna and flora, and their habitats whether it be loch, marsh, moorland or sea-shore.'

*Fig. 109.
Ungrazed land produces wonderfully luxuriant growth (Photo: R. S. Moore).*

Comparison of aerial photographs taken in 1946–48 and in 1967–68, covering 10% of the Orkney Mainland, showed that in this period 29% of the moorland and 11% of the wetland were lost, mainly to agricultural reclamation; between 1967 and 1980 a further 5% of moorland and 4% of wetland disappeared. Experts believe that this process is now approaching a critical point. The Common Scoter ceased to be a regular breeding species in Orkney when the Loch of Doomy on Eday was drained; the Yellowhammer, formerly common, is no longer breeding, almost certainly due to the removal of gorse; the Corncrake, Corn Bunting and Lapwing have all declined.

Several plant species have decreased, notably *Primula scotica*, which has very specific habitat needs and is now found at many fewer sites than earlier in the century. Juniper (*Juniperus communis*), the Stag Horn Moss (*Lycopodium clavatum*) and Alpine Clubmoss (*Diphasiastrum alpinum*) have decreased as a consequence of reclamation or excessive burning of dry heath. (There is a long traddition of muirburn in Orkney, often for no particular purpose.) A number of 'weeds' of cultivation such as the Corn Cockle (*Agrostemma githago*), Greater Yellow-rattle (*Rhinanthus serotinus*) and Cornflower (*Centaurea cyanthus*) have disappeared, and the Long-headed Poppy (*Papaver dubium*) is becoming increasingly rare. In the wetlands, the Blunt-leaved Pondweed (*Potamogeton obtusifolius*) has been lost, and colonies of the Greyish Bulrush (*Schoenoplectus tabernaemontani*) have declined due to drainage and grazing.

In fairness, it must be recorded that numbers of the Hen Harrier and Red-throated Diver have increased during this century, presumably due to statutory protection, and large flocks of Curlews feeding on agricultural land are one of the sights of Orkney. However the situation has now been reached when further reclamation will almost certainly produce a decline in, for example, the Short-eared Owl and Merlin; there has apparently been a decrease in Hen Harrier numbers in the last few years.

There are three organizations concerned with conserving Orkney's threatened terrestrial habitats. The first 'line of defence' are the local organizations in Orkney, of which the most important is the Orkney Field Club, founded in 1959 (p. 206). This body has undoubtedly contributed to a greater awareness of the natural environment of Orkney through field meetings and lectures, and it has now entered a new phase, with its own reserve.

The involvement of the Royal Society for the Protection of Birds with Orkney has been described in Chapter 9. In addition to their highly important site protection work, the RSPB undertakes a considerable amount of survey and education work in the islands.

The most important conservation body is the government's Nature Conservancy Council, which has a statutory duty to identify important areas for nature conservation, and to schedule them as Sites of Special Scientific Interest (SSSIs). On the grounds of their national botanical, zoological, geological or geomorphological importance, 29 such SSSIs have been identified in Orkney (11% of the land area of the county). Unfortunately the review of the SSSIs required by the Wildlife & Country-side Act 1981 caused considerable controversy in Orkney. Nationally about 4% of SSSIs a year were damaged or destroyed during the 1960s and 1970s, largely by agricultural developments. The Orkney sites shared with the

rest of Britain in this. The 1981 Act required specific agricultural operations to be notified three months in advance to the NCC. The intention
was that this would allow time for management agreements to be negotiated
between the NCC and the owner of the land, with compensation paid to
the owner if necessary. The hope was that this procedure would lead to
reasonable compromise rather than confrontation between the conflicting
claims of agriculture and conservation; in Orkney it led instead to aggrava-
tion, because farmers interpreted the requirements to notify as both an
improper restriction on their freedom in their traditional fight with the
environment, and also an unwarranted criticism of their stewardship of
the Orkney environment.

*Fig. 110.
A wrecked ship in
Scapa Flow, sunk
during World War
II, provides a
major roost for shags
(Photo: Gunnie
Moberg).*

The arguments were an unhappy and unfortunate episode. Government
subsidies aimed at increasing agricultural productivity, whatever the cost,
must bear a large amount of blame. Possibly the affair was approached too
mechanically by the conservation bureaucrats, but the heart of the problem
was a re-enactment of Garret Hardin's 'tragedy of the commons': a
demand on the environment which is acceptable when made by one user
becomes wholly intolerable when every user decides, however honestly and

*Fig. 111.
Conservation argu-
ments have been
violent in Orkney.
The land is precious
(Photo: R. S.
Moore).*

necessarily, to make the same demand. The common which was a benefit to all becomes useless, and all suffer. The onus in this situation is on the conservationist to convince those who use the land that the interests of all are best served by a degree of self-denial. Orcadians genuinely love their county; Robert Rendall's poem quoted on p. 25 accurately describes a typical attitude. But it takes a great deal to convince such a person that he should change the tactics of centuries in his battles with the land. Conservationists have earned a bad reputation for crying 'woe', and no woe follows. As long ago as 1910, a special commission appointed by President Theodore Roosevelt claimed that the USA had 'timber for less than 30 years, coal for about 50 years . . . Supplies of iron ore, minerals, oil and natural gas are rapidly being depleted.' Such pessimism has repeatedly characterized the conservationists' case in all countries; to the outsider it has become difficult to know when and how to take seriously pleas of environmental doom. This makes the conservationists' job doubly difficult.

The bitterness that arose in Orkney over SSSI re-sheduling is a microcosm of two general problems: how does one judge, and then persuade others that an environmental situation is a critical one? It is all too easy to answer these questions in 'preservationist' terms: there are now more/less Hen Harriers, Orkney Voles, Otters, Scottish Primroses or whatever than ten years ago, and therefore one's policies are succeeding or failing as the case may be. The real answers involve a much better understanding of the factors which control the numbers and structures in natural communities (in other words, there is a need for good ecological research), and a much wider appreciation of the results of this understanding, an appreciation which includes education but even more important, a moral acceptance of the need for conservation.

Seal-culling

The status and importance of seals in Orkney were described in Chapter 6. A new seasonal element in Orkney life nowadays is an influx of protesters every autumn, objecting on the grounds of 'animal rights' and/or 'conservation', and each year attempting to disrupt the local cull. As often happens in such situations, the issues at stake have become confused.

The increase in numbers of the Grey Seal in the eastern Atlantic at a rate of 6–7% a year can be considered a conservation success story. It led in 1962 to the introduction of an annual pup cull as a fisheries protection measure. The quotas are determined annually by the Secretary of State for Scotland, after consultation with the Sea Mammal Research Unit of the Natural Environment Research Council. They were 735 in 1962, 1000 in 1976, and 1200 in 1982, numbers set at a level which the population could sustain without threatening its conservation. Following the 1970 Conservation of Seals Act, licences could be issued for the purpose of 'utilizing a population surplus as a resource'.

It is unfortunate that a number of organizations have protested against the Orkney seal culls under the conservation banner, since conservation is, by definition, the management of resources, and it cannot be argued that the number of pups killed in Orkney is more than the harvesting of a surplus carried out at a level which the population can easily sustain. This 'conservationist' involvement has hampered the work of nature conservation in general in Orkney, since all 'conservationists' are tarred with the same brush to the outsider.

However the real stimulus for protest in Orkney was not the fairly modest pup cull, but a decision in 1977 by the Department of Agriculture and Fisheries for Scotland to carry out a major cull of Grey Seals on fishery protection grounds. This was a response to pressure from fishing interests, and involved an attempt to reduce the British Isles seal population to its mid-1960s level. This was clearly not a harvest of surplus animals in the normal meaning of the word, and was unsupported by objective information about seal-fish population dynamics. This angered genuine conservation groups, who mounted an agitation which was successful in forcing the DAFS to abandon their plan, and commission a major research programme into the interactions between Grey Seals and fish (p. 100).

Orkney and Radioactivity

Disseminated uranium ore is present in the basal beds of the Stromness Flags in the Yesnaby and Stromness area, and also in the same beds in Caithness. The amount of uranium is unknown. As a part of its investigation of the geochemical resources of Britain, the South of Scotland Electricity Board proposed some years ago to carry out an uranium exploration in Orkney. This was interpreted by the ever-vigilant anti-nuclear lobby as an attempt to begin uranium mining in Orkney and to turn 'green Orkney white'. Considerable emotion was generated as a result, and this was rekindled by rumours that the seas round Orkney were being considered as a depository for radioactive waste. These events showed the alertness of the anti-nuclearists, and confirmed the prejudices of others about conservationists.

Fish Farming

Fish farming grew explosively in Scotland during the 1970s; virtually every sheltered loch seemed to spawn a set of floating tanks. It seems probable that there will be an even greater interest in fish and mollusc culture in coming years. This will need care by the planning authorities, because fish farms can produce waste to an extent that locally-degrading changes in fauna and flora are induced. The problem was different but, in the context of the responsibility of the planning authority, it is worth recording that a proposal to open a mink farm on Westray was rejected following a public enquiry in 1978 on the grounds of the danger to the Westray sea-birds and voles, although it was at first approved by the local planners.

Kelp Harvesting

Collecting kelp has long been important in Orkney (p. 184), but commercial use of kelp in Orkney is currently of little importance. There are, however, considerable areas of shallow waters around Orkney which could be vulnerable if mechanical harvesting of weed was deemed to be viable commercially. Whole communities of animals depend on kelp beds for food and shelter, including economically valuable species such as lobsters and edible crabs. Otters and several seabird species (notably the Black Guillemot) feed almost exclusively on inshore demersal fish, which live in *Laminaria* dominated areas. Certain gastropods and crustaceans closely associated with kelp appear to be of importance in the diet of such wintering wildfowl as the Long-tailed Duck. Any proposed commercial harvesting of the sub-littoral seaweed resources of Orkney must be approached with care; excessive removal of weed could initiate a chain of events leading to the loss of species, together with the physical erosion of shores.

The Case for Conservation

One of the problems about arguing the importance of conservation in Britain is to make a case for it which will stand up to examination. Many habitats are remarkably robust and resistant to disturbance. Few, if any, species which to present knowledge are economically significant, are at risk in Britain. The plea of the World Conservation Strategy (WCS) issued in 1980 was self-interest: a neglect of conservation leads inevitably to an erosion of the genetic and species variability necessary for the continued existence and development of life on this planet. The WCS made a powerful case for this on a global basis. Now the fate of the United Kingdom cannot be separated from that of the rest of the world. But the environmental pressures which are increasingly desperate in some parts of the world, compounded by over-use of renewable resources by human over-population, are not so urgent in Britain, and are less intense in Orkney than in other parts of the country. True, new machinery and techniques are making it possible to change Orkney and its biology more quickly and radically

than ever before, but it would be difficult to maintain that human survival would be affected if the whole of Orkney became (perish the thought) a single vast beef-fattening farm or turnip or rape field. Motives for conservation in Orkney cannot be sought simply on the crude level of self-survival.

Why conserve? In its examination of its raison d'être (*Nature Conservation in Great Britain*, 1984), the NCC's rationale for itself is that the primary reason for conservation in Britain is cultural, defined embracingly as including the scientific, educational, recreational, aesthetic and inspirational value of the countryside. In other words, the whole environment is greater than the sum of its parts. This makes good scientific sense. The Government working party which recognized the need for an official Natural Conservancy in Britain, and whose report (Cmd 7122, 1947) led to its establishment, urged an integrated concept of nature conservation, with the renewable resources of the country developed yet sustained for the manifold benefit of society, through the application of scientific insight to management and control. *Nature Conservation in Great Britain* identified

Fig. 112. Copinsay and the Calf of Copinsay, now a bird sanctuary, were purchased by the RSPB as a memorial to naturalist James Fisher, one of the founders of the New Naturalist *series.*

'the most serious and disappointing shortcoming in nature conservancy practice has been the failure to translate into reality the broad and integrated concept of conservation which was the great vision of Cmd 7122.'

In the context of Orkney this can be interpreted to mean that conservation success or failure should not be judged as to where there are more or less Hen Harriers, Grey Seals or *Primula scotica*, but whether the Orkney known to Edwin Muir, Robert Rendall and George Mackay Brown still exists, whether we can join in sensation with Eric Linklater:

'As I walked downhill, over grass starred with tormentil to a shore where black rocks were parti-coloured with the yellow tangle of the sea, and the sea was still glass-grey, I became aware of an extraordinary physical pleasure. It suffused my body and possessed my mind. Eyes and ears contributed to it, but my lungs were filled with it – I breathed the euphory that blows down from an arctic spring.'

The future of nature conservation in Orkney is inextricably linked with attitudes. We must work to convince people of the threat to the dwindling natural assets around them and of the need to conserve for future generations examples of Orkney habitats and Orkney species. We must gain the confidence of the farming community and the decision makers of the Islands Council. And above all we must implant a sense of respect and responsibility in Orkney's schoolchildren, the decision makers of tomorrow.

Site-based conservation, as reflected in the SSSI system, is inadequate in isolation. What is required is the fostering of a more sympathetic approach to nature conservation generally. Whether or not the Wildlife and Countryside Act survives unchanged, the future must involve some

Fig. 113.
Peace in Orkney
(Photo: *R. S. Moore*).

form of management agreements between the NCC and the owners and occupiers of SSSIs. If it does not, much of Orkney's natural environment seems doomed.

> *What would the world be, once bereft*
> *Of wet and wildness? Let them be left,*
> *Oh let them be left, wildness and wet*
> *Long live the weeds and the wilderness yet.*
> Gerald Manly Hopkins

Getting about Orkney

Orkney is a good county for the naturalist who wants to see a wide range of species and habitats. There is an abundance of good ground for walking; some of the cliff walks rank with the best in the United Kingdom. Most of the land is farmed, but Orcadians are in general very tolerant of people walking on their property, so long as their crops, stock and privacy are properly respected (and it is, of course, only courteous to seek permission if one wants to cross private land).

For newcomers, the Tourist Office in Broad Street near the Cathedral in Kirkwall (phone Kirkwall (0856) 2856) (or its satellite at Stromness Harbour) provides all necessary information about local transport and accommodation. Cars and bicycles can be hired in Kirkwall and Stromness, and cars on most of the islands. There are frequent boat sailings to Hoy, Flotta, Graemsay, Shapinsay, Rousay, Wyre and Egilsay, and less often to the other North Isles (which are also connected by air services with Kirkwall, usually twice daily). The Mainland and South Isles are better served by buses than most rural areas in mainland Britain.

Orkney is covered by three sheets (nos 5, 6, 7) of the Ordnance Survey 1:50,000 series, and by a single sheet (no 61) of Bartholomew's 1:100,000 series. Many of the island Community Councils produce information leaflets setting out places of interest. The Orkney Field Club has produced Car Trails to the West and East Mainland. 'Go-Orkney' provides guided tours of the Mainland, including places of natural history interest (details from the Tourist Office or the *Orcadian* newspaper, published every Thursday).

Many of the archaeological and historical monuments are in the care of the Department of the Environment; a very useful general introduction to them is Anna and Graham Ritchie's *The Ancient Monuments of Orkney* (HMSO, 1978).

The Orkney Museum Service maintains as a museum Tankerness House in Kirkwall, dating from the 16th century and for 300 years the town house of one of the leading merchant-laird families of Orkney; and also a restored farm-house at Corrigall, Harray, featuring some of the characteristic artefacts of Orkney agriculture. The Orkney Natural History Society supports the Stromness Museum (founded 1836), near the south end of the town. Besides exhibitions of the maritime traditions of Orkney, the Stromness Museum houses one of Scotland's best collections of stuffed birds, local birds eggs, the Robert Rendall collection of Orkney shells and seaweed, the Magnus Spence herbarium of Orkney plants, the Ian Lorimer collection of Orkney butterflies and moths, local fossils and geological samples, and a small archaeological display, chiefly from Skara Brae.

References and Further Reading

Chapter 1

A full Bibliography is provided on pages 226–235. References to literature cited or relevant for each chapter are listed below.

GENERAL

Older works: Barry, 1805; Brand, 1701; Low, 1879; Tudor, 1883; Wallace, 1693, 1700; Withrington & Grant, 1978.
Modern works: Bailey, 1971; Brown, 1969, 1979, 1981; Clouston, 1932; Fenton, 1978; Linklater, 1965; Marwick, 1951; Miller, 1976; Thomson, 1980.

There have been two *Orkney Books*, the original one edited by Gunn (1909); the new one by Shearer, Groundwater & Mackay (1966). Older Orkney literature has been listed by Cursiter (1894).

There is also a *Shetland Book* (edited by Cluness, 1967), a *Caithness Book* (edited by Omand, 1972) and a *Sutherland Book* (edited by Omand, 1982).

SHETLAND

General: Cluness, 1951; Cowie, 1871; Nicolson, 1972.
Natural history: Berry & Johnston, 1980; Evans & Buckley, 1899; Goodier, 1974; Spence, 1979; Tulloch, 1978; Tulloch & Hunter, 1972; Venables & Venables, 1955; Williamson, 1965.

FAROE

General: West, 1972; Williamson, 1948.
Natural history: Jensen, 1928–72; Rasmussen, 1952; Reinert, 1971; Williamson, 1948.

ORKNEY

Natural history: Baikie & Heddle, 1848; Balfour, 1972; Booth, Cuthbert & Reynolds, 1984; Buckley & Harvie-Brown, 1891; Bullard, 1975; Dunn, 1837; Goodier, 1975; Groundwater, 1974; Low, 1813; Rendall, 1960; Spence, 1914.
Weather: Douglas, 1980; Plant & Dunsire, 1973.

ISLAND BIOLOGY

General: Berry, 1977, 1983a; Carlquist, 1974; Darling & Boyd, 1964; Gorman, 1980; Lack, 1969, 1976;

MacArthur & Wilson, 1967; Mayr, 1954; Parsons, 1983; Williamson, 1981.

The Royal Society of Edinburgh have held two symposia, one on the Natural Environment of the Outer Hebrides and the other on the Natural Environment of the Inner Hebrides. These are published in the Proceedings of the Royal Society of Edinburgh, series B, volumes 77, 1979 and 83, 1983 respectively.

Chapter 2

Berry, 1985; Berry & Rose, 1975; Bullard, 1975; Chapman & Crawford, 1981; Childe, 1931; Corbet, 1961, 1979; Davidson, Jones & Renfrew, 1976; Flett, 1920; Flinn, 1974; Hoppe, 1965; Huxtable, Hedges, Renfrew & Aitken, 1976; Keatinge & Dickson, 1979; Lorimer, 1982; Mathews, 1952; Moar, 1969; Peach & Horne, 1880; Prentice & Prentice, 1975; Renfrew, 1979; Renfrew, Harkness & Switsur, 1976; Ritchie, 1978; Ritchie & Ritchie, 1974; Steers, 1953; Traill, 1868.

See also the general books on Orkney, listed for Chapter 1.

Chapter 3

GEOLOGY

Agassiz, 1834; Black, 1978; Bott & Browitt, 1975; Brown, 1975; Fannin, 1969; Flett, 1897, 1898, 1920; Flinn, 1969a, 1969b, 1973, 1978, 1981; Gallagher *et al.*, 1971; Geikie, 1877; Goodier & Ball, 1975; Halliday, McAlpine & Mitchell, 1977; Heddle, 1878; Jameson, 1813; Jarvik, 1948; Institute of Geological Sciences, 1978; Kellock, 1969; Laing, 1877; Leask, 1928; McQuillin, 1968; Mather, Ritchie & Smith, 1974, 1975; Michie & Cooper, 1979; Miles & Westoll, 1963; Miller, 1849; Muir & Ridgway, 1975; Murchison, 1859; Mykura, 1975, 1976; Parnell, 1983a, 1983b, 1983c; Peach & Horne, 1880, 1883; Richardson, 1965; Saxon, 1975; Saxton & Hopwood, 1919; Steavenson, 1928; Watson, 1932; Watts, 1971; Wilson *et al.*, 1935; Wilson & Knox, 1936.

Chapter 4

Bullard, 1972, 1975; Bullard & Goode, 1975; Burnett, 1964; Chapman & Crawford, 1981; Crampton, 1911; Dunn, 1837; Goodier & Ball, 1975; Macdonald, 1967;

224

McVean & Ratcliffe, 1962; Moar, 1969; Nicol, 1938; Prentice & Prentice, 1975; Ritchie, 1954; Shirreff, 1814; Spence, D. H. N., 1974, 1979; Spence, M., 1914; Wallace, 1700; Wright, Smith & Fletcher, 1942. The Orkney Field Club work on *Primula scotica* is described in a number of notes by Bullard, E. R. & Shearer, D. H. in the Field Club *Bulletin*: 4, 1965; *1-4*, 1967; *3*, 1969; *1*, 1970; *1*, 1973; *1*, 1975; *3*, 1979.

Chapter 5

Atkins, Jones & Simpson, 1985; Baxter, 1982; Baxter, Jones & Simpson, 1985; Davies, 1985; Dunn, 1938; Jones, 1975; Lyle, 1929; McMillan, 1971; Mason *et al.*, 1985; Nicol, 1938; Rendall, 1956, 1960; Sinclair, 1950; Tait, 1937; Thomson, 1983; Traill, 1890, 1892, 1895; Walker, 1950; Wilkinson, 1975; Winchworth, 1920.

Chapter 6

GENERAL

Buckley & Harvie-Brown, 1891; Corbet & Southern, 1977; Fenton, 1978; Groundwater, 1974; Hewer, 1974; Lockley, 1966.

SEALS

Berry, 1969; Bonner, 1972, 1976, 1978; Bonner, Vaughan & Johnston, 1973; Boyd, 1963; Consultative Committee, 1963; Davis & Anderson, 1976; Flint, 1979; Harwood, 1978; Harwood & Prime, 1978; Hewer, 1964; McConnell, 1985; Marwick, 1975; Sea Mammal Research Unit, 1984; Smith, 1966; Summers, 1978; Summers, Bonner & Van Haaften, 1978; Tickell, 1970; Vaughan, 1969, 1975, 1977.

WHALES

Brown, 1976; De Cock, 1956; Evans, 1976a, 1976b, 1980; Reynolds & Booth, 1985; Sheldrick, 1976; West, 1972.

OTTERS

Baker *et al.*, 1981; Green & Green, 1980; Kruuk & Hewson, 1978; Watson, 1978.

Chapter 7

Balfour-Browne, 1949; Barnes, 1980; Barry, 1805; Britton, 1974; Buckley & Harvie-Brown, 1891; Bullard, 1972, 1975; Bullard & Goode, 1975; Dunn, 1937; Heppleston, 1972, 1983a, 1983b, 1983c, 1984; Kellock & Maitland, 1969; Low, 1813; Maitland, 1979; Maitland & Kellock, 1971; Murray & Pullar, 1908; Nicol, 1938; Sutcliffe, 1974; Trowbridge & Heppleston, 1984; West & West, 1905.

Chapter 8

MAMMALS

Baikie & Heddle, 1848; Berry, 1977; Berry & Rose, 1975; Buckley & Harvie-Brown, 1891; Ellison, 1906; Godfrey, 1905; Groundwater, 1974; Hewson, 1948; Hinton, 1913; Major, 1905; Millais, 1905; Miller, 1908; Rose, 1975; Ryder, 1983; Ryder, Land & Ditchburn, 1974; Turner, 1965; Zimmermann, 1959.

INVERTEBRATES

Bradley & Fletcher, 1979; Cuthbert *et al.*, 1979, 1983; Lorimer, 1975, 1983; Picozzi, 1981; Smith & Smith, 1983; South, 1888; Traill, 1869, 1888; White, 1882. See also the references given in the lists in the Appendix referring to invertebrates.

Chapter 9

GENERAL

Arthur, 1950; Baikie & Heddle, 1848; Balfour, 1968, 1972; Booth, Cuthbert & Reynolds, 1984; Buckley & Groundwater, 1974; Lack, 1942, 1943; Low, 1813; Omond, 1925; Lea & Bourne, 1975; Watson, 1977.

SPECIFIC

Balfour, 1955, 1962, 1970; Balfour, Anderson & Dunnet, 1967; Balfour & Cadbury, 1975, 1979; Balfour & Macdonald, 1970; Birkhead, 1984; Booth, 1979, 1982; Bourne, 1983; Bullock & Gomershall, 1981; Cadbury, 1980; Dunnet, Ollason & Anderson, 1979; Duffey, 1955; Hope-Jones, 1979; Lea & Bourne, 1975; Marler, 1952; Meek *et al.*, 1975; Ollason & Dunnet, 1983; Picozzi, 1980, 1981, 1983a, 1983b; Picozzi & Cuthbert, 1982; Ratcliffe, 1984; Robertson, 1934; Robinson, 1934; Scharf & Balfour, 1970; Slater & Ince, 1979; Tay & Orkney Ringing Groups, 1984; Tomison, 1904.

Chapter 10

BOOKS

Anderson, 1982; Bailey, 1971; Berry, 1985; Brøgger, 1929; Capper, 1937; Childe, 1931; Childe & Clarke, 1983; Clouston, 1932; Coleman & Wheeler, 1980; Fenton, 1978; Forsythe, 1982; Goudie, 1904; Gunn, 1909; Hedges, 1984; Jakobsen, 1897; Laing, 1974; Linklater, 1975; Marwick, 1951; Miller, 1976; Renfrew, 1979, 1985; Ritchie & Ritchie, 1978; Shaw, 1980; Shearer, Groundwater & Mackay, 1966; Shetelig, 1940; Sutherland, 1966; Thomson, 1981, 1983; Wainwright, 1955, 1962.

ARTICLES: ARCHAEOLOGY & ANTHROPOLOGY

Barclay, 1965; Berry & Muir, 1975; Boyce, Brothwell & Holdsworth, 1983; Brothwell, 1985; Davidson,

1979; Davidson, Jones & Renfrew, 1976; Harvev, Suter & Tills, 1985; Hedges, 1975, 1985; Jakobsen, 1901; Marwick, 1930; Ralegh Radford, 1983; Renfrew, Harkness & Switsur, 1976; Ritchie, A., 1983; Ritchie, A. & Ritchie, G., 1974; Ritchie, J., 1978; Roberts, 1985; Roberts, Roberts & Poskanzer, 1979; Small, 1968; Thomas, 1884; Thomson, 1985.

MAN & THE LAND

Calder, 1952; Davidson et al., 1976; Dry, 1985; Dry & Robertson, 1982; Fenton, 1978; Goodier, 1975; Macdonald, 1967; Marwick, 1930; Mooney, 1931; O'Dell, 1939; Senior & Swan, 1972; Spence, 1981; Tait, 1936; Thomson, 1981, 1983; Willis, 1983; Young, 1985.

Chapter 11

Agassiz, 1834; Anderson, 1834; Baikie & Heddle, 1848; Barry, 1805; Ben, 1529; Brand, 1701; Buckley

& Harvie-Brown, 1891; Burkill, 1968; Charleson, 1905; Crichton, 1866; Donaldson, 1966; Dunn, 1837; Groundwater, 1974; Lea, 1976; Love, 1982; Low, 1813, 1879; McMillan, 1968; Millais, 1904; Neill, 1806; Peach & Horne, 1880, 1883; Pennie, 1964; Rendall, 1948, 1956, 1960; Robertson, 1934; Sibbald, 1711; Sinclair, 1950; Spence, 1914; Traill, 1830; Wallace, 1693; Wallace, 1700; Withrington & Grant, 1978.

Chapter 12

Baker et al., 1981; Berry, 1983b; Calder, 1952; Coughtrey, 1983; Flint, 1979; Gallagher et al., 1971; Goodier, 1975; Hardin, 1964; Harwood, 1978; Keatinge & Dickson, 1979; Kruick & Hewson, 1978; Linklater, 1981; Mabey, 1980; Nature Conservancy Council, 1984; O'Dell, 1939; Orkney Islands Council, 1978; Rendall, 1960; Senior & Swan, 1972; Summers, 1978; Walker, 1950; Wanless et al., 1982; Young, 1985.

Bibliography

Agassiz, L. (1834). On the fossil fishes of Scotland. *Rep. Br. Ass. Advmt Sci, 4th Meeting, Edinburgh, Transactions of Sections* 646–649.

Anderson, G. P. (1834). *Guide to the Highlands and Islands of Scotland, including Orkney and Shetland.* London.

Anderson, P. D. (1982). *Robert Stewart, Earl of Orkney, Lord of Shetland 1533–1593.* Edinburgh: John Donald.

Arthur, G. T. (1950). Orkney's birds. *Bird Notes* 24: 130–135.

Ashby, E. (1978). *Reconciling Man with the Environment.* London: Oxford University Press.

Ashmole, N. P. (1979). The spider fauna of Shetland and its zoogeographic context. *Proc. R. Soc. Edin.* 78B: 63–122.

Atkins, S. M., Jones, A. M. & Simpson, J. A. (1985). The fauna of sandy beaches of Orkney: a review. *Proc. R. Soc. Edin.* 87B: 27–45.

Baikie, W. B. & Heddle, R. (1848). *Historia Naturalis Orcadensis. Zoology, Part 1.* Edinburgh: Paterson.

Bailey, P. (1971). *Orkney.* Newton Abbot: David & Charles.

Baker, J. R., Jones, A. M., Jones, T. P. & Watson, H. C. (1981). Otter (*Lutra lutra*) mortality and marine oil pollution. *Biol. Cons.* 20: 311–321.

Balfour, E. (1955). Kestrels nesting on the ground in Orkney. *Bird Notes* 26: 245–53..

Balfour, E. (1962). The nest and eggs of the Hen Harrier in Orkney. *Bird Notes* 30: 69–73.

Balfour, E. (1968). Breeding birds in Orkney. *Scot. Birds* 5: 89–104.

Balfour, E. (1970). Iris colour in the Hen Harrier. *Bird Study* 17: 47.

Balfour, E. (1972). *Orkney Birds. Status and Guide.* Stromness: Senior.

Balfour, E., Anderson, A. & Dunnet, G. M. (1967). Orkney Cormorants – their breeding distribution and dispersal. *Scot. Birds* 4: 481–93.

Balfour, E. & Cadbury, C. J. (1975). A population study of the Hen Harrier, *Circus cyaneus* in Orkney. In *The Natural Environment of Orkney*: 122–8. Goodier, R. (ed.) Edinburgh: Nature Conservancy Council.

Balfour, E. & Cadbury, C. J. (1979). Polygyny, spacing and sex ratio among Hen Harriers *Circus cyaneus* in Orkney, Scotland. *Ornis Scand.* 10: 133–41.

Balfour, E. & Macdonald, M. A. (1970). Food and feeding behaviour of the Hen Harriers in Orkney. *Scot. Birds* 6: 157–66.

Balfour-Browne, F. (1949). The aquatic coleoptera of the Orkney islands with some remarks on water beetle faunas of the Scottish islands. *Proc. R. Phys. Soc.* 23: 143–53.

Barclay, R. S. (1969). *The Population of Orkney.* Kirkwall: W. R. Mackintosh.

Barnes, R. S. K. (1980). *Coastal Lagoons.* Cambridge University Press.

Barry, G. (1805). *The History of the Orkney Islands.* Edinburgh: Constable.

Baxter, J. M. (1982). Population dynamics of *Patella vulgata* in Orkney. *Neth. J. Sea Res.* 16:96–104.

Baxter, J. M., Jones, A. M. & Simpson, J. A. (1985). A study of long-term changes in some rocky shore communities in Orkney. *Proc. R. Soc. Edin.*

Ben, J. (1529). *Descriptio Insularum Orchadearum.* See Appendix VII in Barry, 1805.

Berry, R. J. (1969). Non-metrical variation in two Scottish colonies of the Grey seal. *J. Zool., Lond.* 157:11–18.

Berry, R. J. (1977). *Inheritance and Natural History.* London: Collins New Naturalist.

Berry, R. J. (1983a). Diversity and differentiation: the importance of island biology for general theory. *Oikos* 41:523–9.

Berry, R. J. (1983b). Environmental ethics and conservation action. In *The Conservation and Development Programme for the UK*: 407–38. London: Kogan Page.

Berry, R. J. (ed.) (1985). *The People of Orkney.* Stromness: Orkney Press.

Berry, R. J. & Johnston, J. L. (1980). *The Natural History of Shetland.* London: Collins New Naturalist.

Berry, R. J. & Muir, V. M. L. (1975). Natural history of man in Shetland. *J. biosoc. Sci.* 7:319–44.

Berry, R. J. & Rose, F. E. N. (1975). Islands and the evolution of *Microtus arvalis* (Microtinae). *J. Zool., Lond.* 177:395–409.

Birkhead, T. R. (1984). Distribution of the bridled form of the common guillemot *Uria aalge* in the North Atlantic. *J. Zool., Lond.* 202:165–76.

Black, G. P. (ed.) (1978). *Orkney: Localities of Geological and Geomorphological Importance.* Newbury: Nature Conservancy Council.

Böker, U. von (1964). Bermerkungen zur Vogelwelt der Orkneyinsel Hoy. *Ornith. Mitt.* 16:3–12.

Booth, C. J. (1979). A study of ravens in Orkney. *Scot. Birds* 10:261–7.

Booth, C. J. (1982). *Scot. Birds* 12:33–8.

Booth, C. J., Cuthbert, Mildred & Reynolds, P. (1984). *The Birds of Orkney.* Stromness: Orkney Press.

Bott, M. H. P. & Browitt, C. W. A. (1975). Interpretation of geophysical observations between the Orkney and Shetland Islands. *J. geol. Soc. Lond.* 131:353–71.

Bonner, W. N. (1972). The Grey Seal and Common Seal in European waters. *Oceanogr. Mar. Biol. Ann. Rev.* 10:461–507.

Bonner, W. N. (1976). *Stocks of Grey Seals and Common Seals in Great Britain.* N.E.R.C. Publications Ser. C, no. 16. London: N.E.R.C.

Bonner, W. N. (1978). Man's impact on seals. *Mamm. Rev.* 8:3–13.

Bourne, W. R. P. (1983). Birds, fish and offal in the North Sea. *Mar. Poll. Bull.* 14:294–6.

Boyce, A. J., Holdsworth, V. M. L. & Brothwell, D. R. (1973). Demographic and genetic studies in the Orkney Islands. In *Genetic Variation in Britain*: 109–28. Sunderland, E. & Roberts, D. F. (eds.). London: Taylor & Francis.

Boycott, A. E. (1936). *Neritina fluviatilis* in Orkney. *J. Conchol.* 20:199–200.

Boyd, J. M. (1963). The Grey Seal (*Halichoerus grypus* Fab.) in the Outer Hebrides in October 1961. *Proc. zool. Soc. Lond.* 141:635–62.

Bradley, J. D. & Fletcher, D. S. (1979). *A Recorder's Log Book or Label List of British Butterflies and Moths.* London.

Braendegaard, J. (1958). Araneida. *Zoology Iceland,* 3 (54).

Brand, J. (1701). *A Brief Description of Orkney, Zetland, Pightland Firth and Caithness.* Edinburgh: Brown.

Bristowe, W. S. (1931). The spiders of the Orkney and Shetland Islands. *Proc. Zool. Soc., Lond.* for 1931: 951–6.

Britton, R. H. (1974). The freshwater ecology of Shetland. In *The Natural Environment of Shetland*: 119–29. Goodier, R. (ed.), Edinburgh: Nature Conservancy Council.

Brøgger, A. W. (1929). *Ancient Emigrants.* Oxford: Clarendon.

Brothwell, D. (1976). Further evidence of bone chewing by ungulates: the sheep of North Ronaldsay, Orkney. *J. archaeol. Sc.* 3:179–82.

Brothwell, D. R., Tills, D. & Muir, V. (1985). Evidence of microevolution in the Orkney islanders. In *The People of Orkney*, Berry R. J. (ed.), Stromness: Orkney Press.

Brown, E. S. (1965). Distribution of the ABO and Rhesus (*D*) blood groups in the north of Scotland. *Heredity,* 20:289–303.

Brown, G. M. (1969). *An Orkney Tapestry.* London: Gollancz.

Brown, G. M. (1981). *Portrait of Orkney.* London: Hogarth.

Brown, J. F. (1975). Potassium-argon evidence for a Permian age for the camptonite dykes in Orkney. *Scot. J. Geol.* 11:259–62.

Brown, S. G. (1976). Modern whaling in Britain and the north-east Atlantic Ocean. *Mammal Rev.* 6:25–36.

Buckley, T. E. & Harvie-Brown, J. A. (1891). *A Vertebrate Fauna of the Orkney Islands.* Edinburgh: Douglas.

Bullard, E. R. (1972). *Orkney – A Checklist of Vascular Plants and Ferns.* Stromness: Rendall.

Bullard, E. R. (1972). Lagoons and oyces in Orkney. *Bull. Orkney Fld Club* no. 3, 7–8.

Bullard, E. R. (1975). Orkney habitats: an outline ecological framework. In *The Natural Environment of Orkney*: 19–28. Goodier, R. (ed.). Edinburgh: Nature Conservancy Council.

Bullard, E. R. & Goode, D. A. (1975). The vegetation of Orkney. In *The Natural Environment of Orkney*: 31–46. Goodier, R. (ed.). Edinburgh: Nature Conservancy Council.

Bullock, I. D. & Gomersall, C. H. (1981). The breeding population of terns in Orkney and Shetland in 1980. *Bird Study* 28:187–200.

Burkill, H. M. (1968). James Sinclair, 1913–1968: an obituary and appreciation. *Garden Bull., Singapore*, no. 23.

Burnett, J. H. (ed.) (1964). *The Vegetation of Scotland*. Edinburgh: Oliver & Boyd.

Cadbury, C. J. (1980). The status and habitats of the Corncrake in Britain, 1978–79. *Bird Study* 27: 203–18.

Calder, A. (1952). Orkney's changing agriculture. *Scot. Agriculture*: 37–41.

Capper, D. P. (1937). *The Vikings of Britain*. London: Allen and Unwin.

Carlquist, S. (1974). *Island Biology*. New York & London: Columbia.

Chapman, H. M. & Crawford, R. M. M. (1981). Growth and regeneration in Britain's most northerly natural woodland. *Trans. bot. Soc. Edin.* 43: 327–35.

Charleson, M. M. (ed.) (1905). *Orcadian Papers*. Kirkwall.

Childe, V. G. (1931). *Skara Brae. A Pictish Village in Orkney*. London: Kegan Paul.

Childe, V. G. & Clarke, D. V. (1983). *Skara Brae*. Edinburgh: HMSO.

Clouston, J. S. (1927). *The Orkney Parishes*. Kirkwall.

Clouston, J. S. (1932). *A History of Orkney*. Kirkwall: W. R. Mackintosh.

Cluness, A. T. (1951). *The Shetland Isles*. London: Hale.

Cluness, A. T. (ed.) (1967). *The Shetland Book*. Lerwick: Zetland Education Committee.

Coleman, V. & Wheeler, R. (1980). *Living on an Island*. Findhorn, Moray: Thule.

Comfort, A. (1937). Land shells of the West Mainland. *Orcadian*, 13 May 1937.

Consultative Committee (1963). *Grey Seals and Fisheries*. London: HMSO.

Corbet, G. B. (1961). Origin of the British insular races of small mammals and of the 'Lusitanian' fauna. *Nature, Lond.* 191:1037–40.

Corbet, G. B. (1979). Report on rodent remains. In *Excavations in Orkney*: 135–7. Renfrew, C. (ed.). London: Society of Antiquities.

Corbet, G. B. & Southern, H. N. (1977). *The Handbook of British Mammals*, 2nd edn. Oxford: Blackwell.

Coughtrey, P. J. (ed.) (1983) *Ecological Aspects of Radionuclide Release*. Oxford: Blackwell.

Cowie, J. R. (1871). *Shetland and its Inhabitants*. Aberdeen: Lewis, Smith.

Cramp, S., Bourne, W. R. P. & Saunders, D. (1974). *Seabirds of Britain and Ireland*. London: Collins.

Crampton, C. B. (1911). *The Vegetation of Caithness, considered in relation to the geology*. Cambridge: Committee for the Survey and Study of British Vegetation.

Crichton, W. T. (1866). *A Naturalist's Rambles to the Orcades*. London.

Cursiter, J. W. (1894). *List of Books and Pamphlets relating to Orkney and Shetland*. Kirkwall: Peace.

Cuthbert, O. D., Brostoff, J., Wraith, D. G. & Brighton, W. D. (1979), *Clin. Allergy*, 9:229–36.

Cuthbert, O. D., Jeffrey, I. G., McNeill, H. & Topping, M. D. (1983). Barn allergy among Scottish farmers. *Clin. Allergy*, 13.

Darling, F. F. & Boyd, J. M. (1964). *The Highlands and Islands*. London: Collins New Naturalist.

Davidson, D. A. (1979). The Orcadian environment and cairn location. In *Excavations in Orkney*: 7–20. Renfrew, C. (ed.). London: Society of Antiquities.

Davidson, D. A., Jones, R. L. & Renfrew, C. (1976). Palaeoenvironmental reconstruction and evaluation: a case study from Orkney. *Trans. Inst. Brit. Geog.* 1:346–61.

Davies, I. M. (1985). Marine pollution in Orkney. *Proc. R. Soc. Edin.* 87B:105–112.

Davis, J. E. & Anderson, S. S. (1976). Effects of oil pollution on breeding Grey Seals. *Mar. Pollution Bull.* 7:115–18.

De Cock, L. (1956). The Pilot Whale stranding on the Orkney Island of Westray, 1955. *Scot. Nat.* 68: 63–70.

Dennis, R. W. G. (1972). Fungi of the Northern Isles. *Kew Bull.*, 26:427–32.

Donaldson, G. (1966). *Northwards by Sea*. Edinburgh: Grant.

Douglas, C. K. M. (1952). Synoptic aspects of the storm over N. Scotland on Jan. 15, 1952. *Meteor. Mag.* 81:104–106.

Dry, F. T. (ed.) (1985). *The Soils of Orkney*. Aberdeen: Macaulay Institute.

Dry, F. T. & Robertson, J. S. (1982). *Soil and Land Capability for Agriculture. Orkney and Shetland*. Aberdeen: Macaulay Institute.

Dunn, M. D. (1973). Notes on the flora of Loch Harray and Loch Stenness. *Trans. Proc. bot. Soc. Edin.* 32:368–72.

Dunn, R. (1837). *The Ornithologist's Guide to the Islands of Orkney and Shetland*. Hull.

Dunnet, G. M., Ollason, J. & Anderson, A. (1978).

The estimation of survival rate in the Fulmar, *Fulmarus glacialis. J. anim. Ecol.* 47:507–20.

Duffey, E. (1955). Notes on the natural history of Eynhallow. *Scot. Nat.* 67:40–51.

Ellis, A. E. (1951). Census of the distribution of British non-marine Mollusca (7th edition). *J. Conchol.* 23:171–244.

Ellison, G. (1906). *The Orkney Vole. Microtus orcadensis* (Millais). Kirkwall: Mackintosh.

Evans, A. H. & Buckley, T. E. (1899). *A Vertebrate Fauna of the Shetland Islands.* Edinburgh: Douglas.

Evans, P. G. H. (1976a). An analysis of sightings of Cetacea in British waters. *Mammal Rev.* 6:5–14.

Evans, P. G. H. (1976b). *Guide to Identification of Cetaceans in British Waters.* Reading: Mammal Society.

Evans, P. G. H. (1980). Cetaceans in British waters. *Mamm. Rev.* 10:1–52.

Fannin, N. G. T. (1969). Stromatolites from the Middle Old Red Sandstone of western Orkney. *Geol. Mag.* 106:77–88.

Fenton, A. (1978). *The Northern Isles: Orkney and Shetland.* Edinburgh: John Donald.

Flett, J. S. (1897). On the discovery in Orkney of the John o' Groats horizon of the Old Red Sandstone. *Proc. R. phys. Soc. Edin.* 13:225–57.

Flett, J. S. (1898). The Old Red Sandstone of the Orkneys. *Trans. R. Soc. Edin.* 39:383–424.

Flett, J. S. (1920). The submarine contours around the Orkneys. *Trans. Edin. geol. Soc.* 11:42–9.

Flinn, D. (1969a). A geological interpretation of the aeromagnetic maps of the continental shelf around Orkney and Shetland. *Geol. J.* 6:279–92.

Flinn, D. (1969b). On the development of coastal profiles in the north of Scotland, Orkney and Shetland. *Scot. J. Geol.* 5:393–9.

Flinn, D. (1973). The topography of the sea floor around Orkney and Shetland and in the northern North Sea. *Q. J. Geol. Soc. Lond.* 129:39–59.

Flinn, D. (1974). The coastline of Shetland. In *Natural Environment of Shetland*: 13–23. Goodier, R. (ed.). Edinburgh: Nature Conservancy Council.

Flinn, D. (1978). The most recent glaciation of the Orkney–Shetland Channel and adjacent areas. *Scot. J. Geol.* 14:109–23.

Flinn, D. (1981). A note on the glacial and late glacial history of Caithness. *Geol. J.* 16:175–9.

Flint, S. (1979). *Let the Seals Live!* Sandwick, Shetland: Thule.

Forrest, J. E. (1938). Notes concerning some animals recently obtained from three German warships recently salvaged at Scapa Flow, Orkney. *Scot. Nat.* No. 229:3–8.

Forsythe, D. (1982). *Urban–Rural Migration, Change* and Conflict in an Orkney Island Community. North Sea Oil Panel Occasional Paper No. 14. London: Social Science Research Council.

Gallagher, M. J., Michie, U. McL., Smith, R. T. & Haynes, L. (1971). New evidence of uranium mineralization in Scotland. *Trans. Inst. Min. Met.* 80B:150–7.

Geikie, A. (1877). The glacial geology of Orkney and Shetland. *Nature, Lond.* 16:414–16.

Godfrey, R. (1906). Notes on the Orkney Vole. *Ann. Scot. Nat. Hist.* No. 56:195–8.

Godfrey, R. (1906). Land shells in Orkney. *Ann. Scot Hist for 1906*: 55

Goodier, R. (ed.) (1974). *Natural Environment of Shetland.* Edinburgh: Nature Conservancy Council.

Goodier, R. (ed.) (1975). *The Natural Environment of Orkney.* Edinburgh: Nature Conservancy Council.

Goodier, R. & Ball, D. F. (1975). Ward Hill, Orkney: patterned features and their origin. In *The Natural Environment of Orkney*: 47–56. Goodier, R. (ed.). Edinburgh: Nature Conservancy Council.

Gorman, M. (1979). *Island Ecology.* London: Chapman & Hall.

Goudie, G. (1904). *The Celtic and Scandinavian Antiquities of Shetland.* Edinburgh and London: Blackwood.

Green, S & Green, R. (1980). *Otter Survey of Scotland 1977–1979.* London: Vincent Wildlife Trust.

Grimshaw, P. H. (1905). Diptera Scotica IV. Orkney and Shetland. *Ann. Scot. nat. Hist.*, for 1905, 22–35.

Groundwater, W. (1974). *Birds and Mammals of Orkney.* Kirkwall: Kirkwall Press.

Groves, J. & Bullock-Webster, G. R. (1920). *The British Charophyta* 1. *Nitelleae.* London: Ray Society.

Groves, J. & Bullock-Webster, G. R. (1924). *The British Charophyta* 2. *Chareae.* London: Ray Society.

Gunn, J. (ed.) (1909). *The Orkney Book.* London and Edinburgh: Nelson.

Halliday, A. N., McAlpine, A. & Mitchell, J. G. (1977). The age of the Hoy Lavas, Orkney. *Scot. J. Geol* 13:43–52.

Hammond, C. O. (1983). *The Dragonflies of Great Britain and Ireland.* Colchester: Harley.

Hardin, G. (1964). The tragedy of the commons. *Science, N.Y.*, 162:1243–8.

Harvey, R. G., Suter, D. & Tills, D. (1985). Relationships of the Orcadians: the view from Faroe. In *The People of Orkney*: Berry, R. J. (ed.), Stromness: Orkney Press.

Harwood, J. (1978). The effect of management policies on the stability and resilience of British Grey Seal populations. *J. appl. Ecol.* 15:413–21.

Harwood, J. & Prime, J. H. (1978). Some factors affecting the size of British Grey Seal populations. *J. appl. Ecol.* 15:401–11.

Heddle, M. F. (1878). *The County Geognosy and Mineralogy of Scotland, Orkney and Shetland.* Truro.

Hedges, J. (1975). Excavation of two Orcadian burnt mounds at Liddle and Beaquoy. *Proc. Soc. Ant. Scot.* 106:39–98.

Hedges, J. W. (1982). An archaeodemographical perspective on Isbister. *Scot. archaeol. Rev.* 1:5–20.

Hedges, J. W. (1984). *Tomb of the Eagles.* London: John Murray.

Hedges, J. W. (1985). From the first inhabitants to the Viking settlement. In *People of Orkney*: Berry, R. J. (ed.). Stromness: Orkney Press.

Henshall, A. S. (1963). *The Chambered Tombs of Scotland.* Edinburgh.

Heppleston, P. B. (1972). Life history and population fluctuations of *Lymnaea truncata*, the snail vector of fascioliasis. *J. appl. Ecol.* 9:229–42.

Heppleston, P. B. (1983a). How salty are Orkney's lochs? *Bull. Orkney Fld Club* No. 1:5–6.

Heppleston, P. B. (1983b). Observations on some macro-invertebrates in Orkney freshwaters. *Bull. Orkney Fld Club* No. 1:11–14.

Heppleston, P. B. (1983c). *Gammarus pulex* in Orkney, Scotland. *Crustaceana*, 46:20.

Heppleston, P. B. (1983d). The use of Orkney farmland in winter by wading birds. Orkney Bird Report for 1982, 52–7.

Heppleston, P. B. (1984). Comparative observations on the invertebrate fauna of two Orkney streams. *Scot. Nat.* (in press).

Hewer, H. R. (1964). The determination of age, sexual maturity, longevity and a life-table in the Grey Seal (*Halichoerus grypus*). *Proc. zool. Soc. Lond.* 142:593–624.

Hewer, H. R. (1974). *British Seals.* London: Collins New Naturalist.

Hewson, R. (1948). Some observations on the Orkney Vole, *Microtus o. orcadensis.* Northw. Nat. 23:7–10.

Hillyard, P. D. (1977). The spiders of Orkney. *Bull. Orkney Fld Club*, No. 1:7–8.

Hinton, M. A. C. (1913). Note on the voles of the *orcadensis* group. *Ann. Mag. nat. Hist.* (8), 12:452–62.

Hope-Jones, P. (1979). Roosting behaviour of long-tailed ducks in relation to possible oil pollution. *Wildfowl*, 30:155–8.

Hoppe, G. (1965). Submarine peat in the Shetland Islands. *Geogr. Annlr*, 47A:195–203.

Huxtable, J., Hedges, J. W., Renfrew, C. & Aitken, M. J. (1976). Dating a settlement pattern by thermoluminescence: the burnt mounds of Orkney. *Archaeometry*, 18:4–11.

Hynes, H. B. N. (1958). A key to the adults and nymphs of British Stoneflies (Plecopetera) *Sci. Publ. Freshw. Biol. Ass.* 17:1–86.

Ing. B. (1980). A revised census catalogue of British Myxomycetes, Part I. *Bull. Br. Mycol. Soc.* 14:97–111.

Ing. B. (1982). A revised census catalogue of British Myxomycetes, Part II. *Bull. Br. Mycol. Soc.* 15.

Ing, B. (1982). *Provisional Atlas of the Myxomycetes of the British Isles.* Huntingdon: Biological Records Centre.

Innes, G., Kidd, C. & Ross, H. S. (1968). Mental subnormality in north-east Scotland. *Brit. J. Psychiat.* 114:35–41.

Institute of Geological Sciences (1978). *Regional Geochemical Atlas: Orkney.* London: Institute of Geological Sciences.

Jakobsen, J. (1897). *The Dialect and Place Names of Shetland.* Lerwick: Manson.

Jakobsen, J. (1901). Shetlandsøernes stednavne. *Abøger for nordisk oldkyndighed og historie*, 2nd ser 16:55–258.

Jameson, R. (1813). *Mineralogical Travels through the Hebrides, Orkney and Shetland Islands and Mainland of Scotland.* 2 vols, Edinburgh.

Jarvik, E. (1948). On the morphology and taxonomy of the Middle Devonian osteolepid fishes of Scotland. *K. Svenska vidensk Akad.* (3), 15:1–301.

Jensen, A. D. (ed.) (1928–72). *The Zoology of the Faroes.* Copenhagen: Høst.

Jones, A. M. (1975). The marine environment of Orkney. In *The Natural Environment of Orkney*: 85–94. Goodier, R. (ed.), Edinburgh: Nature Conservancy Council.

Jones, K. H. & Kennard, A. S. (1919). Notes on the non-marine Mollusca observed in East Ross and the Orkney and Shetland Islands. *Proc. malac. Soc. Lond.* 13:146–52.

Keatinge, T. H. & Dickson, J. H. (1979). Mid-Flandrian changes in vegetation on Mainland Orkney. *New Phytol.* 82:585–612.

Kellock, E. (1969). Alkaline basic igneous rocks in the Orkneys. *Scot. J. Geol.* 5:140–52.

Kellock, E. & Maitland, P. S. (1969). Ephemeroptera and Plecoptera from Orkney. *Entomologist* 102:235–44.

Kerney, M. P. (1982). Vice-comital census of the non-marine Mollusca of the British Isles. (18th edition) *J. Conchol.* 30:63–71.

Kruuk, H. & Hewson, R. (1978). Spacing and foraging of otters (*Lutra lutra* L.) in a marine habitat. *J. Zool. Lond.* 195:205–12.

Lack, D. (1942). The breeding birds of Orkney. *Ibis* 85:461–84.

Lack, D. (1943). The breeding birds of Orkney. *Ibis* 86:1-27.

Lack, D. (1969). The numbers of bird species on islands. *Bird Study* 16:193-209.

Lack, D. (1976). *Island Biology*. Oxford: Blackwell.

Laing, L. (1974). *Orkney and Shetland. An archaeological guide*. Newton Abbot: David & Charles.

Laing, S. (1877). Glacial geology of Orkney and Shetland. *Nature, Lond.* 16:418-19.

Lea, D. (1976). Obituary: Eddie Balfour. *Scot. Birds* 9:69-71.

Lea, D. & Bourne, W. R. P. (1975). The birds of Orkney. In *The Natural Environment of Orkney*: 98-121. Goodier, R. (ed.), Edinburgh: Nature Conservancy Council.

Lea, D. & Bourne, W. R. P. (1975). The birds of Orkney. *Brit. Birds* 68:261-82.

Leask, A. (1928). Shell sand deposits in Orkney. *J. Orkney agric. Discuss. Soc.* 3:57-8.

Linklater, E. (1965). *Orkney and Shetland*. London: Hale.

Linklater, M. (1981). Uranium: a questionable commodity. *Orkney Heritage*, 1:7-21.

Locket, G. H., Millidge, A. F. & Merrett, P. (1974). *British spiders, volume III*. London: Roy. Society.

Lockley, R. M. (1966). *Grey Seal, Common Seal*. London: Deutsch.

Lorimer, R. I. (1975). Lepidoptera in Orkney. In *The Natural Environment of Orkney*: 57-79. Goodier, R. (ed.), Edinburgh: Nature Conservancy Council.

Lorimer, R. I. (1983). *The Lepidoptera of the Orkney Islands*. Faringdon: Classey.

Love, J. (1982). Harvie-Brown: a profile. *Scot. Birds*, 12:49-53.

Low, G. (1813). *Fauna Orcadensis*. Edinburgh.

Low, G. (1879). *A Tour through Orkney and Shetland*. Kirkwall.

Lyle, L. (1929). Marine algae of some German warships in Scapa Flow and of the neighbouring shores. *J. Linn. Soc. (Bot.)* 48:231-57.

MacArthur, R. H. & Wilson, E. O. (1963). An equilibrium theory of insular zoogeography. *Evolution* 17:373-87.

MacArthur, R. H. & Wilson, E. O. (1967). *The Theory of Island Biogeography*. Princeton: University Press.

McConnell, B. (1985). Seals in Orkney. *Proc. R. Soc. Edin.* 87B:195-204.

Macdonald, A. (1967). Trial plantations established by the Forestry Commission on the Island of Hoy, Orkney. *J. R. Scot. For. Soc.* 21:163-72.

McMillan, N. F. (1968). Obituary of Robert Rendall. *J. Conchol.* 26:273-74.

McMillan, N. F. (1971). Large *Cardium edule* L. and *Mytilus edulis* L. *J. Conchol.* 26:253.

McMillan, N. F. (1960). *Hygromia hispida* L. on Hoy, Orkney. *J. Conchol.* 24:395-7.

McMillan, N. F. (1966). *Margaritifera margaritifera* L. in hard water in Scotland. *J. Conchol.* 26:69.

McMillan, N. F. (1966). Kennard's record of fossil *Helix nemoralis* L. in Orkney. *J. Conchol.* 26:135-6.

McMillan, N. F. (1967 onwards). (Many notes on Orkney Mollusca in *Bull. Orkney Fld Club*)

McQuillin, R. (1968). Geophysical surveys in the Orkney Islands. *Geophys. Paper No. 4, Inst. geol. Sci.* 1-18.

McVean, D. N. & Ratcliffe, D. A. (1962). *Plant Communities of the Scottish Highlands*. London: HMSO.

Mabey, R. (1980). *The Common Ground*. London: Hutchinson.

Macan, T. T. (1961). A key to the nymphs of the British species of Ephemeroptera. *Sci. Publ. Freshw. Biol. Ass.* 20:1-64.

Maitland, P. S. (1979). *Synoptic Limnology: the analysis of British freshwater ecosystems*. Cambridge: Institute of Terrestrial Ecology.

Maitland, P. S. & Kellock, E. (1971). The freshwater leeches (Hirudinea) of Orkney. *Glasg. Nat.* 18:558-64.

Major, C. I. (1905). The affinities of the Orkney Vole (*Microtus orcadensis* Millais). *Ann. Mag. nat. Hist.* (1) 15:323-4.

Marler, P. (1952). Variations in the song of the Chaffinch, *Fringilla coelebs*. *Ibis* 94:958-72.

Martin & Summers (1984). See Tay & Orkney Ringing Groups (1984).

Marwick, E. (1975). *The Folklore of Orkney and Shetland*. London: Batsford.

Marwick, H. (1923). Celtic place-names in Orkney. *Proc. Soc. Ant. Scot.* 57:251-65.

Marwick, H. (1930). An Orkney Jacobite farmer. *J. Orkney agric. Discussion Soc.* 5:1-12.

Marwick, H. (1951). *Orkney*. London: Hale.

Mason, J., Newton, A. W., McKay, D. W. & Kinnear, J. A. M. (1985). Fisheries in the Orkney area. *Proc. R. Soc. Edin.* 87B:65-81.

Mather, A. S., Ritchie, W. & Smith, J. S. (1974). *Beaches of Orkney*. Aberdeen: Dept. Geography.

Mather, A. S., Ritchie, W. & Smith, J. S. (1975). An introduction to the morphology of the Orkney coastline. In *The Natural Environment of Orkney*: 10-18. Goodier, R. (ed.), Edinburgh: Nature Conservancy Council.

Matthews, L. H. (1952). *British Mammals*. London: Collins New Naturalist.

Matthey, R. (1953). Les chromosomes des Muridae. *Rev. Suisse Zool.* 60:225-83.

Mayr, E. (1954). Change of genetic environment and evolution. In *Evolution as a Process*: 157-80. Huxley, J., Hardy, A. C. & Ford, E. B. (eds). London: Allen & Unwin.

Meade-Briggs, A. R. & Page, R. J. C. (1967). Ectoparasites from hares collected throughout the United Kingdom, January–March 1964. *Entomol. mon. Mag.* 103:26–34.

Meinertzhagen, R. (1939). A note on the birds of Hoy, Orkney. *Ibis*, 14th ser. 3:258–64.

Michie, V. McL. & Cooper, D. C. (1979). Uranium in the Old Red Sandstone of Orkney. *Rep. Inst. geol. Sci.* No. 78:16.

Miles, R. S. & Westoll, T. S. (1963). Two new genera of coccosteid Athrodira from the Middle Old Red Sandstone of Scotland and their stratigraphical distribution. *Trans. R. Soc. Edin.* 66:179–210.

Millais, J. G. (1904). On a new British vole from the Orkney Islands. *Zoologist*, ser 4, 8:241–6.

Millais, J. G. (1905). *Mammals of Great Britain and Ireland*. London: Longmans.

Miller, G. S. (1908). Eighteen new European voles. *Ann. Mag. nat. Hist.* (8) 1:194–206.

Miller, H. (1849). *Footprints of the Creator*. Edinburgh: Nimmo.

Miller, R. (1976). *Orkney*. London: Batsford.

Miller, R. & Luther-Davies, S. (1969). *Eday and Hoy. A Development Study*. Glasgow: Dept. Geography.

Moar, N. T. (1969). Two pollen diagrams from the Mainland Orkney Islands. *New Phytol.* 68:201–208.

Møller, F. H. (1945). *Fungi of the Faeröes Part I*. Copenhagen.

Møller, F. H. (1958). *Fungi of the Faeröes Part II*. Copenhagen.

Moore, J. A. & Greene, D. M. (1983). *Provisional Atlas of the Characeae of the British Isles*. Huntingdon: Biological Records Centre.

Mooney, J. (1931). Notes on agricultural progress in Orkney. *J. Orkney agric. Discussion Soc.* 6:40–49.

Muir, R. O. & Ridgway, J. M. (1975). Sulphide mineralisation of the continental Devonian sediments of Orkney (Scotland). *Mineral Deposita (Berlin)*, 10:205–15.

Murchison, R. I. (1859). On the succession of the older rocks in the northernmost counties of Scotland: with some observations on the Orkney and Shetland Islands. *Q. J. geol. Soc. Lond.* 15:353–418.

Murray, J. & Pullar, L. (1908). *Bathymetric Survey of the Freshwater lochs of Scotland: the Lochs of Orkney*. Edinburgh.

Mykura, W. (1975). The geological basis of the Orkney environment. In *The Natural Environment of Orkney*: 1–9. Goodier, R. (ed.), Edinburgh: Nature Conservancy Council.

Mykura, W. (1976). *British Regional Geology. Orkney and Shetland*. Edinburgh: Institute of Geological Sciences.

Nature Conservancy Council (1984). *Nature Conservation in Great Britain*. London: Nature Conservancy Council.

Neill, P. (1806). *A Tour through some of the Islands of Orkney and Shetland*. Edinburgh.

Nicol, E. A. T. (1938). The brackish-water lochs of Orkney. *Proc. R. Soc. Edin.* 58:181–91.

Nicolson, J. R. (1972). *Shetland*. Newton Abbot: David & Charles.

O'Dell, A. C. (1939). *The Land Utilisation Survey of Britain. Part 4, Orkney*. London: Geographical Publications.

Oldham, C. (1928). *Paludestrina jenkinsi* in Orkney and Caithness. *J. Conchol.* 18:272.

Oldham, C. (1932). Notes on some Scottish and Shetland Pisidia. *J. Conchol.* 19:271–8.

Ollason, J. & Dunnet, G. M. (1983). Modelling annual changes in numbers of breeding Fulmars, *Fulmarus glacialis*, at a colony in Orkney. *J. anim. Ecol.* 52: 185–98.

Omand, D. (ed.) (1972). *The Caithness Book*. Inverness: Highland Printers.

Omand, D. (ed.) (1982). *The Sutherland Book*. Golspie: Northern Times.

Omond, J. (1925). *How to Know the Orkney Birds*. Kirkwall.

Orkney Islands Council (1978). *Orkney Structure Plan*. Kirkwall.

Parnell, J. (1983a). Ancient duricrusts and related rocks in perspective: a contribution from the Old Red Sandstone. *Spec. Publ. geol. Soc. Lond.* No. 12.

Parnell, J. (1983b). The distribution of hydrocarbon minerals in the Orcadian Basin. *Scot. J. Geol.* 19: 205–13.

Parnell, J. (1983c). The summery volcanic 'neck', Hoy. *Scot. J. Geol.* 19.

Parsons, P. A. (1983). *The Evolutionary Biology of Colonizing Species*. Cambridge: University Press.

Peach, B. N. & Horne, J. (1880). The glaciation of the Orkney Islands. *Q. J. geol. Soc. Lond.* 36:648–63.

Peach, B. N. & Horne, J. (1883). The geology of the Orkneys. In *Orkneys and Shetland*: 180–94. Tudor, J. R. (ed.), London: Stanford.

Pennie, I. D. (1964). Scottish ornithologists. I. Sir Robert Sibbald 1641–1722. *Scot. Birds* 3:159–66.

Picozzi, N. (1980). Food, growth, survival and sex ratio of nestling Hen Harriers *Circus cyaneus* in Orkney. *Ornis Scand.* 11:1–11.

Picozzi, N. (1981). Weight, wing-length and iris colour of Hen Harriers in Orkney. *Bird Study* 28: 159–61.

Picozzi, N. (1981). Common gull predation of Winter Moth larvae *Bird Study* 28:68–9.

Picozzi, N. (1983a). Growth and sex of nestling Merlins in Orkney. *Ibis* 125:377–82.

Picozzi, N. (1983b). Two hens, but a single nest: an unusual case of polygyny by Hen Harriers in Orkney. *Brit. Birds* 76:123–8.

Picozzi, N. & Cuthbert, M. F. (1982). Observations

and food of Hen Harriers at a winter roost in Orkney. *Scot. Birds* 12:73–80.

Plant, J. A. & Dunsire, A. (1974). *The Climate of Orkney*. Edinburgh: Meteorological Office.

Poppius, B. R. (1905). Contributions to the knowledge of the Coleopteran fauna of the Shetland and Orkney Islands. *Ofr. Finska Vet. Soc. Forh.* 47:1–13.

Prentice, H. C. & Prentice, I. C. (1975). The hill vegetation of North Hoy, Orkney. *New Phytol.* 75: 313–67.

Racey, P. A. (1977). A vagrant noctule from Orkney. *J. Zool., Lond.* 183:555–6.

Ralegh Radford, C. A. (1983). Birsay and the spread of Christianity to the North. *Orkney Heritage* 2: 13–35.

Rasmussen, R. (1952). *Føroya Flora*. Torshavn: Thomsen.

Ratcliffe, D. A. (1984). The Peregrine breeding population of the United Kingdom in 1981. *Bird Study* 31:1–18.

Reinert, A. (1971). Højere dyr på land. *Danmarks Natur.* 10:537–8.

Rendall, R. (1948). Wallace's list of Orkney mollusca. *J. Conchol.* 23:17–19.

Rendall, R. (1956). Mollusca orcadensia. *Proc. R. Soc. Edin.* 66B:131–201.

Rendall, R. (1960). *Orkney Shore*. Kirkwall: Kirkwall Press.

Renfrew, C. (1979). *Investigations in Orkney*. London: Society of Antiquaries.

Renfrew, C. (1979). The Orcadian monuments and society. In *Excavations in Orkney*: 199–223. Renfrew, C. (ed.), London: Society of Antiquaries of London.

Renfrew, C. (1985). *The Prehistory of Orkney*. Edinburgh.

Renfrew, C., Harkness, D. D. & Switsur, R. (1976). Quanterness, radio-carbon and the Orkney cairns. *Antiquity* 50:194–204.

Reynolds, P. & Booth, C. J. (1985). Cetaceans in Orkney waters, 17th century to 1982. *Scot. Nat.*

Richardson, J. B. (1965). Middle Old Red Sandstone spore assemblages from the Orcadian basin, Northeast Scotland. *Palaeontology* 7:559–605.

Ritchie, A. (1983). Birsay around AD 800. *Orkney Heritage* 2:56–66.

Ritchie, A. & Ritchie, G. (1978). *The Ancient Monuments of Orkney*. Edinburgh: HMSO.

Ritchie, G. & Ritchie, A. (1974). Excavation of a barrow at Queenafjold, Twatt, Orkney. *Proc. Soc. Ant. Scot.* 105:33.

Ritchie, J. C. (1954). *Primula scotica* Hook. *J. Ecol.* 42:623–8.

Ritchie, J. N. G. (1978). The Stones of Stenness, Orkney. *Proc. Soc. Ant. Scot.* 107:1.

Roberts, D. F. (1985). Genetic affinities of the Orkney islanders. In *The People of Orkney*: Berry, R. J. (ed.), Stromness: Orkney Press.

Roberts, D. F., Papiha, S. S. & Poskanzer, D. C. (1979). Polymorphisms and multiple sclerosis in Orkney. *J. Epidem. comm. Hlth*, 33:236–42.

Roberts, D. F., Roberts, M. J. & Cowie, J. A. (1979). Inbreeding levels in Orkney islanders. *J. biosoc. Sci.* 11:391–5.

Roberts, D. F., Roberts, M. J. & Poskanzer, D. C. (1979). Genetic analysis of multiple sclerosis in Orkney. *J. Epidem. comm. Hlth.* 33:229–35.

Robertson, D. J. (1934). *Notes from a Bird Sanctuary*. Kirkwall: Orcadian.

Robinson, H. W. (1934). First nesting of Leach's Fork-tailed Petrel in Orkney. *Scot. Nat. for 1930* 93.

Rose, F. E. N. (1975). A note on the Orkney Vole. In *The Natural Environment of Orkney*: 29–30. Goodier, R. (ed.), Edinburgh: Nature Conservancy Council.

Rosie, J. H. (1976). Some notes on the macrolepidoptera of Caithness. *Ent. Gaz.* 27:13–26.

Ryder, M. L. (1983). *Sheep & Man*. London: Duckworth.

Ryder, M. L., Land, R. B. & Ditchburn, R. (1974). Coat colour inheritance in Soay, Orkney and Shetland Sheep. *J. Zool. Lond.* 173:477–85.

Saxon, J. (2nd edn, 1975). *The Fossil Fishes of the North of Scotland*. Thurso: Humphries.

Saxton, W. I. & Hopwood, A. T. (1919). On a Scandinavian erratic from the Orkneys. *Geol. Mag.* 56:273–4.

Scarth, G. (1911). The grassland of Orkney: an oecological analysis. *Trans. Bot. Soc. Edin.* 24: 143–63.

Scharf, W. C. & Balfour, E. (1970). Growth and development of nestling Hen Harriers. *Ibis*, 113: 323–329.

Sea Mammal Research Unit (1984). *Interactions between Grey Seals and UK Fisheries*. Cambridge: Natural Environmental Research Council.

Seaward, M. R. D. & Hitch, C. J. B. (1982). *Atlas of the Lichens of the British Isles*. Huntingdon: Biological Records Centre.

Senior, W. H. & Swan, W. B. (1972). *Survey of Agriculture in Caithness, Orkney and Shetland*. Special Report No. 8. Inverness: Highland Development Board.

Shaw, F. J. (1980). *The Northern and Western Islands of Scotland*. Edinburgh: John Donald.

Shearer, J., Groundwater, W. & Mackay, J. D. (1966). *The New Orkney Book*. London: Nelson.

Sheldrick, M. C. (1976). Trends in the strandings of Cetacea on the British coasts. *Mammal Rev.* 6: 15–23.

Shetelig, H. (1940). *Viking Antiquities in Great Britain and Ireland*. Oslo: Ascheoug.

Shirreff, J. A. (1814). *A General View of the Agriculture of the Orkney Islands*. Edinburgh.

Sibbald, R. (1711). *The Description of the Isles of Orkney and Zetland*. Edinburgh.

Sinclair, J. (1950). The marine algae of Stronsay. *Notes from R. Bot. Garden* 20:160–79.

Skene, A. (1984). Marine Mollusca recording. *Bull. Orkney Fld Club* No. 2:17–19.

Slater, P. J. B. & Ince, S. A. (1979). Cultural evolution in Chaffinch song. *Behaviour* 71:146–66.

Small, A. (1968). The historical geography of the Norse Viking colonization of the Scottish Highlands. *Norsk geogr. Tidsskr*, 22:1–16.

Smith, E. A. (1966). A review of the world's Grey Seal population. *J. Zool., Lond.* 150:463–89.

Smith, K. & Smith, V. (1983). *A Bibliography of the Entomology of the Smaller British Offshore Islands*. Faringdon: Classey.

South, R. (1888). Distribution of lepidoptera in the Outer Hebrides, Orkney, and Shetland. *Entomologist* 21:28–30; 98–9.

Spence, D. H. N. (1974). Sub-arctic debris and scrub vegetation in Shetland. In *The Natural Environment of Shetland*: 73–88. Goodier, R. (ed.). Edinburgh: Nature Conservancy Council.

Spence, D. H. N. (1979). *Shetland's Living Landscape: a Study in Island Plant Ecology*. Lerwick: Thuleprint.

Spence, M. (1914). *Flora Orcadensis*. Stromness: Spence.

Spence, P. F. (1981). An eye-witness account of the division of the Birsay Commons. *Orkney Heritage* 1:92–8.

Steavenson, A. G. (1928). The geology of Stronsay Parish, Orkney. *Proc. Orkney nat. Hist. Soc.* 1–19.

Steers, J. A. (1953). *The Sea Coast*. London: Collins New Naturalist.

Summers, C. F. (1978). Trends in the size of British Grey Seal populations. *J. appl. Ecol.* 15:395–400.

Summers, C. F., Bonner, W. N. & Van Haaften, J. (1978). Changes in the seal populations of the North Sea. *Rapp. P.-v. Réun. Couns. int. Explor. Mer.* 172:278–85.

Surtees, M. J. (1976). The spiders of Hoy. *Bull. Orkney Fld Club* No. 2:11–12.

Sutcliffe, D. W. (1974). On *Gammarus* from freshwaters in the islands of Orkney and Shetland. *Crustaceana* 27:109–11.

Sutherland, D. (1966). *Against the Wind*. London: Heinemann.

Tait, J. B. (1937). The surface water drift in the northern and middle areas of the North Sea and in the Faroe–Shetland Channel. *Sci. Invest. Fish. Scot. for 1937*, No. 1.

Tait, W. S. (1936). Farming in a bygone day. *J. Orkney agric. Discussion Soc.* 11:13–18.

Tay & Orkney Ringing Groups (1984). *The Shorebirds of the Orkney Islands*. Perth: Tay Ringing Group.

Thomas, F. W. L. (1884). What is a pennyland? *Proc. Soc. Ant. Scot.* 18:253–85.

Thomson, G. (1980). *The Other Orkney Book*. Edinburgh: Northabout.

Thomson, W. P. L. (1981). *The Little General and the Rousay Crofters*. Edinburgh: John Donald.

Thomson, W. P. L. (1983). *Kelp-Making in Orkney*. Stromness: the Orkney Press.

Thomson, W. P. L. (1985). Settlement and identity. In *The People of Orkney*: Berry, R. J. (ed.), Stromness: Orkney Press.

Tickell, W. L. N. (1970). The exploitation and conservation of the Common Seal (*Phoca vitulina*) in Shetland. *Biol. Conservation* 2:179–84.

Tomison, J. (1904). Sule Skerry, Orkney and its bird life. *Ann. Scot. nat. Hist. for 1904*: 16–98.

Tomlin, J. R. le B. (1937). Orkney land and freshwater shells. *J. Conchol.* 20:341.

Traill, G. W. (1890). The marine algae of the Orkney Islands. *Trans. Proc. bot. Soc. Edin.* 18:302–42.

Traill, G. W. (1892). Supplementary notes on the marine algae of the Orkney Islands. *Trans. Proc. bot. Soc. Edin.* 19:544–6.

Traill, G. W. (1895). Supplementary notes (number 2) on the marine algae of the Orkney Islands. *Trans. Proc. bot. Soc. Edin.*, 20:341–5.

Traill, J. W. H. (1869). Notes on the Lepidoptera of Orkney. *Entomologist* 4:197–200.

Traill, J. W. H. (1888). The lepidoptera of the Outer Hebrides, Orkney and Shetland. *Scot. Nat.* 8:298–304.

Traill, J. W. H. (1889). The Peronosporeae of Orkney. *Scot. Nat.* 10:30–32.

Traill, J. W. H. (1890). Revision of the Uredineae and the Ustilagineae of Scotland. *Scot. Nat.* 10:302–27.

Traill, T. S. (1806). Observations chiefly mineralogical on the Shetland Islands made in the course of a tour through these islands in 1803. *Nicholson's J.* 15:353–67.

Traill, T. S. (1830). Orkney Islands. In *Brewster's Edinburgh Encyclopaedia*. Edinburgh.

Traill, W. (1868). On submarine forests and other remains of indigenous wood in Orkney. *Trans. bot. Soc. Edin.* 9:146.

Trowbridge, R. & Heppleston, P. B. (1984). Lochs Harray and Stenness, Orkney: their salinity and associated invertebrate fauna in 1936 and 1978. *Scot. Nat.* (in press).

Tudor, J. R. (1883). *The Orkneys and Shetland: their past and present state*. London: Stanford.

Tulloch, R. J. (1978). *A Guide to Shetland Mammals*. Lerwick: Shetland Times.

Tulloch, R. & Hunter, F. (1972). *Guide to Shetland Birds*. Lerwick: Shetland Times.

Turner, D. T. L. (1965). A contribution to the ecology and taxonomy of *Microtus arvalis* on the island of Westray, Orkney. *Proc. zool. Soc.*, Lond. 144:143–50.

Vaughan, R. W. (1969). Grey Seal numbers in Orkney. *Bull. Mamm. Soc. Br. Is.* No. 32:11–15.

Vaughan, R. W. (1975). Seals in Orkney. In *Natural Environment of Orkney*. 95–97. Goodier, R. (ed.). Edinburgh: Nature Conservancy Council.

Vaughan, R. W. (1977). A review of the status of the Common Seal, *Phoca vitulina*, in Scotland. *I.C.E.S. Marine Mammals Committee* 18:1–5.

Venables, L. S. V. & Venables, U. M. (1955). *Birds and Mammals of Shetland*. Edinburgh & London: Oliver & Boyd.

Wainwright, F. T. (ed.) (1955). *The Problem of the Picts*. Edinburgh & London: Nelson.

Wainwright, F. T. (ed.) (1962). *The Northern Isles*. Edinburgh & London: Nelson.

Walker, F. T. (1950). Sublittoral seaweed survey of the Orkney Islands. *J. Ecol.* 38:139–45.

Wallace, J. (1693). *A Description of the Isles of Orkney*. Edinburgh.

Wallace, J. (1700). *An Account of the Islands of Orkney*. London: Tonson.

Wanless, S., French, D. D., Harris, M. P. & Langslow, D. R. (1982). Detection of annual changes in the number of cliff-nesting seabirds in Orkney 1976–1980. *J. anim. Ecol. 51*, 785–795.

Waterston, J. (1903). Mollusca observed at Stromness, Orkney. *Ann. Scot. nat. Hist.* for 1903: 52–3.

Watson, D. M. S. (1932). On three new species of fish from the Old Red Sandstone of Orkney and Shetland. *Mem. geol. Surv. Summ. Prog.* for 1931, part 2: 157–66.

Watson, A. D. (1977). *The Hen Harrier*. Berkhamsted: Poyser.

Watson, H. (1978). *Coastal Otters in Shetland*. Privately printed.

Watts, A. B. (1971). Geophysical investigations on the continental shelf and slope north of Scotland. *Scot. J. Geol.* 7:189–218.

West, J. F. (1972). *Faroe: the Emergence of a Nation*. London: Hurst.

West, W. & West, G. S. (1905). Freshwater algae from the Orkneys and Shetlands. *Trans. Bot. Soc. Edin.* 23:3–41.

White, F. B. (1882). The Lepidoptera of Orkney, Shetland and the Outer Hebrides. *Scot. Nat.* 2: 289–91; 337–44.

Wiener, G., Suttle, N. F., Field, A. C., Herbert, J. G. D. & Williams, J. A. (1978). Breed differences in copper metabolism in sheep. *J. agric. Sci, Camb.* 91:433–41.

Wilkinson, M. (1975). The marine algae of Orkney. *Brit. phycol. J.*

Williamson, K. (1948). *The Atlantic Islands*. London: Collins.

Williamson, K. (1965). *Fair Isle and its Birds*. Edinburgh & London: Oliver & Boyd.

Williamson, M. H. (1981). *Island Populations*. Oxford: University Press.

Willis, D. P. (1983). *Moorland and Shore. Their place in the human geography of old Orkney*. O'Dell Memorial Monogr. No. 14. Aberdeen: Dept. Geography.

Wilson, G. V., Edwards, W., Knox, J., Jones, R. C. B. & Stephens, J. V. (1935). *The Geology of the Orkneys. Mem. geol. Surv. GB.*

Wilson, G. V., & Knox, J. (1936). The geology of the Orkney and Shetland Islands. *Proc. Geol. Ass.* 47:270–82.

Wilson, M. (1934). The distribution of the Uredineae in Scotland. *Trans. bot. Soc. Edin.* 31:345–49.

Winchworth, R. (1920). Giant race of *Cardium edule*. *J. Conchol.* 26:569.

Withrington, D. J. & Grant, I. R. (eds) (1978). *The Statistical Account of Scotland 1791–1799*. Vol. XIX. *Orkney & Shetland*. Wakefield: E.P. Publishing.

Wood, R. D. & Imahori, K. (1965). *A Revision of the Characeae*. Weinheim: J. Cramer.

Wright Smith, W. & Fletcher, H. R. (1942). Genus *Primula*: section Farinosae. *Trans. R. Soc. Edin.* 61:1–69.

Young, D. (1985). Agriculture. In *The Soils of Orkney*. Dry, F. T. (ed.) Aberdeen: Macaulay Institute.

Zimmermann, K. (1959). Über eine Kreuzung von Unterarten der Feldmans *Microtus arvalis*. *Zool. Jb. (Syst.)* 87:1–12.

Appendices

This Appendix contains lists of all the species recorded in Orkney for all the groups which have been relatively well studied in the islands. There is little point in listing species from groups which have not been intensively collected. For example, the national Biological Records Centre holds records of the occurrence in Orkney of only five species of millipedes, one centipede, one dermapteran (the common Earwig, *Forficula auricularia*), three cladocerans, one copepod, and five isopods. On the other hand, it may be true that only five species of Dragonflies are found in Orkney (p. 264). Notwithstanding, it has to be recognized that the lists that follow vary greatly in their completeness. This is especially true of the invertebrates. It is to be hoped that their inclusion (and perhaps even more, those taxa which are not included) will stimulate efforts to fill the gaps.

Most of the tables have been compiled by specialists in the different groups. They are acknowledged at the head of each section. Each group follows an arrangement conventional to it. In drawing together this information, it is a pleasure to acknowledge the help of Mr Paul Harding and the staff of the Biological Records Centre at the Monks Wood Experimental Station of the Institute of Terrestrial Ecology, Huntingdon. It is worth noting also that an index of published Scottish insect records is maintained at the Royal Scottish Museum in Edinburgh.

MYXOMYCETES

This list is based on the *Provisional Atlas of the Myxomycetes of the British Isles* (Ing, 1982), which was designed to illustrate a number of points about the distribution of the group. It should not, therefore, be taken to be a complete list of Orkney species.

Arcyria cinerea (Bull.) Pers. A common and widespread species found on mossy, rotten logs and the bark of living trees.

A. denudata (L.) Wettst. A common species found on well rotted logs.

A. ferruginea Sauter. An uncommon species found on dead wood.

A. incarnata (Pers.) Pers. A very common species of broad-leaved woodland.

A. minuta Buchet. An uncommon species.

A. obvelata (Oeder) Onsberg. A common and conspicuous species, found in summer, often in exposed places.

A. oerstedtii Rost. An uncommon but conspicuous species, rare in the north.

A. pomiformis (Leers) Rost. A common species on sticks of oak and bark of living trees.

Badhamia utricularis (Bull.) Berk. A common and familiar species found on *Stereum* and similar fungi on logs of broad-leaved trees.

B. versicolor A.List. A rare species found on mossy bark of living trees.

Ceratiomyxa fruticulosa (Mull.) Macbr. A common species, especially in wet summer, on very rotten wood.

Comatricha nigra (Pers.) Schroet. Ubiquitous on all kinds of dead wood.

Craterium minutum (Leers) Fr. Common litter species.

Cribraria argillacea (Pers.) Pers. More or less confined to coniferous woodland.

C. cancellata (Batsch) Nann.-Brem. Largely confined to coniferous woodland.

Diderma chondrioderma (*de Bary & Rost.*) G. List. A rare species of mossy bark of living trees.

Didymium difforme (Pers.) S.F. Fray. Widespread species of soil and litter.

D. squamulosum (Alb. & Schw.) Fr. Widespread and abundant species of all kinds of litter.

Echinostelium minutum de Bary. Common and widespread species on the bark of living trees.

Enerthenema papillatum (Pers.) Rost. Common species of both rotting wood and the bark of living trees.

Enteridium lycoperdon (Bull.) Found in spring on many kinds of rotten wood.

Hemitrichia minor G. List. Uncommon species associated with liverworts on the bark of living trees.

Lamproderma scintillans (Berk & Br.) Morg. Common species characteristic of holly litter.

Licea minima Fr. Widespread species on bark of living trees.

L. parastica (Zukal) Martin. Widespread corticolous species.

L. variabilis Shrad. More or less confined to small conifer sticks.

Lycogala epidendrum (L.) Fr. Widespread and very common.

Mucilago crustacea Wiggers. Characteristic of grassland on chalk and limestone; rarely found on lime-deficient soils.

Paradiacheopsis fimbriata (G. List & Cram.) Hertel. Common bark species.

P. solitaria (Nann.-Brem.) Nann.-Brem. On bark, often with mosses and lichens.

Perichaena corticalis (Batsch) Rost. Characteristic of mossy bark on fallen trees.

P. depressa Libert. Southern species; only three Scottish records.

Physarum crateriforme Petch. Rare species found on bark of living trees in the north and west.

P. leucophaeum Fr. Common and widespread species.

P. nutans Pers. Common and widespread on all kinds of dead wood.

P. pusillum (Berk. & Curt.) G. List. Widespread.

Stemonitis axifera (Bull.) Macbr. Common species, especially on well rotted logs.

S. flavogenita Jahn. Common.

S. fusca Roth. Abundant species of rotting logs and stumps.

S. typhina (Wiggers) Nann.-Brem. Common on very rotten logs.

Trichia contorta (Ditm.) Rost. Widespread species on dead wood and sticks.

T. decipiens (Pers.) Macbr. Very common on all kinds of dead wood.

T. flavicoma (A. List) B. Ing. Leaf litter, mainly southern species.

T. floriformis (Schw.) G. List. On all kinds of dead wood; a very abundant species.

T. persimilis Karst. Common on rotten logs that are still firm.

T. scabra Rost. On rotten logs; commoner in the south of Britain than in the north.

T. varia (Pers.) Pers. Abundant on dead wood, especially if rather damp.

FUNGI
(based on Dennis, 1972)

Ironically, the true fungi have been less well studied than the myxomycetes. Certainly the Orkney fungi are under-recorded. The following list (based on collections made by Dr R. W. G. Dennis of the Royal Botanic Gardens, Kew and including earlier records from J. W. H. Traill (1889, 1880) and M. Wilson (1934) contains only about 70 species although Moller (1945, 1958) catalogues 547 species from Faroe.

Chytridiales

Synchytrium taraxaci de By. & Wor. on *Taraxacum*. Finstown and South End, Stromness.

Peronsporales

Albugo lepigoni Kze. on *Spergularia media*, Egilsay.

Peronospora alsinearum Casp. (*P. media* Gaum), on *Stellaria media*, Brough of Deerness; St Magnus, Egilsay.

Peronospora fulva Syd. on *Lathyrus pratensis*, Egilsay and Wyre.

Peronospora minor (Casp.) Gaum. on *Atriplex* seedlings, Kirkwall. It was probably this which Traill recorded under the collective name *P. effusa* on *A. babingtonii* from Stromness, Bay of Firth and Orphir.

Peronospora radii de By. recorded by Traill on *Chrysanthemum segetum* from three localities in Orkney.

Peronospora ranunculi Gaum. Curwell Hill Cairn; between north pier and the Dwarfie Stane, Hoy;

Wyre, and by Traill, as *P. ficariae* Tul. on *R. repens* at Birsay.

Peronospora rumicis Cda. Trail recorded *P. rumicis* on *Polygonum aviculare* in Orkney but this would now be regarded as a distinct species, *P. polygoni* Thuem.

Peronospora trifolii-repentis Syd. on *Trifolium repens*, Curwell Hill Cairn; Wyre.

Plasmopara densa (Rab.) Schroet. on *Rhinanthus minor*, Egilsay.

Agaricales

Agaricus campester L. ex Fr. pasture at the Broch of Gurness, Aikerness.

Aphyllophorales

Cyphella cf *orthospora* (Bourd. & Galz.) on *Ulex europeaus*, Banks, Rousay.

Pellidiscus pallidus (Berk. & Br.) Donk, on *Ulex europaeus*, Banks, Rousay.

Ustilaginales

Ustilago violacea (Pers.) Roussel on *Lychnis flos-cuculi*, Head of Work.

Uredinales

Puccinia acetosae Kornicke, on *Rumex acetosa*, Wyre.

Puccinia calthae Link, on *Caltha palustris*, Wyre, recorded by Traill.

Puccinia cnici Mart. on *Cirsium vulgare*, Head of

Work, Egilsay; recorded from Burray by Wilson (1934).

Puccinia dioica Magn. in *Cirsium palustre*, Wideford Hill; north end of Hoy; south shore of Rousay; recorded by Traill.

Puccinia glomerata Grev. on *Senecio aquaticus*, Egilsay.

Puccinia galii-verni Ces. listed by Traill as *P. valantiae* Pers.

Puccinia hieracii var. *hypochaeridis* (Oud.) Jørst, on *Hypochaeris radicata*, Ring of Brogar; *P. hieraccii* var. *hieracii* was recorded by Traill.

Puccinia obscura Svhroet, on *Bellis perrenis*, Egilsay; on *Luzula sylvatica* between north pier and the Dwarfie Stane, Hoy; recorded by Wilson (1934) and it was probably this that Traill had from Orkney under the name *O. oblongata* Wint.

Puccinia poae-nemoralis Otth. on *Arrhenatherum elatius*, south coast of Rousay; on *Anthoxanthum odoratum* Egilsay; on *Agrostis canina*, Egilsay.

Puccinia poarum Niels, on *Tussilago farfara*, Wideford Hill; north end of Hoy; Wyre; recorded by Traill.

Puccinia primulae Duby, on *Primula vulgaris*, roadside near Dwarfie Stane, Hoy.

Puccinia punctata Link, on *Galium verum*, Skaill Bay.

Puccinia punctiformis (Str.) Röhl. on *Cirsium arvense*, north end of Hoy; Rousay; Egilsay and Wyre; recorded by Wilson (1934).

Puccinia recondita Rob. & Desm. on *Holcus*, Wyre; recorded as *P. holcina* Erikss. by Wilson (1934).

Puccinia variabilis Grev. on *Taraxacum*, Taiverso Tuick, Rousay; recorded by Traill.

Puccinia violae DC. on *Viola* sp. road to the Dwarfie Stane, Hoy.

Trachyspora intrusa (Grev.) Arth. on *Alchemilla* sp. Banks, Rousay; listed by Traill.

Uromyces acetosae Schroet., on *Rumex acetosa*, road to the Dwarfie Stane, Hoy.

Uromyces anthyllidis Schroet, on *Anthyllis vulneraria*, Egilsay; recorded by Wilson (1934).

Uromyces armeriae Kickx, on *Armeria maritima*, Brough of Birsay; Brough of Deerness; Egilsay.

Uromyces nerviphilus (Grogn.) Hots. on *Trifolium repens*, north end of Hoy; Egilsay.

Uromyces poae Rabh. on *Poa trivialis*, Egilsay; recorded by Wilson (1934).

Protomycetales

Taphridium umbelliferarum (Rostr.) Lag. & Juel. on *Heracleum sphondylium*; north end of Hoy; Egilsay.

Perizales

Ascobolus albidus Crouan, on rabbit droppings, Brough of Deerness; recorded by Traill as *A. glaber*.

Ascobolus stictoideus Speg., on rabbit dropping, Brough of Deerness.

Ascophanus aurora (Crouan) Boudier, on rabbit dropping, Brough of Deerness.

Lasiobolus ciliatus (Schmidt ex Fr.) Boudier, recorded by Traill.

Rhyparobius pachyascus Zukal, on rabbit droppings, Brough of Deerness.

Heliotiales

Dasyscyphus diminutus (Rob.) Sacc., on *Juncus* sp., road to the Dwarfie Stane, Hoy.

Hysteropezizella prahliana (Jaap) Nannf., on *Ammophila arenaria*, Egilsay.

Phaeangellina empetri (Phill.) Dennis, on *Empetrum* sp., Brough of Deerness; the type came from Orkney, August 1888.

Phialea cyathoidea (Bull. ex. Mérat) Gillet; recorded by Traill.

Pseudopeziza trifolii (Biv., Bern.) Fuckel, on *Trifolium pratense*, Egilsay.

Sphaeriales

Endodothella junci (Fr.) Theiss. & Syd. on *Juncus* sp., north end of Hoy.

Phyllachora silvatica Sacc. & Speg. on *Festuca rubra*, Brough of Birsay.

Plagiospaera immersa (Trail) Petrak, on *Urtica dioica*, Egilsay.

Podospora minuta (Fuckel) Niessl., Brough of Deerness.

Pgdospora tetraspora (Wint.) Cain, on rabbit droppings, Brough of Deerness.

Plectascales

Erysiphe cichoracearum DC. ex Mérat, on *Plantago maritima*, Kirkwall.

Eryiphe graminis DC. ex Mérat, on *Agropyron repens*, Egilsay.

Sphaeronemella fimicola Marchal, on rabbit droppings, Brough of Deerness.

Pleosporales

Leptosphaeria (Phaeosphaeria) litoralis Sacc. on *Ammophila arenaria*, Egilsay.

Leptosphaeria culmorum Auersw. on *Ammophila arenaria*, Egilsay.

Ophiobolus erythrosporus (Reiss) Wint, on *Urtica dioica*, Egilsay.

Sporormia australis Speg. on rabbit droppings, Brough of Deerness.

Sporormia intermedia Auersw. on rabbit droppings, Brough of Deerness.

Venturia rumicis (Desm.) Wint., on *Rumex* sp., north end of Hoy.

Spaeropsidales

Dilophospora alopecuri (Fr.) Fr. on *Holcus lanatus*, south coast of Rousay.
Septoria nodorum Berk., on *Ammophila arenaria*, Egilsay.
Septoria oxyspora Penz. & Sacc. on *Dactylis glomerata*, Egilsay.

Moniliales

Fusarium avenaceum (Fr.) Sacc. on *Deschampsia caespitosa*, Egilsay.
Isariopsis carnea Oud. on *Lathyrus pratensis*, Egilsay.
Ovularia decipiens Sacc. on *Ranunculus acris*, Wyre.

Ovularia obliqua (Cke.) Oud. on *Rumex* sp. Wyre.
Ovularia primulana Karst., on *Primula vulgaris*, road to the Dwarfie Stane, Hoy; south coast of Rousay.
Passalora graminis (Fuckel) von Höhnel, on *Glyceria fluitans*, Wyre.
Ramularia alborosella (Desm.) Gjaerum, on *Cerastium holosteoides*, Wyre.
Ramularia calthea (Erikss.) Lindr., on *Caltha palustris*, road to the Dwarfie Stane, Hoy; Wyre.
Ramularia heraclei (Oud.) Sacc., on *Heracleum sphondylium*, Egilsay.
Ramularia pratensis Sacc., on *Rumex acetosa*, road to the Dwarfie Stane, Hoy.

MARINE ALGAE
(based on Wilkinson, 1975)

A comprehensive list of marine algae recorded from Shetland has been compiled by David Irvine (in Berry & Johnston, 1980). In it he noted that 'several southern species appear to come no further north than the Orkneys, for instance *Bostrychia scorpioides* and *Nemalion helminthoides*'. The following table lists species collected during a visit of the British Phycological Society to Orkney in 1973, when 45 species not previously recorded in the county were found. Earlier accounts of Orkney marine algae are given by Traill (1891, 1893, 1895), Lyle (1929), Dunn (1937) and Sinclair (1950).

Chlorophyceae

Acrosiphonia arcta (Dillw.) J. Ag.
eulittoral, in pools.
Blidingia minima (Nag. ex Kütz.) Kylin.
littoral fringe.
Bolbocoleon piliferum N. Pringsh.
sublittoral; in *Laminaria digitata*, *L. saccharina*, *Dumontia incrassata* and *Asperococcus* sp.
Bryopsis hypnoides Lamour.
eulittoral, in pools.
B. plumosa (Huds.) C. Ag. eulittoral, in pools.
Capsosiphon fulvescens (C. Ag.) Setch. et Gardn.
Chaetomorpha capillaris (Kütz.) Børg.
eulittoral, rocks, pools and mud.
C. linum (O. F. Müll.) Kütz.
eulittoral, rocks, pools and mud.
C. melagonium (Web. et Mohr) Kütz.
eulittoral, in pools.
Chara sp.
brackish loch.
Chlorochytrium cohnii Wright.
eulittoral; in tubes of *Schnizonema*.
C. inclusum Kjellm.
eulittoral.

C. willwi Printz
littoral fringe; in *Blidingia minima*.
Cladophora aegagropila (L.) Rabenh.
brackish loch.
C. albida (Huds.) Kütz.
eulittoral.
C. dalmatica Kütz.
eulittoral.
C. laetevirens (Dillw.) Kütz.
eulittoral.
C. rupestris (L.) Kütz.
eulittoral, rocks and pools, sublittoral.
C. sericea (Huds.) Kütz.
eulittoral, in pools.
Codiolum phases.
eulittoral, sublittoral; in mollusc shells.
Codium fragile (Sur.) Hariot subsp. *atlanticum* (Cotton) Silva
eulittoral, in pools.
Codium fragile (Sur.) Hariot subsp. *tomentosoides* (Goor) Silva
eulittoral, in pools.
Enteromorpha clathrata (Roth) Grev.
eulittoral.
E. flexuosa (Wulf. ex Roth) J. Ag.
eulittoral.
E. intestinalis (L.) Link
eulittoral.
E. linza (L.) J. Ag.
eulittoral.
E. prolifera (O. F. Müll.) J. Ag.
eulittoral.
E. ralfsii Harv.
eulittoral.
E. ramulosa (Sm.) Hook.
eulittoral.
Entocladia perforans (Huber) Levr.
eulittoral; in mollusc shells.
E. viridis Reinke.
eulittoral.

Epicladia flustrae Reinke
eulittoral; in hydroids.
Eugomontia sacculata Kornm.
sublittoral; in mollusc shells.
Monostroma oxyspermum (Kütz.) Doty.
eulittoral, in pools.
Percursaria percursa (C. Ag.) Rosenv.
eulittoral.
Prasiola stipitata Suhr in Jessen
littoral fringe.
Pringsheimiella scutata (Reinke) Marchew.
eulittoral; on *Codium*.
Rhizoclonium implexum (Dillw.) Kütz.
eulittoral, pools, mud and salt-marsh.
R. riparium (Roth) Harv.
eulittoral, rocks, pools, mud and salt-marsh.
Rosenvingiella polyrhiza (Rosenv.) Silva
eulittoral.
Spirogyra sp.
brackish loch.
Spongomorpha aeruginosa (L.) Hoek
eulittoral.
Tellamia intricata Batt.
eulittoral; in shells of *Littorina littoralis*.
Ulva lactuca L.
eulittoral.
U. rigida (C. Ag.) Thur.
eulittoral.

Phaeophyceae

Acrothrix gracilis Kylin.
eulittoral.
Alaria esculenta (L.) Grev.
eulittoral, sublittoral; in exposed positions.
Ascophyllum nodosum (L.) Le Jol.
eulittoral.
Asperococcus compressus Griff. ex Hook.
eulittoral.
A. fistulosus (Huds.) Hook.
eulittoral; on rocks and various algae.
A. turneri (Sm.) Hook.
drift.
Chorda filum (L.) Stackh.
eulittoral, sublittoral.
Chordaria flagelliformis (O. F. Müll.) C. Ag.
eulittoral.
Cladostephus spongiosus (Huds.) C. Ag.
eulittoral.
C. spongiosus f. *verticillatus* (Lightf.) C. Ag.
eulittoral.
Colpomenia peregrina Sauv.
eulittoral.
Cylindrocarpus berkeleyii (Grev. in Berk.) Crouan frat.
eulittoral; on *Ralfsia*.
Desmarestia aculeata (L.) Lamour.
drift.

D. ligulata (Lightf.) Lamour.
drift.
D. viridis (O. F. Müll.) Lamour.
eulittoral.
Dictosiphon foeniculaceus (Huds.) Grev.
eulittoral.
D. chordaria Aresch.
eulittoral.
Dictyota dichotoma (Huds.) Lamour.
eulittoral.
Ectocarpus fasciculatus Harv.
eulittoral; on *Himanthalia* and *Laminaria*.
E. siliculosus (Dillw.) Lyngb.
eulittoral; on *Chorda, Himanthalia* and *Scytosiphon*.
Elachista flaccida (Dillw.) Aresch.
eulittoral; on *Halidrys siliquosa*.
E. fucicola (Vell.) Aresch.
eulittoral; on *Asperococcus, Fucus* and *Himanthalia*
E. scutulata (Sm.) Aresch.
eulittoral; on *Himanthalia*.
Endodictyon infestans Gran
eulittoral; in hydroids.
Eudesme virescens (Carm. ex Harv. in Hook.) J. Ag.
eulittoral.
Feldmannia simplex (Crouan frat.) Hamel
eulittoral; on *Codium*.
Fucus ceranoides L.
eulittoral; in channels flowing with fresh water; fertile.
F. distichus L. subsp. *anceps* (Harv. et Ward ex Carr.) Powell
eulittoral, rocks on exposed shore; fertile.
F. serratus L.
eulittoral; fertile.
F. spiralis L.
eulittoral; fertile.
F. vesiculosus L.
eulittoral; fertile.
Giffordia granulosa (Sm.) Hamel
eulittoral.
Halidrys siliquosa (L.) Lyngb.
eulittoral.
Himanthalia elongata (L.) S. F. Gray.
eulittoral.
Laminaria digitata (Huds.) Lamour.
eulittoral, sublittoral.
L. hyperborea (Gunn.) Fosl.
sublittoral.
L. saccharina (L.) Lamour.
sublittoral.
Leathesia difformis (L.) Aresch.
eulittoral.
Litosiphon laminariae (Lyngb.) Harv.
eulittoral; on *Alaria esculenta*.
L. pusillus (Carm. ex Hook.) Harv.
eulittoral; on *Chorda filum*.

Mesogloia lanosa Crouan frat.
eulittoral.
M. vermiculata (Sm.) S. F. Gray.
eulittoral.
Microspongium globosum Reinke.
eulittoral; on *Enteromorpha* and *Asperococcus*.
Myrionema strangulans Grev.
eulittoral; on *Enteromorpha* and *Ulva*.
Myriotrichia filiformis Harv.
eulittoral; on *Asperococcus* and *Litosiphon*.
Pelvetia canaliculata (L.) Dcne et Thur.
eulittoral; fertile.
Petalonia fascia (O. F. Müll.) Kuntze.
eulittoral.
P. zosterifolia (Reinke) Kuntze.
eulittoral.
Pilayella littoralis (L.) Kjellm.
eulittoral; on various algae.
P. littoralis var. *varia* Kjellm.
eulittoral; on *Scytosiphon*.
Protectocarpus speciosus (Børg.) Kuck.
eulittoral; on *Laminaria*.
Ralfsia clavata (Harv. in Hook.) Crouan frat.
eulittoral; on rocks and on *Patella*.
R. verrucosa (Aresch) J. Ag.
eulittoral.
Saccorhiza polyschides (Lightf.) Batt.
sublittoral.
Sauvageaugloia griffithsianus (Grev. ex Harv. in Hook.) Hamel ex Kylin.
eulittoral.
Scytosiphon lomentaria (Lyngb.) Link
eulittoral.
Spermatochnus paradoxus (Roth.) Kütz.
eulittoral.
Sphacelaria bipinnata (Kütz.) Sauv.
eulittoral; on *Halidrys siliquosa*.
S. britannica Sauv.
eulittoral, salt marsh.
S. cirrosa (Roth.) C. Ag.
eulittoral.
S. fusca (Huds.) C. Ag.
eulittoral; on *Corallina officinalis*.
S. radicans (Dillw.) C. Ag.
eulittoral.
Spongonema tomentosum (Huds.) Kütz.
eulittoral; on various algae.
Stictyosiphon tortilis (Rupr.) Reinke
eulittoral.
Ulonema rhizophorum Fosl.
eulittoral; on *Dumontia incrassata*.

Rhodophyceae

Acrochaetium alariae (Jónss.) Born.
eulittoral.
A. daviesii (Dillw.) Näg.

eulittoral; on *Rhodymenia palmata*.
A. secundatum (Lyngb.) Näg.
eulittoral; on *Porphyra umbilicalis*.
Ahnfeltia plicata (Huds.) Fries
eulittoral.
Apoglossum ruscifolium (Turn.) J. Ag.
drift.
Asparagopsis armata Harv. (*Falkenbergia* phase)
eulittoral; on rocks and on *Halidrys siliquosa*.
Audouinella membranacea (Magn.) Papenf.
eulittoral; in hydroids.
Bonnemaisonia asparagoides (Woodw.) C. Ag.
drift.
B. hamifera Hariot (*Trailliella* phase)
eulittoral; on rocks and other algae.
Bostrychia scorpiodes (Huds.) Mont.
salt-marsh.
Brongniartella byssoides (Good. et Woodw.) C. Ag.
eulittoral, in pools.
Callithamnion arbuscula (Dillw.) Lyngb.
eulittoral; on rocks, *Balanus* and *Mytilus*.
C. granulatum (Ducluz.) C. Ag.
eulittoral.
C. hookeri (Dillw.) S. F. Gray.
eulittoral, rocks.
C. tetragonum (With.) S. F. Gray.
eulittoral, sublittoral; on *Laminaria digitata*.
Callophyllis laciniata (Huds.) Kütz.
eulittoral, rocks.
Catenella repens (Lightf.) Batt.
eulittoral, littoral fringe.
Ceramium ciliatum (Ellis) Ducluz.
eulittoral, rocks.
C. diaphanum Agg.
eulittoral, rocks.
C. rubrum Agg.
eulittoral; on rocks and other algae.
C. shuttleworthianum (Kütz.) Silva.
eulittoral.
Chondrus crispus Stackh.
eulittoral.
Chylocladia verticillata (Lightf.) Bliding.
eulittoral.
Conchocelis phases.
eulittoral; in mollusc shells.
Corallina officinalis L.
eulittoral.
Cryptopleura ramosa (Huds.) Kylin ex Newton.
eulittoral.
Cystoclonium purpureum (Huds.) Batt.
eulittoral.
Delesseria sanguinea (Huds.) Lamour.
eulittoral.
Dilsea carnosa (Schmidel) Kuntze
eulittoral.
Dumontia incrassata (O. F. Müll.) Lamour.
eulittoral.

Erythrotrichia boryana (Mont.) Berth.
eulittoral; on *Porphyra leucosticta*.
E. carnea (Dillw.) J. Ag.
eulittoral; on various algae.
Erythrocladia irregularis Rosenv.
eulittoral; on *Cladophora rupestris* and *Bryopsis plumosa*.
Fosliella sp.
eulittoral.
Furcellaria fastigiata (L.) Lamour.
eulittoral.
Gelidium crinale Agg.
eulittoral.
Gigartina stellata (Stackh.) Batt.
eulittoral.
Heterosiphonia plumosa (Ellis) Batt.
drift.
Hildenbrandia protypus Nardo.
eulittoral.
Laurencia hybrida (DC.) Lenorm. ex Duby.
eulittoral.
L. pinnatifida (Huds.) Lamour.
eulittoral.
Lithothamnion glaciale Kjellm.
eulittoral.
Lomentaria articulata (Huds.) Lyngb.
eulittoral.
L. clavellosa (Turn.) Gaill.
eulittoral.
L. orcadensis (Harv.) Coll. ex Taylor.
eulittoral; on sponge.
Membranoptera alata (Huds.) Stackh.
eulittoral.
Nemalion helminthoides (Vell. in With.) Batt.
eulittoral; on *Patella* in exposed positions.
Nitophyllum bonnemaisonii (C. Ag.) Grev.
eulittoral, sublittoral; on *Laminaria hyperborea*.
N. punctatum (Stackh.) Grev.
drift.
Odonthalia dentata (L.) Lyngb.
eulittoral, in pools.
Palmaria palmata (L.) Stackh.
eulittoral, sublittoral; on *Fucus serratus* and *Laminaria digitata*.
Phycodrys rubens (L.) Batt.
eulittoral; on *Laminaria hyperborea*.
Phyllophora crispa (Huds.) Dixon.
eulittoral.
P. pseudoceranoides (Gmelin) Newroth et A. R. A. Taylor.
eulittoral.
P. traillii Holm. ex Batt.
eulittoral.
P. truncata (Pallas) Zinova.
eulittoral.
Phymatolithon lenormandii (Aresch.) Adey.
eulittoral.

P. polymorphum (L.) Foslie.
eulittoral.
Plocamium cartilagineum (L.) Dixon.
eulittoral.
Plumaria elegans (Bonnem.) Schm.
eulittoral.
Polyoides rotundus (Huds.) Grev.
eulittoral.
Polysiphonia brodiaei (Dillw.) Spreng.
eulittoral, in pools on exposed shores.
P. elongata (Huds.) Spreng.
drift.
P. lanosa (L.) Tandy.
eulittoral; on *Fucus vesiculosus* and *Ascophyllum nodosum*.
P. nigrescens (Huds.) Greb.
eulittoral.
P. urceolata (Lightf. ex Dillw.) Grev.
eulittoral; on rocks and on *Laminaria hyperborea*.
P. violacea (Roth.) Spreng.
eulittoral.
Porphyra leucosticta Thur. in Le Jol.
eulittoral; on *Fucus serratus* and *Gigartina stellata*.
P. miniata (C. Ag.) C. Ag.
drift.
P. umbilicalis (L.) J. Ag.
eulittoral; on *Fucus serratus* and *Gigartina stellata*.
Pterosiphonia parasitica (Huds.) Falkenb.
eulittoral, sublittoral; on *Laminaria hyperborea*.
P. thuyoides (Harv. in Mackay) Schm.
eulittoral.
Ptilota plumosa (Huds.) C. Ag.
eulittoral; on rocks and on *Laminaria hyperborea*.
Rhodochorton floridulum (Dillw.) Näg.
eulittoral, binding sand on rocks.
R. purpureum (Lightf.) Rosenv.
eulittoral, on rocks.
Rhodomela confervoides (Huds.) Silva.
eulittoral.
R. lycopodioides (L.) C. Ag.
eulittoral; on *Laminaria hyperborea*.

Cyanophyceae

Agmenellum thermale (Kütz.) Dr. et D.
salt-marsh.
Anacystis dimidiata (Kütz.) Dr. et D.
salt-marsh.
A. marina (Hansg.) Dr. et D.
salt-marsh.
Calothrix aeruginea Born. et Flah.
salt-marsh.
C. scopulorum Born. et Flah.
littoral fringe, on rocks.
Endophysalis conferta (Kütz.) Dr. et D.
salt-marsh.

E. deusta (Menegh.) Dr. et D.
  salt-marsh; in mollusc shells.
Lyngbya lutea Gom.
  littoral fringe, on rocks.
L. rivularianum Gom.
  on mud in brackish loch.
Microcoleus lyngbyaceus Gom.
  salt-marsh.
M. othonoplastes Gom.
  salt-marsh.
Nodularia harveyana Born. et Flah.
  salt-marsh.
Nostoc sp.
  salt-marsh.
Oscillatoria brevis Gom.
  salt-marsh.
O. nigroviridis Gom.
  salt-marsh.
Phormidium fragile Gom.
  littoral fringe, on rocks.
Plectonema terebrans Gom.
  eulittoral; in mollusc shells.
Rivularia biasolettiana Born. et Flah.
  on mud by brackish loch.
Schizothrix calcicola Gom.
  salt-marsh.
Spirulina subsalsa Gom.
  salt-marsh.

Haptophyceae

Apistonema pyrenigerum Pasch.
  salt-marsh.

Xanthophyceae

Vaucheria arcassonensis P. Dang.
  salt-marsh.
V. coronata Nordst.
  salt-marsh.
V. intermedia Nordst.
  salt-marsh and on mud by brackish loch.
V. subsimplex Crouan frat.
  salt-marsh.
V. synandra Woron.
  on mud by brackish loch.

Dinophyceae

Amphidinium carterae Hulb.
  in sand.
A. herdmanii Kof. et Swezy.
  in sand.
Amphidium spp.
  inshore waters, in sand and harbour.
Ceratium furca (Ehrenb.) Clap. et Lachm.
  inshore waters, harbour.

C. fusus (Ehrenb.) Dujard
  inshore waters, harbour.
C. horridum (Cleve) Gran.
  inshore waters, harbour.
C. lineatum (Ehrenb.) Cleve.
  inshore waters, harbour.
C. longipes (Bail.) Gran.
  inshore waters, harbour.
C. macroceros (Ehrenb.) Vanhoffen.
  inshore waters.
C. tripos (O. F. Müll.) Nitzsch.
  inshore waters, harbour.
Coolia monotis Meun.
  inshore waters.
Dinophysis acuminata Clap. et Lachm.
  inshore waters, harbour.
D. acuta Ehrenb.
  inshore waters.
D. norvegica Clap. et Lachm.
  inshore waters, harbour.
D. rotundata Clap. et. Lachm.
  inshore waters, harbour.
Diplopsalis lenticula Bergh.
  inshore waters.
Glenodinium sp.
  inshore waters.
Gonyaulax digitale (Pouchet) Kof.
  inshore waters, harbour.
G. tamarensis Lebour.
  in harbour.
Gonyaulax spp.
  inshore waters, harbour.
Gymnodinium spp.
  inshore waters, harbour.
Gyrodinium spp.
  inshore waters, harbour, littoral fringe pools.
Hemidinium nasutum Stein.
  in sand, inshore waters.
Katodinium rotundatum (Lohm.) Loeblich III.
  in sand, harbour, inshore waters.
Oblea rotundata (Lebour) Balech.
  inshore waters, harbour.
Oxyrris marina Dujard.
  inshore waters, harbour; littoral fringe pools.
Peridiniopsis asymmetrica Mangin.
  inshore waters.
Peridinium brevipes Pauls.
  inshore waters.
P. cerasus Pauls.
  inshore waters.
P. curtipes Jorg.
  inshore waters.
P. depressum Bail.
  inshore waters, harbour.
P. diabolus Cleve.
  in harbour.

P. leonis Pav.
inshore waters.
P. mite Pav.
harbour.
P. ovatum (Pouchet) Schutt.
inshore waters.
P. pallidum Ostenf.
inshore waters.
P. pellucidum (Bergh) Schutt.
inshore waters, harbour.
P. pyriforme (Pauls.) Pauls.
inshore waters.
P. subinerme Pauls.
harbour.

P. trochoideum (Stein) Lemm.
inshore waters, harbour.
Polykrikos lebourae C. Herdm.
in sand.
P. schwartzii Butschli.
harbour.
Prorocentrum marinum (Cienk.) Dodge et Bibby.
in sand, harbour, inshore waters.
P. micans Ehrenb.
inshore waters, harbour.
Pyrocystis lunula (Schutt) Schutt.
in sand, harbour, inshore waters.
Pyrophacus horologicum Stein.
harbour.

CHARACEAE

(Compiled by Mrs Jenny Moore of the Botany department of the British Museum (Natural History) from the *Provisional Atlas of the Characeae of the British Isles* (Moore & Greene, 1983))

The charophytes (more correctly Characeae) are an unusual group of macroscopic green algae that have been sadly neglected by botanists in recent years. They have been poorly collected so it is not surprising that the status of charophytes in Orkney is less well known now than it was at the time of Henry Halcro Johnston. Johnston made regular collections on many of the islands from 1920–1926, and his herbarium is housed at the British Museum (Natural History). This major contribution along with other collections from the turn of the century and a few sporadic records from the 1930s, 1960s and 1970s form the data base for the Orkney section of the *Provisional Atlas*. The nomenclature used is that of Wood & Imahori (1965) with the more familiar names used by Groves and Bullock-Webster (1920, 1924) added, where appropriate, in parentheses.

Chara canescens Desv. & Lois.
L. Stenness, 1920.
Bay of Voy, L. Stenness, 1926.
Nether Bigging, L. Stenness, 1921.
C. globularis Thuill. (*C. fragilis*)
Standing stones, Stenness, 1881.
L. Harray, 1882.
C. globularis var. *aspera* (Deth. ex Willd.) R. D. Wood (*C. aspera*)
South Dam, Hoy, 1886.
Hoy, 1911.
Mill Dam, Vensilly Hill, South Ronaldsay, 1914.
L. Harray, 1881, 1882, 1936.
Bay of Islands, L. Harray, 1912.
L. Harray, Waterhall, 1925.
L. Harray, Brodgar, 1961.
Stream near the Manse, Harray, 1883.
Kettle hole, Brodgar, 1961.

L. Skaill, 1881, 1888, 1901, 1921, 1973.
L. Stenness, 1973.
Bay of Voy, L. Stenness, 1924.
L. Rango, 1926.
Kirbister L., 1920.
Pond near Mill Dam of Voy, 1886.
Mill Dam of Voy, 1900.
L. Boardhouse, Birsay, 1888, 1913.
L. Ayre, St. Mary's Holm, 1916.
Graemeshall, St. Mary's Holm, 1921.
L. Burness, Westray, 1913.
L. Saintear, Westray, 1913.
L. Swartmill, Westray, 1913.
L. St. Tredwell, Westray, 1913.
C. globularis var. *aspera* f. *curta* (Nolte ex Kütz.) R. D. Wood (*C. desmacantha*)
L. Stenness, 1900, 1920.
L. Harray, 1920,
Mill Dam of Rango, 1925.
Pool at the Loons, Birsay, 1921.
Near Twatt, 1973.
Kirbister, Orphir, 1920.
Loch of the Riv, Burness, Sanday, 1920.
Bardister L., Walls, 1920.
C. globularis var. *virgata* (Kütz.) R. D. Wood (*C. delicatula*)
Rotten Loch, Waas, Hoy, 1913.
Pegal Burn, Hoy, 1931.
Braebuster Burn, Hoy, 1961.
Holm of Wasbuster, L. Harray, 1881.
Brodgar, L. Harray, 1961.
Around islands in L. Harray, 1881.
L. Harray, 1882, 1886, 1900, 1936, 1979.
Reservoir, Stromness, 1925.
Inholm, Stromness, 1912.
Burn of Salta, Stromness, 1912.
Near Stromness, 1900.
In a peat bog near East Bigging, 1964.
L. Boardhouse, 1973.
Burn near Naversdale Loch, Kirbister, 1921.
L. Swannay, Birsay, 1883.
Burn of Sourin, Rousay, 1921.

Berstane St. Ola, 1913.
In pools near standing stones, Stenness, 1881.
Marsh at Cringla Fiold, 1912.
Pool near Hewing Firth, 1926.
C. hispida L.
L. Langamay, Sanday, 1920.
C. hispida var. *baltica* (Bruz.) R. D. Wood (*C. baltica*)
L. Harray, 1936.
L. Stenness, 1900, 1901, 1911.
Bay of Voy, L. Stenness, 1912, 1924.
Nether Bigging, L. Stenness, 1913.
C. vulgaris L.
Bog-pool near the Dwarfie Stone, Hoy, 1886, 1900.
Quarry pool, Quoys, Graemsay, 1924.
Reservoir, Stromness, 1925.
Bog ditch at Brodgar, 1961.
Quarry pool, Odinstone, Shapinsay, 1925.
Fidge, Swanbister, Orphir, 1880.
Quarry pool, Whinpark Gyre, Orphir, 1886.
C. vulgaris var. *vulgaris* f. *contraria* (A. Br. ex Kütz.)
R. D. Wood (*C. contraria*)
L. Harray, Mill of Rango, 1925.
L. Hundland, 1973.
L. Bosquoy, Dounby, 1921.
C. vulgaris var. *vulgaris* f. *hispidula* (A. Br.) R. D.
Wood (*C. contraria* var. *hispidula*)
The Loons, Birsay, 1923.
Orr Shun, Sandwick, 1922.
L. Wasdale, Firth, 1981.
C. vulgaris var. *vulgaris* f. *longibracteata* (Kütz.) H. &
J. Gr. (*C. vulgaris* var. *longibracteata*)
Near Stromness, 1900.
C. vulgaris var. *vulgaris* f. *muscosa* (J. Gr. & Bull.-
Webst.) R. D. Wood (*C. muscosa*)
L. Rango, 1925.
Nitella flexilis (L.) C. A. Ag. (*N. opaca*)
Pool near Rottenloch, Hoy, 1913.
Blind burn, Hoy, 1886.
Pool at Garth Head, South Walls, Hoy, 1913.
Pool between Orgil and Rackwick, Hoy, 1900.
Sandy Loch, Orgil, Hoy, 1900.
East Gairy Loch, South Ronaldsay, 1914.
Stream near Mill of Rango, 1886.
Bog-pool near waterworks, Stromness, 1900.
Bog-pool near the Loons, Stromness, 1914.
Quarry pool, Swanbister, Orphir, 1883.
Pool near Meikle water, Stronsay, 1923.

Tolypella nidifica (O. Müll.) Leonh.
Bay of Voy, L. Stenness, 1926.
Nether Bigging, L. Stenness, 1921.
L. Stenness, 1920.
Langa Ness, L. Boardhouse, 1923.
The abundance of fresh and brackish water on the islands provides a wide range of habitats suitable for the growth of charophytes. However, most of the records are from sheltered bays of the larger lochs and, to a lesser extent, from burns. Some species are characteristic of brackish lakes, ponds and ditches near the sea (*C. canescens*, *C. hispida* var. *baltica* and *T. nidifica*, all comparatively rare in the British Isles). Charophytes are rarely found in running water but two species that are capable of filling this niche are *N. flexilis* (*N. opaca* in Groves & Bullock-Webster; typical *N. flexilis* is not found on Orkney but the 'opaca' form is fairly common) and *C. globularis* var. *virgata*.

The majority of charophytes grow in clear water on a sand/silt substrate, often with little organic deposit, although some species are more often found on mud. Many species are restricted to water with a high pH but some are tolerant of acid conditions, particularly where there is water movement as in a burn or peat runnel.

Three species that do not accumulate surface lime occur on Orkney, *C. hispida* var. *baltica*, *C. vulgaris* f. *muscosa* and *T. nidifica*, and other species, which are normally heavily encrusted, are often less so in Orkney material.

The most common taxa on the islands are *C. globularis* var. *aspera* and var. *virgata* whilst the type variety, *C. globularis* var. *globularis*, is rare. Climatic and habitat conditions would probably favour var. *aspera* and var. *virgata* at the expense of var. *globularis* as they may also favour *C. hispida* var. *baltica* at the expense of *C. hispida* var. *hispida*, which is a rarity on the islands, despite its widespread occurrence in mainland Britain.

The polymorphic *C. vulgaris* is a ubiquitous, cosmopolitan and complex species which is reasonably well represented on Orkney but is far more common on the mainland of the British Isles. *C. vulgaris* f. *muscosa* is a very rare taxon described by Groves & Bullock-Webster from Donegal and only recorded in two other localities, N. Uist and Orkney.

LICHENS

Compiled by C. J. B. Hitch from the *Atlas of Lichens of the British Isles* (Seaward & Hitch, 1982) and the record cards of the mapping scheme of the British Lichen Society.

Lichens are found in a wide range of habitats, from mountain top to sea floor, from dry rocks to river beds, also trees, wood, bog, moorland, soil, etc. but norm-ally they are very strict regarding substrate requirements, a useful pointer in their determination. They may prefer sun or shade, but generally will disappear, when under pressure from other organisms.

If circumstances alter, they may be found on different substrates. For instance, some species that normally grow on trees, can be found on soil. In the Orkneys where there are very few trees, weathered worked wood, becomes an important substrate.

Range of distribution may alter too. It is noticeable for example that *Lichina confinis*, normally in sheltered areas, at or above high tide level, may be found 100 yards up exposed hillsides in Orkney due to excessive winds for much of the year and concomitant salt water spray.

Distribution of lichens *per se* is important. Species may be present in Orkney, but rare, because they are at the edge of their range, e.g. *Diploicia canescens* and *Candelariella medians*, which are both abundant in the south east of the British Isles. Conversely they

may develop more. For example, *Xanthoria candelaria* is often found abundantly fertile in the Orkneys, whereas it is virtually sterile in the south.

All lichens are very sensitive to atmospheric pollution, particularly in the form of acid precipitation, but it is evident that the Orkneys have a very clean air due to the prevailing winds coming from the Atlantic. This is borne out by the fact that *Lecanora coniziaeoides*, a species that tolerates or even benefits from pollution and is abundant on trees and wood in most of the British Isles, is virtually absent in Scotland and the out-lying islands.

Acarospora fuscata
A. smaragdula
A. veronensis
Alectoria nigricans
Anaptychia fusca
Anisomeridium biformis
Arthonia phaeobaea
A. radiata
Arthropyrenia halodytes
A. laburni
A. lapponina
A. punctiformis
Aspicilia calcarea
A. leprosescens
Baeomyces roseus
B. rufus
Bryoria fuscescens
B. subcana
Buellia aethalea
B. disciformis
B. punctata
B. stellutata
B. verruculosa
Caloplaca aurantia
C. caesiorufa
C. cerina
C. cerinella
C. citrina
C. decipiens
C. ferruginea
C. flavescens
C. flavovirescens
C. granulosa
C. holocarpa
C. marina
C. microthallina
C. ochracea
C. saxicola
C. thallincola
Candelariella aurella
C. medians
C. vitellina
Catapyrenium lachneum
Catillaria chalybeia

C. lenticularis
C. littorella
Cetraria chlorophylla
C. islandica
C. sepincola
Cladonia anomaea
C. arbuscula
C. bellidiflora
C. cervicornis
C. c. subsp. *verticillata*
C. chlorophaea
C. ciliata
C. c. var. *tenuis*
C. coccifera
C. coniocraea
C. crispata
C. digitata
C. fimbriata
C. floerkeana
C. furcata
C. f. subsp. *subrangiformis*
C. gracilis
C. luteoalba
C. macilenta
C. ochrochlora
C. polydactyla
C. portentosa
C. pyxidata
C. rangiferina
C. rangiformis
C. scabriuscula
C. squamosa
C. strepsilis
C. subcervicornis
C. sulphurina
C. uncialis subsp. *biuncialis*
Cliostomum griffithii
Coelocaulon aculeata
C. muricata
Collema auriculatum
C, tenax var. *ceranoides*
C. t. var. *vulgare*
Coriscium viride
Dermatocarpon miniatum

Diploicia canescens
Diplotomma alboatra
Evernia prunastri
Fuscidea cyathoides
F. kochiana
Graphis scripta
Haematomma ochroleucum
H. ventosum
Huilia albocaerulescens
H. crustulata
H. macrocarpa
H. platycarpoides
H. tuberculosa
Hymenelia lacustris
Hypogymnia physodes
H. tubulosa
Icmadophila ericetorum
Lecania aipospila
L. cyrtella
L. erysibe
Lecanora actophila
L. atra
L. badia
L. campestris
L. carpinea
L. chlarotera
L. confusa
L. conizaeoides
L. crenulata
L. dispersa
L. expallens
L. fugiens
L. gangaleoides
L. helicopis
L. intricata
L. intumescens
L. jamesii
L. muralis
L. poliophaea
L. polytropa
L. pulicaris
L. rupicola
L. soralifera
L. symmicta

L. varia
Lecidea cinnabarina
L. confluens
L. granulosa
L. immersa
L. lapicida
L. leucophaea
L. lithophila
L. sulphurea
Lecidella elaeochroma
L. e. var. *soralifera*
L. scabra
L. stigmatea
L. subincongrua
Lepraria incana
Leptogium sinuatum
L. tenuissimum
Lichina confinis
L. pygmaea
Lobaria pulmonaria
Micarea lignaria
M. prasina
Nephroma laevigatum
Normandina pulchella
Ochrolechia androgyna
O. frigida
O. parella
O. tartarea
Opegrapha atra
O. calcarea
O. chevallieri
O. confluens
O. gyrocarpa
O. herbarum
O. niveoatra
O. persoonii
O. saxatilis
O. saxicola
O. varia
O. vulgata
Parmelia crinita
P. elegantula

P. exasperatula
P. glabratula
P. g. subsp. *fuliginosa*
P. omphalodes
P. perlata
P. saxatilis
P. subaurifera
P. sulcata
Peltigera canina agg
P. hymenina
P. rufescens
*P. scabrosa**
Pertusaria amara
P. corallina
P. leioplaca
P. pertusa
P. pseudocorallina
Phaeophyscia nigricans
P. orbicularis
Phlyctis argena
Physcia adscendens
P. aipolia
P. caesia
P. dubia
P. tenella
P. tribacia
Physconia pulverulacea
Placynthiella ichmalea
Placynthium nigrum
Platismatia glauca
Polyblastia cupularis
Porina aenea
P. chlorotica
Protoblastenia rupestris
Pseudephebe pubescens
Pseudevernia furfuracea
Psorotichia schaereri
Pycnothelia papillaria
Pyrenula chlorospila
Ramalina baltica
R. cuspidata
R. duriaei

R. farinacea
R. fastigiata
R. fraxinea
R. siliquosa
R. subfarinacea
Rhizocarpon concentricum
R. constrictum
R. geographicum
R. obscuratum
Rinodina exigua
R. gennarii
Sarcogyne regularis
Schaereria tenebrosa
Scoliciosporum umbrinum
Sphaerophorus globosus
S. melanocarpus
Thamnolia vermicularis var *subuliformis*
Toninia aromatica
T. caeruleonigricans
T. lobulata
Trapelia coarctata
Umbilicaria cylindrica
U. proboscidea
U. torrefacta
Usnea fragilescens
U. inflata
U. subfloridana
Verrucaria fusconigrescens
V. glaucina
V. maura
V. mucosa
V. muralis
V. striatula
V. viridula
Xanthoria calcicola
X. candelaria
X. elegans
X. parietina
X. polycarpa
Xylographa vitiligo

BRYOPHYTA
(Compiled by Mrs Ann Thomson of Kirkwall)

Mosses

Sphagnum palustre
S. magellanicum
S. papillosum
S. imbricatum
S. compactum
S. recurvum
S. tenellum

S. cuspidatum
S. subsecundum
S. s. inundatum
S. s. auriculatum
S. fimbriatum
S. girgensohnii
S. robustum
S. rubellum
S. capillaceum
S. quinquefarium
S. plumulosum
Andreaea rupestris
A. rothii

Atrichum undulatum
Oligotrichum hercynicum
Polytrichum nanum
P. aloides
P. a. minimum
P. urnigerum
P. alpinum
P. piliferum
P. juniperinum
P. alpestre
P. auranticum
P. formosum
P. commune

* Only known site is the Orkney Isles.

P. c. perigoniale
Diphyscium foliosum
Fissidens bryoides
F. osmundoides
F. taxifolius
F. christatus
F. adianthoides
Archidium alternifolium
Pleuridium acuminatum
Ditrichum cylindricum
D. heteromallum
D. flexicaule
Distichium capillaceum
D. inclinatum
Ceratodon purpureus
C. p. purpureus
Seligeria recurvata
Blindia acuta
Pseudephemerum nitidum
Dicranella palustris
D. schreberana
D. varia
D. rufescens
D. crispa
D. subulata
D. cerviculata
D. heteromalla
Cynodontium jenneri
Dichodontium pellucidum
Dicranum scottianum
D. fuscescens
D. majus
D. bonjeanii
D. scoparium
Campylopus subulatus
C. schimperi
C. fragilis
C. pyriformis
C. flexuosus
C. atrovirens
C. introflexus
C. brevipilus
Leucobryum glaucum
Encalypta streptocarpa
Tortula ruralis
T. ruraliformis
T. subulata
T. s. angustata
T. muralis
Pottia heimii
P. truncata
P. starkeana ssp minutula
P. recta
P. davalliana
Phascum cuspidatum
Cinclidotus fontinaloides
Barbula convoluta

B. unguiculata
B. revoluta
B. hornschuchiana
B. fallax
B. reflexa
B. spadicea
B. rigidula
B. tophacea
B. cylindrica
B. ferruginascens
B. recurvirostra
Gymnostomum aeruginosum
G. recurvirostrum
G. calcareum
Eucladium verticillatum
Tortella tortuosa
T. flavovirens
Trichostomum crispulum
T. brachydontium
T. b. var littoralle
Weissia controversa
W. rutilans
W. microstoma
Leptodontium flexifolium
Grimmia maritima
G. apocarpa
G. stricta
G. alpicola var rivularis
G. pulvinata
G. trichophylla
G. stirtonii
Rhacomitrium aciculare
R. aquaticum
R. fasciculare
R. heterostichum
R. h. var gracilescens
R. canescens
R. c. varericoides
R. lanuginosum
Funaria hygrometrica
F. hygrometrica
F. attenuata
F. fascicularis
F. obtusa
Tetraplodon mnioides
Splachum sphaericum
Pohlia nutans
P. rothii
P. bulbifera
P. wahlenbergii
P. delicatula
Plagiobryum zieri
Anomobryum filiforme
Bryum pendulum
B. inclinatum
B. pallens
B. weigelii

B. pseudotriquetrum
B. caespiticium
B. argentium
B. a. var lanatum
B. bicolor
B. micro-erythrocarpum
B. klinggraeffii
B. alpinum
B. capillare
Mnium hornum
M. marginatum
M. stellare
M. longirostrum
M. rugicum
M. seligeri
M. undulatum
M. punctatum
M. pseudopunctatum
Aulacomnium palustre
Amblyodon dealbatus
Bartramia ithyphylla
Philonotis fontana
P. seriata
P. calcarea
Breurelia chrysocoma
Ptychomitrium polyphyllum
Amphidium mougeotii
Zygodon viridissimus
Z. v. var stirtonii
Orthotrichum rupestre
O. anomalum
O. pulchellum
O. diaphanum
Ulota phyllantha
U. crispa
U. bruchii
U. drummondii
Fontinalis antipyretica
Climacium dendroides
Antitrichia curtipendula
Neckera crispa
N. complanata
Omalia trichomanoides
Thamnium alopecurum
Hookeria lucens
Heterocladum heteropterum
Thuidium tamariscinum
Cratoneuron filicinum (var fallax)
C. f. var fallax
C. commutatum
C. c. var commutatum
C. c. var falcatum
Campylium stellatum
C. protensum
C. chrysophyllum
Leptodictyum riparium
Hygroamblystegium tenax

Amblystegium serpens
A. juratzkanum
Drepanocladus aduncus
D. lycopodioides
D. fluitans
D. f. var fluitans
D. f. var falcatus
D. exannulatus
D. e. var exannulatus
D. revolvens
D. r. var revolvens
D. uncinatus
Hygrohypnum ochraceum
H. luridum
Scorpidium scorpioides
Acrocladium straminium
A. cordifolium
A. gigantium
A. sarmentosum
A. cuspidatum
Isothesium myurum
I. myosuroides
I. m. var brachythecioides
Camptothecium sericeum
C. lutescens
Brachythecium albicans
B. mildeanum
B. rutabulum
B. rivulare
B. populeum
B. plumosum
Cirriphyllum piliferum
C. crassinervium
Eurhynchium striatum
E. praelongum
E. p. var stokesii
E. swartzii
E. riparioides
E. murale
E. confertum
Rhynchostegiella pumila
R. teesdalei
Orthothecium rufescens
O. intricatum
Pseudoscleropodium purum
Pleurozium schreberi
Isopterygium pulchellum
I. elegans
Plagiothecium succulentum
P. sylvaticum
P. undulatum
Hypnum cupressiforme
P. c. resupinatum
P. c. ericetorum

P. c. tectorum
P. c. lacunosum
Ctenidium molluscum
C. m. condensatum
Hyocomium flagellare
Rhytidiadelphus triquetrus
R. squarrosus
R. loreus
Hylocomium splendens

Liverworts

Conocephalum conicum
Lunularia cruciata
Preissia quadrata
Marchantia polymorpha
Riccardia multifida
R. sinuata
R. palmata
R. pinguis
Pellia epiphylla
P. endiviifolia
Metzgeria furcata
M. fruticulosa
M. conjugata
M. hamata
Blasia pusilla
Anthelia julacea
Herberta staminea
H. adunca
Ptilidium ciliare
Trichocolea tomentella
Blepharostoma trichophyllum
Bazzania trilobata
B. tricrenata
Lepidozia pinnata
L. reptans
L. pearsonii
L. setacea
L. trichoclados
Calypogeia fissa
C. sphagnicola
C. arguta
Lophozia ventricosa
L. porphyroleuca
L. incisa
Leiocolea turbinata
L. badensis
L. muelleri
Barbilophozia floerkei
B. atlantica
Tritomaria quinquedentata
Sphenolobus minutus
Eremonotus myriocarpus

Anastrepta orcadensis
Gymnocolea inflata
Solenostoma triste
S. pumilum
S. crenulatum
Plectolea subelliptica
P. hyalina
Nardia compressa
N. scalaris
Marsupella emarginata
M. aquatica
Gymnomitrion crenulatum
Mylia taylori
M. anomala
Plagiochila carringtonii
P. asplenioides
P. a. var asplenioides
P. a. var major
P. spinulosa
P. s. var inermis
Lophocolea bidentata
L. cuspidata
Chiloscyphus polyanthos
C. pallescens
Saccogyna viticulosa
Cephaloziella rubella
Cephalozia bicuspidata
C. b. var lammersiana
C. connivens
C. media
Nowellia curvifolia
Odontoschisma sphagni
O. denudatum
O. elongatum
Diplophyllum albicans
Scapania curta
S. irrigua
S. umbrosa
S. gracilis
S. nemorea
S. undulata
S. subalpina
S. compacta
Radula complanata
R. lindbergiana
Pleurozia purpurea
Porella thuja
Lejeunea cavifolia
L. patens
Frullania tamarisci
F. t. var robusta
F. t. var cornubica
F. dilatata

FLOWERING PLANTS AND FERNS

(Compiled by Miss E. R. Bullard of St Ola, Kirkwall, based on her *Checklist of Vascular Plants* (1972, revised 1975, 1979)).

Attempts were made to list the flora of Orkney from the end of the 17th century and although there were often gaps in time between the compilation of one list and the next, most people tended to make use of those of their predecessors in a somewhat uncritical fashion. It was the late Col. Henry Halcro-Johnstone who, in the early part of the present century, backed up all his own records with herbarium specimens and made strenuous attempts to check all earlier unauthenticated records. He sent specimens to all the major Herbaria in Great Britain and his own very extensive collection is now housed at the Royal Botanic Garden, Edinburgh. While knowledge of the Orkney flora was increased immeasurably by his painstaking work, there were losses as the result of over-zealous collecting. It was not unknown for the Colonel to collect as many as 90 specimens from one colony of a single species and as he often took and pressed a whole plant, roots and all, some very rare plants, e.g. *Hammarbya paludosa*, were probably exterminated.

A group of islands poses problems in obtaining thorough coverage and inevitably some of the early suspect records have been proved to be correct since his time. The apparently unlikely *Atriplex littoralis* turns up occasionally as strand-line seedlings which fail to overwinter, and many other unconfirmed records – omitted from the following list – may yet appear. Although it is known that Halcro-Johnstone and other earlier botanists explored very close to the sites where the species now exist, they managed to miss such rarities as *Rubus chamaemorus*, *Poa alpina* and *Heirochloë odorata*. New understandings from time to time disclose a species hitherto unrecognized in the UK, e.g. *Puccinellia capillaris* was passed over by earlier specialists as a form of *P. distans*. The real possibility of other European species appearing in Orkney is to some extent offset by the failure of visiting botanists to recognize the replacement there of familiar southern species by ones of northern distribution, so that false records of *Poa pratensis* appear in lieu of the widespread *P. subcaerulea*, and *Festuca ovina* in lieu of *F. tenuifolia*. Other common plants are slightly different in appearance, being larger or smaller, or differently coloured than their southern counterparts. Some others occupy unfamiliar habitats: visitors simply do not expect to find *Thalictrum alpinum* in low-lying fen or maritime heath, nor *Galium sterneri* in machair or on grassy banks.

Apart from two *Euphrasia* species and *Hierochloë odorata*, Orkney appears to have no 'nationally rare' plants, but does have a special abundance of northern species such as *Dryopteris expansa*, *Ligusticum scoti-cum*, *Mertensia maritima*, *Saussurea alpina* and *Carex maritima*; it shares with Caithness and north Sutherland one of the UK's few endemics, *Primula scotica*; and has such oddities of distribution as *Ophioglossum azoricum*, *Dryopteris aemula*, *Pyrola rotundifolia* and *Jasione montana*.

Many groups, genera and microspecies require further work and there are good opportunities for searchers of *Equisetum* (hybrids), *Fumaria*, *Atriplex*, *Salix* (hybrids), *Epilobium* (hybrids), *Rhinanthus*, *Odontites*, *Pilosella* (microspecies), *Taraxacum* (microspecies – only one, *T. rubellum*, has been discovered in recent years, but there must be more), *Zostera*, *Dactylorhiza* and perhaps *Festuca*.

As can be seen from the Orkney list, a large number of plants definitely known in Orkney in the early part of this century are probably now extinct. At first the losses were mostly of 'weeds of cultivation', probably originally introduced with improperly cleaned crop seeds. More serious is the loss now taking place of truly native plants of wetland, heath and machair as these habitats are lost to agricultural development and sand extraction. The spread of such recently introduced aliens as *Montia sibirica*, *Mimulus* species and London Pride, however pretty, can in no way compensate future generations of Orcadians for these losses.

The nomenclature follows in most cases that used in the *Excursion Flora of the British Isles* (3rd ed.), as these names are to be used for botanical recording in the foreseeable future. This has meant that some familiar names have been changed from those given in popular handbooks and previously published lists of Orkney flora. Synonyms are given in most cases. It should be noted that a large number of plants found in Orkney, particularly those with a restricted or northern distribution, are not fully described in the *Excursion Flora*.

Huperzia selago (L.) Schrank & Mart. = *Lycopodium selago* L. Fir Clubmoss. Frequent.
Lycopodium annotinum L. Interrupted Clubmoss. Hoy, not seen since 1920.
L. clavatum L. Stag's-horn Clubmoss. Local, stony heaths.
Diphasiastrum alpinum (L.) Holub. = *Lycopodium alpinum* L. Alpine Clubmoss. Local, stony heaths.
Selaginella selaginoides (L.) Link. Lesser Clubmoss. Frequent.
Isoetes lacustris L. Quill-wort. Rare, Hoy and Rousay.
Equisetum hyemale L. Dutch Rush. Rare, first recorded, in Hoy, in 1960 but probably there before 1940.
E. fluviatile L. Water Horsetail. Common.
E. arvense L. Common Horsetail. Common.
E. × litorale Rupr. Hybrid Horsetail. Rare, Hoy and Birsay.

E. pratense Ehrh. Shady Horsetail. Very rare, Rousay.

E. sylvaticum L. Wood Horsetail. Frequent.

E. palustre L. Marsh Horsetail. Common.

Botrychium lunaria (L.) Swartz. Moonwort. Occasional.

Ophioglossum vulgatum L. Adder's Tongue. Local, usually on dune slacks.

O. azoricum C. Presl. = *Ophioglossum vulgatum* ssp. *ambiguum* (Coss & Germ.) E. T. Warb. Adder's Tongue. Local, on thin peat near the sea.

Hymenophyllum wilsonii Hook. Wilson's Filmy Fern. Local, Hoy.

Polypodium vulgare L. Polypody. Occasional.

P. × mantoniae Rothm. Hybrid Polypody. Rare.

Pteridium aquilinum (L.) Kuhn. Bracken. Locally common.

Phegopteris connectilis (Michx) Watt = *Thelypteris phegopteris* (L.) Slossum. Beech Fern. Very rare, Hoy, first recorded 1969.

Oreopteris limbosperma (All.) Holub. = *T. oreopteris* (Ehrh.) Slossum. Lemon-scented Fern. Occasional.

Phyllitis scolopendrium (L.) Newm. Hart's-tongue Fern. Very rare, Hoy and Rousay.

Asplenium adiantum-nigrum L. Black Spleenwort. Occasional.

A. marinum L. Sea Spleenwort. Occasional.

A. trichomanes L. ssp. *quadrivalens* D. E. Meyer em Lovis. Maiden-hair Spleenwort. Occasional.

A. ruta-muraria L. Wall-rue. Rare, Rousay, Wyre, Westray.

Athyrium filix-femina (L.) Roth. Lady Fern. Frequent.

Cystopteris fragilis (L.) Bernh. Brittle Bladder-fern. Rare, Hoy, Rousay, Westray.

Polystichum lonchitis (L.) Roth. Holly Fern. Very rare. Hoy.

P. aculeatum (L.) Roth. Hard Shield Fern. Very rare, perhaps extinct. Hoy.

Dryopteris filix-mas (L.) Schott. Male Fern. Frequent.

D. affinis (Lowe) Fraser-Jenkins. = *D. borreri* Newm. Scaly Male-fern. Frequent.

D. aemula (Ait.) Kuntze. Hay-scented Buckler-fern. Occasional, especially near Scapa Flow.

D. dilatata (Hoffm.) A. Gray. Broad Buckler-fern. Common.

D. × ambrosiae Fraser-Jenkins & Jermy. Hybrid Buckler-fern. Rare.

D. expansa (C. Presl.) Fraser-Jenkins & Jermy. = *D. assimilis* S. Walker. Northern Buckler-fern. Occasional.

Blechnum spicant (L.) Roth. Hard Fern. Common.

Pinus contorta Dougl. Lodgepole Pine, and *P. mugo* Turra. Mountain Pine, were planted in Hoy in 1954 and seedlings now appear outside the plantations.

Juniperus communis L. ssp. *communis*. Juniper. May be confused with next.

J. communis L. ssp. *nana* Syme. Juniper. Occasional.

Caltha palustris L. Marsh Marigold. Common.

Aconitum stoerchianum Reichb. Monkshood. Garden escape, Stromness 1920.

Anemone nemorosa L. Wood anemone. Introduced, Binscarth Plantation.

Ranunculus acris L. Meadow Buttercup. Common.

R. repens L. Creeping Buttercup. Common.

R. bulbosus L. Bulbous Buttercup. Very local, on links (machair).

R. flammula L. Lesser Spearwort. Common.

R. sceleratus L. Celery-leaved Crowfoot. Extinct since 1906.

R. hederaceus L. Ivy-leaved Water Crowfoot. Local.

R. trichophyllus Chaix. Water Crowfoot. Frequent.

R. aquatilis L. Water Crowfoot. Frequent.

R. baudotii Godr. Brackish Water Crowfoot. Local, usually near the sea.

R. ficaria L. ssp. *ficaria*. Lesser Celandine. Common.

R. ficaria ssp. *bulbifer* Lawalree. Rare, probably introduced, first recorded c. 1959.

Aquilegia vulgaris L. Columbine. Garden escape.

Thalictrum alpinum L. Alpine Meadow Rue. Locally common, often on low ground.

T. minus L. ssp. *arenarium* (Butcher) Clapham. Lesser Meadow Rue. Local, on dunes.

Papaver dubium L. Long-headed Field Poppy. Occasional, in sandy fields.

P. somniferum L. Opium Poppy. Garden escape.

Meconopsis cambrica (L.) Vig. Welsh Poppy. Garden escape, perhaps sometimes naturalized.

Fumaria capreolata L. Ramping Fumitory. Occasional.

F. purpurea Pugsl. Ramping Fumitory. Occasional.

F. bastardii Bor. Fumitory. Occasional.

F. muralis Kock ssp. *boraei* (Jord.) Pugsl. Fumitory. Occasional.

F. officinalis L. Fumitory. Common.

Brassica napus L. Swede. Escape.

B. rapa L. Turnip. Escape.

B. nigra (L.) Koch. Black Mustard. Rare escape.

Sinapsis arvensis L. Charlock. Common.

Diplotaxis muralis (L.) DC. Wall Rocket. Casual, 1920.

Raphanus raphanistrum L. var *aureus*. Runch, Wild Mustard. Common. Yellow.

R. sativus L. Radish. Occasional escape.

Cakile maritima Scop. Sea Rocket. Frequent.

Lepidum virginicum L. Pepperwort. Casual, 1960.

L. perfoliatum L. Pepperwort. Casual, 1920.

Cardaria draba (L.) Desv. Hoary Cress. Rare, Hoy and Birsay. First recorded 1957.

Thlaspi arvense L. Field Penny Cress. Now very rare.

Capsella bursa-pastoris (L.) Medic. Shepherd's Purse. Common.

Cochlearia officinalis L. Scurvy-grass. Common.

Draba incana L. Hoary Whitlowgrass. Rare, rock outcrops.

Erophila verna (L.) Chevall. Common Whitlowgrass. Occasional.

Armoracia rusticana Gaertn., Mey & Scherg. Horse Radish. Rare escape.

Cardamine pratensis L. Lady's Smock. Common.

C. flexuosa With. Wood Bitter-cress. Frequent.

C. hirsuta L. Hairy Bitter-cress. 'Poppers'. Frequent.

Barbarea vulgaris R. Br. Winter Cress. Local populations fluctuate.

B. intermedia Bor. Intermediate Yellow Rocket. Casual.

Arabis causcasica Schlecht. Garden Arabis. Rare escape.

Nasturtium officinale R.Br. Watercress. Frequent.

N. microphyllum × officinale. Very rare, probably introduced.

Rorippa islandica (Oeder) Borbas. Northern Yellow-cress. Somewhat sporadic, mainly dried-out pools and muddy loch margins in the North Isles.

Hesperis matronalis L. Dame's Violet, Sweet Rocket. Common escape.

Sisymbrium officinale (L.) Scop. Hedge Mustart. Presumably casual but common in Pierowall, Westray, in 1974.

Arabidopsis thaliana (L.). Heynh. Thale Cress. Rare.

Reseda luteola L. Dyer's Rocket. Casual, St Ola 1916.

Viola riviniana Reichb. Common Violet.
   ssp. *riviniana.* Occasional.
   ssp. *minor* (Gregor) Valentine. Common.

V. canina L. Dog Violet. Very rare, Evie.

V. palustris L. Marsh Violet. Common.

V. cornuta L. Escape.

V. tricolor L. Heart's Ease, WildPansy.
   ssp. *tricolor.* Common.
   ssp. *curtisii* (E. Forst.) Syme. Local, on dunes.

V. arvensis Murr. Field Pansy. Rare.

Polygala vulgaris L. Common Milkwort. Occasional.

P. serpyllifolia Hose. Heath Milkwort. Common.

Hypericum tetrapterum Fr. Square-stemmed St John's Wort. Rare, Hoy, probably introduced.

H. pulchrum L. Slender St John's Wort. Common.

H. hirsutum L. Hairy St John's Wort. Rare, Hoy and Firth, perhaps introduced.

Silene vulgaris (Moench) Gacke. Bladder Campion. Rare casual.

S. maritima With. Sea Campion. Common.

S. dichotoma Ehrh. Forked Catchfly. Escape, Deerness 1904.

S. acaulis (L.) Jacq. Moss Campion. Very local, Hoy and Westray. In the latter, plants of *Primula scotica* grow in the *Silene* cushions.

S. dioica (L.) Clairv. Red Campion. Common in most areas.

S. alba (Mill.) E. H. L. Krause. Perhaps native in Sanday, occasional casual elsewhere.

S. alba × dioica. Rare, but some colonies of Red Campion, especially in the South Isles, show signs of introgression.

Lychnis viscaria L. Sticky Catchfly. as the cvr. *flore-pleno*, escape 1967.

L. flos-cuculi L. Ragged Robin. Common.

L. coronaria Rose Campion. Escape, 1914.

Agrostemma githago L. Corn Cockle. Probably now extinct as a cornfield weed.

Cerastium arvense L. Field Mouse-ear Chickweed. Apparently extinct since 1929.

C. fontanum Baumg. ssp. *glabrescens* (G. F. W. Meyer) Salman = *C. holosteoides* Fr. Common Mouse-ear Chickweed. Common.

C. glomeratum Thuill. Sticky Mouse-ear Chickweed. Common.

C. diffusum Pers. = *C. atrovirens* Bab. Dark-green Mouse-ear Chickweed. Common.

Stellaria media (L.) Vill. Chickweed. Very abundant.

S. holostea L. Greater Stitchwort. Probably introduced, on a Firth roadside date unknown.

S. graminea L. Lesser Stitchwort. Occasional, almost entirely on roadsides.

S. alsine Grimm. Bog Stitchwort. Common.

Sagina maritima Don. Sea Pearlwort. Frequent.

S. procumbens L. Procumbent Pearlwort. Common.

S. subulata (SW.) C. Presl. Awl-leaved Pearlwort. Occasional, on stony heaths.

S. nodosa (L.) Fenzl. Knotted Pearlwort. Frequent.

Honkenya peploides (L.) Ehrh. Sea Sandwort. Frequent.

Arenaria serpyllifolia L. Apparently extinct, last certain record before 1914.

Spergula arvensis L. Corn Spurrey. Common.

Spergularia media (L.) C. Presl. Greater Sea-spurrey. Frequent.

S. marina (L.) Griseb. Lesser Sea-spurrey. Occasional.

Montia fontana L. Blinks. ssp. *fontana.* Common.
   ssp. *chondrosperma* (Fenzl) Walters. Occasional.
   ssp. *variabilis* Walters. Occasional.

M. perfoliata (Willd.) Howell. Winter Purslane. Casual 1884.

M. sibirica (L.) Howell. Pink Purslane. Widespread in plantations in Orkney, probably preventing establishment of a native ground flora.

Chenopodium album L. Fat Hen. Casual.

Atriplex littoralis L. Shore Orache. Strandline seedlings appear occasionally.

A. patula L. Iron-root. Casual.

A. prostrata DC. Spear-leaved Orache. Exact status uncertain owing to confusion with next and possibly other unnamed sp.

A. glabriuscula Edmonst. Babington's Orache. See above.

A. laciniata L. Frosted Orache. Rare and apparently spasmodic.

Suaeda maritima (L.) Dumort. Sea-blite. Occasional to frequent on sheltered shores.

Salsola kali L. Salt-wort. Apparently extinct, last recorded 1905.

Salicornia dolichstachya Moss. Glasswort.

S. nitens P. W. Ball & Tutin. Glasswort.

S. europaea L. Glasswort.

S. ramosissima J. Woods. Glasswort. Sanday 1974. The exact status of each of the above spp. is uncertain. *Salicornia* spp. as a whole are 'occasional' in Orkney.

Tilia sp. Lime. Planted.

Malva moschata. L. Musk Mallow. Casual or escape.

M. pusilla Sm. Small Mallow. Casual, 1933.

Linum catharticum L. Purging Flax. Common.

L. usitatissimum L. Flax. Escape, now rare.

Radiola linoides Roth. All-seed. Occasional, damp heaths.

Geranium pratense L. Escape, North Ronaldsay and probably elsewhere.

G. sylvaticum L. Wood Cranesbill. Rare; doubtfully native.

G. dissectum L. Cut-leaved Cranesbill. Occasional but probably decreasing.

G. molle L. Dove's-foot Cranesbill. Frequent.

G. pusillum L. Small-flowered Cranesbill. Rare casual.

G. lucidum L. Shining Cranesbill. Occasional. Appears to be a recent introduction as a garden weed.

G. robertianum L. ssp. *robertianum* Herb Robert. Occasional garden weed and in plantations.

G. robertianum L. ssp. *maritimum* (Bab.) H. G. Bak. Very rare. St Ola.

Erodium cicutarium (L.) L'Herit. spp. *cicutarium* Common Storksbill. Seems to be becoming very rare. North Isles only.

Oxalis acetosella L. Wood-sorrel. Rare, apparently confined to Scapa Flow islands.

Impatiens glandulifera Royle. Policeman's Helmet. Escape.

Acer pseudoplatanus L. Sycamore, Scots 'Plane'. Much planted but scarcely naturalised.

Ilex aquifolium L. Holly. Planted.

Aesculus hippocastanum L. Horse Chestnut. Planted.

Lupinus nootkatensis Sims. Nootka Lupin. Originally sown for soil improvement and locally naturalised; now decreasing.

Ulex europaeus L. Whin, Gorse. Probably not native but frequently naturalised.

Cytisus scoparius (L.) Link. Broom. Planted and scarcely naturalised.

Ononis repens L. Restharrow. Sandwick, now nearly extinct.

Medicago sativa ssp. *sativa* L. Lucerne. Occasional escape from sown crops.

M. sativa ssp. *falcata* (L.) Arcangeli. Sickle Medick. Casual, St Ola, 1920.

M. lupulina L. Black Medick. Rare casual.

Melilotus officinalis (L.) Pall. Common Melilot. Casual, St Ola 1916.

M. indica (L.) All. Small Melilot. Casual.

Trifolium pratense L. Red Clover. Common.

T. medium L. Zigzag Clover. Apparently frequent last century but not recorded recently.

T. hybridum L. Alsike Clover. Occasional.

T. repens L. White Clover. Common.

T. campestre Schreb. Hop Trefoil. Casual, pre-1950.

T. aureum Poll. Casual, 1912.

T. dubium Sibth. Lesser Yellow Trefoil. Common.

Anthyllis vulneraria L. ssp. *vulneraria*. Kidney Vetch, Ladies' Fingers. Occasional.

A. vulneraria L. ssp. *lapponica* (Hyland) Jalas. Frequent.

Lotus corniculatus L. Bird's-foot Trefoil, Cocks-and-Hens. Common.

L. uliginosus Schkuhr. Large Bird's-foot Trefoil. Occasional, apparently increasing.

Vicia hirsuta (L.) Gray. Hairy Tare. Casual.

V. cracca L. Tufted Vetch. Frequent.

V. sepium L. Bush Vetch. Frequent.

V. sativa L. Common Vetch. Casual.

V. sativa L. ssp. *nigra* (L.) Ehrh = *V. angustifolia* L. Narrow-leaved Vetch. Rare.

Lathyrus pratensis L. Meadow Vetchling. Common.

L. montanus Bernh. Bitter Vetch. Apparently a rare casual, last seen 1961 in Shapinsay.

Filipendula ulmaria (L.) Maxim. Meadowsweet. Common.

Rubus chamaemorus L. Cloudberry. Rare, Hoy and Firth.

R. saxatilis L. Stone Bramble. Occasional.

R. idaeus L. Raspberry. Relict of cultivation and introduced Binscarth Plantation.

R. spectabilis Pursh. Salmonberry. Frequently planted and spreading rapidly.

R. fruticosus L. *sensu lato*. Naturalized in several places although method of introduction seems uncertain. Any truly native sp. almost certainly extinct.

Potentilla palustris (L.) Scop. Marsh Cinquefoil. Occasional.

P. anserina L. Silverweed. Common.

P. erecta (L.)Rausch. Common Tormentil, Hillbark. Common.

Fragaria vesca L. Wild Strawberry. Rare. Rousay.

F. ananassa Duchesne. Strawberry. Garden escape.

Geum urbanum L. Herb Bennet. Naturalized in Binscarth Plantation.

G. rivale L. Water Avens. Frequent.

Dryas octopetala L. Mountain Avens. Rare and decreasing. Hoy only.

Alchemilla filicaulis Buser. Lady's Mantle. Occasional.

A. glabra Neygenf. Lady's Mantle. Presumably naturalized as is confined to roadsides. Occasional.

Aphanes arvensis L. Parsley Piert. Rare.

A. microcarpa (Boiss. & Reut.) Rothm. Slender Parsley Piert. Occasional.

Sanguisorba minor Scop. Salad Burnet. Has been sown for fodder. Recorded 1903.

Rosa arvensis Huds. Field Rose. Rare, probably planted.

R. pimpinellifolia × sherardii. Scotch Rose–Downy Rose hybrid. Rare.

R. rugosa Thnb. Ramanas Rose, Japanese Rose. Much planted and spreading.

R. canina L. (*sensu stricto*) Dog Rose. Rare.

R. dumetorum Thuill. Dog Rose. Rare.

R. afzeliana Fr. Dog Rose. Frequent.

R. tomentosa Sm. Downy Rose. Rare.

R. sherardii Davies. Downy Rose. Occasional.

R. mollis Sm. Downy Rose. Occasional.

R. mollis × pimpinellifolia. Rare.

R. mollis × rubiginosa Downy Rose–Sweet Briar hybrid. Rare.

R. mollis × sherardii. Rare.

R. micrantha Sm. Sweet Briar. Rare, perhaps introduced.

Cotoneaster microphyllus Wall ex Lindl. Occasionally naturalized, especially in the Finstown area.

Crataegus monogyna Jacq. Hawthorn, Quick. Occasionally planted for hedging, not naturalized.

Sorbus aucuparia L. Rowan. Native only in Hoy, where spreading. Planted elsewhere.

Sedum rosea (L.) Scop. Rose-root. Occasional, both on inland rock outcrops and on sea cliffs.

S. album L. White Stonecrop. Escape.

S. acre L. Wall Pepper. Rare native but also escape from gardens.

Saxifraga spathularis Brot. × *umbrosa* L. London Pride. Escape.

S. aizoides L. Yellow Saxifrage. Occasional, Hoy.

S. oppositifolia L. Purple Saxifrage. Occasional, Hoy only.

Chrysoplenium oppositifolium L. Opposite-leaved Golden Saxifrage. Occasional but absent from North Isles.

Parnassia palustris L. Grass-of-Parnassus. Frequent.

Escallonia macrantha Hook. & Arn. Escape, first recorded 1972.

Ribes rubrum L. = *Ribes sylvestre* (Lam.) Mert. & Koch. Red Currant. Garden relict.

R. nigrum L. Black Currant. Garden relict.

R. uva-crispa L. Gooseberry. Garden relict.

Drosera rotundifolia L. Sundew. Frequent.

D. anglica Huds. Great Sundew. Occasional, Hoy, Orphir and perhaps St. Andrews.

Lythrum portula (L.) D. A. Webb ssp. *longidentata* (Gay) P. D. Sell. Water Purslane. Becoming rare.

Epilobium hirsutum L. Great Hairy Willow-herb. Not native in Orkney but occasionally naturalized.

E. parviflorum Schreb. Small-flowered Willow-herb. Occasional.

E. montanum L. Broad-leaved Willow-herb. Common.

E. obscurum Schreb. Short-fruited Willow-herb. Occasional.

E. palustre L. Marsh Willow-herb. Frequent.

E. brunnescens (Cn) Raven & Engelhorn. A creeping Willow-herb, native to New Zealand. Occasional in Hoy and St Ola, first recorded 1956.

Chamerion angustifolium (L.) J. Holub. Rosebay Willow-herb. Frequent.

Fuchsia magellanica Lam. Fuchsia. Planted and naturalized.

Circaea × intermedia Ehrh. Intermediate Enchanter's Nightshade. Rare.

Myriophyllum spicatum L. Spiked Water-milfoil. Occasional.

M. alterniflorum DC. Alternate Water-milfoil. Frequent.

Hippuris vulgaris L. Mare's-tail. Frequent.

Callitriche stagnalis Scop. Common Water-starwort. Common.

C. platycarpa Koch. Various-leaved Water-starwort. Common.

C. hamulata Koch. = *C. intermedia* Hoffm. Intermediate Water-starwort. Occasional.

C. hermaphroditica L. Autumnal Water-starwort. Occasional.

Cornus suecica L. = *Chamaepericlymenum suecicum* (L.) Aschers & Graebn. Dwarf Cornel. Rare, Hoy.

Hedera helix L. Ivy. Doubtfully native but planted and naturalized. (*H. hibernica*, the Irish Ivy, is commonly planted.)

Hydrocotyle vulgaris L. Marsh Pennywort. Common.

Anthriscus sylvestris (L.) Hoffm. Cow Parsley. Common.

Scandix pecten-veneris L. Shepherd's Needle. Casual, last recorded 1921.

Myrrhis odorata (L.) Scop. Sweet Cicely. Naturalized.

Conium maculatum L. Hemlock. Rare, last seen around Kirkwall in 60's and perhaps now extinct.

Apium inundatum (L.) Reichb. Lesser Marshwort. Frequent.

Carum carvi L. Caraway. Occasional casual.

Conopodium majus (Guan) Loret. Pignut. Local.

Bunium bulbocastanum L. Great Pignut. Casual, Hoy 1925.

Pimpinella saxifraga L. Burnet Saxifrage. Rare, St Ola.

Aegopodium podagraria L. Ground Elder, Bishop Weed. Common.

Berula erecta (Huds.) Coville. Narrow-leaved Water-parsnip. Rare, Sanday.

Ligusticum scoticum L. Scottish Lovage. Frequent, sea cliffs and rocky shores.

Angelica sylvestris L. Wild Angelica. Common and often very luxurient.

A. archangelica L. Angelica. Escape or garden relict, especially in Westray.

Levisticum officinale Koch. Lovage. Escape or garden relict.

Peucedanum ostruthium (L.) Koch. Masterwort. Escape or garden relict.

Heracleum sphondylium L. Hogweed. Common.

Daucus carota L. Wild Carrot. Rare.

Euphorbia helioscopia L. Sun Spurge. An occasional garden weed.

E. peplus L. Petty Spurge. Casual, last recorded 1933.

Polygonum aviculare L. Knotgrass. Occasional.

P. boreale (Lange) Small. Northern Knotgrass. Frequent.

P. arenastrum Bor. Small-leaved Knotgrass. Frequent.

P. oxyspermum Ledeb. Ray's Knotgrass. An immature specimen from Copinsay 1933.

P. viviparum L. Alpine Bistort. Occasional.

P. bistorta L. Bistort. Not native; escape or garden relict.

P. amphibium L. Amphibious Bistort. Frequent.

P. persicaria L. Persicaria. Occasional.

P. lapathifolium L. Pale Persicaria. Casual.

Fallopia convolvulus (L.) A. Löve, Black Bindweed. Occasional garden weed.

Reynoutria japonica Houtt. Japanese Knotweed. Occasional escape.

Rheum rhaponticum L. Rhubarb. Garden relict.

Oxyria digyna (L.) Hill. Mountain Sorrel. Rare, Hoy.

Rumex acetosella L. Sheep's Sorrel. Common.

R. acetosa L. Sorrel. Common.

R. longifolius DC Long-leaved Dock. Rare.

R. crispus L. Curled Dock. Common.

R. obtusifolius L. Broad-leaved Dock. Common.

Soleirolia soleirolii (Req.) Dandy. Mind-your-own-business. Rare escape.

Urtica urens L. Small Nettle. Occasional on sandy soils.

U. dioica L. Stinging Nettle. Common.

Cannabis sativa L. Hemp. Escape, Hoy 1933.

Humulus lupulus L. Hop. Relict of cultivation.

Ulmus glabra Huds. Wych Elm. Planted.

Myrica gale L. Bog Myrtle. Very rare, Eday.

Betula pubescens Ehrh. ssp. *odorata* (Bechst) E. F. Warb. Native only in Hoy where it appears to be increasing.

Alnus glutinosa (L.) Gaertn. Alder. Planted.

Corylus avellana L. Hazel. Native, but only three or four bushes remain, in Hoy.

Fagus sylvatica L. Beech. Planted.

Castanea sativa Mill. Sweet Chestnut. Planted.

Quercus sp. Oak. Planted.

Populus tremula L. Aspen. Occasional, confined to Hoy and to Scapa Flow cliffs.

Populus spp. Poplars. Planted.

Salix pentandra L. Bay Willow. Planted.

S. alba L. White Willow. Planted.

S. fragilis L. Crack Willow. Planted.

S. viminalis L. Common Osier. Planted.

S. caprea L. Goat Willow. Planted.

S. caprea × *viminalis*. Planted (see also *S. cinerea* × *viminalis* below).

S. cinerea L. ssp. *oleifolia* Macreight = *S. atrocinerea* (Brot) Silva & Sobrinho. Common Sallow, 'Rice'. Frequent.

S. cinerea × *viminalis*. Planted. The most commonly planted hybrid Osier in Orkney has been variously named this or *S. caprea* × *viminalis* by different authorities.

S. aurita L. Eared Willow, 'Rice'. Frequent.

S. aurita × *viminalis*. Planted, or may have been incorrectly identified. Rare.

S. aurita × *cinerea*. Rare.

S. aurita × *repens*. Occasional.

S. nigricans. Sm. Very rare, perhaps planted.

S. phylicifolia L. Tea-leaved Willow, 'Rice'. Frequent.

S. phylicifolia × *repens*. Occasional.

S. repens L. ssp. *repens*. Creeping Willow. Common.

S. repens ssp. *argentea* (Sm) G. & A. Camus. Silver Creeping Willow. Common.

S. myrsinites L. Myrtle-leaved Willow. Only one, female, plant remains in Hoy.

S. herbacea L. Least Willow. Occasional, but confined to Hoy, Rousay and Westray. Other *Salix* hybrids probably occur, both wild and planted.

Loiseleuria procumbens (L.) Desv. Trailing Azalea. Very rare, Hoy only.

Arctostaphylos uva-ursi (L.) Spreng. Bearberry. Occasional, Hoy.

A. alpinus (L.) Spreng. Alpine Bearberry. Occasional, Hoy, Rousay and Westray, though perhaps extinct now in the last through cultivation.

Calluna vulgaris (L.) Hull. Heather. Common. Occurs as var. *incana* in Hoy and St Ola.

Erica tetralix L. Cross-leaved Heath. Frequent.

E. cinerea L. Bell-heather. Frequent.

Vaccinium vitis-idaea L. Cowberry. Occasional.

V. myrtillus L. Blaeberry. Frequent.

V. uliginosum L. Bog Blaeberry. Rare.

Pyrola rotundifolia L. ssp. *rotundifolia* Large Wintergreen. Occasional.

Orthilia secunda (L.) House. Serrated Wintergreen. Rare, Rousay, where first recorded in 1963.

Empetrum nigrum L. Crowberry. Common.

Armeria maritima (Mill.) Willd. Sea-pink, Thrift. Common.

Primula scotica Hook. Scottish Primrose. Occasional, decreasing as sites are lost to cultivation.

P. veris L. Cowslip. Rare and decreasing.

P. veris × *vulgaris*. False Oxlip. Rare.

P. vulgaris Huds. Primrose. Common in most areas but absent from some smaller islands.

Lysimachia nemorum L. Yellow Pimpernel. Occasional, Rousay, Hoy and Orphir.

L. punctata L. Occasional escape.

Trientalis europaea L. Chickweed Wintergreen. Rare, and apparently decreasing.

Anagallis tenella (L.) L. Bog Pimpernel. Frequent.

A. arvensis L. Scarlet Pimpernel. Rare casual.

Glaux maritima L. Sea Milkwort. Frequent.

Samolus valerandi L. Brookweed. Rare, Stronsay.

Fraxinus excelsior L. Ash. Planted.

Gentianella campestris (L.) Borner. Field Gentian. Occasional.

G. amarella (L.) Borner ssp. *druceana* Pritchard. Felwort, Autumn Gentian. Frequent, especially on links (machair).

Menyanthes trifoliata L. Bogbean. Frequent.

Symphytum × uplandicum Nyman. Russian Comfrey. Introduced. Occasional.

S. tuberosum L. Tuberous Comfrey. Rare. Garden outcast.

Anchusa arvensis (L.) Bieb = *Lycopsis arvensis* L. Bugloss. Frequent on sandy soils.

Myosotis scorpioides L. Water Forget-me-not. Frequent, but said to have been introduced into Orkney.

M. secunda A. Murr. Creeping Forget-me-not. Occasional.

M. laxa Lehm = *M. caespitosa* K. F. Schultz. Lesser Water Forget-me-not. Frequent.

M. arvensis (L.) Hill. Field Scorpion-grass. Field Forget-me-not. Common.

M. discolor Pers. Changing Forget-me-not. Frequent.

M. ramosissima Rochel. Early Forget-me-not. Rare, perhaps casual.

Mertensia maritima (L.) Gray. Oysterplant. Occasional, increasing and colonizing new sites.

Echium vulgare L. Viper's Bugloss. Rare, presumably escape.

Convolvulus arvensis L. Bindweed. Introduced, but occasionally well-established.

Calystegia sepium (L.) R. Br. Great Bindweed. Introduced, but frequently well-established.

C. soldanella (L.) R.Br. Sea Bindweed. Rare, South Ronaldsay, first recorded 1963.

Lycium barbarum L. = *L. halimifolium* Mill. Duke of Argyll's Teaplant. Escape or garden relict.

Hyocyamus niger L. Henbane. Rare casual, 1933.

Solanum dulcamara L. Woody Nightshade. Introduced but occasionally well-established.

S. nigrum L. Black Nightshade. Rare casual.

Verbascum thapsus L. Great Mullein, Aaron's Rod. Rare casual.

Linaria vulgaris Mill. Introduced, occasional.

Scrophularia nodosa L. Figwort. Apparently now extinct.

Mimulus guttatus DC. Monkey-flower. Naturalized, frequent.

M. cupreus D'Ombr. × *guttatus*. Monkey-flower. Naturalized, occasional.

M. luteus L. Blood-drop Emlets. Naturalized. Rare. Other unidentified *Mimulus* hybrids occur.

Digitalis purpurea L. Foxglove. Frequent, except in some North Isles.

Veronica beccabunga L. Brooklime. Frequent.

V. anagallis-aquatica L. Water-speedwell. Frequent.

V. catenata Pennell. Pink Water-speedwell. Rare.

V. scutellata L. Marsh Speedwell. Occasional.

V. officinalis L. Common Speedwell. Common.

V. chamaedrys L. Germander Speedwell. Assumed by earlier botanists to have been introduced. Occasional.

V. serpyllifolia L. Thyme-leaved Speedwell. Common.

V. arvensis L. Wall Speedwell. Occasional.

V. hederifolia L. Ivy-leaved Speedwell. Frequent.

V. persica Poir. Buxbaum's Speedwell. Frequent.

V. polita Fr. Grey Speedwell. Probably extinct.

V. agrestis L. Field Speedwell. Frequent.

V. filiformis Sm. Slender Speedwell. Introduced, widespread, probably never seeds but can establish from tiny scraps.

Hebe × franciscana Souster. 'Veronica'. Occasionally naturalized near seashores.

Pedicularis palustris L. Red Rattle, Marsh Lousewort. Frequent.

P. sylvatica L. Lousewort. Frequent except in outer North Isles.

Rhinanthus serotinus (Scheonh.) Orbony. Greater Yellow-rattle. Probably extinct.

R. minor L. ssp. *minor*. Yellow-rattle. Common.

R. minor L. ssp. *stenophyllus* (Schur) O. Schwarz. Yellow-rattle. Common.

R. minor L. ssp. *monticola* (Sterneck) O. Schwarz. Yellow-rattle. Occasional.

Melampyrum pratense L. ssp. *pratense*. Common Cow-wheat. Rare, Hoy hills.

Euphrasia officinalis L. Eyebright. The *Euphrasia* situation in Orkney has been revised several times and is, moreover, confused by the abundance of hybrids. The following is merely an attempt at distribution.

E. arctica Rostrup ssp. *arctica*. Occasional?

E. arctica Rostrup ssp. *borealis* (Towns.) P. F. Yeo. Occasional?

E. nemorosa (Pers.) Wallr. Frequent, often on roadsides.

E. confusa Pugsl. Frequent, often on dunes.

E. foulaensis Wettst. Occasional, especially on stony grassland near the sea.

E. marshalli Pugsl. Various 'possible' determinations; presumably doubtful or rare.

E. rotundifolia Pugsl. This is a nationally 'rare species' and has only been found once in Orkney, in 1963.

E. micrantha Reichenb. Common, especially on heaths.

E. scottica Wettst. Frequent, on flushes and saltmarsh.

E. heslop-harrisonii Pugsl. This is another 'rare species' but has been found on at least five sites in Orkney, where it occurs on sloping banks near the sea, in very short turf.

Odontites verna (Bellardi) Dumort. ssp. *verna*. Red Bartsia. Frequent.

Pinguicula vulgaris L. Common Butterwort. Frequent, except in outer North Isles.

Utricularia australis R.Br. = *U. neglecta* Lehm. Bladderwort. Occasional.

U. minor L. Lesser Bladderwort. Occasional. There appear to be no records of Bladderworts flowering in Orkney.

Mentha aquatica L. Water-mint. Common.

M. aquatica × spicata. Peppermint. Escape, more or less naturalized.

M. spicata L. Spearmint. Escape, more or less naturalized.

M. × villosa Huds. nm. *alopecuroides* (Hull) Briq. Mint. Occasional garden outcast.

M. × villosa Huds. nm. *webberi* (Frase) Ined. Mint. Rare garden outcast.

M. × suaveoloens Ehrh. Apple-scented Mint. Rare? garden outcast, easily confused with *M. × villosa*.

Thymus pracox Opiz. ssp. *arcticus* (Durand) Jalis. = *T. drucei* Ronn. Thyme. Frequent.

Prunella vulgaris L. Self-heal. Common. White flowered f. occur.

Stachys arvensis (L.) L. Field Woundwort. Rare casual.

S. palustris L. Marsh Woundwort. Occasional.

S. palustris × sylvatica = S. × ambigua Sm. Hybrid Woundwort. Common, usually in the absence of both parents.

S. sylvatica L. Hedge Woundwort. Rare.

Lamium amplexicaule L. Henbit. Rare.

L. moluccellifolium Fr. Intermediate Dead-nettle. Common.

L. purpureum L. Red Dead-nettle. Common.

L. album L. White Dead-nettle. Extinct.

L. maculatum L. Spotted Dead-nettle. Escape.

Galeopsis tetrahit L. Common Hemp-nettle. Common.

G. bifida Boenn. Hemp-nettle. Rare.

G. speciosa Mill. Large-flowered Hemp-nettle. Rare casual, 1924.

Glechoma hederacea L. Ground Ivy. Introduction. Rare.

Scuttellaria galericulata. L. Skull-cap. Rare, North Isles only.

Teucrium scorodonia L. Wood Sage. Occasional, not in outer North Isles.

Ajuga reptans L. Bugle. Occasional.

A. pyramidalis L. Rare, Hoy and Orphir.

A. pyramidalis × reptans = A. × hampeana Braun & Vatke. Recorded in Harray but apparently extinct there. A vigorous plant occurring on some Scapa Flow cliffs could be this.

Plantago major L. Great Plantain. Common.

P. media L. Hoary Plantain. Rare, presumably introduced (in a lawn). Holm. First recorded 1984.

P. lanceolata L. Ribwort. Common.

P. maritima L. Sea Plantain. Common, often at considerable distances from the coast.

P. indica L. Casual, 1932.

P. coronopus L. Buck's-horn Plantain. Common, entirely coastal.

Littirella uniflora (L.) Aschers. Shore-weed. Frequent.

Campanula rapunculoides L. Creeping Campanula. Garden outcast.

C. rotundifolia L. Harebell, Scots Bluebell. Appears sporadically but has never persisted in Orkney for more than a few years.

Jasione montana L. Sheep's-bit. Occasional, but very local – Eday, the east side of Sanday and South Ronaldsay.

Lobelia dortmanna L. Water Lobelia. Rare. Unknown if truly native anywhere as introductions have been made.

Sherardia arvensis L. Field Madder. Was an occasional weed of sandy North Isles fields until late 1960s, since apparently extinct.

Galium mollugo L. Common Hedge Bedstraw. Naturalized, Burray.

G. album Mill = *G. erectum* Syme. Upright Hedge Bedstraw. Naturalized on roadsides in Twatt.

G. verum Lady's Bedstraw. Frequent.

G. saxatile L. Heath Bedstraw. Common.

G. sterneri Ehrend. Limestone Bedstraw. Frequent.

G. palustre L. Great Marsh Bedstraw. Common.

G. elongatum C Presl. Marsh Bedstraw. Rare.

G. aparine L. Goosegrass, Cleavers. Frequent, but almost confined to seashores.

Sambuscus ebulus L. Danewort. Rarely planted.

S. nigra L. Elder, Bourtree. Has been commonly planted but probably never seeds.

Symphoricarpos rivularis Suksd. Snowberry. Commonly planted and semi-naturalized.

Lonicera periclymenum L. Honeysuckle. A frequent native in the South Isles and Scapa Flow coast, probably planted elsewhere.

Valerianella locusta (L.) Betke. Lamb's Lettuce. Common in Westray near Pierowall, in the early 1960s, but apparently disappeared since.

Valeriana officinalis L. Valerian. Occasional.

V. pyrenaica L. Pyrenean Valerian. Occasionally naturalized.

Knautia arvensis (L.) Coult. Field Scabious. Casual or introduction.

Succisa pratensis Moench. Devil's-bit Scabious. Common.

Senecio jacobaea L. Ragwort. Only common on very sandy soils.

S. aquaticus Hill. Marsh Ragwort. Frequent.

S. aquaticus × jacobaea = S. ostenfeldii Druce. Ragwort. Common.

S. sylvaticus L. Wood Groundsel. Not seen post-1950 and probably always rare.

S. vulgaris L. Groundsel. Common.

S. smithii DC. Magellan Ragwort. Occasional, always

planted or escape. Probably introduced from the Falkland Isles in the early part of the 20th century.

Tussilago farfara L. Coltsfoot. Common.

Petasites hybridus (L.) Gaert. *et al.* Butterbur. A few large colonies.

P. fragrans (Vill.) C. Presl. Winter Heliotrope. Rare, naturalized, first recorded 1950.

Calendula officinalis L. Pot Marigold. Escape.

Inula helenium L. Elecampane. Occasional. Escape.

Gnaphalium sylvaticum L. Wood Cudweed. Rare, possibly extinct.

G. uliginosum L. Marsh Cudweed. Occasional.

Anaphalis margaritacea (L.) Benth. Pearly Everlasting. Garden outcast, occasionally naturalized.

Antennaria dioica (L.) Gaertn. Cat's-foot, Mountain Everlasting. Frequent.

Solidago virgaurea L. Golden-rod. Frequent except in the east of Orkney.

Aster tripolium L. Sea Aster. Occasional; sometimes on sea cliffs.

A.× salignus Willd. A Michaelmas Daisy. A rare garden outcast, recorded pre-1950.

Bellis perennis L. Daisy. Common.

Eupatorium cannabinum L. Hemp Agrimony. Rare. South Ronaldsay. First recorded 1964.

Anthemis cotula L. Stinking Mayweed. Casual.

A. arvensis L. Corn Chamomile. Casual, pre-1950.

Chamaemelum nobile (L.) All. Chamomile. Garden escape. Last recorded 1927.

Achillea millefolium L. Milfoil, Yarrow. Common.

A. ptarmica L. Sneezewort. Frequent.

Tripleurospermum maritimum (L.) Koch = *Matricaria maritima* L. Sea Mayweed. Common.

Matricaria recutita L. Wild Chamomile. Casual.

M. matricarioides (Less.) Porter. Pineapple Weed. Common, first recorded 1931.

Chrysanthemum segetum L. Corn Marigold. Common in the west of Orkney.

Leucanthemum vulgare Lam. = *C. leucanthemum* L. Ox-eye Daisy. Occasional.

Tanacetum parthenium (L.) Schultz Bip. = *C. parthenium* (L.) Bernh. Feverfew. Escape.

T. vulgare L. Tansy. Occasional relict of cultivation.

Cotula soualida Hook *fil.* A New Zealand Pincushion plant, reported from 'a lawn in St Ola' in the 60's.

Artemesia vulgaris L. Mugwort. Occasional.

Arctium minus Bernh. Burdock. Occasional.

Cirsium vulgare (Savi) Ten. Spear Thistle. Common.

C. palustre (L.) Scop. Marsh Thistle. Common.

C. arvense (L.) Scop. Creeping Thistle. Common.

C. helenoides (L.) Hill = *C. heterophyllum* (L.) Hill. Melancholy Thistle. Occasional, almost certainly introduced and not recorded before 1964.

Saussurea alpina (L.) DC. Alpine Saw-wort. Rare, Hoy and Rousay.

Centaurea cyanus L. Cornflower. Now a rare cornfield weed.

C.× drucei C. E. Britton. Rare casual, 1928.

C. nigra L. Hardheads. Occasional.

C. solstitalis L. St Barnaby's Thistle. Rare casual, 1927.

Chicorum intybus L. Chicory. Occasional escape.

Lapsana communis L. Nipplewort. Rare casual.

Hypochoeris radicata L. Cat's Ear. Common.

Leontodon autumnalis. Autumnal Hawkbit. Common.

Sonchus arvensis L. Corn Sowthistle. Frequent.

S. oleraceus L. Common Sowthistle. Occasional.

S. asper (L.) Hill. Prickly Sowthistle. Frequent.

Hieracium murorum L. *sensu lato.* Hawkweed. *Hieracia*, as a group, are occasional in Orkney. The following are from Sell & West's revision in *Watsonia*, Vol. 5 Pt. 4.

H. anglicum L. Occasional. Hoy and Rousay.

H. iricum Fr. Rare. Hoy.

H. sarcophylloides Dahlst. Occasional. Hoy.

H. argenteum Er. Rare. Hoy.

H. caledonicum F. J. Hanb. Occasional.

H. scoticum F. J. Hanb. Occasional.

H. orimeles W. R. Linton. Rare. Orphir.

H. euprepes F. J. Hanb. Occasional. Hoy.

H. lactobrigorum (Zahn) Roffey. Occasional.

H. maritimum (F. J. Hanb.) F. J. Hanb. Rare, South Walls.

H. pilosella L. Mouse-ear Hawkweed. Frequent.

H. aurantiacum L. Fox-and-cubs. Rare garden escape.

Crepis biennis L. Rough Hawk's-beard. Rare casual, before 1914.

C. capillaris (L.) Wallr. Smooth Hawk's-beard. Occasional.

C. nicaeensis Balb. French Hawk's-beard. Rare casual, pre-1950.

Taraxacum officinale group (i.e. Section Vulgaria Dahlst.) Common Dandelion. Frequent, mainly on roadsides and in cultivated areas.

T. spectabile group (Section Spectabilia Dahlst.) Broad-leaved Marsh Dandelion. Common.

Elodea canadensis Michx. Canadian Pondweed. Rare, introduced.

Triglochin palustris. Marsh Arrow-grass. Frequent.

T. maritima L. Sea Arrow-grass. Frequent, often inland.

Zostera marina L. Grass-wrack. Apparently frequent.

Z. angustifolia (Hornem.) Reichb. Narrow-leaved Grass-wrack. Status uncertain.

Z. noltii Hornem. Dwarf Grass-wrack. Apparently rare.

Potamogeton natans L. Broad-leaved Pondweed. Common.

P. polygonifolius Pourr. Bog Pondweed. Common.

P. lucens L. Shining Pondweed. Rare, Rousay.

P. gramineus L. Various-leaved Pondweed. Occasional.

Potamogeton gramineus × lucens = P. × zizii Roth. Rare, Rousay.

P. gramineus × perfoliatus = P. × nitens Weber. Rare.

P. praelongus Wulf. Long-stalked Pondweed. Rare and declining. Tankerness.

P. perfoliatus L. Perfoliate Pondweed. Common.

P. friesii Rupr. Flat-stalked Pondweed. Occasional.

P. pusillus L. Lesser Pondweed. Occasional.

P. obtusifolius Mert & Koch. Extinct through drainage.

P. berchtoldii Fieb. Small Pondweed. Frequent.

P. crispus L. Curled Pondweed. Occasional.

P. filiformis Pers. Slender-leaved Pondweed. Common.

P. pectinatus L. Fennel-leaved Pondweed. Frequent.

Ruppia cirrhosa (Petagna) Grande = *R. spiralis* Dumort. Spiral Tasselweed. Rare.

R. maritima L. Tasselweed. Frequent.

Zannichellia palustris L. Horned Pondweed. Frequent.

Narthecium ossifragum (L.) Huds. Bog Asphodel. Common.

Lilium pyrenaicum Gouan. Persists in derelict gardens.

Scilla verna Huds. Spring Squill. Frequent.

Hyacinthoides hispanica × non-scripta. Garden escape.

(*H. non-scripta* (L.) Chuard ex Rothm. = *Endymion non-scriptus* (L.) Garcke. Bluebell, Wild Hyacinth. Not a wild plant in Orkney.)

Juncus squarrosus L. Heath Rush. Common.

J. tenuis Willd. Slender Rush. Rare casual 1957, not seen since.

J. gerardi Lois. Mud Rush. Coastal and saltmarsh.

J. bufonus L. Toad Rush. Common.

J. effusus L. Soft Rush. Common.

J. conglomeratus L. Common Rush. Common.

[*J. balticus* Willd.] Baltic Rush. Reported from Loch of Harray 1937 by one person but not seen since.

J. acutiflorus Hoffm. Sharp-flowered Rush. Occasional.

J. acutiflorus × articulatus = J. × surrejanus Druce. Status uncertain but some large colonies apparently occur.

J. articulatus L. Jointed Rush. Common.

J. kochii F. W. Schultz (has been previously recorded as *J. bulbosus* L). Bulbous Rush. Common.

J. bulbosus var. *fluitans.* Common.

J. triglumis L. Three-flowered Rush. Seen in 1909. Probably extinct.

Luzula pilosa (L.) Willd. Hairy Woodrush. Rare.

L. sylvatica (Huds.) Gaudin. Greater Woodrush. Common.

L. campestris (L.) DC. Field Woodrush. Common.

L. multiflora (Retz.) Lejeune. Many-headed Woodrush. Common.

Allium schoenoprasum L. Chives. Garden escape.

A. paradoxum (Bieb.) G. Don. Flowering Garlic. Escape.

A. ursinum L. Ramsons. Rare. Presumably garden escape.

Iris pseudacorus L. Yellow Flag, Segs. Common.

Tritonia × crocosmiflora (Lemoine) Nicholson = *Crocosmia × crocosmiflora* (Lemoine) N. E. Br. Montbretia. Planted in waste places.

Listera ovata (L.) R. Br. Twayblade. Occasional, often on roadsides where it is destroyed by mowing.

L. cordata (L.) R. Br. Lesser Twayblade. Occasional.

Goodyera repens (L.) R. Br. Creeping Lady's Tresses. Specimens collected in Harray and Stromness 1877 and 1896 and plants presumably destroyed.

Hammarbya paludosa (L.) Kuntze. Bog Orchid. A clump found and collected in Hoy in 1933. Seen again in 1936 but not since.

Coeloglossum viride (L.) Hartm. Frog Orchid. Occasional.

Gymnadenia conopsea (L.) R. Br. ssp. *conopsea.* Fragrant Orchid. Occasional.

G. conopsea ssp. *densiflora* (Wahlenb.) Camus *et al.* Occasional, wet places.

Pseudorchis albida (L.) A. & D. Loeve = *Leuchorchis albida* (L.) E. Mey ex Schur. Small White Orchid. Rare.

Orchis mascula (L.) L. Early Purple Orchid. Rare. Hoy and St Ola.

Dactylorhiza fuchsii (Druce) Soo. = *Dactylorchis fuchsii* (Druce) Vermeul. Spotted Orchid. Rare. Only found in St Ola although possible hybrids occur elsewhere.

D. maculata (L.) Soo ssp. *ericetorum* (E. F. Linton) Hunt & Summerh. Moorland Spotted Orchid. Common.

D. maculata × purpurella = D. × formosa (T. & T. A. Steph.) Vermeul. Occasional, sometimes very large spikes.

D. incarnata (L.) Soo. Early Marsh Orchid. Occasional.

D. purpurella (T. & T. A. Steph.) Soo. Northern Fen Orchid. Common.

D. maculata × Pseudorchis albida. Hybrid orchid. Very rare.

Arum maculatum L. Lords-and-Ladies. Introduced in gardens but spreading.

Lemna minor L. Duckweed. Occasional.

Sparganium erectum L. Bur-reed. Frequent.

S. angustifolium Michx. Floating Bur-reed. Occasional.

Typha latifolia L. Great Reedmace. Introduced at one site in Evie.

Eriophorum angustifolium Honck. Common Cottongrass. Common.

E. latifolium Hoppe. Broad-leaved Cotton-grass. Rare. Hoy.

E. vaginatum L. Hare's-tail. Common.

Trichophorum cespitosum (L.) Hartman. Deer-grass. Common.

Scirpus maritimus L. Sea Club-rush. A small colony in Westray seen in 1960s and 70s now appears to be extinct.

Schoenoplectus lacustris (L.) Palla. Bulrush. Occasional but decreasing in many places.

S. tabernaemontani (C. G. Gmel.) Palla. Glaucus Bulrush. Occasional but also decreasing. Both these species are affected by draining and grazing of habitat.

Isolepis setacea (L.) R. Br. Bristle Scirpus. Occasional.

Elegiton fluitans (L.) Link. Floating Scirpus. Rare.

Eleocharis quinqueflora (F. X. Hartmann) Schwarz. Few-flowered Spike-rush. Occasional.

E. multicaulis (Sm.) Sm. Many-stemmed Spike-rush Occasional.

E. palustris (L.) Roem. & Schult. Common Spike-rush. Common.

E. uniglumis (Link) Schult. One-glumed Spike-rush. Occasional.

Blysmus rufus (Huds.) Link. Narrow Blysmus. Occasional.

Schoenus nigricans L. Black Bog-rush. Frequent.

Carex hostiana DC. Tawny Sedge. Frequent.

C. hostiana × lepidocarpa. Occasional.

C. binervis Sm. Green-ribbed Sedge. Common.

C. lepidocarpa Tausch. Long-stalked Yellow Sedge. Frequent.

C. demissa Hornem. Yellow Sedge. Frequent.

C. serotina Meret. Small-fruited Yellow Sedge. Frequent, mainly coastal.

C. extensa Gooden. Long-bracted Sedge. Occasional. Saltmarsh.

C. sylvatica Hudson. Wood Sedge. Rare, Shapinsay, almost certainly introduced.

C. rostrata Stokes. Bottle Sedge. Frequent.

C. riparia Curt. Greater Pond Sedge. Rare, Stronsay.

C. panicea L. Carnation Sedge. Common.

C. limosa L. Mud Sedge. Occasional.

C. flacca Schreb. Glaucous Sedge. Common.

C. lasiocarpa. Ehrh. Slender Sedge. Grew, until late 1960s in two sites in West Mainland, now both drained. Believed extinct.

C. pilulifera L. Pill Sedge. Frequent.

C. nigra (L.) Reichard. Common Sedge. Common.

C. bigelowii Schwein. Stiff Sedge. Occasional, higher hills.

C. paniculata L. Greater Tussock Sedge. Occasional.

C. diandra Schrank. Lesser Tussock Sedge. Rare.

C. disticha Huds. Brown Sedge. Rare.

C. arenaria L. Sand Sedge. Frequent.

C. maritima Gunn. Curved Sedge. Occasional.

C. spicata Huds. Spiked Sedge. Recorded by Magnus Spence, not seen since.

C. echinata Murr. Star Sedge. Common.

C. curta Gooden. White Sedge. Rare.

C. ovalis Gooden. Oval Sedge. Occasional.

C. pulicaris L. Flea Sedge. Common.

C. dioica L. Dioecious Sedge. Frequent.

Phragmites australis (Cav.) Strud. = *P. communis* Trin. Common Reed. Occasional.

Molinia caerulea (L.) Moench. Purple Moor-grass. Common.

Danthonia decumbens (L.) DC. = *Sieglingia decumbens* (L.) Bernh. Heath Grass. Frequent.

Glyceria fluitans (L.) R. Br. Floating Sweet-grass. Frequent.

G. fluitans × plicata Hybrid Sweet-grass. Rare.

G. plicata Fr. Plicate Sweet-grass. Rare.

G. declinata Breb. Glaucous Sweet-grass. Rare.

Festuca pratensis Huds. Meadow Fescue. Rare, probably introduced.

F. arundinacea Schreb. Tall Fescue. Occasional, probably introduced.

F. rubra L. Red Fescue. Common.

F. ovina L. Sheep's Fescue. Rare, South Isles only.

F. tenuifolia Sibth. Fine-leaved Sheep's Fescue. Occasional.

F. vivipara (L.) Sm. Viviparous Fescue. Common.

Lolium perenne L. Perennial Rye-grass. Frequent, often sown.

L. multiflorum Lam. Italian Rye-grass. Rare, sown.

Vulpia bromoides (L.) Gray. Squirrel-tail Fescue. Casual, last recorded 1928.

Puccinellia maritima (Huds.) Parl. Common Saltmarsh Grass. Common.

P. capillaris (Liljebl) Jansen. Northern Saltmarsh Grass. Frequent.

Desmazeria marina (L.) Druce. Stiff Sand Grass. Rare.

Poa annua L. Annual Meadow-grass. Common.

P. alpina L. Alpine Meadow-grass. Rare, Hoy, first recorded 1963. Became very plentiful during first myxomatosis outbreak but now declining as rabbits return.

P. pratensis L. Smooth Meadow-grass. Rare, probably introduced.

P. subcaerulea Sm. Spreading Meadow-grass. Common.

P. trivialis L. Rough Meadow-grass. Common.

Catabrosa aquatica (L.) Beauv. Water Whorl-grass. Occasional.

Dactylis glomerata L. Cocksfoot. Common, frequently sown.

Cynosurus cristatus L. Crested Dog's-tail. Common.

Briza media L. Common Quaking-grass. Rare, doubtfully native.

Bromus hordeaceus L. ssp. *pseudothominii* (P. Smith) Scholz. Soft Brome. Occasional.

B. sterilis L. Barren Brome. Rare casual.

Brachypodium sylvaticum (Huds.) Beauv. Slender False-brome. Occasional, usually on sea cliffs.

Elymus repens (L.) Gould = *Agropyrum repens* (L.) Beauv. Couch. Common.

E. farctus (Viv.) Runemark ex Melderis = *Agropyron junceiforme* (A. & D. Loeve) A. & D. Loeve. Sand Couch. Frequent.

E. farctus × repens. Occasional.

Leymus arenarius (L.) Hochst = *Elymus arenarius* L. Lyme Grass. Frequent.
Koeleria cristata (L.) Pers. Crested Hair-grass. Rare.
Trisetum flavescens (L.) Beauv. Yellow Oat Grass. A 19th century record, perhaps doubtful.
Avena fatua L. Common Wild Oat. Casual.
A. fatua × *sativa* L. Oat. Casual.
A. strigosa Schreb. Bristle Oat. Casual.
Avenula pubescens (Huds.) Dumort. = *Helictotrichon pubescens* (Huds.) Pilg. Hairy Oat-grass. Frequent.
Arrhenatherum elatius (L.) J. & C. Presl. False Oat-grass, including 'swine-beads'. Common.
Holcus lanatus L. Yorkshire Fog. Common.
H. mollis L. Creeping Soft-grass. Rare.
Deschampsia cespitosa (L.) Beauv. Tufted Hair-grass, 'Burrowy to'ers'. Common.
D. flexuosa (L.) Trin. Wavy Hair-grass. Frequent.
Aira praecox L. Early Hair-grass. Common.
A. caryophylla L. ssp. *multiculmis* (Dumort.) Hegi. Silvery Hair-grass. Occasional.
Ammophila arenaria (L.) Link. Marram. Frequent.
Agrostis canina L. ssp. *canina*. Brown Bent. Common, mainly pastures.

A. vinealis Schreber = *A. canina* L. ssp. *montana* (Hartm.) Hartm. Brown Bent. Common.
A. capillaris L. = *A. tenuis* Sibth. Brown Top. Common.
A. capillaris × *A. canina* Rare, first recorded 1971.
A. gigantea Roth. Black Bent. Occasional, possible introduction. First recorded 1972.
A. gigantea × *A. stolonifera*. Rare, first recorded 1982.
A. stolonifera L. Creeping Bent. Common.
A. stolonifera × *capillaris*. Rare, first recorded 1971.
Phleum pratense L. Timothy. Sown or escape.
Alopecurus pratensis L. Meadow Fox-tail. Probably sown or escape.
A. geniculatus L. Marsh Fox-tail. Frequent.
Hierochloë odorata (L.) Beauv. Holy-grass. Rare, first recorded 1980 though obviously overlooked previously.
Anthoxanthum odoratum L. Sweet Vernal-grass. Common.
Apuelii Lecoq & Lamott. Annual Vernal-grass. Rare casual, 1933.
Phalaris arundinacea L. Reed Canary-grass. Frequent.
Nardus stricta L. Mat-grass. Frequent.

HIRUDINEA
(based on Maitland & Kellock, 1971, and data held by the Biological Records Centre)

Piscicola geometra
Haementeria costata
Threomyzon tessulatum
Hemiclepis marginata
Glossiphonia heteroclita
G. complanata

Batracobdella paludosa
Boreobdella verrucata
Helobdella stagnalis
Haemopis sanguisuga
Hirudo medicinalis
Erpobdella testacea

E. octoculata
Dina lineata
Trocheta subviridis
T. bykowskii

COLEOPTERA
The Orkney beetles have been most collected in recent years by Mr Vincent Lorimer of Orphir and Dr Stuart Ball of the Nature Conservancy Council. The following list has been compiled by Mr Lorimer with the help of Mr M. Bacchus of the British Museum (Natural History). Dr Colin Welch of the Institute of Terrestrial Ecology has also worked on beetles in Orkney, and he has compared their status in Orkney and Shetland (basing his comments on the latter on Bacchus' data in Berry & Johnston, 1980):

Carabidae
Very similar lists of species from the two groups.

Water beetles
Half as many again on Orkney as listed for Shetland, largely as a result of the work of Balfour-Browne (1949).

Staphylinidae
128 species listed for Shetland, about 90 for Orkney.

Minor families
Under collecting probably accounts for the slight differences between the recorded faunas, although Cantharidae are significantly better represented on Orkney (9 species, as compared with only one in Shetland). This probably reflects the presence of more woodland in Orkney, since 6 of the species are woodland species.

Chrysomelidae
Three times as many species recorded in Orkney as in Shetland. This is difficult to explain as only one or two are woodland species.

Curculionidea
The weevil fauna is very similar in both island groups.

Carabidae

Cicindela campestris (L.)
Cychrus caraboides (L.)
Carabus arvensis (Herbst)
C. nemoralis (Müller)
C. problematicus (Herbst)
Leistus rufescens (Fab.)
Pelophila borealis (Paykull)
Nebria brevicollis (Fab.)
N. gyllenhali (Schoenher)
N. salina Fairmaire & Laboulbène
Notiophilus aquaticus (Fab.)
N. biguttatus (Fab.)
N. germingi (Fauvel)
N. palustris (Duftschmid)
Elaphrus cupreus (Duftschmid)
E. lapponicus (Gyllenhal)
Loricera pilicornis (Fab.)
Clivina fossor (L.)
Broscis cephalotes (L.)
Patrobus assimilis (Chaudoir)
P. atrorufus (Ström)
Trechus obtusus Erichson
T. quadristriatus (Schrank)
Bemidion litorale (Olivier)
B. bipunctatum (L.)
B. tibiale (Duftschmidt)
B. tetracolum (Say)
Pterostichus diligens (Sturm)
P. melanarius (Illiger)
P. niger (Schaller)
P. nigrita (Paykull)
P. strenuus (Panzer)
Calathus erratus (Sahlberg)
C. fuscipes (Goeze)
C. melanocephalus (L.)
C. mollis (Marsham)
Olisthopus rotundatus (Paykull)
Agonum albipes (Fab.)
A. muelleri (Herbst)
Amara bifrons (Gyllenhal)
A. apricaria (Paykull)
A. aulica (Panzer)
A. ovata (Fab.)
A. plebeja (Gyllenhal)
Harpalus rufipes (Degeer)
H. latus (L.)
Dicheirotrichus gustavi (Crotch)
Trichocellus placidus (Gyllenhal)
Bradycellus harpalinus (Serville)
B. ruficollis (Stephens)

Haliplidae

Haliplus confinis (Stephens)
H. obliquus (Fab.)
H. fulvus (Fab.)

H. lineatocollis (Marsham)
H. ruficollis (Degeer)
H. wehnckei (Gerhardt)

Dytiscidae

Hygrotus inaequalis (Fab.)
Coelambus novemlineatus
  (Stephens)
Hydroporus discretus (Fairmaire)
H. erythrocephalus (L.)
H. gyllenhali (Schiödte)
H. incognitus (Sharp)
H. memnonius (Nicolai)
H. morio (Aubé)
H. nigrita (Fab.)
H. obscurus (Sturm)
H. palustris (L.)
H. pubescens (Gyllenhal)
H. striola (Gyllenhal)
H. tristis (Paykull)
Potamodytes assimilis (Paykull)
P. depressus (Fab.)
P. elegans (Panzer)
P. griseostriatus (Degeer)
Oreodytes sanmarki (Sahlberg)
O. septentrionalis (Sahlberg)
Agabus arcticus (Paykull)
A. bipustulatus (L.)
A. chalconotus (Panzer)
A. congener (Thunberg)
A. guttatus (Paykull)
A. melanocornis (Zimmermann)
A. nebulosus (Forster)
A. sturmi (Gyllenhal)
Ilybius fuliginosus (Fab.)
Rhantus bistriatus (Bergstraesser)
Colymbetes fuscus (L.)
Acilius sulcatus (L.)
Dyticsus semisulcatus (Müller)
D. lapponicus (Gyllenhal)

Gyrinidae

Gyrinus natator (L.)

Hydrophilidae

Helophorus flavipes (Fab.)
H. aquaticus (L.)
H. grandis (Illiger)
H. flavipes (Fab.)
H. granularis (L.)
H. rufipes (Boss D'Antic)
H. griseus (Marsham)
H. brevipalpis (Bedel)
H. brevipalpis f. bulbipalpis (Kuwert)
Cercyon analis (Paykull)

C. atomarius (Fab.)
C. haemorrhoidalis (Fab.)
C. littoralis (Gyllenhall)
C. marinus C. G. Thomson
C. melanocephalus (L.)
C. quisquilius (L.)
C. unipunctatus (L.)
Cryptopleurum minutum (Fab.)
Megasternum obscurum (Marsham)
Hydrobius fuscipes (L.)
H. fuscipes f. picicrus C. G. Thomson
Anacaena globulus (Paykull)
Laccobius minutus (L.)
L. striatulus (Fab.)
Enochrus quadripunctatus (Herbst)
  f. fuscipennis (C. G. Thomson)

Hydraenidae

Ocththebius dilatatus (Stephens)
O. exsculptus (Germar)
O. minimis (Fab.)
Hydraena rufipes (Curtis) f. longior
  Rey.
H. britteni (Joy)
Limnebius nitidus (Marsham)
L. papposus (Mulsant)
L. truncatellus (Thunberg)

Ptiliidae

Ptenidium nitidum (Heer)
P. pusillum (Gyllenhal)
Acrotrichis atomaria (Degeer)
A. grandicollis (Mannerheim)
A. sericans (Heer)

Leiodidae

Leiodes dubis (Kugelann)
Ptomaphagus subvillosus (Goeze)
Choleva jeanneli (Britten)
Sciodrepoides watsoni (Spence)
Catops chrysomeloides (Panzer)
C. fuliginosus Erichson
C. grandicollis Erichson
C. coracinus Kellner
C. morio (Fab.)

Silphidae

Necrophorus humator (Gleditsch)
N. investigator Zetterstedt
N. vespilloides Herbst
Aclypea opaca (L.)
Silpha atrata (L.) f. brunnen
  (Herbst)
Thanatophilus rugosus (L.)

Scymaenidae

Stenichnus collaris (Müller & Kunze)

Staphylinidae

Megarthrus denticollis (Beck)
M. depressus (Paykull)
M. sinuatocollis (Boisduval & Lacordaire)
Olophrum piceum (Gyllenhal)
Lesteva longelytra (Goeze)
Omalium caesum (Gravenhorst)
O. excavatum (Stephens)
O. laeviusculum (Gyllenhal)
O. riparium (C. G. Thomson)
O. rivulare (Paykull)
Philorinum sordidum (Stephens)
Carpelimus pusillus (Gravenhorst)
Platystethus arenarius (Fourcroy)
Anotylus nitidulus (Gravenhorst)
A. rugosus (Fab.)
Oxytelus laqueatus (Marsham)
Stenus aceris (Stephens)
S. impressus (Garmar)
S. latifrons (Erichson)
S. brunnipes (Scopoli)
S. clavicornis (Stephens)
S. crassus (Stephens)
S. juno (Fab.)
S. pricipes (Stephens)
S. nanus (Stephens)
S. nitidusculus (Stephens)
S. ossium (Stephens)
Lathrobium fulvipenne (Gravenhorst)
Othius punctulatus (Goeze)
O. angustus (Stephens)
Gyrohypnus punctulatus (Paykull)
Xantholinus linearis (Olivier)
X. glabratus (Gravenhorst)
Philonthus addendus Sharp
P. decorus (Gravenhorst)
P. laminatus (Creutzer)
P. marginatus (Ström)
P. succicola (C. G. Thomson)
P. umbratilis (Gravenhorst)
P. varians (Paykull)
P. varius (Gyllenhal)
P. varius var. shetlandicus (Poppius)
Cafius xantholoma (Gravenhorst)
Staphylinus ater (Gravenhorst)
S. brunnipes (Fab.)
S. erythropterus (L.)
S. olens (Müller)

Creophilus maxillosus (L.)
Ontholestes murinus (L.)
Quedius cinctus (Paykull)
Q. fuliginosus (Gravenhorst)
Q. mesomelinus (Marsham)
Q. molochinus (Gravenhorst)
Q. semioeneus (Stephens)
Q. tristis (Gravenhorst)
Q. umbrinus (Erichson)
Mycteporus longulus (Mannerheim)
Tachinus elongatus (Gyllenhal)
T. laticollis (Gravenhorst)
T. marginellus (Fab.)
T. signatus (Gravenhorst)
Tachyporus hypnorum (Fab.)
T. pusillus (Gravenhorst)
T. nitidulus (Fab.)
T. chrysomelinus (L.)
Autalia puncticollis (Sharp)
Tachyusa atra (Gravenhorst)
Aloconota currax (Kraatz)
A. gregaria (Erichson)
Amischa analis (Gravenhorst)
Geostiba circellaris (Gravenhorst)
Atheta atramentaria (Gyllenhal)
A. fungi (Gravenhorst)
A. incognita (Sharp)
A. macrocera (C. G. Thomson)
A. melanocera (C. G. Thomson)
A. pertyi (Heer)
A. triangulum (Kraatz)
A. trinotata (Kratz)
A. nigra (Kraatz)
A. longicornis (Gravenhorst)
A. vestita (Gravenhorst)
Oxypoda elongatula (Aubé)
O. opaca (Gravenhorst)
Aleochara brevipennis (Gravenhorst)
A. lanuginosa (Gravenhorst)
A. sparsa (Heer)

Geotrupidae

Geotrupes stercorarius (L.)

Scarabeidae

Aphodius ater (Degeer)
A. contaminatus (Herbst)
A. depressus (Kugelann)
A. lapponicum (Gyllenhal)
A. prodromus (Brahm)
A. rufipes (L.)
A. rufus (Moll.)
Serrica brunnea (L.)

Ptinidae

Ptinus fur (L.)

Clambidae

Clambus pubescens (Redtenbacher)

Scirtidae

Elodes marginata (Fab.)
E. minuta (L.)
Cyphon coarctatus (Paykull)
C. variabilis (Thunberg)

Byrrhidae

Cytilus sericeus (Forster)
Simplocoria semistriata (Fab.)

Elmidae

Elmus aenea (Müller)
Limnius volkmari (Panzer)
Oulimnius tuberculatus (Müller)

Elateridae

Hypnoidus riparius (Fab.)
Athous hirtus (Herbst)
A. haemorrhoidalis (Fab.)
Ctenicera cuprea var. aeruginosa (Fab.)
C. pectinicornis (L.)
Selatosomus incanus (Gyllenhal)
Dalopius marginatus (L.)
Agriotes obscurus (L.)
Adrastus pallens (Fab.)

Cantharidae

Cantharis paludosa (Fallén)
Rhagonycha elongata (Fallén)
R. femoralis (Brullé)
R. pallida (Fab.)
Malthinus flaveolus (Paykull)
Malthodes flavoguttus (Kieschwetter)
M. fuscus (Walton)
M. mysticus (Kieschwetter)
M. pumilus (Brébisson)

Anobiidae

Anobium punctatum (Degeer)

Nitidulidae

Brachypterus urticae (Fab.)
Meligethes aeneus (Fab.)
M. viridescens (Fab.)
Epuraea depressa (Gyllenhal)

Rhizophagidae

Rhizophagus cribratus (Gyllenhal)
R. dispar (Paykull)

Cryptophagidae

Cryptophagus pseudodentatus
  (Bruce)
C. dentatus (Herbst)
C. pilosus (Gyllenhal)
C. scanicus (L.)
Micrambe villosus (Heer)
M. vini (Panzer)
Atomaria atricapilla (Stephens)
A. fuscipes (Gyllenhal)
A. nitidula (Marsham)
A. borealis (Sjöberg)

Coccinellidae

Coccinella septempunctata (L.)
Propylea quatuordecem punctata
  (L.)

Lathridiidae

Aridius nodifer (Westwood)
Lathridius minutus (L.)
Enicmus transversus (Olivier)
Corticarina fuscula (Gyllenhal)

Tenebrionidae

Isomita murina (L.)

Salpingidae

Rhinusimus planirostris (Fab.)

Scraptiidae

Anaspis ruficollis (Fab.)

Cerambycidae

Acanthocinus aedilis (L.)

Cyrysomelidae

Plateumaris discolor (Panzer)
Oulema melanopa (L.)
Chrysolina latecincta (Demaison)
C. sanguinolenta (L.)
C. fastuosa (Scopoli)
C. staphylaea (L.)
Gastroidea viridula (Degeer)
Phaedon armoraciae (L.)
P. concinnis (Stephens)
Hydrothassa hannoveriana (Fab.)
H. glabra (Herbst)
Phyllotreta flexuosa (Illiger)
Phyllodecta olivacea (Forster)
Chaetocnema hortensis (Fourcroy)
Galeruca tanaceti (L.)
Longitarsus lycopi (Foudras)
L. succineus (Foudras)
Derocrepis rufipes (L.)
Psylliodes chrysocephala (L.)
P. cuprea (Koch)
P. marcida (Illiger)

Apionidae

Apion punctigerum (Paykull)
A. assimile (Kirby)
A. reyi (Blackburn)
A. ervi (Kirby)

A. frumentarium (Paykull)
A. dissimile (Germar)
A. violaceum Kirby

Curculionidae

Otiorhynchus arcticus (Fab.)
O. atroapterus (Degeer)
O. nodosus (Müller)
O. singularis (L.)
O. sulcatus (Fab.)
Phyllobius roboretanus (Gredler)
P. viridicollis (Fab.)
Polydrosus cervinus (L.)
Barypeithes areneiformis (Schrank)
Strophosomus melanogrammus
  (Forster)
Philopedon plagiatus (Schaller)
Barynotus moerens (Fab.)
B. squamosus (Germar)
Sciaphilus asperatus (Bonsdorff)
Tropiphorus elevatus (Herbst)
T. terricola (Newman)
Sitona lepidus Gyllenhal
Hypera arator (L.)
H. plantaginis (Degeer)
H. nigrirostris (Fab.)
H. punctata (Fab.)
Notaris acridulus (L.)
Grypus equiseti (Fab.)
Cidnorhinus quadrimaculatus (L.)
Micrelus ericae (Gyllenhal)
Ceuthorhynchus pollinarius (Fors-
  ter)
C. constrictus (Marsham)
C. punctiger (Sahlberg)
C. contractus (Marsham)
Rhynchaenus fagi (L.)
R. foliorum (Müller)
Rhinonchius pericarpius (L.)

ODONATA
(Biological Records Centre and Hammond, 1983)

There are only 37 species of Dragonflies which breed
regularly in the U.K.

Enallagma cyathigerum (Charpentier)
Pyrrhosoma nymphula (Sulzer)
Ischnura elegans (Van Linden)
Aeschna juncea (L.)
Sympetrum danae (Sulzer)

ORTHOPTERA

Chorthippus parallelus
Omocestus viridulus
Tetrix undulata

TRICHOPTERA
(collected by J. D. Walker of Kirkwall)

Phryganeidae

Phryganea grandis (Linnaeus)
P. varia (Fabricius)

Limnephilidae

Limnephilus marmoratus (Curtis)
L. luridus (Curtis)
L. incisus (Curtis)
L. stigma (Curtis)
L. affinis (Curtis)
L. sparsus (Curtis)
L. griseus (Linnaeus)
L. flavicornis (Fabricius)
L. extricatus (McLachlan)
Stenophylax sequax (McLachlan)
S. permistus (McLachlan)
Mesophylax impunctatus (McLachlan)
Drusus annulatus (Stephens)
Potamophylax rotundipennis (Brauer)
P. cingulatus (Stephens)
P. latipennis (Curtis)
Chaetopteryx villosa (Fabricius)
Glyphotaelius pellucidus (Retzius)
Limnephilus politus McLachlan.
Putative, one specimen only

Polycentropodidae

Cyrnus flavidus (McLachlan)
C. trimaculatus (Curtis)
Holocentropus picicornis (Stephens)
Plectrocnemia conspersa (Curtis)
Polycentropus flavomaculatus (Pictet)

Glossomatidae

Agapetus fuscipes (Curtis)
A. delicatulus (McLachlan)

Lepidostomatidae

Lepidostoma hirtum (Fabricius)

Hydropsychidae

Hydropsyche pellucidula (Curtis)

Psychomyiidae

Tinodes waeneri (L.)
T. maculicornis (Pictet)
Metalype fragilis (Pictet)

Leptoceridae

Triaenodes reuteri (McLachlan)
T. conspersa (Rambur)
T. bicolor (Curtis)
T. simulans (Tjeder)
Arthripsodes nigrinervosus (Retzius)
A. fulvus (Rambur)
A. cinereus (Curtis)
A. aterrimus (Stephens)
A. annulicornis (Stephens)
Mystacides azurea (L.)
M. longicornis (L.)
Oecetis ochracea (Curtis)

Sericostomatidae

Silo pallipes (Fabricius)
Sericostoma personatum (Spence)

Hydroptilidae

Hydroptila tineoides Dalman

EPHEMEROPTERA
(based on Kellock & Maitland, 1969)

Macan (1961) has listed 47 species of Ephemeroptera in the British Isles, 36 of them in Scotland. He recorded none from Orkney and only two from Caithness. This list has 13 species.
Caenis horaria
C. moesta
Ephemerella ignita
Rhithrogena semicolorata

Heptagenia lateralis
Leptophlebia marginata
Cenbtroptilum luteolum
C. pennulatum
Procloeon pseudorufulum
Cloeon simile
Baetis pumilus
B. rhodani
B. tenax

PLECOPTERA
(Based on Kellock & Maitland, 1969)

Hynes (1958) has listed 34 species of Plecoptera in the British Isles, 29 of them in Scotland. This list contains 10 species.

Amphinemura sulcicollis
Nemoura cinerea

N. avicularis
Leuctra inermis
L. hippopus
L. fusca
Perlodes microcephala
Diura bicaudata
Isoperla grammatica
Chloroperla torrentium

SYRPHIDAE (Hoverflies)
(collected by A. D. J. Meeuse, and published in the Orkney Field Club Bulletin)

Platychirus manicatus Meigen
P. peltatus Meigen
P. albimanus Fab.
Melanostoma mellinum L.
Leucozona lucorum L.
Rhingia campestris Meigen

Neoascia podagrica Fab.
Cheilosia illustata Harris
C. bergmenstammi Becker
Eristalis pertinax Scop.
E. intricarius L.
E. abusivus Collin
E. arbustorum L.
Tubifera pendula L.
Syritta pipiens L.
Cinxia borealis Fallen

LEPIDOPTERA
(compiled by R. I. Lorimer of Orphir)

The first list of Orkney lepidoptera was published by J. Traill in 1869 when he was only 18 (he produced a more complete list in 1888). Weir (1882) listed the results of a season's work on Hoy by a professional collector, probably H. McArthur. The next visitor was E. R. Curzon, who also spent a summer on Hoy, in 1885. His captures were listed independently by Gregson (1885) and South (1888).

A few other lepidopterists worked in Orkney before the turn of the century (details are given by Lorimer, 1983), but it was the publication of E. B. Ford's New Naturalist on *Butterflies* in 1945 that really stimulated interest in Orkney's butterflies and moths. Current knowledge is summarized in Lorimer's *Lepidoptera of the Orkney Islands* (1983).

The following list is in accordance with the order and nomenclature of Kloet & Hincks (1972) as amended by Bradley & Fletcher (1979). The Roman numerals indicate the months when each species is flying.

Micropterigidae

Micropterix aureatella Scop.: Resident, vi.
M. aruncella Scop.: Resident, vii–viii.
M. calthella L.: Probably resident. Hoy, 1895, a single recent confirmation.

Hepialidae

Hepialus humuli L. Ghost Moth: Resident, well distributed, vii. Males white.
H. lupulinus L. *Common Swift*: Hoy, 1882 record unconfirmed. May refer to pale sandhill form of *H. fusconebulosa*.

H. fusconebulosa Degeer. Map-winged Swift: Resident, moors and plantations, vi–vii.

Nepticulidae

Stigmella hybnerella Hübn. Resident, probably imported with Hawthorn, vi.
S. auritella Skala. Mining *Salix aurita*, late viii.
S. sorbi Staint.: Resident. Mines on Rowan wherever examined, viii.
S. confusella Wood: Resident, Hoy. Mines on Birch, viii–ix.
S. lapponica Wocke: Resident. Hoy. Mines on Birch, early viii.

Incurvariidae

Lampronia oehlmanniella Hübn.: Resident, Hoy, vi.
L. praelatella D. & S.: Resident, local in marshes, vii–viii.

Psychidae

Psyche casta Pall.: Resident; a single larval case found on Hoy.

Tineidae

Monopis rusticella Hübn.: Resident; moors, farm buildings, houses, vi–vii.
M. weaverella Scott: Resident; habitat and season as *M. rusticella*.
Niditinea fuscipunctella Haw.: Resident; hen-houses, barns, etc., x.
Tinea pallescentella Staint. Probably immigrant; once recorded, viii. 80.

Ochsenheimeriidae

Ochsenheimeria bisontella L. & Z.: Resident; moors and marshes.

Gracillariidae

Caloptilia elongella L.: Resident, probably originally introduced on Alder.

C. betulicola Hering: Resident; local among Birch, Hoy: larval cones early viii.

C. stigmatella F.: Resident; moors, among Sallows and Aspen, ix–v.

C. syringella F.: Resident, probably originally introduced with Ash; now common in plantations and on Privet in gardens.

Aspilapteryx tringipennella Zell.: Resident. Well distributed, moors and marginal land.

Phyllonorycter messaniella Zell., *P. maestingella* Mull. Mines collected from Beech have been assigned to both species; so far only *maestingella* has actually been bred. Probably originally imported.

P. junoniella Zell.: Resident; Hoy, vi.

P. ulmifoliella Hübn.: Resident; local among Birch; larval mines viii.

P. emberizaepenella Bouché: Resident; local, Hoy, vii.

P. spinolella Dup.: Resident; well distributed moors, vi.

Choreutidae

Anthophila fabriciana L. Resident, widely distributed, vii.

Glyphipterigidae

Glyphipterix simpliciella Steph.: Resident; widely distributed, vi–vii.

G. haworthana Steph.: Resident; local, among cotton grass, vi.

G. thrasonella Scop.: Resident; Recorded from Hoy and Orphir, vii.

Yponomeutidae

Argyresthia brockeella Hübn.: Resident; local among Birch, Hoy, vii–viii.

A. goedartella L.: Resident; local among Birch, Hoy, vii.

A. pygmaeella Hübn.: Resident; well distributed on moors, vii.

A. retinella Zell.: Resident; local among Birch, Hoy, viii.

A. conjugella Zell.: Resident; Hoy and Orphir, vi–vii.

A. semifusca Haw.: Resident; local among Rowan, Hoy, viii.

A. curvella L.: Resident, probably originally imported with Hawthorn, viii.

Yponomeuta evonymella L.: Immigrant; in large numbers in 1980, vii–viii.

Y. padella L.: Immigrant; both white and grey-forewing forms, viii.

Swammerdamia caesiella L.: Resident; local among Birch, Hoy, vi–vii.

Ypsolopha paranthesella L.: Resident; local among Birch, Hoy, viii.

Y. vittella L.: Resident, probably originally imported with Beech, ix.

Plutella xylostella L. Diamond-back Moth: Resident, often reinforced by immigration in large numbers, iv–x.

P. porrectella L. Resident; well distributed, vii–viii.

Rhigognostis senilella Zett.: Resident; well distributed and common, viii–vi.

R. annulatella Curt.: Resident; mainly coastal, viii–v.

Epermeniidae

Phaulernis fulviguttella Zell.: Resident; well distributed, viii.

Epermenia chaerophyllella Goeze: Resident; well distributed; Larvae vi.

Coleophoridae

[*Coleophora anatipennella* Hübn., *C. albidella* D. & S.] Record dubious; Gregson (1885) recorded the former species, but Meyrick (1928) arbitrarily altered this to the latter; expert opinion thinks neither to be likely.

C. albicosta (Haworth): Resident; Orphir, among *Ulex*.

C. discordella Zell.: Resident; well distributed, viii.

C. virgaureae Staint.: Resident; locally common among Golden Rod, vii–viii.

C. benanderi Kanerva: Resident; apparently local, viii.

C. striatipennella Tenger: Probably resident; once recorded, Hoy, viii.

Elachistidae

Elachista argentella Cl.: Resident; apparently well distributed, vii–viii.

E. bisulcella Dup.: Resident; well distributed, viii.

E. pulchella Haw.: Resident; well distributed, vii.

E. kilmunella Staint.: Probably resident; once recorded, Hoy, viii.

E. alpinella Staint.: Probably resident. Once recorded, Orphir, viii.

Oecophoridae

[*Dafa formosella* (D. & S.)]: Probably incorrect determination (Cheesman, 1898); the moth is southern in distribution and very rare.

Endrosis sarcitrella L. White-shouldered Housemoth. Resident; household pest, but also common on moors. Main emergence vi–vii.

Pleurota bicostella Cl.: Resident; common on moors, vi–viii.

Hofmannophila pseudospretella Staint.: Resident, originally imported. A household pest, main emergence vii–viii.

Agonopterix heracliana L.: Resident; well distributed, viii–vi.

A. eiliella Staint.: Resident; well distributed, viii–vi.

A. liturella D. & S.: Probably immigrant; once recorded, viii. 81.

A. assimilella Treits.: Resident, probably originally imported with Broom. Local, viii & ix.

A. ulicetella Staint.: Resident, rather local, ix & x.

A. nervosa Haw.: Resident; common and well distributed, viii & ix.

Deprassaria badiella Hübn.: Resident, Hoy.

D. weirella Staint.: Status uncertain. One record, Orphir.

Gelechiidae

Xenolechia aerhiops H. & W.: Resident; moors, iv & v.

Teleiodes proximella Hübn.: Resident: local among Birch, Hoy, vi.

Teleiopsis diffinis Haw.: Resident; moors, vii & viii.

Bryotropha desertella (Douglas): Resident; Burray, on dunes.

B. terrella D. & S.: Resident; well distributed, viii.

B. politella Staint.: Probably resident, but only once recorded, vii.

Mirificarma mulinella Zell.: Resident; locally common among Gorse, vii.

Neofaculta ericetella Hübn.: Resident; common on moors, v & vi.

Scrobipalpa samadensis plantaginella Staint.: Resident, well distributed, viii.

[*S. instabilella* Dougl.]: Record (Cheesman 1898) probably refers to previous species. This is a local, southern salt-marsh species.

S. acuminatella Sirc.: Resident, well distributed, vi.

Caryocolum marmoreum Haw.: Probably resident; recorded only from Yesnaby, viii.

Momphidae

Mompha raschkiella Zell.: Resident; common wherever Rosebay grows, vi–vii.

Cochylidae

Aethes piercei Obrazt.: Status uncertain; recorded by Weir (1882) and Gregson (1885), but not seen since.

A. cnicana Westw.: Resident; well distributed, vi–vii.

Eupoecilia angustana angustana Hübn.: Resident; generally common, vi–vii.

Falseuncaria ruficiliana Haw.: Resident; common among Primroses, vi–vii.

Agapeta hamana L. Resident, local.

Tortricidae

Pandemis cerasana (Hübn.) Barred Fruit-tree Tortrix: Resident; Hoy, Berrie Dale.

Archips rosana L.: Resident, probably imported. A minor pest of deciduous shrubs in gardens, viii.

Syndemis musculana musculinana Kennel: Resident; well distributed, vi.

Aphelia viburnana D. & S.: Resident; common and well distributed, vii–viii.

A. paleana Hübn.: Resident; distribution uncertain, as so far only larvae found; Orphir, viii.

Clepsis senecionana Hübn.: Resident; well distributed, vi.

Philedonides lunana Thunb.: Resident; well distributed, vii–viii.

[*Ditula angustiorana* Haw.]: Dubious record (Cheesman, 1898), not accepted either by Barrett (1905) or Bradley (1973); the possibility of accidental introduction with garden shrubs should be noted, as much of Cheesman's work was in Stromness.

Cnephasia stephensiana Doubled.: Probably immigrant. A single record, viii. 80.

C. interjectana Haw.: Resident, well distributed, viii.

Eana osseana Scop.: Resident; especially common on sandhills, viii & ix.

Penziana colquhounana Barr.: Univoltine resident; coasts, viii–ix.

[*Aleimma loeflingiana* L.]: Only recorded by Weir (1882); probably a misidentification, as there is no confirmation and main foodplants absent.

Croesia bergmanniana L.: Resident; rather local, Hoy and South Ronaldsay, vi.

Acleris comariana Lienig & Zeller. Strawberry Tortrix: Resident; South Ronaldsay and Orphir.

A. caledoniana Steph.: Resident; abundant on moors, viii.

A. sparsana D. & S.: Resident, possibly imported with Beech; plantations and gardens, viii–ix.

A. rhombana D. & S.: Resident; mainly plantations, viii–ix.

A. aspersana Hübn.: Resident; well distributed, viii.

A. variegana D. & S.: Resident; most common in gardens and plantations, ix.

A. hastiana L.: Resident; local among Sallow, ix–iv.

A. hyemana Haw.: Resident; common on moors, ix–vi.

A. emargana F.: Resident; local among willows, viii.

Olethreutes schulziana F.: Resident; moors, vi–vii.

O. lacunana D. & S.: Resident; well distributed vii–viii.

Apotomis sororculana Zett.: Resident; local among Birch, Hoy, viii.

Endothenia marginana Haw.: Resident; well distributed, v–vi.

E. quadrimaculana Haw.: Resident; well distributed, not common, viii.

Lobesia littoralis Humph. & Westw.: Resident, mainly coastal, vii–viii.

Bactra furfurana Haw.: Resident; local, Hoy and mainland viii.

B. lancealana Hübn.: Bivoltine resident; marshes iv and vi–viii.

Ancylis unguicella L.: Resident; well distributed, v–vi.

A. geminana subarcuana Doug.: Resident; local among Dwarf Sallow, vi.

A. badiana D. & S.: Resident; well distributed, vi.

A. myrtillana Treits.: Resident; local and uncommon, vi.

Epinotia subocellana Don.: Resident; common among Sallows, vi.

E. ramella L.: Resident; local among Birch, Hoy, viii.

E. tetraquetrana Haw.: Resident; local among Birch, Hoy, vi.

E. nisella Cl.: Probably immigrant; two at m.v.l., viii, 80.

E. tenerana D. & S.: Resident; local, viii. (see text).

E. nemorivaga Tengst.: Resident; very local, Hoy, ?vii.

[*E. tedella* Cl.]: Incorrect determination of *E. nemorivaga* – the very specimens which provided the previous record. Gregson (1884) described the larvae feeding on Bearberry.

E. cruciana L.: Resident; well distributed and common, viii.

E. mercuriana Fröl.: Resident; common and well distributed vii–viii.

E. stroemiana F.: Resident; local among Birch, Hoy, viii.

E. maculana F.: Resident; local among Aspen, Hoy, vi.

[*E. sordidana* Hübn.]: Probably an incorrect determination of *E. caprana*, of which there are no published 19th century records, although 'Hoy, 1895' specimens exist.

E. caprana F.: Resident; well distributed among Sallow, viii–ix.

E. solandriana L.: Resident; local among Birch, Hoy, viii.

Rhopobota naevana Hübn.: Status uncertain; two to m.v.l., viii. 80, but as foodplants are present, could either be resident or immigrant.

Griselda stagnana D. & S.: Status uncertain; recorded from Hoy (Gregson, 1885), but no subsequent confirmation; record probably correct.

Zeiraphera diniana Guen.: Resident, imported with conifers; now breeding in small conifer plantations, viii.

Epiblema cynosbatella L.: Resident; well distributed, viii.

E. scutulana D. & S.: Resident; well distributed vi–vii, including small proportion of f. *cirsiana* Zell. on moors.

E. farfarae Fletch.: Probably resident, although only a single record, vii.

[*Eucosma hohenwartiana* D. & S., *E. fulvana* Steph.]: Probably incorrect determinations of *E. cana*, below.

E. cana Haw.: Resident; well distributed and common, vi–vii.

Cydia succedana D. & S.: Resident, possibly partly bivoltine; well distributed, vi & viii.

C. gallicana Guen.: Probably resident; once recorded, vii.

Dichrorampha montanana Dup.: Resident; well distributed, common on dunes, vii–viii.

Pyralidae

Crambus pascuella L.: Status uncertain, probably not resident; once recorded, vii.

C. ericella Hübn.: Resident; locally common, Hoy moors, vii–viii.

C. nemorella Hübn.: Resident; well distributed, vi.

Agriphila straminella D. & S.: Resident; generally abundant, vii–viii.

A. tristella D. & S.: Resident; common on dunes, occasional elsewhere, viii.

A. inquinatella D. & S. Status uncertain; recorded by Cheesman (1898), but not seen since; Barret (1905) accepted this record.

Catoptria margaritella D. & S.: Resident; very local, Hoy, vii–viii.

Scoparia subfusca Haw.: Resident: locally common, vi–vii.

S. ambigualis Treits.: Resident; well distributed and common, vi–vii.

Eudonia pallida Curt.: Status uncertain; only listed by South (1888) without details.

E. alpina Curt.: Status uncertain; the only record is by Weir (1882).

E. murana Curt.: Resident; local among exposed rocks, Hoy, viii.

E. truncicolella Staint.: Status uncertain; once to m.v.l., viii.

[*E. lineola* Curt.]: Record (Cheesman, 1898) probably refers to *E. murana*.

E. angustea Curt.: Resident; well distributed, viii–ix.

[*Paraponyx diminutalis* Snellen] Tropical species
[*Nymphula enixalis* Swinhoe] accidentally imported with pondweed.

Pyrausta cespitalis D. & S.: Resident; locally common, vi.

Opsibotys fuscalis D. & S.: Resident; locally common, vi–vii.

Udea elutalis Hübn.: Resident; generally common, especially in marshes and on marginal land, viii.

U. prunalis D. & S.: Resident; local on moors, vi.

U. olivalis D. & S.: Probably immigrant; twice recorded, on consecutive nights, from sites five miles apart, viii.

U. uliginosalis D. & S. (*alpinalis* aver.) Resident, very local, moors, viii.

U. ferrugalis Hübn.: Immigrant species; twice recorded, ix. 80, and xi. 82.

Nomophila noctuella D. & S. Rush Veneer: Regular immigrant, vii–ix.

Pleuroptya ruralis Scop. Mother of Pearl: Probably immigrant; of seven records, five were during periods of major immigration, viii.

Aphomia sociella L. Bee Moth: Resident; locally common, viii–ix.

Pyla fusca Haw.: Resident; moors, viii.

Dioryctria abietella D. & S.: Immigrant, twice recorded.

Pterophoridae

Platyptilia gonodactyla D. & S.: Resident; well distributed and common, viii.

P. isodactylus Zell.: Resident; local in marshes, viii.

Stenoptilia bipunctidactyla Scop.: Resident; well distributed and common, vii–viii.

[*S. pterodactyla* L.]: Probably incorrect determination (South, 1888); Gregson assigned the identical specimens to *S. bipunctidactyla*.

[*Emmelina monodactyla* L.]: Probably a misidentification; Cheesman (1898) lists this species as 'common', but omits *S. bipunctidactyla*.

Pieridae

Colias croceus Fourc.: Clouded Yellow. Rare immigrant, vii–viii.

Pieris brassicae L.: Large White: Resident, reinforced by immigration. Generally distributed and common from early vi–viii.

P. rapae L. Small White: Rare immigrant; once reliably recorded in this century.

P. napi thomsoni Warren. Green-veined White: Resident, partly bivoltine; believed to have colonized Orkney c. 1936, now well distributed; vi and viii.

Lycaenidae

Lycaena phlaeas L. Small Copper: Once recorded, Hoy, 1895.

Polyommatus icarus Rott. Common Blue: Resident; common and well distributed, vi–viii.

Nymphalidae

Vanessa atalanta L. Red Admiral: Regular immigrant; occasionally breeds.

Cynthia cardui L. Painted Lady: Fairly regular immigrant; has bred.

Aglais urticae L. Small Tortoiseshell: Resident; well distributed, viii–vi.

Nymphalis antiopa L. Camberwell Beauty: Very rare immigrant; two records (1949 & 1932).

Inachis io L. The Peacock: Once recorded (1939), during a period of extension of the species' range.

Argynnis aglaja scotica Watkins. Dark Green Fritillary: Resident; well distributed, vii–viii.

Satyridae

Maniola jurtina splendida White. Meadow Brown: Resident; well distributed but favouring sunny banks and cliffs, vii–viii.

Coenonympha tullia scotica Staud. Large Heath: Resident; local on moors; habitats suffering from drainage on Mainland, vii–viii.

Danaidae

[*Danaus plexippus* L. The Milkweed:] Geographically incorrect record (Entomologist 75:60) 'The Orkney Isles . . . Lerwick'.

Lasiocampidae

Lasiocampa quercus callunae Palmer. Northern Eggar: Resident, biennially brooded; Hoy only; imago in 'odd' years, vi–viii.

Saturniidae

Saturnia pavonia L. Emperor Moth: Resident; common moors and marshes, v–vi.

Thyatiridae

Ochropacha duplaris L. Common Lutespring: Resident; very local among indigenous Birch on Hoy, but one larva found on planted Birch at Binscarth; vii.

Achlya flavicornis L. Yellow Horned. Larva common on Birch, in May. Hoy.

Geometridae

Timandra griseata Pet. Blood-vein: Rare immigrant; two records on same night, 10 miles apart, viii. 69.

Idaea biselata Hufn. Small Fan-footed Wave: Probably immigrant; one record, viii. 80.

Orthonama vittata Borkh. Oblique Carpet: Probably immigrant; one record, vii. 80.

O. obstipata F. The Gem: Immigrant species; once recorded, viii. 80.

[*Xanthorhoe designata* Hufn. Flame Carpet.]: Status uncertain; recorded by Trail (1869) but accompanying detail is more appropriate to *X. munitata*, of which one form strongly resembles this species.

X. munitata Hübn. Red Carpet: Resident; very

common and well distributed; no resemblance to ssp. *hethlandica* Prout; viii.

X. spadicearia D. & S. Red Twin-spot Carpet: Resident; local and uncommon, vi–vii.

X. montanata D. & S. Silver-ground Carpet: Resident; well distributed and common; no resemblance to ssp. *shetlandica* Weir, vi–vii.

X. fluctuata L. Garden Carpet: Resident, partly bivoltine; locally common, vi and viii–ix; no resemblance to ssp. *trules* Prout.

Scotopteryx chenopodiata L. Shaded Broad-bar: Resident, probably a recent colonizer, now well distributed and common, vii–viii.

Epirrhoe tristata L. Small Argent & Sable: Status uncertain; once recorded, v.

E. alternata Müll. Common Carpet: Resent; locally common, vi–vii.

Camptogramma bilineata L. Yellow Shell: Resident; common, especially on low cliffs and dunes, vi–vii.

Entephria flavicinctata Hübn. Yellow-ringed Carpet: Present status uncertain but 19th century specimens extant. This species should not be collected, at least until more is known of its range.

E. caesiata D. & S. Grey Mountain Carpet: Resident; very common on moors, vi–viii.

Anticlea derivata D. & S. The Streamer: Resident; locally common, Hoy, vi.

Cosmorhoe ocellata L. Purple Bar: Resident; well distributed, but not common, vii–viii.

Coenotephria salicata latentaria Curt. Striped Twin-spot Carpet: Resident; recently recorded only from Hoy, vi.

Eulithis prunata L. The Phoenix: Resident; locally common, mainly gardens, viii.

E. testata L. The Chevron: Resident; common on moors, viii–ix.

E. populata L. Northern Spinach: Resident; very common on moors; over 50% melanic to some degree, vi–viii.

E. pyraliata D. & S. Barred Straw: Status uncertain; once recorded, vii.

Ecliptoptera silaceata D. & S. Small Phoenix: Status uncertain, twice recorded, vi. 80 and vi. 83.

Chloroclysta siterata Hufn. Red-green Carpet: Status uncertain; only once recorded, but the moth is sluggish and can exist undetected, ix.

C. miata L. Autumn Green Carpet: Resident; very local, Hoy, ix–vi.

C. citrata pythonissata Mill. Dark Marbled Carpet: Resident; common, especially in marshes, viii.

C. truncata Hufn. Common Marbled Carpet: Resident; there are probably two races in Orkney – a large, pale low-ground and a small, dark montane race; vii–viii.

Cidaria fulvata Forst. Barred Yellow: Resident, locally common, vii–viii.

Thera obeliscata Hübn. Grey Pine Carpet: Probably

immigrant; one at m.v.l., viii. The moth is common in the conifer plantations of Caithness.

T. firmata Hubn.: Probably immigrant. Two records, ix & x 1932.

T. cognata Thunb. Chestnut-coloured Carpet: Resident, locally common on Hoy, vii–viii.

T. juniperata orcadensis Cock. Juniper Carpet: Resident. This moth has not been seen since 1895, when McArthur collected the type-series on Hoy, but this is probably because there has been no collecting at the correct time of year.

Colostygia multistrigaria Haw. Mottled Grey: Resident; on the wing in iii.

C. pectinataria Knoch. Green Carpet: Resident; well distributed and common, vi–vii.

Hydriomena furcata Thunb. July Highflyer: Resident; generally common among Willows, viii.

H. impluviata D. & S. May Highflyer: Resident, probably imported with foodplant in 19th century: Binscarth, vi.

H. ruberata Frey. Ruddy Highflyer. Resident; local, Hoy, vi.

[*Epirrita dilutata* D. & S.] November Moth: Incorrect record, arbitrarily substituted by Meyrick (1928) for *E. filigrammaria*.

E. filigrammaria H.-S. Small Autumnal Moth: Resident; local on moors, viii.

Operophtera brumata L. Winter Moth: Resident; a pest in gardens and plantations, locally defoliating moorland heather, xi–i.

[*Perizoma affinitatum* Steph. The Rivulet]: Status uncertain; recorded only by Gregson (1885), but probably misidentification of *P. alchemillata*.

P. alchemillata L. Small Rivulet: Resident; rather local, often in gardens, vi–vii.

P. minorata ericetata Steph. Heath Rivulet: Probably resident. No records this century.

P. blandiata D. & S. Pretty Pinion: Resident; locally common, vi–vii.

P. albulata D. & S. Grass Rivulet. Well distributed and common, vi–vii.

P. didymata L. Twin-spot Carpet: Resident; generally abundant and showing ecological variation, viii.

Eupithecia pulchellata Steph. Foxglove Pug: Resident; locally common, vi–vii.

E. pygmaeata Hübn. Marsh Pug. Resident; extremely local; known only from one locality in S. Ronaldsay, where it is common; vi.

E. venosata ochracae Gregs. Netted Pug. Resident; common wherever there is *Silene maritima*, vi.

E. satyrata Hübn. Satyr Pug: Common, especially on moors; most are f. *callunaria* Doubled, but a few approach f. *curzoni* Gregs. vi.

E. goossensiata Mab. Ling Pug: Resident; recorded only from Hoy, vii.

E. assimilata Doubled. Currant Pug: Probably resident; only one record, but lack of darkness at mid-summer makes sampling at m.v.l. rather inconsistent.

E. vulgata scotica. Common Pug: Cockayne: Local resident, vi.

[*E. denotata jasioneata* Crew. Jasione Pug]: Two specimens taken, but later proved to have been accidentally imported by a visitor, as pupae.

E. nanata angusta Prout. Narrow-winged Pug: Resident, possibly bivoltine; common on moors, v–viii.

E. fraxinata Crew. Ash Pug: Resident, probably originally imported; recorded only from Binscarth, vii.

E. pusillata D. & S. H.-S. Juniper Pug: Resident; only on Hoy, viii.

Gymnoscelis rufifasciata Haw. Double-striped Pug: Resident; moors, vi–vii.

Chesias legatella D. & S. The Streak. Probably immigrant. Two, x-1932.

Carsia sororiata anglica Prout. Manchester Treble-bar: Resident; local on moors, viii.

Aplocera plagiata scotica Rich. Treble-bar: Resident; well distributed, vii.

Abraxas grossulariata L. The Magpie: Immigrant; although common in Caithness there are only two Orkney records and the larva does not appear to have been seen on currants etc. vii.

Plagodis pulveraria L. Barred Umber: Probably resident; Hoy, 1895, not since.

Opisthograptis luteolata L. Brimstone Moth: Resident, probably recent colonizer, now well distributed and common, vi.

Selenia dentaria F. Early Thorn: Resident; local on Hoy, v–vi.

S. lunularia Hübn. Lunar Thorn. Status doubtful: recorded from Hoy, 1895, but no trace of larvae among Birch on Hoy in recent years.

Odoptopera bidentata Cl. Scalloped Hazel: Resident; local on Hoy, vi.

Agriopis aurantiaria Hübn. Scarce Umber: Resident; apparently loak, but little collecting done at time of emergence, x.

A. marginaria F. Dotted Border: Resident; locally common on moors; iii.

Erannis defoliaria Cl. mottled Umber: Resident, well distributed.

Ematurga atomaria L. Common Heath: Resident, moors: most common on Hoy, v–vi.

Cabera pusaria L. Common White Wave: Resident, local on Hoy.

Campaea margaritata L. Light Emerald: Resident; local on Hoy, vii–viii.

Hylaea fasciaria (L.) Barred Red: Probably immigrant; once recorded.

Dyscia fagaria Thunb. Grey Scalloped Bar: Resident; moors, vi–viii.

Sphingidae

Agrius convolvuli L. Convolvulus Hawk-moth: Immigrant species, seen almost every year, viii–ix.

Acherontia atropos L. Death's-head Hawk-moth: Immigrant species; rather rare, viii–ix.

Macroglossum stellatarum L. Humming-bird Hawk-moth: Immigrant species; only six Orkney records.

Hyles gallii Rott. Bedstraw Hawk-moth. Immigrant species; three records, all early vii, 1973.

Notodontidae

Cerura vinula L. Puss Moth: Resident; well distributed on Poplars and Willows, v–vi.

Furcula furcula Cl. Sallow Kitten: Resident; once recorded as a larva, Hoy, vii.

Eligmodonta ziczac L. Pebble Prominent: Resident; only a few records, but covering a wide area.

Notodonta dromedarius L. Iron Prominent: Resident, local on Hoy.

Lymantriidae

Orgyia antiqua L. The Vapourer: Resident; one larva found Hoy, and Orphir.

Leucoma salicis L. White Satin: Probably immigrant, temporarily resident. Several were taken on Hoy, in 1948.

Arctiidae

Parasemia plantaginis insularum Seitz Wood Tiger: Resident; mainly moors, but well distributed; apparently less common than in 19th century, vi–vii.

Arctia caja L. Garden Tiger: Resident; common and well distributed, vii–viii.

Spilosoma lubricipeda L. White Ermine: Resident; locally common, vi.

Phragmatogia fuliginosa borealis Staud. Northern Ruby Tiger: Resident; common, especially on moors and sandhills, v–vi.

Tyria jacobaeae L. The Cinnabar: Status uncertain. Once recorded, vi. 1985.

Noctuidae

[*Euxoa obelisca* D. & S. Square-spot Dart]: Incorrect determination by Gregson; South (1888) assigned the identical specimens to *E. tritici*.

E. tritici L. White-line Dart: Resident; very common on sandhills, occasional elsewhere, viii.

E. cursoria Hufn. Coast Dart: Resident; extremely local; McArthur found it commonly on Hoy in 1895, but despite several searches, it has not been seen since; several specimens still exist.

Agrotis vestigialis Hufn. Archer's Dart: Resident; locally common on sandhills, viii.

A. exclamationis L. Heart & Dart: Status uncertain; recorded by Gregson (1885), not seen since.

A. ipsilon Hufn. Dark Sword-grass: Regular immigrant; recorded every month from iv to x.

A. segetum Hufn.: Turnip Moth. Probably immigrant. One record, ix. 1982.

Ochropleura plecta L. Flame Shoulder: Resident; well distributed and common, v–vii.

Standfussiana lucernea L. Northern Rustic: Resident; well distributed, but not common, vii–viii.

Rhyacia simulans Hufn. Dotted Rustic: Resident, locally common; often enters houses to aestivate, vii–ix.

Noctua pronuba L. Large Yellow Underwing: Resident; generally abundant, viii.

N. comes Hübn. Lesser Yellow Underwing: Resident; recorded only from Hoy; all are f. *curtisii* Newman.

N. janthina D. & S. Lesser Broad-bordered Yellow Underwing: Resident; most common in plantations, occasional elsewhere, viii.

Spaelotis ravida D. & S. Stout Dart: Immigrant; two came to m.v.l. viii. 80. There are very few Scottish records.

Graphiphora augur F. Double Dart: Resident; rather local; mainly gardens and plantations.

Paradiarsia glareosa Esp. Autumnal Rustic: Resident; generally common; f. *edda* Staud. occurs at varying frequency.

Lycophotia porphyrea D. & S. True Lover's Knot: Resident; very common on moors, vi–vii.

Peridroma saucia Hübn. Pearly Underwing: Uncommon immigrant; recorded in vi, ix & x.

Diarsia mendica orkneyensis B.-Salz. Ingrailed Clay: Resident; common in all habitats, very variable, vii–viii.

[*D. dahlii* Hübn. Barred Chestnut]: Probably recorded in error; both Weir and Gregson list this species, but doubtfully, and there has been no confirmation.

Diarsia rubi (Vieweg) Small Square-spot: Immigrant. A single male of the second brood, along with other moths of more southern distribution. Orphir, viii. 83.

D. florida Schmidt. Fen Square-spot: Common and well distributed, vii.

D. brunnea D. & S. Purple Clay: Resident, locally common, viii.

Xestia alpicola alpina Humph. & Westw. Northern Dart: Resident, probably biennial; found on Hoy by McArthur in 1895, not really searched for since.

X. c.-nigrum L. Setaceous Hebrew Character: Resident; well distributed and common, vii–viii.

X. triangulum D. & S. Double Square-spot: Status uncertain, possibly immigrant; only three records, all during periods of immigration.

X. baja D. & S. Dotted Clay: Resident; locally common in plantations, viii.

X. castanea Esp. Neglected Rustic: Resident; common on moors, viii–ix.

X. sexstrigata Haw. Six-striped Rustic: Status uncertain; there are four records, all from different areas and all of very worn specimens, vii–viii.

X. xanthographa D. & S. Square-spot Rustic: Resident; generally common, viii.

X. agathina Dup. Heath Rustic: Resident; local on moors, preferring deep heather, viii–ix.

Naenia typica (L.) The Gothic: Probably immigrant; one, Orphir, viii.

Eurois occulta L. Great Brocade: Immigrant, sometimes in large numbers, viii.

Cerastis rubricosa D. & S. Red Chestnut: Resident; well distributed and common, iv.

Anarta myrtilli L. Beautiful Yellow Underwing: Resident; local on moors, vi.

Discestra trifolii Hufn. The Nutmeg: Immigrant, temporarily resident, 1969–77.

Hada nana Hufn. The Shears: Resident; well distributed and common, v–vii.

Mamestra brassicae L. Cabbage Moth: Resident, fairly common; may hibernate as imago in Orkney, viii–ix.

[*Lacanobia contigua* D. & S. Beautiful Brocade]: Incorrect determination of an aberrant *Apamea remissa* Hübn.

L. thalassina Hufn. Pale-shouldered Brocade: Resident; local and uncommon, vi.

L. oleracea L. Bright-line Brown-eye: Resident; rather uncommon, viii.

Papestra biren Goeze. Glaucous Shears: Resident; common on moors, v–vi.

Ceramica pisi L. Broom Moth: Resident; uncommon, only recorded from Hoy and mainland, vi.

Hadena rivularis F. The Campion: Resident; well distributed on moors and coastal shingle, vi–vii.

H. confusa Hufn. Marbled Coronet: Resident; common wherever there is Sea Campion, v–vi.

H. bicruris Hufn. The Lychnis: Resident; well distributed and common, vi–viii.

Cerapteryx graminis L. Antler Moth: Resident; abundant in all habitats, xii–ix.

Panolis flammea D. & S. Pine Beauty: Probably immigrant from Caithness, where is a forestry pest. Once recorded.

Orthosia gracilis D. & S. Powdered Quaker: Resident; the only record is of a moth bred from a larva found on Hoy.

O. incerta Hufn. Clouded Drab: Possibly immigrant; one record, at m.v.l., 16. iv.: on the same night the definitely immigrant *Agrotis ipsilon* Hufn. was recorded.

O. gothica L. Hebrew Character: Resident; well distributed and common, iv–v.

Mythimna conigera D. & S. Brown-line Bright-eye: Status uncertain; four records, all from Orphir, at m.v.l., vii–viii.

M. impura Hübn. Smoky Wainscot: Resident; locally common, especially on sandhills, vii–viii.

Cucullia umbratica L. The Shark: Present status uncertain: recorded as 'not common' in Stromness (Cheesman, 1898). The moth is more often seen feeding at flowers during twilight than coming to light.

Brachylomia ximinalis F. Minor Shoulder-knot: Resident; local on Hoy, viii.

Dasypolia templi Thunb. Brindled Ochre: Resident; locally common, ix–iv.

Aporophyla lutulenta lueneburgensis Frey. Northern Deep-brown Dart. Resident; locally common on moors and sandhills, viii.

A. nigra Haw. Black Rustic: Resident; locally common, viii–ix.

Lithomoia solidaginis (Hübn.) Golden-rod Brindle: Probably immigrant; one, of Scottish form, Orphir.

Xylena vetusta Hübn. Red Sword-grass: Status uncertain; few records, all in 'migrant years'.

X. exsoleta L. Sword-grass. Status as preceding species; several recent records, Orphir.

Blepharita adusta Esp. Dark Brocade: Resident; well distributed; the resident population is ab. *duplex* Haw., v–vii.

Eupsilia transversa Hufn. The Satellite: Resident; local and uncommon, x–iv.

Agrochola circellaris Hufn. The Brick: Resident; local and uncommon, viii–ix.

Parastichtis suspecta Hübn. The Suspected: Probably immigrant; it has occurred in two recent years, both times during periods of immigration from the east, viii?

[*Xanthia citrago* L. Orange Sallow]: Recorded by McArthur (South, 1895), but probably a lapsus calami for *X. togata* Esp.: x, which was not recorded, but of which two specimens bearing McArthur's 'Hoy, 1895' labels exist.

X. togata Esp. Pink-barred Sallow: Well distributed, but uncommon, ix.

X. icteritia Hufn. The Sallow: Resident; fairly common, viii–ix.

[*Acronicta tridens* D. & S.] Dark Dagger: Almost certainly incorrect as there are no Scottish records of this moth and at the time when it was recorded (Cheesman, 1898), there was no infallible way of determining the imago.

Amphipyra tragopogonis Probably immigrant. Orphir, Clerck & Kirkwall.

Euplexia lucipara L. Small Angle Shades: Resident; apparently local and uncommon, vii.

Phlogophora meticulosa L. Angle Shades: Probably immigrant; usually occurs viii–x, sometimes commonly, but overwintering larvae have not been found.

Cosmia trapezina L. Dun-bar: Immigrant; occurred in numbers and over a wide area in viii. 1980; other immigrant species arrived at the same time.

Apamea monoglypha Hufn. Dark Arches: Resident; well distributed and common, vii–viii.

A. lithoxylaea D. & S. Status uncertain; only once recorded, viii. 68.

A. exulis assimilis Doubled. Northern Arches: Resident; local on Orphir moors, vii–viii.

A. crenata Hufn. Clouded-bordered Brindle: Resident; generally common; about 20% melanic specimens, vi–viii.

A. furva britannica Cockayne. The Confused: Resident; well distributed, but most common on moors and coast, viii.

A. remissa Hübn. Dusky Brocade: Resident; well distributed and common, vii.

[*A. unanimis* Hübn. Small Clouded Brindle]: Probably a misidentification of *A. remissa* to which the circumstantial details given by Trail (1869) seem more appropriate; there are no subsequent records.

A. sordens Hufn. Rustic Shoulder-knot: Status uncertain; recorded from Hoy by Gregson (1885) and once this century, from Orphir; vi.

A. ophiogramma Esp. Double-lobed: Probably a very local resident; two records, ten years apart, from the same site in St Ola; viii.

Oligia fasciuncula Haw. Middle-barred Minor: Resident; well distributed and common, vii–viii.

[*O. furuncula* D. & S. Cloaked Minor]: Probably a misidentification of *O. fasciuncula*; several 19th century authors list this species, but none list the very common *O. fasciuncula*.

O. literosa (Haw.) Rosy Minor: Probably immigrant; twice recorded, Orphir.

Mesapamea secalis L. Common Rustic: Resident; well distributed and common, vii–viii.

M. secalella Orphir, Remon. Recently separated from two preceding species on genatalic grounds. One Orkney specimen has been detected.

Photedes minima Haw. Small Dotted Buff: Resident; well distributed and fairly common, vii–viii.

P. pygmina Haw. Small Wainscot: Resident; most abundant in marshes and on moors, viii–ix.

Luperina testacea D. & S. Flounced Rustic: Resident; well distributed, but not common, viii–ix.

Amphipoea lucens Frey. Large Ear: Resident; well distributed and fairly common, viii.

A. oculea L. Ear Moth: Resident; only two records have been confirmed by examination of genitalia, so range is not known.

Hydraecia micacea Esp. Rosy Rustic: Resident; well distributed and very common, viii–ix.

Celaena haworthii Curt. Haworth's Minor: Resident; local, moors and marshes, viii–ix.

C. leucostigma Hübn. The Crescent: Immigrant; both the nominate subspecies and the small ssp. *scotica* Cockayne have occurred, although in different years, viii.

Rhizedra lutosa Hübn. Large Wainscot: Resident, maily near lochs, ix.

Caradrina clavipalis Scop. Pale Mottled Willow: Resident, probably sometimes reinforced by immigration; common and well distributed, vii–x.

Stilbia anomala Haw. The Anomalous. Resident; moors and sandhills, viii.

Diachrysia chrysitis L. Burnished Brass: Resident, probably a recent colonizer, as no 19th century records; now generally common, vii–viii.

Macdunnoughia confusa Steph. Dewick's Plusia: Very scarce immigrant; the Orkney specimen (8. viii. 69) was the seventh British record.

Plusia festucae L. Gold Spot: Resident; well distributed and common, vii–viii.

Autographa gamma L. Silver Y: Immigrant, sometimes in vast numbers; has bred; vi–x.

A. pulchrina Haw. Beautiful Golden Y: Resident; well distributed and common, vii–viii.

A. jota L. Plain Golden Y: Probably immigrant; only two positive records, both in 'migrant years'.

A. bractea D. & S.: Resident; well distributed, but uncommon, vii–viii.

Syngrapha interrogationis L. Scarce Silver Y: Immigrant. Although the species is resident in northern Scotland, all three Orkney specimens are of the Scandinavian race, viii.

Abrostola triplasia L. The Spectacle: Resident; well distributed and common, vi–vii.

[*A. trigemina* Werneb. Dark Spectacle]: Incorrect record by Traill (1869), tacitly corrected by him (1888).

Catocala fraxini L. Clifden Nonpareil: Very rare immigrant, once recorded (1896).

S. libatrix Resident, Orphir.

Rivula sericealis Scop. Straw Dot: Probably immigrant. Two records, St Ola, vi & viii. 69.

Hypena proboscidalis L. The Snout: Resident; like *D. chrysitis*, apparently a recent colonist, now well distributed and common, vii.

ARACHNIDA

The spiders of the eastern North Atlantic form a 'common faunal area' (Braendegaard, 1958). However there are species which are certainly limited by climate. For example *Segestria senoculata* (Dysderidae) and *Dictyma arundinacea* (a cribellate) occur in Orkney, but have not been recorded in Shetland, Faroe or Iceland; the former does not occur much to the north of 60°N in Fennoscandia. Similarly, *Amaurobius fenestralis* is highly successful in Orkney and Shetland, but is absent from both the Faroes and Iceland (which have been well-studied for spiders); it has been recorded only a little north of 60°N in Norway.

Several species are absent in particular groups for reasons difficult to understand. For example, *Pardosa amentata* occurs in Orkney and up to the Arctic Circle in Scandinavia, but it has not been found in Shetland, Faroe or Iceland despite the presence of apparently suitable habitats. Presumably its absence is due to a failure in colonization.

The first major spider collecting in Orkney was done by W. S. Bristowe in 1927 and 1931 (Bristowe, 1931). Apart from a single species record made by Duffy in 1955, the next study of spiders was by M. J. Surtees in 1975, who added 22 new County Records out of 35 species found, mainly from Rackwick in Hoy. He was followed by P. D. Hillyard, who colected on the Mainland, Hoy and Burray in 1976, and added another 30 species to the Orkney list (with the help of Miss A. M. Coyle). There are now 93 species which have been found in Orkney, similar to the 90 for Shetland listed by Ashmole (1979). The Orkney and Shetland lists are given together in the following table, together with some of the 616 British species noted by Locket, Millidge and Merrett (1974).

	Scottish mainland	Orkney	Shetland
Family AMAUROBIIDAE			
Amaurobius fenestralis (Stroem)	*	*	*
Amaurobius similis (Blackw.)	*	*	
Family DICTYNIDAE			
Dictyna arundinacea (Linn.)	*	*	
Family OONOPIDAE			
Dysderina loricata Simon			
Family DYSDERIDAE			
Segestria senoculata (Linn.)	*	*	
Family GNAPHOSIDAE			
Drassodes lapidosus (Walck.)	*		*
Gnaphosa lapponum (L. Koch)			
Gnaphosa leporina (L. Koch)	*		*
Micaria pulicaria (Sund.)	*	*	
Haplodrassus signifer (C. L. Koch)	*		*
Family CLUBIONIDAE			
Agroeca proxima (Cambr.)	*	*	*
Clubiona phragmitis C. L. Koch	*	*	*
Clubiona reclusa Cambr.	*	*	
Clubiona trivialis C. L. Koch	*	*	*
Clubiona diversa Cambr.	*	*	
Family THOMISIDAE			
Oxyptila trux (Blackw.)	*	*	*
Xysticus cristatus (Clerck)	*	*	*
Family SALTICIDAE			
Neon reticulatus (Blackw.)	*	*	*
Salticus scenicus (Clerck)	*		
Family LYCOSIDAE			
Alopecosa pulverulenta (Clerck)	*	*	*
Arctosa perita (Latr.)	*		*
Pardosa amentata (Clerck)	*	*	
Pardosa eiseni (Thor.)			
Pardosa furcifera (Thor.)			
Pardosa groenlandica (Thor.)			
Pardosa hyperborea (Thor.)			
Pardosa nigriceps (Thor.)	*	*	*
Pardosa palustris (Linn.)	*	*	*
Pardosa pullata (Clerck)	*	*	*
Pardosa sphagnicola (Dahl)			
Pirata piraticus (Clerck)	*	*	*
Tricca alpigena (Dol.)	*		
Trochosa terricola Thor.	*	*	*
Family AGELENIDAE			
Anitistea elegans (Blackw.)	*		*
Cryphoeca silvicola (C. L. Koch)	*		*
Hahnia montana (Blackw.)	*	*	*
Tegenaria domestica (Clerck)	*	*	*
Textrix denticulata (Oliv.)	*	*	*
Family NIMETIDAE			
Ero cambridgei Kulcz.	*	*	

	Scottish mainland	Orkney	Shetland
Family THERIDIIDAE			
Achaearanea tepidariorum (C. L. Koch)	*		
Enoplognatha ovata (Clerck)	*	*	*
Pholcomma gibbum (Westr.)	*	*	
Robertus arundineti (Cambr.)	*	*	*
Robertus lividus (Blackw.)	*	*	*
Steatoda bipunctata (Linn.)	*		
Theridion bellicosum Simon	*		
Theridion varians Hahn	*		
Family TETRAGNATHIDAE			
Meta mengei (Blackw.)	*	*	?
Meta merianae (Scop.)	*	*	*
Meta segmentata (Clerck)	*	*	*
Pachygnatha clercki Sund.	*	*	
Pachygnatha degeeri Sund.	*	*	*
Tetragnatha extensa (Linn.)	*	*	*
Family ARANEIDAE			
Araneus cornutus Clerck	*		
Araneus diadematus Clerk	*	*	*?
Araneus marmoreus Clerck	*		
Araneus patagiatus Clerck	*		
Araneus quacratus Clerck	*	*	
Hyposinga pygmaea (Sund.)	*	*	
Zygiella x-notata (Clerck)	*	*	
Family LINPHIIDAE, Subfamily ERIGONINAE			
Araeoncus crassiceps (Westr.)	*		*
Aulacocyba subitanea (Cambr.)	*		
Caledonia evansi Cambr.	*		
Ceratinella brevipes (Westr.)	*	*	*
Cnephalocotes obscurus (Blackw.)	*	*	
Collinsia holmgreni (Thor.)	*		
Collinsia spetsbergensis (Thor.)			
Conigerella borealis (Jacks.)			
Dicymbium brevisetosum Locket	*	?	*
Dicymbium nigrum (Blackw.)	*	*?	
Dicymbium tibiale (Blackw.)	*		
Diplocentria bidentata (Emerton)	*		
Diplocephalus cristatus (Blackw.)	*	*	*
Diplocephalus permixtus (Cambr.)	*	*	*
Dismodicus bifrons (Blackw.)	*		
Eboria fausta (Cambr.)	*		
Entelecara errata Cambr.	*		
Entelecara erythropus (Westr.)	*		
Erigone arctica (White)	*	*	*
Erigone atra (Blackw.)	*	*	*
Erigone capra Simon	*		
Erigone dentipalpis (Wider)	*	*	*
Erigone longipalpis (Sund.)	*	*	
Erigone promiscua (Cambr.)	*	*	*
Erigone psychrophila Thor.	*		

	Scottish mainland	Orkney	Shetland
Erigone tirolensis L. Koch	*		
Erigonella hiemalis (Blackw.)	*	*	*
Erigonidium graminicola (Sund.)	*		
Erigonopterna globipes (L. Koch)			
Gonatium rubens (Blackw.)	*	*	*
Gongulidielium vivum (Cambr.)			
Micrargus herbigradus (Blackw.)	*	*	
Hypomma bituberculatum (Wider)	*	*	*
Islandiana princeps (Braend.)			
Lophomma punctatum (Blackw.)	*	*	
Maso sundevalli (Westr.)	*	*	
Minyriolus pusillus (Wider)	*	*	
Monocephalus casteneipes (Simon)	*		*
Monocephalus fuscipes (Blackw.)	*	*	
Oedothorax gibbosus (Blackw.)	*	*	
Oedothorax fuscus (Blackw.)	*		*
Oedothorax retusus (Westr.)	*	*	*
Tricopterna thorelli (Westr.)	*	*	
Pelecopsis nemoralis (Blackw.)	*	*	*
Pocadicnemis pumila (Blackw.)	*	*	*
Rhaebothorax morulus (Cambr.)	*	*	*
Savignya frontata (Blackw.)	*	*	*
Silometopus ambiguus (Cambr.)	*	*	*
Tapinocyba pallens (Cambr.)	*		
Thyreosthenius parasiticus (Westr.)	*		
Tiso aestivus (L. Koch)	*		
Tiso vagans (Blackw.)	*	*	*
Tmeticus affinis (Blackw.)			
Typhochrestus digitatus (Cambr.)	*	*	*
Walckenaera acuminata Blackw.	*	*	*
Walckenaera antica (Wider)	*	*	*
Walckenaera capito (Westr.)	*	*	
Walckenaera clavicornis (Emerton)	*	*	*
Walckenaera cuspidata Blackw.	*	*	
Walckenaera incisa (Cambr.)			
Walckenaera melanocephala Cambr.	*		
Walckenaera nodosa Cambr.	*		
Walckenaera nudipalpis (Westr.)	*	*	*
Walckenaera obtusa Blackw.			
Pepocranium ludicrum (Cambr.)			
Family LINYPHIIDAE, Subfamily LINYPHIINAE			
Agyneta conigera (Cambr.)	*	*	
Agyneta decora (Cambr.)	*	*	*
Agyneta subtilis (Cambr.)	*		

	Scottish mainland	Orkney	Shetland
Agyneta cauta (Cambr.)	*	*	
Allomengea scopigera (Grube)	*		*
Bathyphantes approximatus (Cambr.)	*	*	
Bathyphantes gracilis (Blackw.)	*	*	*
Bolyphantes alticeps (Sund.)	*	*	*
Bolyphantes index (Thor.)			
Bolyphantes luteolus (Blackw.)	*	*	*
Centromerita bicolor (Blackw.)	*	*	*
Centromerita concinna (Thor.)	*	*	*
Centromerus arcanus (Cambr.)	*		
Centromerus prudens (Cambr.)	*	*	*
Diplostyla concolor (Wider)	*		*
Drepanotylus uncatus (Cambr.)	*	*	
Halorates reprobus (Cambr.)	*	*	*
Helophora insignis (Blackw.)	*		
Hilaira frigida (Thor.)	*	*	*
Hilaira nubigena Hull	*		
Kaestneria pullata (Cambr.)	*	*	
Labulla thoracica (Wider)	*	*	
Lepthyphantes complicatus (Emerton) = umbraticola Keys.	*		
Lepthyphantes cristatus (Menge)	*		
Lepthyphantes ericaeus (Blackw.)	*	*	*
Lepthyphantes leprosus (Ohlert)	*	*	*
Lepthyphantes mengei Kulcz.	*	*	*
Lepthyphantes minutus (Blackw.)	*	*	
Lepthyphantes obscurus (Blackw.)	*	*	
Lepthyphantes pallidus (Cambr.)			
Lepthyphantes tenuis (Blackw.)	*	*	*
Lepthyphantes zimmermanni Bertkau	*	*	*
Leptorhoptrum robustum (Westr.)	*	*	*
Maro lehtineni Saaristo			
Maro minutus Cambr.	*		
Meioneta beata (Cambr.)	*		*
Meioneta gulosa (L. Koch)	*		*
Meioneta nigripes (Simon)	*	*	*
Meioneta saxatilis (Blackw.)	*		*
Meioneta rurestris (C. L. Koch)	*		
Oreonetides abnormis (Blackw.)	*		
Oreonetides vaginatus (Thor.)	*		*
Phaulothrix hardyi (Blackw.)	*		*
Poeciloneta globosa (Wider)	*	*	*
Porrhomma convexum (Westr.)	*		
Porrhomma egeria Simon	*		*
Porrhomma montanum (Jacks.)	*		

MOLLUSCA

Compiled by Mrs Norah F. MacMillan (Merseyside County Museums, Liverpool)

For convenience the marine and non-marine (i.e. terrestrial and freshwater) species are given in two separate lists.

The marine Mollusca

Any account of the marine Mollusca of Orkney must rely heavily upon Rendall's excellent list (1956) which included earlier records. Since then, however, much field work, notably diving, has been done by Alan Skene (Marine Recorder for Sea Area 3 of the Conchological Society's Recording Scheme), Alastair Skene, I. F. and K. Smith (all Orkney residents) as well as by G. H. Brown, C. Glendinning, D. Heppell, D. W. McKay, B. E. Picton, A. Simpson, Shelagh Smith and the writer. This has greatly increased the number of species taken alive and the following list is largely due to the generous co-operation of those workers named above.

Where shells or single valves only have been obtained this has been indicated; where the matter is uncertain this has also been stated. *Unless otherwise stated the species has been taken alive.*

'Orcadian' has been used in rather a restricted sense; some rare species included by Rendall were dredged far to the west of Orkney and have not been listed here. Nomenclature follows that of the *Sea Area Atlas of the Marine Mollusca of Britain and Ireland* (ed. Seaward 1982).

Polyplacophora

Lepidopleurus asellus (Gmelin)
L. cancellatus (Sowerby)
Tonicella marmorea (Fabricius)
T. rubra (L.)
Lepidochitona cinereus (L.)
Callochiton achatinus (Brown)
Acanthochitona crinitus (Pennant)
Ischnochiton albus (L.)

Gastropoda: Prosobranchia

Scissurella crispata Fleming. ? live-taken.
Emarginula reticulata Sowerby.
E. crassa Sowerby. One doubtful record.
Puncturella noachina (L.) one shell.
Diodora apertura (Montagu)
Patella vulgata L.
P. aspera Röding
Patina pellucida (L.)
Acmaea testudinalis (Müller)
A. virginea (Müller)
Lepeta fulva (Müller). Shells only.

Margarites helicinus (Fabricius)
M. groenlandicus (Gmelin)
Calliostoma zizyphinum (L.)
C. occidentale (Mighels) old records only, ? live-taken.
Gibbula magus (L.). NOT on Atlantic shores.
G. tumida (Montagu)
G. cineraria (L.)
G. umbilicalis (da Costa)
Cantharidus montagui (W. Wood)
C. clelandi (W. Wood)
Skenea serpuloides (Montagu)
S. nitens (Philippi) ? live-taken.
S. cutleriana (Clark) shells only.
Tricolia pullus (L.) shells only.
Lacuna vincta (Montagu)
L. crassior (Montagu)
L. parva (da Costa)
L. pallidula (da Costa)
Littorina littorea (L.)
L. saxatilis (Olivi), the aggregate species.
L. nigrolineata Gray
L. neglecta Bean
L. rudis (Maton)
L. tenebrosa (Montagu)
L. groenlandica Menke recorded by Winckworth 1917.
L. littoralis (L.), the aggregate species.
L. mariae Sacchi & Rastelli
L. obtusata (L.) s.s.
L. neritoides (L.)
NOTE: *Hydrobia ulvae*, *H. ventrosa*, *H. neglecta* and *Potamopyrgus jenkinsi* are listed among the land and freshwater species.
Cingula cingillus (Montagu)
C. alderi (Jeffreys) shells only, one record.
C. semistriata (Montagu) shells only, one record.
C. semicostata (Montagu)
C. aculeus (Gould)
Alvania crassa (Kanmacher)
A. beanii (Thorpe)
A. calathus (Hanley)
A. cimicoides (Forbes)　Of these six species only shells have so far been obtained.
A. cancellata (da Costa)
A. zetlandica (Montagu)
A. punctura (Montagu)
A. carinata (da Costa) shells only.
Rissoa parva (da Costa) and var. *interrupta* (J. Adams)
R. inconspicua Alder
R. albella Lovén and var. *sarsii* Lovén, shells only.
R. violacea Desmarest, the aggregate species.
R. porifera Lovén
R. rufilabrum Alder
R. membranacea (J. Adams)
Rissoella diaphana (Alder)
R. opalina (Jeffreys)
Omalogyra atomus (Philippi)
Ammonicera rota (Forbes & Hanley), one shell.

Skeneopsis planorbis (Fabricius)
Caecum glabrum (Montagu), a shell.
Turritella communis Risso
Bittium reticulatum (da Costa), shells only.
Cerithiopsis tubercularis (Montagu), shells only.
Triphora perversa (L.), the aggregate species, shells
only.
Clathrus trevelyanus (Johnston), ? ever taken alive.
C. clathratulus (Kanmacher)
Janthina janthina (L.) one old doubtful record but as
the species' prey *Velella* drifts to Orkney the
record may be correct.
Graphis albida (Kanmacher) ⎤ Of these four species
Aclis minor (Brown) ⎟ only shells have so far
A. walleri (Jeffreys) ⎰ been obtained.
Pherusina gulsonae (Clark) ⎦
Cima minima (Jeffreys)
Eulima glabra (da Costa), ? live-taken.
E. trifasciata (J. Adams) shells only.
Balcis alba (da Costa)
B. monterosatoi (Monterosato) shells only.
B. devians (Montersato) shells only.
Trichotropis borealis Broderip & Sowerby, shells only.
Capulus ungaricus (L.)
Aporrhais pespelicani (L.)
A. serresianus (Michaud)
Amauropsis islandica (Gmelin) shells only.
Natica catena (da Costa)
N. alderi Forbes
N. montagui Forbes
Velutina velutina (Müller)
V. plicatilis (Müller) an old record ? live-taken.
Lamellaria perspicua (L.)
L. latens (Müller)
Erato voluta (Montagu) shells only, on Atlantic coasts.
Trivia arctica (Pulteney)
T. monacha (da Costa)
Simnia patula (Pennant) rare, shells only.
Trophon truncatus (Ström)
T. barvicensis (Johnson) shells only.
T. muricatus (Montagu)
Nucella lapillus (L.)
Colus islandicus (Gmelin) 'East Orkneys' ? live-taken.
C. gracilis (da Costa)
C. howsei (Marshall)
Neptunea antiqua (L.)
Buccinum undatum L.
Nassarius reticulatus (L.)
N. incrassatus (Ström)
Lora turricula (Montagu)
L. trevelliana (Turton) one 1850 record ? live-taken.
L. rufa (Montagu)
Thesbia nana (Lovén) two old records ? live-taken.
Mangelia attenuata (Montagu)
M. coarctata (Forbes) shells only.
M. nebula (Montagu) one record, shells only.

Philbertia gracilis (Montagu) one pre-1850 record
? live-taken.
P. leufroyi (Michaud)
P. purpurea (Montagu) shells only.
P. asperrima (Brown) dredged Pentland First ? live-
taken.
P. linearis (Montagu)
P. teres (Reeve)

Gastropoda: Opisthobranchia

Acteon tornatilis (L.) shells only.
Diaphana minuta Brown
Colpodaspis pusilla M. Sars
Retusa obtusa (Montagu)
R. truncatula (Bruguière)
R. mammillata (Philippi) shells only.
R. umbilicata (Montagu)
Rhizorus acuminatus (Bruguière) 'West Orkneys',
? live-taken.
Cylichna cylindracea (Pennant) shells only.
Roxania utriculus (Brocchi) two records, ? live-taken.
Scaphander lignarius (L.) shells only.
Akera bullata Müller
Philine aperta (L.)
P. angulata Jeffreys 'West Orkneys' ? live-taken.
P. catena (Montagu), as *P. angulata* q.v.
P. punctata (J. Adams)
P. quadrata (S. Wood) shells only.
P. scabra (Müller) shells only.
Runcina coronata (Quatrefages)
Chrysallida obtusa (Brown)
C. indistincta (Montagu)
C. decussata (Montagu) 'West Orkneys' ? live-taken.
C. spiralis (Montagu) shells only.
Menestho divisa (J. Adams) shells only.
M. warreni (Thompson) one record ? live-taken.
Odostomia nivosa (Montagu) one record ? live-taken.
O. turrita Hanley
O. unidentata (Montagu)
O. conspicua Alder, recorded ex Pentland Firth, ? live-
taken.
O. acuta (Lovén) ? live-taken.
O. umbilicaris (Malm) 'West Orkneys', ? live-takeff.
O. conoidea (Brocchi) shells only.
O. lukisii Jeffreys, shells only.
O. albella Lovén
O. scalaris Macgillivray
O. perezi Dautzenberg & Fischer, two records, ? live-
takeff.
Eulimella macandrei (Forbes) one record.
E. laevis (Brown) one shell.
E. nitidissima (Montagu), one record, ? live-taken.
Turbonilla elegantissima (Montagu), one record, ? live-
taken.
T. fulvocincta (Thompson), a shell dredged.

T. jeffreysii (Forbes & Hanley) one record, ? live-taken.

T. rufescens (Forbes) one record, ? live-taken.

Limacina retroversa (Fleming)
Pneumodermopsis paucidens (Boas)
Clione limacina (Phipps)
Aplysia punctata Cuvier
Berthella plumula (Montagu)
Elysia viridis (Montagu)
Hermaea bifida (Montagu)
Placida dendritica (Alder & Hancock)
Limapontia capitata (Müller)
L. depressa Alder & Hancock
L. senestra (Quatrefages)
Alderia modesta (Lovén)
Tritonia hombergi Cuvier
T. plebeia Johnston
Lomanotus marmoratus (Alder & Hancock)
Dendronotus frondosus (Ascanius)
Doto coronata (Gmelin), the aggregate species.
D. dunnei Lemche
D. millbayana Lemche
D. fragilis (Forbes)
Goniodoris nodosa (Montagu)
Ancula cristata (Alder)
Acanthodoris pilosa (Müller)
Adalaria proxima (Alder & Hancock)
Onchidoris bilamellata (L.)
O. muricata (Müller)
O. depressa (Alder & Hancock)
O. sparsa (Alder & Hancock)
O. pusilla (Alder & Hancock)
Aegires punctilucens (Orbigny)
Polycera quadrilineata (Müller)
P. faeroensis Lemche
Palio dubia (M. Sars)
P. nothus (Johnston)
Limacia clavigera (Müller)
Cadlina laevis (L.)
Archidoris pseudoargus (Rapp)
Jorunna tomentosa (Cuvier)
Antiopella cristata (Chiaje)
Coryphella browni Picton
C. gracilis (Alder & Hancock)
C. verucosa (M. Sars)
C. lineata (Lovén)
C. pedata (Montagu)
C. pellucida (Alder & Hancock)
Facelina bostoniensis (Couthouy)
F. coronata (Forbes & Goodsir) s.s.
F. auriculata (Müller), the aggregate species.
Favorinus branchialis (Rathke)
Aeolidia papillosa (L.)
Eubranchus tricolor Forbes s.s.
E. farrani (Alder & Hancock)
E. pallidus (Alder & Hancock)
E. cingulatus (Alder & Hancock)

E. exiguus (Alder & Hancock)
Cuthona nana (Alder & Hancock)
C. foliata (Forbes & Goodsir)
C. viridis (Forbes)
C. pustulata (Alder & Hancock)
C. caerulea (Montagu)
C. gymnota (Couthouy)
C. amoena (Alder & Hancock)
C. rubescens Picton & Brown
Tergipes tergipes (Forskal)

Gastropoda: Pulmonata

The semi-marine species *Leucophytia bidentata* (Montagu) and *Phytia myosotis* (Draparnaud) (sub *Ovatella myosotis*) are listed among the land and freshwater species.

Scaphopoda

Dentalium entalis L.
Siphonodentalium lofotense (M. Sars) an old record, ? live-taken.

Bivalvia

Nucula nucleus (L.)
N. turgida Leckenby & Marshall, shells only.
N. tenuis (Montagu)
Nuculana minuta (Müller) shells only.
'*Leda buccata* Stimpson' (det. Tomlin). Two valves dredged Hoy Sound. Probably Pleistocene fossils.
Yoldiella tomlini Winckworth. A shell.
Arca tetragona Poli
A. pectunculoides Scacchi. Old record 'Orkneys' ? live-taken.
Glycymeris glycymeris (L.)
Anomia ephippium L. Very doubtful!
Monia patelliformis (L.)
M. squama (Gmelin)
Heteranomia squamula (L.)
Mytilus edulis L.
Modiolus modiolus (L.)
M. barbatus (L.) var. *gallicus* Dautzenberg
M. phaseolinus (Philippi)
Musculus discors (L.)
M. marmoratus (Forbes)
M. niger (Gray)
Crenella decussata (Montagu)
Pinna fragilis Pennant
Ostrea edulis L.
Pecten maximus (L.)
Chlamys varia (L.). Represented by a giant white form up to 85 mm high: the 28 ribs mark it off from *C. nivea* (Macgillivray)

C. distorta (da Costa)
C. opercularis (L.)
C. tigerina (Müller)
C. furtiva (Lovén) shells only.
G. striata (Müller) shells only.
Similipecten similis (Laskey)
Lima hians (Gmelin) shells only.
L. loscombi Sowerby
L. sulcata Brown, shells only.
L. subauriculata (Montagu)
Astarte sulcata (da Costa)
A. montagui (Dillwyn)
A. triangularis (Montagu)
A. borealis (Schumacher). Valves dredged Hoy Sound. Probably Pleistocene fossils.
Myrtea spinifera (Montagu) shells only.
Lucinoma borealis (L.)
Thyasira flexuosa (Montagu)
T. ferruginea Winckworth, shells only.
T. subtrigona (Jeffreys) one record, 'West Orkneys' ? live-taken.
Kellia suborbicularis (Montagu)
Lasaea rubra (Montagu)
Lepton nitidum Turton
Montacuta substriata (Montagu)
M. ferruginosa (Montagu) shells only.
Mysella bidentata (Montagu)
M. dawsoni (Jeffreys) '5 valves West Orkneys'
Arctica islandica (L.)
Acanthocardia echinata (L.)
Parvicardium minimum (Philippi)
P. ovale (Sowerby)
P. scabrum (Philippi)
P. exiguum (Gmelin)
Cerastoderma edule (L.)
Laevicardium crassum (Gmelin)
Dosinia exoleta (L.)
D. lupinus (L.)
Gafrarium minimum (Montagu)
Venus casina L.
V. ovata Pennant
V. fasciatu (da Costa)
V. striatula (da Costa)
Venerupis rhomboides (Pennant)
V. pullastra (Montagu)
V. saxatilis (Fleuriau)
Turtonia minuta (Fabricius)
Mysia undata (Pennant)
Mactra corallina (L.) shells only.
Spisula elliptica (Brown)
S. solida (L.)
S. subtruncata (da Costa)
Lutraria lutraria (L.)
Donax vittatus (da Costa) shells only.
Tellina squalida Montagu, a single valve.
T. tenuis da Costa
T. fabula Gmelin

T. donacina L.
T. pygmaea Lovén
T. crassa Pennant
T. magna Spengler. An American/Caribbean species. A specimen with valves still connected was found cast-up on the West Shore, Stromness, Easter 1947. Specimen in the Royal Scottish Museum.
Macoma balthica (L.)
M. calcarea (Gmelin). Valves dredged Hoy Sound. Probably Pleistocene fossils.
Abra alba (Wood)
A. nitida (Müller)
A. prismatica (Montagu)
Gari fervensis (Gmelin)
G. tellinella (Larmarck)
G. costulata (Turton) shells only.
Solecurtus scopula (Turton) two single valves.
Ensis arcuatus (Jeffreys)
E. siliqua (L.)
Cultellus pellucidus (Pennant)
Mya truncata L.
M. arenaria L. A very small form lives in the brackish Loch of Stenness.
Corbula gibba (Olivi) valves only.
Hiatella arctica (L.)
Saxicavella jeffreysi Winckworth, valves dredged Scapa Flow.
Zirfaea crispata (L.)
Nototeredo norvagicus (Spengler)
Psiloteredo megotara (Forbes & Hanley)
Teredora malleolus (Turton) shells only.
Cochlodesma praetenue (Pulteney)
Thracia phaseolina (Lamarck)
T. villosiuscula (MacGillivray)
T. convexa (Wood). Large fragments tentatively assigned to this species were taken off Flotta, 1973.
T. distorta (Montagu)
Lyonsia norwegica (Gmelin). The only record is 'The Orkneys (McAndrew)' in Forbes & Hanley's *Hist. Brit. Moll.* vol. 1, p. 217. 1848.

Cephalopoda

Ommastrephes caroli Furtado
Sagittatus sagittatus (Lamarck)
Illex illecebrosus (Lesueur)
Taonius megalops (Prosch)
Alloteuthis media (L.)
A. subulata (Lamarck)
Loligo forbesii Steenstrup
Sepia officinalis L.
Sepiola atlantica Orbigny
Sepietta oweniana (Orbigny)
Rossia macrosoma (Chiaje)
R. glaucopis Lovén
Octopus vulgaris Lamarck
Eledone cirrhosa (Lamarck)

The land and freshwater Mollusca

Orkney's group of islands affords a variety of habitats suitable for Mollusca, both aquatic and terrestrial, and the non-marine fauna is therefore relatively rich. Orkney is also fortunate in possessing resident conchologists; visiting workers, unfortunately, have usually confined their activities to the main island (Mainland) and two of the larger islands (Westray and Stronsay) are almost unknown, conchologically speaking. On the other hand, of the South Isles group, the large hilly island of Hoy has been well searched, and of the North Isles Egilsay and little flat North Ronaldsay likewise have been fairly well investigated.

As the fauna of each island, no matter how small, is a separate entity, I have noted the major islands in which each species occurs.

Earlier workers include E. A. T. Nicol, R. Godfery, K. Hurlston Jones, C. Oldham, A. W. Stelfox, J. R. le B. Tomlin and J. Waterston. Rendall in his *Mollusca Orcadensia* (1956) mentioned a few land and freshwater species.

In the following list I have made use of all published records as well as my own (from 1957 onwards) and those of several friends, Orcadian and otherwise. To all these I am most grateful.

Nomenclature follows that of the *Atlas of the non-marine Mollusca of the British Isles* (1976).

Theodoxus fluviatilis (L.). Lochs of Stenness and Harray on Mainland, the only Scottish localities.

Valvata cristata Müller. Apparently only in Mainland.

Hydrobia ventrosa (Montagu) the aggregate species. Jeffreys (*Brit. Conch.* vol. 5, p. 151. 1869) recorded this species from 'Orkneys (Thomas' but possibly the next species (not recognized in Jeffreys' time) was that obtained.

H. neglecta Muus. Oyce of Isbister 1966 and Ouse of Finstown 1975, both Mainland; Cata Sound, Sanday 1876.

H. ulvae (Pennant). Common.

Potamopyrgus jenkinsi (Smith). First recorded as Orcadian in 1927 (by C. Oldham) but now widely distributed.

Carychium minimum Müller s.s. At Loch of Skaill (Mainland).

C. tridentatum (Risso). Binscarth and Grimsquoy, both Mainland.

Leucophytia bidentata (Montagu). This semi-marine species is probably not uncommon, though only taken so far from Hoy (Longhope), Bay of Firth (Mainland) and Otterswick (Sanday).

Ovatella myosotis (Draparnaud). St Margarets Hope, South Ronaldsay, 1974, a shell.

Lymnaea truncatula (Müller). Common.

L. peregra (Müller). Common. A near-involute form lives in the Loch of Swannay, Mainland.

L. stagnalis (L.). This species has been recorded from an acid peat pool on Mainland (Heppleston 1983) but there is some doubt about the species and unfortunately no specimens are available.

Anisus leucostoma (Millet). Apparently rather uncommon. Four Mainland localities and two on Egilsay.

Bathyomphalus contortus (L.). In five Mainland lochs.

Gyraulus laevis (Alder). In three Mainland lochs, in Welland Loch (Egilsay) and Garson Loch (North Ronaldsay).

Armiger crista (L.). Mainland, Egilsay, Burray and North Ronaldsay.

Ancylus fluviatilis Müller. Frequent in suitable burns and in the Loch of Bosquoy, Mainland.

Succinea pfeifferi (Rossmässler). Widely distributed. Specimens from the Loch of Brockan (Mainland) and from Selwick (Hoy) have been confirmed by Dr Lloyd-Evans and Dr Quick.

Cochlicopa lubrica (Müller). Common.

C. lubricella (Porro). Mainland, Hoy, Sanday and North Ronaldsay.

Columella edentula (Draparnaud), the aggregate species. Mainland (Stenness, coll. Stelfox 1907).

C. aspera Waldén. Mainland (Binscarth 1966, *det.* Waldén).

Vertigo pygmaea (Draparnaud). Only four records, three of them (all west Mainland) old. Egilsay, a fresh shell 1966.

V. lilljeborgi Westerlund. By Loch of Skaill, Mainland, one, 1966.

Pupilla muscorum (L.). Rare? Four Mainland records. SW Sanday 1961.

Lauria cylindracea (da Costa/. Common.

Leiostyla anglica (Wood). Recorded from Orkney in Conchological Society's 7th. Census (1951).

Vallonia pulchella (Müller) s.s. Recorded from Orkney in the Conchological Society's 8th. Census (1982).

V. excentrica Sterki. Bay of Skaill, Mainland (Stelfox 1907).

Punctum pygmaeum (Draparnaud). ? overlooked. Only four records, all Mainland.

Discus rotundatus (Müller). Fairly widely distributed but nowhere common.

Arion ater (L.), s.l. Common.

A. ater (L.) s.s. Specimens from north Hoy conf. Dr Quick and some from South Ronaldsay conf. Miss Davies.

A. subfuscus (Draparnaud). As the last sp. (q.v.)

A. circumscriptus Johnston s.s. Apparently not uncommon.

A. silvaticus Lohmander. Three Mainland records (det. A. E. Ellis) and Egilsay (in garden 1967, det. Ellis).

A. fasciatus (Nilsson). Melsetter Lodge garden (Hoy) 1965 and South Ronaldsay (garden 1979, det. Miss Davies).

A. intermedius Normand. Apparently widespread but under-recorded.

A. hortensis Férussac s.l. Widely distributed.

A. distinctus Mabille. South Ronaldsay (garden 1979, det. Miss Davies).

Vitrina pellucida (Müller/. Common.

Vitrea crystallina (Müller) s.s. Recorded from Orkney in the *Atlas.*

V. contracta (Westerlund). Fairly widespread.

Nesovitrea hammonis (Ström). Mainland and Hoy.

Aegopinella pura (Alder). Mainland (Binscarth), Burray and a shell on Swona.

A. nitidula (Draparnaud). Widely distributed.

Oxychilus draparnaudi. (Beck). Recorded in Conchological Society's 7th. Census (1951) coll. J. G. Milne.

O. cellarius (Müller). Both common.

O. alliarius (Miller).

Milax gagates (Draparnaud), Widespread. var. *rava* Williams (det. Ellis) in an Egilsay garden.

M. sowerbyi (Férussac). Mainland (in a Kirkwall garden 1969, det. Ellis.

M. budapestensis (Hazay). Mainland (in a Stromness garden 1971). Egilsay (garden, 1964, conf. Dr Quick.)

Limax maximus L. Widespread.

L. cinereoniger Wolf. Rousay, Aug. 1967. One specimen on wild ground.

L. flavus L. the aggregate species. Probably quite widespread although only seen Mainland and North Ronaldsay.

L. marginatus Müller. Common.

Deroceras laeve (Müller). Common.

D. reticulatum (Müller). The most common slug!

D. caruanae (Pollonera). In three gardens; Mainland (Isbister, 1963, det. Quick); Egilsay 1967, det. Ellis, and South Ronaldsay 1979 det. Miss Davies.

Euconulus fulvus (Müller), s.l. At School Loch, South Ronaldsay, 1905 (Godfery).

Clausilia bidentata (Ström). Apparently scarce; recorded only from Binscarth (Mainland), Hoy, and at Windwick (South Ronaldsay).

Balea perversa (L.). Scarce ? Binscarth (Mainland);

north Hoy; and a shell W. of Stromness (Stelfox 1907). Burwick churchyard (South Ronaldsay) common, 1905 (Godfery).

Candidula intersecta (Poiret). Birsay (Mainland) and SW Sanday. Possibly a recent immigrant.

Trichia striolata (Pfeiffer). Burray 1966, apparently first Orkney record. There seems to be no specimen extant to substantiate Comfort's 1937 Stenness record.

Trichia hispida (L.) Rare. Near Stromness Harbour, a colony Sept. 1907 (Stelfox). The Bothiegill, north Hoy 1957 and subsequently. Roadside near airport, one specimen 1966.

Arianta arbustorum (L.) Fairly common.

Cepaea hortensis (Müller). On all the islands, only bandless yellow shells and yellow 5-banded shells found.

C. nemoralis (L.). Recorded in error from Papa Westray (*The Orcadian* 7 June 1973) and as subfossil from Howmae, North Ronaldsay. All the specimens have been examined and all are *C. hortensis.*

Helix aspersa Müller. Only about Kirkwall; said to have been established there since about 1910.

Margaritifera margaritifera (L.). One record; three live specimens taken Loch of Stenness 1957. Perhaps now extinct in Orkney.

Sphaerium corneum (L.) In six Mainland lochs and also in two in Egilsay.

Pisidium casertanum (Poli) Fairly frequent; Mainland, Egilsay and North Ronaldsay.

P. personatum Malm. Common.

P. obtusale (Lamarck). Apparently scarce; about Brodgar (Mainland) and on Egilsay.

P. milium Held. Mainland only.

P. subtruncatum Malm. Rather uncommon.

P. lilljeborgii Clessin. Mainland only.

P. hibernicum Westerlund. Fairly frequent, Mainland and Hoy.

P. nitidum Jenyns. Also fairly frequent.

NOTE: all the above *Pisidium* specimens were determined by the late A. W. Stelfox.

P. pulchellum Jenyns. One record; Loch of Kirbister, Orphir, (Mainland) (Oldham 1932).

BIRDS

(compiled by Eric Meek of Stenness, RSPB Orkney Officer)

Red-throated Diver (Rain Goose) *Gavia stellata* Regular migrant breeder in smallish numbers. Has increased since 1925 to a population size of about 90 pairs. Breeds chiefly on elevated moorland tarns or lochans on the Mainland, Hoy and Rousay, but also on a few lower waters and on some other islands as, for example, on Eday where there is an important concentration of some eight pairs on Mill Loch. Very scarce in winter.

Black-throated Diver *Gavia arctica* Mainly a passage visitor in both spring (up to 21 in Echnaloch Bay) and autumn, perhaps irregular and numbers are always small. Now winters in very small numbers.

Great Northern Diver (Immer Goose) *Gavia immer* Regular and fairly common winter visitor; total Orkney wintering population believed to be around 450 (Lea, D., unpub.) Frequents many bays, firths and sounds such as Scapa Flow, Wide Firth and Eynhallow Sound. Large numbers gather in March and early April and these are known to consist of birds in wing moult. Individuals occasionally stay throughout the summer. Rumours of possible breeding have always proved to be unfounded.

White-billed Diver *Gavia adamsii* One in Rousay Sound on 20th April 1976, another in the same locality on 26th January 1984. One off Churchill Barrier no. 3, 18th and 19th December 1984. One adult in summer plumage on the sea off Birsay on 1st October 1984.

Little Grebe (Dabchick) *Tachybaptus ruficollis* Resident breeder in small numbers on suitable reedy lochs. Most common on the North Isles, but also breeds on the Mainland and Burray, and in recent years on South Ronaldsay.

Great Crested Grebe *Podiceps cristatus* Very scarce visitor. Omond reckoned it to be a rare visitor, sometimes seen in autumn or winter and Baxter and Rintoul said it was occasional in Orkney. One on Harray Loch on 16th October 1938 and four more records since 1972 (February, March, June and November).

Red-necked Grebe *Podiceps grisegena* Rather scarce, perhaps irregular winter and passage visitor. Since 1965 there have been about 23 sitings of 1–3 birds scattered throughout the year.

Slavonian Grebe *Podiceps auritus* Mainly a winter (population size around 100 (Lea, D., unpub.)) and

passage visitor in limited numbers. Frequents both fresh and salt water. A doubtful, but possible breeder. G. T. Arthur lists one nesting record (no date) at Quanterness.

Black-necked Grebe *Podiceps nigricollis* Very scarce visitor. Buckley and Harvie-Brown state that one was obtained in Orkney in 1873 and Howard Saunders and W. Eagle Clark say that it has occurred in Orkney. There seems to be no recent reliable record.

Black-browed Albatross *Diomedea melanophrys* Very scarce oceanic wanderer from the southern hemisphere. G. T. Arthur reported one off the Old Man of Hoy on 16th November 1933, but this was not included in the B.O.U. list (1971). One seen from the deck of the ferry boat St Ola off Hoy on 13th August 1969, one in Scapa Flow on 21st August 1975 and another recorded off Hoy on 28th August 1977; however, this last appears not to have been accepted by B.B.R.C.

Fulmar (Mallimack) *Fulmarus glacialis* Mainly oceanic, but present around coasts and off cliffs for most of the year. First bred about 1900. Rapidly increased to be the commonest cliff breeder by the late 1970s, now showing signs of stabilisation. Also nests on inland cliffs, old buildings and even on flat ground as at Auskerry.

Cory's Shearwater *Puffinus diomedea* Oceanic and very scarce visitor to offshore waters. One off Hoy on 24th September 1970, one off the Brough of Birsay on 27th August 1982 and another (not yet accepted by BBRC) in the same locality on 17th August 1984.

Great Shearwater *Puffinus gravis* Oceanic and very scarce visitor to offshore waters. Three records since 1972 (August, September and October).

Sooty Shearwater *Puffinus griseus* Oceanic wanderer from the southern hemisphere. Passes round coasts mainly in August and September. Formerly considered to be rare, but in recent years regular and in considerable numbers; 900 in one day off North Ronaldsay in September 1969 and 1,360 in three hours off Mull Head, Papa Westray on 30th August 1983.

Manx Shearwater (Lyre) *Puffinus puffinus* Oceanic. Migrant breeder and passage visitor to coastal waters. Status not well known, but there seems to have been a gradual decline in breeding numbers from before 1925. Von U. Boker (1964) estimated one colony on the west coast of Hoy at 15 to 20 pairs. The best known colony is still estimated at below 50 pairs although rafts of up to 400 birds have been seen off Rackwick,

Hoy during summer in the last 20 years. Small numbers frequent the North Isles. Variable numbers on offshore passage in autumn, there being very occasional records of Balearic Shearwaters (*P.p. mauretaflicus*) at this time.

Storm Petrel *Hydrobates pelagicus* Oceanic and regular breeder. Thriving colony on Auskerry and a large one on Sule Skerry. Also breeds on some other small islands such as Pentland Skerries, Rusk Holm and Faray Holm, and on Green Holms, Switha, Eynhallow, Skea Skerries, Wart Holm and Holm of Papa Westray in recent years.

Leach's Petrel *Oceanodroma leucorrhoa* Oceanic. Probably regular in Orkney waters. At least six were seen between Sule Skerry and Brough of Birsay on 16th July 1967. Individuals occasionally get blown or lost inland. Robinson's (1934) record of a pair breeding on Sule Skerry has not been generally accepted. The island would seem to be a suitable breeding place and indeed an adult was caught there near a Storm Petrel colony on 15th July 1967. 28 were trapped on Sule Skerry in July 1975, 6 in July 1980 and 18 in July 1982. One in 1980 and several in 1982 showed well-developed brood patches but breeding was not proved. The early autumn of 1984 produced an unprecedented series of records of birds seen from the St Ola on the Pentland Firth crossing.

Gannet (Solan Goose) *Sula bassana* Oceanic in the winter season, but inshore among the islands from early spring to late autumn. The only breeding colony, on Sule Stack, was counted at 4018 pairs in 1969 (Cramp, Bourne and Saunders, 1974). Noted ashore on Copinsay, South Ronaldsay and Westray in recent years but no hint of breeding yet.

Cormorant (Hibling) *Phalacrocorax carbo* Resident and migrant breeder and passage visitor. Some decline at main colonies in recent years e.g. Calf of Eday: 308 nests in 1976, 175 in 1982; Taing Skerry/Boray Holm: 369 nests in 1976, 170 in 1982. Other colonies exist on Seal Skerry (N. Ronaldsay); Muckle Green Holm/Little Green Holm (off Eday); The Brough (Stronsay); Horse of Copinsay; Little Skerry (Pentland Skerries). Single pairs have also bred at Marwick Head and on the Barrel of Butter. Nests are either on flat cliff tops, or on small, rocky skerries.

Shag (Scarf) *Phalacrocorax aristotelis* Resident, migrant breeder and winter and passage visitor. Breeds fairly abundantly on many cliffs; often on low ledges and in caves. The 'Seafarer' survey of 1968–70 put the population at some 3,600 pairs, but Lea & Bourne (1975) give a total of 5,631 pairs from the same survey.

Bittern *Botaurus stellaris* Scarce visitor. One said to have been killed at Melsetter in 1851 (Buckley and Harvie-Brown). One obtained at Voy, Stromness on 22nd February 1934 (Stromness Museum).

Little Bittern *Ixobrychus minutus* Scarce visitor. An old record from Baikie and Heddle of a specimen having been shot at Sanday in 1806. One from Stenness Loch 1910 in Stromness Museum. An adult male was at Hooking Loch, North Ronaldsay on 31st May 1971.

Night Heron *Nycticorax nycticorax* Scarce visitor. Only two records: a full plumaged adult at Lower Crowar, Rendall on 1st November 1961, and one on Mainland on 23rd and 24th May 1982.

Squacco Heron *Ardeola ralloides* Very scarce visitor. One obtained at North Ronaldsay on 7th September 1896.

Little Egret *Egretta garzetta* Very scarce visitor. One at Isbister Oyce, Rendall from 30th July–5th August 1961; two more records since 1972 (May and October/November).

Great White Egret *Egretta alba* One on North Ronaldsay on 28th and 29th April 1978.

Grey Heron *Ardea cinerea* Resident breeder and a passage and winter visitor. The one small sea-cliff colony at Yesnaby on the West Mainland is now deserted and only one small colony of 4 pairs is now left in the islands.

Purple Heron *Ardea purpurea* One on North Ronaldsay from 1st–8th September 1980 and one on South Ronaldsay from 2nd–5th August 1982. A record of one on Eday in May 1976 does not appear to have been submitted to BBRC.

Black Stork *Ciconia fligra* Very rare wanderer. One at Swartland, Sandwick on 7th–12th June 1972.

White Stork *Ciconia ciconia* Very scarce visitor. One caught on South Ronaldsay in 1840 (Baikie and Heddle). One stayed near Burness Loch, Westray for about a week from 20th May 1971. One badly injured found at Innister, Rousay 6th and 7th June 1972. One from 29th April to 14th June 1979, and another from 18th –20th April 1983.

Glossy Ibis *Plegadis falcinellus* Scarce visitor. One shot near Kirkwall in 1857 and another near Stromness on 19th September 1903. Out of a flock of 20 in Sandwick in September 1907 twelve were shot of which one is in Stromness Museum.

Spoonbill *Platalea leucorodia* Scarce visitor. In October 1859 one in Peerie Sea, Kirkwall and nine at Shapinsay. One was killed near Kirkwall in 1861 and on 10th October 1889 there were four at Burness Loch, Westray (Buckley and Harvie-Brown). One in Stromness Museum was shot in Evie, October 1939. Most recent sighting on 10th–13th June 1975.

Mute Swan *Cygnus olor* Common resident breeder. Breeds on the majority of lochs and small waters 67–68 nests being found in a 1983 survey. Considerable numbers on Harray and Stenness Lochs including many non-breeders; from July–December 1983, for example, numbers there fluctuated between 199–261 with a peak in August.

Bewick's Swan *Cygnus columbianus* Scarce and irregular winter visitor. Only two records in the last decade.

Whooper Swan *Cygnus cygnus* Common winter and passage visitor. Formerly bred in small numbers. Birds arrive from mid-September on, numbers usually declining after the turn of the year. November counts in 1976, 1979 and 1981 averaged just over 500. Occasional birds stay through the summer.

Bean Goose *Anser fabalis* Rather scarce and irregular passage visitor. One at Isbister, Rendall in October 1945; another six records of 1–8 birds since 1972, mainly from October to March, but with two on Papa Westray, June 1982.

Pink-footed Goose *Anser bachyrhynchus* Common and numerous passage visitor from Iceland usually in late September and early October. A few occasionally stay the winter.

White-fronted Goose *Anser albifrons* Regular passage visitor in both spring and autumn. Two small flocks of the Greenland race (*A.a. flaviforostris*) regularly winter. The nominate race *A.a. albifrons* occurs only occasionally.

Greylag Goose *Anser anser* Common passage visitor in variable numbers depending on the weather. A few hundred regularly winter in the West Mainland and odd birds and pairs have stayed through the summer but there has been no satisfactory proof of breeding.

Snow Goose *Anser caerulescens* Scarce and irregular visitor. Eight at Onston, Stenness on 18th and 19th May 1968. One on North Ronaldsay on 12th–13th May 1967, another on 13th May 1971, six near Harray Lodge on 16th November 1971, two at Deerness in November 1974, six on Westray in May

1977 and one at Kirkwall in May 1980. In 1983 three were on Sanday in mid-May, one on Hoy on 9th July and one on Papa Westray on 6th October.

Canada Goose *Branta canadensis* Very rare visitor. One old record of a small flock at Graemeshall Loch in 1883 and several recent records of small parties, mainly in summer. A small individual, probably *B.c. minima*, in South Walls in March 1981 was almost certainly a genuine Nearctic vagrant rather than a bird of feral origin.

Barnacle Goose *Branta leucopsis* Mainly a regular passage visitor in modest numbers in both spring and autumn. The wintering flock in the Switha-Swona-South Walls area now numbers some 600 and is believed to be part of the Greenland population.

Brent Goose *Branta bernicla* Rather scarce passage and occasional winter visitor. Almost invariably in association with salt water. Two forms occur in roughly equal numbers – the Pale-bellied *B.b. hrota* from Arctic Canada, Greenland and Spitzbergen and the Dark-bellied *B.b. bernicla* from Siberia.

Ruddy Shelduck *Tadorna ferruginea* Very scarce visitor. A female was shot at Sule Skerry on 18th June 1909. One in Stromness Museum from Sanday 4th May 1932. More recently a pair was observed on Burray on 4th May 1966.

Shelduck *Tadorna tadorna* Common migrant breeder. Frequents most estuaries, lochs and dune areas, but also breeds regularly well inland among heather. Breeding population about 80 pairs.

Mandarin Duck *Aix galericulata* A pair on North Ronaldsay on 8th May 1979.

Wigeon *Anas penelope* Mainly a common and numerous winter and passage visitor frequenting both fresh and salt water. The small but widespread breeding population nests in a variety of habitats from low-lying bogs to high moorland.

American Wigeon *Anas americana* One in Stenness on 13th May 1980 and one at Birsay on 3rd May 1982.

Gadwall *Anas strepera* Mainly a rather scarce winter and passage visitor but has bred on Loch of Banks 1976, 1977 and probably 1983; probably bred on North Ronaldsay in 1977 and 1980 and certainly did in 1979 and 1981.

Teal *Anas crecca* Fairly common resident breeder, winter visitor and passage visitor. Found in the majority of islands. One of the Nearctic race, *A.c.*

carolinensis, was on Eynhallow on 2nd November 1973 and one on the Loch of Bosquoy on 13th and 14th February 1976.

Mallard (Wild Duck or Stock Duck) *Anas platyrhynchos* Fairly numerous resident breeder and winter visitor. Found on most islands and in a variety of habitats.

Pintail *Anas acuta* Mainly a winter and passage visitor in small numbers but, in addition, Orkney now holds perhaps 15–20 breeding pairs which is some 50% of the known British breeding population.

Garganey *Anas querquedula* Somewhat irregular and scarce passage visitor. Usually in spring but occasionally in summer and autumn. G. T. Arthur records seeing a female with two young on a loch at North Ronaldsay on 20th July 1943 and Baxter and Rintoul (1953) quote a record of five being flushed from a marsh on the same island. Since 1972 there have been 11 records involving 13 birds in April–June and Aug–Sept.

Blue-winged Teal *Anas discors* Rare American vagrant. Adult drake on North Ronaldsay 10th November 1966 and five records involving at least six birds since 1966.

Shoveler *Anas clypeata* Rather scarce resident and perhaps migrant breeder and occasional winter and passage visitor. Breeds in limited numbers; mainly on the North Isles. Winters only in the North Isles and not on Mainland.

Red-crested Pochard *Netta rufina* A new Orkney species. A female or immature present on the Loch of Harray for at least a week from 23rd November 1984.

Pochard *Aythya ferina* Common and numerous winter visitor to fresh-water lochs. A small remnant usually stays throughout the summer and occasionally breeds. The lochs of Harray and Boardhouse hold the largest wintering concentration in the U.K., 1982–83 maxima being respectively 4500 and 1105 on the two lochs.

Ring-necked Duck *Aythya collaris* A drake found on Ayre Loch, St Mary's on 7th May 1984 was the first Orkney record. What was presumably the same individual was later seen on Loch of Kirbister and Echnaloch.

Ferruginous Duck *Aythya nyroca* Very rare visitor. Although mentioned by Baikie and Heddle, Buckley and Harvie-Brown and Omond, there was no satisfactory record of its occurrence until one was seen at Birsay on 24th May 1981.

Tufted Duck *Aythya fuligula* Common and numerous winter visitor to most fresh-water lochs. Smallish resident population breeds regularly at a number of waters. Loch of Harray held the third largest British flock in winter 1982–83 showing a maximum of 2279 birds.

Scaup *Aythya marila* Regular and fairly common winter visitor and passage visitor. Sizeable flocks on West Mainland lochs in late winter and early spring. Spasmodic breeder. Bred on Papa Westray in 1954, and continued until 1959 (two pairs). A female with four young was seen on North Ronaldsay in the summer of 1965 and a female and three young on a pool in West Mainland in summer 1969. Bred on Loch of Isbister, Birsay in 1973 and in Birsay in 1978 and 1979.

Eider (Dunter) *Somateria mollissima* Common resident breeder. Has decreased over a longish period but still a widespread breeder and found on most of the islands. Winter population believed to be around 5400.

King Eider *Somateria spectabilis* Very scarce visitor. Apparently scarcer in recent times than formerly. Bullock claims to have taken six eggs of this species on Papa Westray in June 1812. One adult drake seen in March 1884, February 1906 and June 1933. One in Stromness Museum dated 19th January 1925 and G. T. Arthur recorded a pair in Kirkwall Bay in the winter of 1930. A drake accompanied by a duck possibly of the same species, was seen at Longhope on 8th February 1975. A drake was at North Ronaldsay on 19th October 1978 and a duck frequented Kirkwall harbour from 10th December 1982 until February 1983. A drake at Evie on 27th May 1979 does not appear to have been accepted by BBRC.

Steller's Eider *Polysticta stelleri* Very scarce visitor. Two sightings recorded by G. T. Arthur of adult males; one in Wide Firth from 5th to 19th January 1947 and one off Deerness on 13th November 1949. An immature drake was found in the Westray, Papa Westray area on 25th October 1974 and what may well be the same individual has been seen in most summers since. A duck was present off North Ronaldsay on 16th and 17th April 1976.

Harlequin *Histrionicus histrionicus* Very rare visitor. Baikie and Heddle say that a young female was shot in Orkney but give no date. A. Wood and G. T. Arthur record seeing a full plumaged male off Papa Westray in June 1937, although this was not included in the B.O.U. list (1971), and is therefore unacceptable.

Long-tailed Duck *Clangula hyemalis* Regular and common winter visitor – total Orkney wintering population believed to be in the region of 6000. Mainly frequents salt water all round the coast, but also brackish water and occasionally fresh water. Congregates in closely packed flocks just prior to northward migration in early May. A few occasionally stay the summer. Breeding has occurred in 1911, 1912 and possibly also in 1926.

Common Scoter *Melanitta nigra* A winter and passage visitor in very small numbers. A few pairs bred regularly at Loch of Doomy, Eday until 1958 but not since. One pair present at Swona in the summer of 1969. A drake showing the characteristics of the Nearctic race (*M.n. americana*) was seen in Waulkmill Bay on 17th July 1984; not yet accepted by BBRC.

Surf Scoter *Melanitta perspicillata* Scarce visitor. Omond's claim that it was the commonest of the scoters around Orkney must be an error. In recent times it is certainly by far the rarest. An adult male at Echnaloch Bay, Burray on 21st October 1962 was believed to be the first for Orkney since 1905; another was in the same place on 4th and 5th May 1980 and a duck was at the Dam of Hoxa on 18th June 1984.

Velvet Scoter *Melanitta fusca* Fairly common winter visitor (winter population *c.* 350: Lea, D., unpub.) and passage visitor. Usually in small groups on salt water in a number of localities as in Scapa Flow, Wide Firth, Eynhallow Sound, Fara Sound and Papa Sound. Sometimes present in summer. A. Wood was confident that the species bred on Sweyn Holm in 1914.

Bufflehead *Bucephala albeola* Very rare visitor. One specimen said to have been obtained in Orkney in 1841 (Baikie and Heddle). No recent records.

Goldeneye *Bucephala clangula* Common and regular visitor, widespread though not in large numbers. Frequents both fresh and salt or brackish water. Occasionally seen in summer.

Smew *Mergus albellus* Scarce winter visitor. Less frequent than the last species. Balfour (1972) records a male on Stenness Loch in March and April 1958 and a male on Swartmill Loch, Westray in March 1968. Since 1972 there have been sitings of some 10 individuals.

Red-breasted Merganser (Sawbill) *Mergus serrator* Common resident breeder and passage visitor. Breeds regularly on loch margins, along burns well

up into the hills and on small holms. Gatherings of up to 50 or more moulting drakes may be found in certain localities such as Waulkmill and Echnaloch Bays in late summer and early autumn.

Goosander *Mergus merganser* Mainly a scarce winter visitor. Since 1970 there have been 23 records including, in May 1981, one which was watched displaying with a Red-breasted Merganser.

Ruddy Duck *Oxyura jamaicensis* A pair in Holm from 3rd–6th May 1980 and one on Stronsay during late May 1984.

Honey Buzzard *Pernis apivorus* Scarce, but perhaps almost regular, passage visitor. Most sightings have been in May and June though also in July and September. Six records in 1981 (two in May, one in June, one in July and two in September) were exceptional for one year.

Black Kite *Milvus migrans* Very scarce visitor. Four recent sightings – one in Lyde area of Harray on 18th and 19th May 1966 and one at Trumland, Rousay on 15th May 1968. One at North Ronaldsay on 28th September 1970 and another on Eday on 3rd May 1975.

Red Kite *Milvus milvus* Very scarce visitor. Only two old records from Sanday in 1877 and 1878 (Buckley and Harvie-Brown).

White-tailed Eagle (Erne) *Haliaetus albicilla* Formerly a resident breeder nesting at a number of coastal cliff sites on several islands up to at least the late 1880s. One on Hoy on 6th May 1976, one on North Ronaldsay on 15th April 1982 and a first-year bird wing-tagged on Rhum as part of the re-introduction scheme there was present in various localities during the summer of 1983. One over South Ronaldsay on 11th March 1984.

Marsh Harrier *Circus aeruginosus* Very scarce passage visitor. Was perhaps more common formerly as Baikie and Heddle cite a number of occurrences on Rousay and Sanday. One shot on Sanday on 6th April 1944, in Stromness Museum. A male was seen at North Ronaldsay in October 1965. Since 1972 there have been records in 1977 (one), 1978 (two), 1979 (one) and 1981 (six).

Hen Harrier *Circus cyaneus* Fairly common resident and migrant breeder and passage and winter visitor. Was rather scarce during the early part of the century until the 1940s when it greatly increased during the war years and reached a peak about 1950 and again in the late 1970s. Since females greatly outnumber males in the breeding population, polygyny has become widespread and regular. Breeding is mainly confined to the moors of the Mainland and Rousay, although a few also nest on Hoy and, occasionally, on Eday.

Montagu's Harrier *Circus pygargus* Very scarce visitor. Said by Baxter and Rintoul to have occurred in Orkney but should be regarded as doubtful.

Goshawk *Accipiter gentilis* Very scarce passage visitor. A female came to grief at Finstown by colliding with overhead wires on 14th May 1968. One in Rendall on 12th April 1976, one in Birsay on 15th December 1977, one in Rendall in February 1978, one in Evie in May 1978, and others on North Ronaldsay, May–July 1981 and mid June 1984.

Sparrowhawk *Accipiter nisus* Regular passage and irregular winter visitor. Most often in spring and autumn. Formerly a few pairs bred but for many years there were none. However, a pair bred unsuccessfully in 1978 and other pairs bred successfully in different localities in 1983 and 1984.

Buzzard *Buteo buteo* Mainly a scarce occasional visitor. Was extremely rare up to about 1955 but since then one or two pairs have been resident and have bred since about 1961.

Rough-legged Buzzard *Buteo lagopus* Rather scarce passage and irregular winter visitor. Occurs most frequently in April/May and October/November. More numerous in the 1930s and 40s than recently.

Golden Eagle *Aquila chrysaetos* Mainly a scarce occasional visitor. Formerly one or two pairs were resident and bred up to about 90 years ago. In 1966 a pair became established on Hoy and have attempted to breed every year, usually successfully. Immature birds have been seen in a number of localities over the past few years.

Osprey *Pandion haliaetus* Scarce passage visitor. Has occurred most regularly in April and May but also in autumn. Annual in recent years.

Kestrel (Moosie Haak) *Falco tinnunculus* Fairly common resident and migrant breeder. Increased in the early 1940s and adapted to ground nesting among heather. Numbers appear to have fallen considerably recently.

Red-footed Falcon *Falco vespertinus* Very scarce visitor. A female at Stromness on 8th May 1962 and a juvenile in the Lyde area of Rendall from 12th

August 1967 for about five weeks. There are now additional records of birds on South Ronaldsay in May 1973, on Papa Westray in August 1977 and on Rousay in May/June 1981. Birds in Rendall in June 1983 and on Papa Westray in June 1984 the latter not yet having been accepted by BBRC.

Merlin *Falco columbarius* Rather scarce resident and migrant breeder and passage and winter visitor. Decreased slightly after the 1940s and drastically during the 1980s. The 1983 population was only 11 or 12 pairs and that of 1984 only six pairs. Taking Mainland alone a survey in 1974 found 13 pairs; in 1983 this population had fallen to just 7 or 8 pairs and in 1984 to only 4 pairs. Breeding pairs are scattered thinly over moorland areas; chiefly on Mainland, Hoy and Rousay.

Hobby *Falco subbuteo* Very scarce visitor. One was recorded at Dale of Cottasgarth, Rendall on 26th June 1957 and another at Melsetter on 12th May 1959. Since 1972 there have been five recorded, all in June–August.

Gyr Falcon *Falco rusticolus* Scarce irregular visitor. Several old records including a specimen in Stromness Museum. More recently one over Burrien Hill on 13th May 1966. In 1984, birds seen on Graemsay in January, and in Rendall in April.

Peregrine *Falco peregrinus* Rather scarce resident and migrant breeder and also passage and winter visitor. Has nested on at least nine of the islands; mainly on sea-cliffs. Low breeding success in the 1960s was attributed to toxic chemicals in the food chain when some pairs failed to produce eggs and some of those that did failed to hatch. In 1981 twenty-four apparently-occupied territories were found but seven of these (29%) were occupied only by single birds. The remaining 17 territories (71%) were occupied by pairs and at least 13 and perhaps as many as 16 pairs attempted to breed. Nine pairs are believed to have produced young. These figures show an improvement on 1971 when only 15 occupied territories were found, 12 of them by pairs; between 8 and 10 pairs attempted to breed but only five produced young.

Red Grouse *Lagopus lagopus* Resident breeder. Not very numerous. Was much more common during the period between the wars. Breeds chiefly on the Mainland, Rousay and Hoy.

Ptarmigan *Lagopus mutus* Former breeder. Confined to Hoy where they were apparently shot out sometime between 1830 and 1840.

Black Grouse *Lyrurus tetrix* Scarce irregular visitor. A male was shot in St Andrews in September 1958 and one was seen on Pentland Skerries in October 1962. Attempted introduction during last century failed.

Red-legged Partridge *Alectoris rufa* Introduced near Kirkwall in 1840, but quickly became extinct.

Grey Partridge *Perdix perdix* Scarce irregular visitor. Single birds have occurred from time to time and there have been some attempted introductions without success.

Quail *Coturnix coturnix* Very scarce and irregular migrant breeder or passage visitor. Has nested on a small number of occasions, notably Shapinsay 1923 Rendall 1937 and 1953, Rousay 1958 and Firth 1982.

Pheasant *Phasianus colchicus* Introduced breeder, scarce, but breeding wild in a few widely scattered places.

Water Rail *Rallus aquaticus* Regular passage and winter visitor. Formerly a regular breeder and resident. Scarcer now, but did breed in St Ola in 1968 and may still do so in one or two localities.

Spotted Crake *Porzana porzana* Very scarce passage visitor. Mentioned by Baikie and Heddle, Buckley and Harvie-Brown, and Omond as having been observed at Sanday. Recorded on North Ronaldsay in September 1884 and September 1892. Heard calling at Rothiesholm, Stronsay in late May 1968. The only recent records involve single birds on North Ronaldsay in October 1980, in Birsay in April 1981, on North Ronaldsay in September 1983 and in St Ola in November 1984.

Corncrake *Crex crex* Migrant breeder. Was very common in the early part of the century but has gradually decreased. Still breeds on most islands but most commonly in the North Isles. A 1977 survey organized with the help of Radio Orkney, revealed calling birds in the following areas: West Mainland, 30; East Mainland, 3; Hoy, 3; South Ronaldsay, 6; Westray, 8; Sanday, 2; Stronsay, 5; Papa Westray, 10; Rousay, 1; Shapinsay, 15; North Ronaldsay, 10. Cadbury (1980) recorded 102–104 calling birds. Has probably further declined on Mainland and South Isles but seems to be holding its own in North Isles.

Moorhen (Water-hen) *Gallinula chloropus* Common resident breeder. Breeds in wet situations on the majority of the islands.

Coot *Fulica atra* Resident breeder and winter visitor on Lochs of Bosquoy and Harray. Decreased

as a breeder on the Mainland since about 1930. Now common only on a few of the North Isles' reedy lochs. Wintering flock in excess of 200 birds regular on Loch of Harray.

Crane *Grus grus* Scarce irregular visitor. Most occurrences have been in May or early June but also in August and September. Most recent sightings have been at Birsay, May 1955; Stronsay, May 1969; Swannay Loch, August/September 1969 and also at Papa Westray and Mainland in May/June 1971. 1972 records for South Ronaldsay in March and from North Ronaldsay in May and December do not appear to have been accepted by BBRC. Since then authenticated records involve two in Deerness from May until September 1978, two in Stenness in April 1980, one in Birsay in April 1982 and one in Firth the following month. In 1983 there were records from Birsay in April/May and in the East Mainland from June to October. Two on Sanday in late March 1984.

Great Bustard *Otis tarda* Very scarce visitor. One was shot at Holland, Stronsay in the spring of 1876 and is believed to be the specimen stuffed in Balfour Castle, Shapinsay. Omond states that there is one in the Royal Scottish Museum from Stronsay dated 1892. The latest Orkney record was in January 1924.

Oystercatcher (Skeldro or Scottie) *Haematopus ostralegus* Common resident and migrant breeder and also passage visitor. Has greatly increased since about the 1930s when it began to nest inland on cultivated fields and dry hill ground as well as on the coast. Wintering population on the shoreline of around 2770 birds (Martin and Summers, 1984). Most local breeders, however, move out in winter; many ringing recoveries in south-west England and South Wales.

Black-winged Stilt *Himantopus himantopus* Very scarce visitor. Two killed at Lopness, Sanday in 1814. (Baikie and Heddle).

Avocet *Recurvirostra avosetta* Very scarce irregular visitor. One in June 1934, one at North Ronaldsay on 5th May 1965, two on Westray in May 1974 and singles in Toab in July 1975 and on North Ronaldsay in March/April 1980.

Collared Pratincole *Glareola pratincola* Very scarce visitor. Omond cites one old record of one being shot by Mr Bullock. One on South Ronaldsay with Golden Plover on 6th October 1963.

Ringed Plover (Sand-lark or Sinloo) *Charadrius hiaticula* Resident and migrant breeder and passage and winter visitor. Mainly found on or near the coast. Breeds in some numbers, a 1984 census revealing almost 550 pairs on territories. Wintering population around 1615 (14% of British population) (Martin and Summers, 1984).

Greater Sand Plover *Charadrius leschenaultii* One in Deerness 9th–16th June 1979.

Dotterel *Charadrius morinellus* Must be regarded as a very scarce and irregular visitor. Though mentioned by Baikie and Heddle, Buckley and Harvie-Brown, and Omond little is known about the species. Said to have nested on Hoy in 1850. In 1935 two boys took three eggs from a plover-type nest on Milldoe in Rendall. This is at least suggestive as the bird was said to be very tame and the eggs were smaller than those of a Lapwing. Single birds on N. Ronaldsay in October 1976 and May 1978 and 3 in S. Ronaldsay in May 1977 are the only records since 1972.

Lesser Golden Plover *Charadrius dominicus* Very rare visitor. One was shot in Stenness in 26th November 1887 (Howard Saunders and W. Eagle Clark).

Golden Plover (Pliver) *Chardrius apricarius* Resident and migrant breeder and passage and winter visitor. Breeds in scattered pairs over the higher moors. Much reduced in numbers since about the 1930s. The winter 1982/83 shoreline survey suggested a population of 2500 on or near the coast (Martin and Summers, 1984).

Grey Plover *Charadrius squatarola* Regular passage visitor in very small numbers. Seen mainly on or near the coast. A few winter, mainly on Sanday; total population of *c.* 20.

Sociable Plover *Chettusia gregaria* Scarce visitor. A 1st-winter female was shot on North Ronaldsay on 3rd November 1926. One was seen with a party of Lapwings in Rendall in early December 1949 and one in Eday in mid-January 1969.

Lapwing *Vanellus vanellus* Mainly a resident and migrant breeder. Also a passage and winter visitor. Though still a reasonably common breeder it was probably three or four times as numerous prior to 1930. Land drainage is undoubtedly the major contributory factor in its decline. In mild winters many stay throughout but in hard winters, many move S.W. to Ireland.

Knot *Calidris canutus* Regular passage visitor. Usually in small parties. More rarely in big flocks. Strangely scarce as a wintering species. Up to 100 can occur in the Deer Sound area.

Sanderling *Calidris alba* Regular passage visitor in small parties. Usually in early autumn. Now shown to have an important wintering population on some of the North Isles; total *c.* 900 (9% of British population).

Little Stint *Calidris minuta* Passage visitor. Regular, but in very small numbers, chiefly in September.

Temminck's Stint *Calidris temminckii* Very scarce passage visitor. One at North Ronaldsay on 21st May 1964 and another on Papa Westray in June 1981.

White-rumped Sandpiper *Calidris fuscicollis* Very scarce passage visitor from North America. One at North Ronaldsay on 31st October 1969 and one at Tankerness on 11th and 12th October 1970. Single birds have occurred on Sanday in July 1973, in Deerness in October 1973 on North Ronaldsay in October 1978 and in Evie in October 1983.

Pectoral Sandpiper *Calidris melanotos* Very scarce visitor. One at Loch of Burness, Westray on 26th August 1889 (Buckley and Harvie-Brown) and one at North Ronaldsay on 6th and 7th September 1971. Recent records of single birds are given for Firth in October 1980, Tankerness in August/September 1981 and in Birsay in September 1981 and in September 1983. In 1984 birds were seen in Tankerness in July and Evie in September.

Curlew Sandpiper *Calidris ferruginea* Scarce passage visitor, most frequent in August and September.

Purple Sandpiper *Calidris maritima* Regular passage and winter visitor. Frequents rocky shores in small flocks. The winter 1982/83 survey showed clearly the importance of the Orkney shoreline for this species. The population is aout 5600 which represents over 30% of the known British total.

Dunlin *Calidris alpina* Regular and common passage visitor. Also winter visitor and regular breeder in small numbers widely scattered. Wintering population of around 2100.

Buff-breasted Sandpiper *Tryngites subruficollis* One at Row Head Sandwick on 25th and 26th June 1976.

Ruff *Philomachus pugnax* Regular passage visitor in small numbers. Usually in autumn, but occasional breeding plumage birds occur in spring and summer.

Jack Snipe *Lymnocryptes minimus* Regular passage and winter visitor. Occurs in very limited numbers, most usually in October.

Snipe (Horse-gowk) *Gallinago gallinago* Common resident breeder and passage and winter visitor. Breeds commonly on most of the islands. Meinertzhagen (1939) ascribed the Orkney breeding birds to the Faroe form *G.g. faroensis.*

Great Snipe *Gallinago media* Scarce visitor. Buckley and Harvie-Brown state that about six had been seen or shot. The most recent sighting was on Wastlee Moor, Hoy on 19th May 1959, although this record was never submitted to BBRC.

Long-billed Dowitcher *Limnodromus scolopaceus* Very scarce visitor from North America. One at Ancum Loch, North Ronaldsay on 4th April 1970 could only be identified as Dowitcher (sp?). One *L. scolopaceus* at Carness, Kirkwall on 24th and 25th September 1983, and one at Kirkwall on 26th and 27th October 1984.

Woodcock *Scolopax rusticola* Regular passage and winter visitor. Usually single birds on open dry hillsides, but on occasions up to about a dozen in Binscarth and Trumland Woods. Said to have bred in 1896, and on Rousay in 1888 and 1923. At Carrick Wood, Eday on 20th June 1963 one was injury feigning but no young could be located in the dense unergrowth. Similar behaviour was noted in two different localities on Hoy in 1984.

Black-tailed Godwit *Limosa limosa* Mainly a passage visitor in small numbers. Bred on Sanday in 1956 and at two sites in 1975 but although birds have been seen in suitable areas since, nesting is not known to have occurred.

Bar-tailed Godwit *Limosa lapponica* Regular passage visitor. Almost exclusively frequents sandy and muddy beaches, as on Sanday and Deer Sound and Scapa Beach on Mainland. The wintering population is about 800.

Whimbrel *Numenius phaeopus* Regular passage visitor in small numbers. Most usual in May/June and August/September. Bred on Eday in 1968 (three pairs), on the Mainland in 1970 and in recent years again on Eday where up to six pairs have become established.

Curlew (Whaup) *Numenius arquata* Common resident and migrant breeder and also passage and winter visitor. Has increased enormously since the 1930s. Now about the commonest moorland breeding bird. Considerable flocks present during the winter. Heppleston (1981) in the *Orkney Bird Report*, charts the increase of the species in the islands and suggests a minimum breeding population of 1000 pairs. The true figure is surely far in excess of this when one considers that an RSPB survey of its Hobbister reserve revealed a population of 96 pairs there alone. Phenomenal numbers winter in Orkney, the figure being put at 18,000 (20% of British population: Martin and Summers, 1984). This figure only applies to those on the shore and on fields immediately inland.

Spotted Redshank *Tringa erythropus* Regular passage visitor but in very small numbers. Most usual in August and September.

Redshank *Tringa totanus* Mainly a resident and migrant breeder but also passage and winter visitor. Breeds commonly. The winter 1982/83 shoreline survey revealed a population of 7000 (7% of British population).

Marsh Sandpiper *Tringa stagnatilis* One on North Ronaldsay on 23rd August 1979.

Greenshank *Tringa nebularia* Regular passage visitor in both spring and autumn. Not numerous. Has bred at least twice, on Heddle Hill, Firth in 1926 and on Hoy in 1951.

Green Sandpiper *Tringa ochropus* Passage visitor. Probably regular but in small numbers. Most usual in early autumn, but also occasional in spring.

Wood Sandpiper *Tringa glareola* Scarce passage visitor in both spring and autumn.

Common Sandpiper (Boondie) *Actitis hypoleucos* Migrant breeder and passage visitor. In the first third of this century it was a pretty common breeder on the banks of most burns and lochs, but now is only known to breed at three Mainland lochs, on Rousay and on Hoy; total population probably less than 10 pairs.

Turnstone (Stoney-putter) *Arenaria interpres* Common passage and winter visitor. Regular on most coasts. A few stay throughout the summer and although birds have been seen displaying in recent years, breeding has never occurred. Wintering population believed to be 6000 (24% of British population) (Martin and Summers, 1984).

Wilson's Phalarope *Phalaropus tricolor* One at Birsay on 3rd September 1981.

Red-necked Phalarope *Phalaropus lobatus* Formerly a scarce migrant breeder and passage visitor; now only a scarce, irregular visitor only one or two a year occurring 1976–1983 and none at all in 1978 and 1980. Formerly bred in smallish numbers on some of the North Isles and even the Mainland, but lost as a breeding species in Orkney about 1970, there being only one hint that breeding may have occurred since (on Stronsay in 1975).

Grey Phalarope *Phalaropus fulicarius* Scarce and irregular passage visitor. Most occurrences have been in autumn but one in breeding plumage was seen at Bay of Skaill in early June 1956. Although still rare, up to 15 occurred in September 1977 on North Ronaldsay.

Pomarine Skua *Stercorarius pomarinus* Irregular passage visitor in small numbers. Up to ten per day passing Auskerry in last week of September 1966.

Arctic Skua (Skootie Allen) *Stercorarius parasiticus* Migrant breeder and passage visitor. Has increased and spread to breed on most of the islands. A 1982 survey revealed a total Orkney population of 1034 pairs, a 44% increase since 1974. Hoy remains the stronghold with 407 pairs (38% of the total). Other important islands are Eday (101 pairs), Papa Westray (95 pairs), Rousay (94 pairs) and Mainland (67 pairs).

Long-tailed Skua *Stercorarius longicaudus* Scarce, irregular passage visitor. One stayed on a farm in Rendall (well inland) for over a week from 2nd June 1955. One on 25th and two on 28th September 1966 at Auskerry. 14 records of single birds between 1973–82 including one in June/July 1982 which exhibited territorial behaviour. In 1983 an unprecedented passage was witnessed off Papa Westray when a total of 45 were seen between 11th and 15th August with a peak of 34 on the 12th.

Great Skua (Bonxie) *Stercorarius skua* Migrant breeder and passage visitor. A 1982 survey revealed a total Orkney population of 1652 pairs, an increase of 242% since 1974. Hoy with 1573 pairs held 96% of the total.

Little Gull *Larus minutus* Rather scarce passage visitor. Formerly considered to be of doubtful occurrence. Small number seen since 1960. Five sightings on North Ronaldsay between 19th May and 13th June 1971. Becoming a little more regular, 2–6 being recorded in each of the last five years.

Sabine's Gull *Larus sabinii* One off North Ronaldsay on 16th October 1979, four off Birsay in late August/early September 1983 and in August/September 1984 there were three records involving five birds.

Black-headed Gull *Larus ridibundus* Common resident breeder. Widespread in smallish colonies in marshy places, on loch margins and on smaller islands.

Ring-billed Gull *Larus delawarensis* One in Stromness harbour on 27th March 1983.

Common Gull *Larus canus* Common resident breeder. Widespread in small colonies in moorland situations and on some smaller uninhabited islands.

Lesser Black-backed Gull *Larus fuscus* Migrant breeder and passage visitor. Breeds at a number of moorland sites in colonies often associated with Herring Gulls, sometimes well inland. The darker Scandinavian form, *L.f. fuscus*, occurs occasionally as a migrant.

Herring Gull (White Maa) *Larus argentatus* Numerous resident breeder and winter visitor. Breeds commonly; widespread on coasts and small islands and in a few inland moorland localities.

Iceland Gull *Larus glaucoides* Irregular winter visitor. One from Birsay 1935 in Stromness Museum. Considerable influxes in the winters of 1982/83 and 1983/84 with perhaps 40+ in the former and 30+ in the latter. Birds tend to be much more confined to the harbour areas than Glaucous Gulls which they greatly outnumbered in both the latter winters. Three birds in Stromness Harbour in winter 1982/83 showed the characteristics of Kumlien's Gull *L.g. kumlienii*; these records are currently under consideration by BBRC.

Glaucous Gull *Larus hyperboreus* Regular winter visitor in small numbers, mainly immature birds.

Great Black-backed Gull (Baakie) *Larus marinus* Rather numerous resident breeder. Numbers were not high 30 years ago, but the species has since increased greatly. Large numbers on Hoy, where there have been up to 4000 pairs; big colonies also occur on Calf of Eday, Rothiesholm (Stronsay) with smaller numbers in several other places.

Kittiwake *Rissa tridactyla* Common resident and migrant breeder and also passage and winter visitor. Following a period of expansion has shown a dramatic decline in recent years, the monitoring counts indicating a breeding population decrease of almost one third since 1976.

Ivory Gull *Pagophila eburnea* Very scarce visitor. Individuals have occurred from time to time; the most recent being one at Kirkwall Bay from 29th April to 6th May 1949.

Gull-billed Tern *Gelochelidon nilotica* Very scarce visitor. One on Pentland Skerries on 7th May 1913.

Sandwich Tern *Sterna sandvicensis* Regular migrant breeder. Numbers vary considerably from year to year. Breeds in very closely packed colonies; often in association with other species such as Black-headed Gulls and Arctic and Common Terns. Has nested most consistently on North Ronaldsay and Sanday, but also occasionally on other islands such as Burray, Holm of Rendall, Wyre, Eday, Stronsay and Pentland Skerries. The 1980 tern census gave a total of 119 pairs at four colonies. This was a decrease from a 1977 count which gave 298 pairs.

Roseate Tern *Sterna dougallii* Scarce occasional visitor. Up to three pairs carrying fish and displaying at an Arctic Tern colony on Sanday in mid-June 1969. One in Arctic Tern colony on Sanday May 1976. One on Pentland Skerries in July 1980 and one on Papa Westray in June 1983.

Common Tern *Sterna hirundo* Regular migrant breeder. Breeding numbers not large. Often nests in association with Arctic Terns. A 1980 census gave a total of 231 pairs in 28 colonies.

Arctic Tern (Pickie-terno; Ritto) *Sterna paradisaea* Common migrant breeder. Breeds in fairly dense colonies on coasts and small islands. The 1980 census gave a population of 33,000 pairs in 215 colonies. North Hill, Papa Westray; Auskerry; Quandale North, Rousay; Pentland Skerries; Wastlee Moor, Hoy and Flotta all held over 1,000 pairs each. The mean overall colony size was 158 pairs.

Bridled Tern *Sterna anaethetus* One at Stromness on 6th and 7th August 1979.

Sooty Tern *Sterna fuscata* Very scarce visitor. One at Isbister, Rendall on 22nd April 1954.

Little Tern *Sterna albifrons* Irregular passage visitor. A few seen in recent years. The statement in the *Handbook* (Witherby *et al.*, 1941) that it is an Orkney breeder is an obvious mistake although a pair bred unsuccessfully on Sanday in 1984.

Black Tern *Chlidonias niger* Scarce and irregular passage visitor. Recent occurrences involve one at North Ronaldsay on 7th May 1965, four on 9th May 1967, one at Yesnaby late May 1968, one at Tanker-

ness on 15th September 1968 and one at North Ronaldsay on 27th August 1971. One to three recorded in five years since 1972; all May–September.

White-winged Black Tern *Chlidonias leucopterus* Very scarce visitor. One at North Ronaldsay 11th to 13th June 1966, and another on North Ronaldsay on 24th and 26th May 1976.

Guillemot (Aak) *Uria aalge* Resident and migrant breeder and perhaps winter visitor. Breeds in several large colonies and many smaller ones on suitable sea-cliffs. Between 1976 and 1980 numbers increased annually at all colonies monitored but since 1980 this increase has halted and numbers have become stable or even declined slightly.

Brunnich's Guillemot *Uria lomvia* One found dead in Stenness on 29th December 1981 and another found dead near Stromness on 3rd April 1982. One found dead in Birsay on 20th March 1984.

Razorbill (Coulter-neb) *Alca torda* Resident and migrant breeder. Breeds fairly commonly on most sea-cliffs, but not nearly as numerous as the Guillemot. Following a period of expansion in the late 1970s they have since slightly declined.

Great Auk *Alca impennis* Extinct. The last pair (perhaps only pair) was killed at Papa Westray in the summer of 1813 or thereby. Buckley and Harvie-Brown give a long account in their *Fauna*.

Black Guillemot *Cepphus grylle* Resident breeder. Breeds in smallish widely spread colonies on rocky coasts. Best colonies were formerly on Eynhallow and Auskerry but in 1984 128 nests were found on the Holm of Papay which is now the largest of the Orkney colonies. The 'Seafarer' figure of 342 for Auskerry has often been quoted as being of breeding pairs but this is obviously incorrect and is simply a count of individuals on and around the island.

Little Auk (Rotchie) *Plautus alle* Winter visitor. Small and irregular numbers. A few get blown inland after storms in most winters. Occasionally seen swimming or flying off-shore.

Puffin (Tammy-norrie) *Fratercula arctica* Migrant breeder. Breeds in smallish numbers at a number of places round the coast as at Costa Head, St John's Head, The Berry and Swona. The largest colony, however, is on Sule Skerry where work by D. Budworth and A. Blackburn suggests that the population there (in 1975 and 1982) is about 44,000 pairs.

Pallas's Sandgrouse *Syrrhaptes paradoxus* Very scarce irruptive visitor. Seen in 1863, but a large scale irruption in 1888 when many occurred and several were shot and preserved. The most recent irruption was in 1908.

Rock Dove *Columba livia* Common resident breeder. Widespread. Some inter-breeding with domestic birds gone feral.

Stock Dove *Columba oenas* There have been no records since 1972; there is no evidence for Balfour's (1972) statement that it was formerly a passage visitor.

Woodpigeon *Columba palumbus* Common resident breeder. In addition to breeding in trees and bushes the species has adapted to nesting among heather and in rushes in a number of places.

Collared Dove *Streptopelia decaocto* Resident breeder. First reached Orkney in 1982 and soon began to breed and spread. Now established in many localities, but most numerous in Kirkwall, Finstown and Stromness.

Turtle Dove *Streptopelia turtur* Regular passage visitor in small numbers in both spring and autumn.

Great Spotted Cuckoo *Clamator glandarius* Very rare visitor. One in Rendall in August 1959 where it stayed for over a week feeding on caterpillars of the Large White Butterfly.

Cuckoo *Cuculus canorus* Passage visitor and occasional migrant breeder. Regular in very small numbers.

Yellow-billed Cuckoo *Coccyzus americanus* Very rare visitor from America. One at Birsay on 22nd October 1936 (Stromness Museum); one at Sandwick on 12th October, 1956.

Barn Owl *Tyto alba* Very scarce visitor. The dark-breasted form *T.a. guttata* has occurred near Stromness in February 1925, near Kirkwall in February 1928 at North Ronaldsay on 2nd November 1944, and on Sanday on 22nd May 1979. In addition an individual (not sub-specifically identified) was recorded at Yesnaby (Sandwick) in 1900.

Scops Owl *Otus scops* Very scarce visitor. At least four acceptable records. One caught on North Ronaldsay on 2nd June 1892, one at Westray on 30th April 1948; one in Kirkwall on 11th June 1965 and one found dead at Holm, November 1970.

Eagle Owl *Bubo bubo* Very scarce visitor. One said to have been killed in Sanday in 1830 (Buckley and Harvie-Brown).

Snowy Owl *Nyctea scandiaca* Irregular visitor. Generally in winter but sometimes in summer. A pair stayed on the high moorland of Eday throughout the summer of 1963 and possibly have attempted to breed. Recent accepted records have been from Eday and Papa Westray in mid-May 1972; Papa Westray (2) in November 1974; Birsay in May 1977; Papa Westray and North Ronaldsay in May 1981 and another on North Ronaldsay in June 1981; and one in Evie in June 1982.

Little Owl *Athene noctua* Extremely doubtful if it ever occurred. Confusion with Tengmalm's Owl likely.

Tawny Owl *Strix aluco* Very rare visitor. Omond's statement that there was an Orkney specimen in Stromness Museum cannot now be verified. It must therefore be regarded as doubtful.

Long-eared Owl *Asio otus* Winter and passage visitor and resident breeder. No breeding records in recent years. Communal winter roosts at Binscarth (Finstown), Berstane (Kirkwall) and occasionally at Norseman Garage (Rendall) can each hold up to 25 birds with smaller numbers in other localities.

Short-eared Owl (Cattieface) *Asio flammeus* Regular resident and migrant breeder and also passage and winter visitor. Breeds fairly commonly in fluctuating numbers. Mainland population in the region of 60 pairs, two pairs on Rousay in 1981, while a pair which nested recently on Eday was seen to fly to Sanday to hunt, presumably the result of Eday's lack of Orkney Voles. Several pairs may nest on Sanday in some years.

Tengmalm's Owl *Aegolius funereus* Very scarce visitor. Three recent records involving four birds: one at Cruan, Rendall in late December 1959, one in Stromness on 1st May 1961, one was in Binscarth Wood 13th–20th October 1980, while another was there on 18th November 1980.

Nightjar *Caprimulgus europaeus* Scarce and irregular passage visitor. The latest two occurrences have been on North Ronaldsay, one in early September 1968 and one in early June 1971. No records since 1972.

Common Nighthawk *Chordeiles minor* One trapped near Kirkwall on 12th September 1978.

Needle-tailed Swift *Hirundapus caudacutus* One at Windwick, South Ronaldsay on 11th and 12th June 1983.

Swift *Apus apus* Passage visitor. Fairly regular in small numbers in spring, summer and autumn.

Alpine Swift *Apus melba* Very rare visitor. One caught at North Ronaldsay Lighthouse on 8th June 1965.

Kingfisher *Alcedo althis* Scarce, irregular visitor. Only a few occurrences, mainly in autumn. The most recent record is of one at Scapa Distillery on 10th May 1975.

Bee-eater *Merops apiaster* Very scarce visitor. Three at Binscarth on 5th June 1966. One dead on Sanday on 25th May 1969 and one seen at Skaill, Westray 29th and 30th May 1969. More recently one was in Kirkwall 15th–26th July 1979 and another was on Rousay on 7th June 1982.

Roller *Coracias garrulus* Very scarce visitor. A few occurrences. Most recently one at Isbister, Rendall on 27th May 1958 and one in east Mainland 5th June–21st July 1958 (assuming all sightings were of the same individual). One bird on North Ronaldsay, 11th June 1966.

Hoopoe *Upupa epops* Scarce passage visitor. Irregular in very small numbers in spring and autumn.

Wryneck *Jynx torquilla* Rather scarce but more or less regular passage visitor; both spring and autumn.

Green Woodpecker *Picus viridis* Very rare visitor. Apparently no acceptable record since July 1885 when T. W. Rankin observed one in a Kirkwall garden (Buckley and Harvie-Brown).

Great Spotted Woodpecker *Dendrocopos major* Passage visitor and occasional winter visitor. Most usual from September to November. Tends to be irruptive. Recently noticeable in 1962 and 1968; a few wintered until early May 1969. One present and 'drumming' in Trumland Woods, Rousay during June but breeding not proved.

Lesser Spotted Woodpecker *Dendrocopos minor* Listed by Baikie and Heddle, Buckley and Harvie-Brown, and Omond, but no recent reliable records. Must be regarded as very doubtful.

Short-toed Lark *Calandrella brachydactyla* Very scarce visitor. One at Auskerry on 1st October 1913 and one on North Ronaldsay in late September 1983.

Woodlark *Lullula arborea* Very scarce visitor. One at Pentland Skerries in October 1911, one at Auskerry in October 1912, and on 11th and 21st October 1913.

Skylark (Lavero) *Alauda arvensis* Common resident breeder. Fairly widespread though now less numerous than formerly.

Shore Lark *Eremophila alpestris* Scarce passage and winter visitor. One at Pentland Skerries and one or two at Auskerry in October/November 1913; one at Graemsay in March 1915 and two on Swona in autumn 1915. A pair on Papa Westray 18th May 1972. Recently recorded more regularly than formerly but still in only very small numbers. The exception was in October 1976 when up to 60 were present on North Ronaldsay.

Sand Martin *Riparia riparia* Passage visitor. Fairly regular but in very small numbers.

Swallow *Hirundo rustica* Passage visitor and migrant breeder. Breeds regularly in small numbers, especially in farm buildings and old air-raid shelters.

Red-rumped Swallow *Hirundo daurica* One on North Ronaldsay on 7th October 1976.

House Martin *Delichon urbica* Mainly a passage visitor. Has bred on a few occasions, at Finstown in 1969 (one pair) and most recently again at Finstown in 1983.

Richard's Pipit *Anthus novaeseelandiae* Scarce visitor. One on North Ronaldsay 13th April 1967, singles on 2nd and 26th October 1968, from 1st to 3rd November 1969 and 28th September 1970. There are more recent records from Deerness on 2nd November 1975 and 12th September, 1981 and North Ronaldsay on 20th and 21st September 1983. A Stronsay record 26th–29th September 1977 does not appear to have been submitted to BBRC.

Tree Pipit *Anthus trivialis* Passage visitor. Usually in very small numbers but occasionally large falls of migrants occur as in early May 1969 when there were hundreds.

Meadow Pipit *Anthus pratensis* Common resident breeder and passage visitor.

Red-throated Pipit *Anthus cervinus* Very rare visitor. One on Auskerry on 1st October 1913 and one on Papa Westray on 4th June 1978.

Rock Pipit (Tang Sparrow) *Anthus spinoletta* Resident breeder and passage and winter visitor, common on most coasts.

Yellow Wagtail *Motacilla flava* Scarce passage migrant. Said to have bred in 1864 at Melsetter; a pair bred successfully on Papa Westray in 1979 and probably on Westray in 1980.

Citrine Wagtail *Motacilla citreola* One on North Ronaldsay 19th–21st September 1983; not yet accepted by BBRC.

Grey Wagtail *Motacilla cinerea* Rather scarce passage visitor. Has bred on a few occasions; in Firth in 1974–76, St Ola 1976–81 and in Hoy 1981–83. It appears that no more than two pairs have bred in any one year although an extra pair may have bred in Evie in 1976.

Pied Wagtail *Motacilla alba* Regular migrant breeder and passage visitor. The Pied Wagtail *M.a. yarellii* was a pretty common breeder until the late 1930s when it became scarce, but has recently been increasing. It has increased and expanded its range on North Isles during the 1970s. Very few remain in winter, migrants returning in March. The White Wagtail *M.a. alba* is a regular migrant and has also bred on rare occasions.

Waxwing *Bombycilla garrulus* Passage visitor; irruptive. Some years fair numbers, others very few if any; usually in late autumn, early winter.

Dipper *Cinclus cinclus* Former regular breeder in limited numbers. Apparently absent from about 1940 or 1941 until the late 1960s when it seemed to be making a comeback. One or two present in Hoy in 1968, 1969, 1970, May 1973 and a pair there during the summer of 1974. Not reported since. One Black-bellied Dipper (*C.c. cinclus*) seen on North Ronaldsay on 4th April 1965.

Wren *Troglodytes troglodytes* Common breeding resident. Widespread, even found far up along moorland burns.

Dunnock *Prunella modularis* Resident breeder and passage visitor. Breeds regularly in small numbers in woods and gardens.

Robin *Erithacus rubecula* Resident breeder and passage and winter visitor. Breeds in small numbers in woods and gardens. Apparently the British race *E.r. melophilus*. The passage and winter visitors are generally ascribed to the Continental race *E.r. rubecula*.

Thrush Nightingale *Luscinia luscinia* One in Holm 12th–16th May 1983.

Nightingale *Luscinia megarhynchos* Very rare visitor. The only reliable record is of one caught at North Ronaldsay on 11th May 1967.

Bluethroat *Luscinia svecica* Scarce passage visitor. Fairly regular in very small numbers. The great majority of Orkney records are of the Red-spotted form *L.s. svecica* but there are two records of the White-spotted form *L.s. cyanecula*, in St Ola on 31st March 1958 and on North Ronaldsay on 6th May 1967. Following a considerable influx in May 1981, two males were heard singing in moorland localities.

Black Redstart *Phoenicurus ochruros* Scarce passage visitor. More or less regular in very small numbers. A female laid a clutch of four eggs on Copinsay in 1973; no male was ever seen and the eggs were infertile.

Redstart *Phoenicurus phoenicurus* Regular passage visitor. Variable numbers in both spring and autumn.

Whinchat *Saxicola rubetra* Mainly a regular passage visitor. Occasionally a summer visitor and has bred on a number of occasions. Present on Hoy in the summer of 1969 although breeding was not proved. A pair possibly bred on Hoy in 1975 and held territory there in 1976. A number of other summer records in the islands have raised hopes of breeding but it has never been proved in recent years.

Stonechat *Saxicola torquata* Resident breeder and perhaps passage visitor. Increased during the 1960s and 1970s but following the hard winter of 1978/79 the only regular breeding haunts appear to be on Hoy and at Hobbister, Mainland. A bird of one of the eastern races *S.t. maura* or *stejnegeri* was seen in Birsay on 21st October 1981. This is the first accepted record of this race in Orkney, one on Stronsay in October 1977 apparently not having been submitted to BBRC.

Wheatear (Chachie) *Oenanthe oenanthe* Migrant breeder and passage visitor. Breeds in smallish numbers, widely scattered. Regular on passage in fair numbers including the Greenland race *O.o. leucorrhoa*.

Pied Wheatear *Oenanthe pleschanka* Very rare visitor. A female on Swona on 1st November 1916.

Desert Wheatear *Oenanthe deserti* Very rare visitor. One (male) at Pentland Skerries on 2nd June 1906 was of the Eastern form *O.d. atrogularis*.

Rock Thrush *Monticola saxatilis* Very rare visitor. One male obtained and another seen on Pentland Skerries on 17th May 1910.

White's Thrush *Zoothera dauma* Doubtful. One said to have occurred on North Ronaldsay on 1st October 1965 but rejected by BBRC.

Siberian Thrush *Zoothera sibirica* First Orkney record; one adult male on South Ronaldsay, 13th November 1984.

Ring Ouzel *Turdus torquatus* Regular passage visitor in small numbers. Also an irregular migrant breeder. One or two pairs regular on Hoy in recent years, holding territory and with breeding proved on several occasions. During the enormous influx of thrushes in October 1976 quite unprecedented numbers occurred with up to 200 in Orphir and 100 in Kirkwall.

Blackbird (Blackie) *Turdus merula* Common resident breeder and passage visitor. A more numerous and widespread breeder than the Song Thrush and using a greater variety of nesting habitat.

Eye-browed Thrush *Turdus obscurus* An immature bird present in Evie on 25th/26th September 1984.

Fieldfare *Turdus pilaris* Regular passage and winter visitor; occasionally very large flocks in autumn. One pair bred in Stenness in 1967 (first British breeding record) and a pair bred in Evie in 1969. Also a pair were seen feeding two young on Westray in mid-June 1974.

Song Thrush (Mavis) *Turdus philomelos* Resident breeder and passage visitor. Breeds fairly commonly in woods and gardens; occasionally along ditches, stone walls and old quarries. Migrants most numerous in late September/early October.

Redwing *Turdus iliacus* Rare occasional breeder and regular passage visitor. Sometimes in huge flocks in autumn. About 15,000 on North Ronaldsay on 14th October 1970. A pair bred successfully in Orphir in 1975, the only Orkney breeding record. In the same year a pair held territory at Binscarth. In 1976 a phenomenal influx occurred, in October, involving many tens of thousands of birds.

Mistle Thrush *Turdus viscivorus* Passage visitor and scarce irregular breeder. Passage birds rather few and no breeding records since 1972.

American Robin *Turdus migratorius* Very rare visitor. One at Kirkwall Airport on 27th May 1961.

Lanceolated Warbler *Locustella lanceolata* Very rare visitor. One at Pentland Skerries on 26th October 1910.

Grasshopper Warbler *Locustella naevia* Scarce passage visitor. Very inconspicuous. Heard singing in St Ola and in Hoy during the summer of 1971. Only five recent records: May 1975, August 1980, September 1981 (two) and June 1982.

Sedge Warbler *Acrocephalus schoenobaenus* Migrant breeder and passage visitor. Small numbers breed in suitable marshy places on the Mainland and a few other islands. A census of the Durkadale area during 1983 revealed a total of 23 pairs, undoubtedly the largest concentration in Orkney.

Blyth's Reed Warbler *Acrocephalus dumetorum* One in Holm on 5th and 13th October, 1979.

Marsh Warbler *Acrocephalus palustris* Very scarce passage visitor. One on Sanday (North End) on 21st September 1968. One found dead on Copinsay on 1st June 1979 had been ringed as a nestling in Denmark the previous year. One was trapped in Orphir on 20th/21st June 1979; in 1983 birds were caught on North Ronaldsay and South Ronaldsay in early June and in 1984 three were noted in June (one on North Ronaldsay and two in the east Mainland) and one on 23rd September (again on North Ronaldsay).

Reed Warbler *Acrocephalus scirpaceus* Scarce passage visitor. One at Auskerry on 28th September 1912. One at North Ronaldsay on 31st August 1966. In recent years it has become more regularly recorded passage migrant. One in August 1973, four in September/October 1979, four in August/September 1980, at least 12 in September 1981, at least 10 in September 1982 and five in September 1984.

Icterine Warbler *Hippolais icterina* Scarce but regular passage visitor. Two at Pentland Skerries in June 1914; one at North Ronaldsay on 2nd September 1966 and two trapped on North Ronaldsay on 23rd May and 19th June 1971. There have been eight documented records between 1972 and 1983 all in fact since 1977; five have been in May/June and three in August/September.

Melodious Warbler *Hippolais polyglotta* Very rare visitor. One caught on North Ronaldsay on 23rd August 1971, one on Papa Westray on 11th June 1979, one trapped in St Ola on 10th September 1983 and another in Holm on 2nd October 1983.

Subalpine Warbler *Sylvia cantillans* Very scarce visitor. One trapped on North Ronaldsay on 14th–17th September 1967, one at Auskerry on 29th May 1968, another caught at Binscarth Wood on 26th April 1971, and one trapped at Windwick, South Ronaldsay on 7th May 1983.

Barred Warbler *Sylvia nisoria* Passage visitor. Apparently regular and in small numbers. About 22 recorded over the past four years, all in the autumn.

Lesser Whitethroat *Sylvia curruca* Regular passage visitor. Smallish numbers but generally more numerous than Whitethroat on passage.

Whitethroat *Sylvia communis* Passage visitor in limited numbers. A pair found nesting at Smoogro, Orphir in 1941.

Garden Warbler *Sylvia borin* Regular passage visitor in both spring and autumn. A pair bred at Binscarth Wood in 1964 and probably also in 1965. The most recent such record is of a bird holding territory in Trumland Woods, Rousay in 1976 but breeding was not proved.

Blackcap *Sylvia atricapilla* Regular passage visitor. Varying numbers in spring and autumn. Has bred once, in the gardens of Balfour Castle, Shapinsay in 1949.

Greenish Warbler *Phylloscopus trochiloides* Very rare visitor. The first Orkney records were in 1981 with one on North Ronaldsay on 17th September, one in Holm on 26th and 27th September and another on North Ronaldsay on 10th October.

Arctic Warbler *Phylloscopus borealis* Very rare visitor. One at Sule Skerry on 5th September 1902. One seen at Heldale Burn, Hoy from 17th to 20th May 1969 was apparently never submitted to BBRC. One was trapped in Stenness on 3rd September 1972, others in Holm on 15th September 1981 and 9th September 1983, and one (not yet accepted by BBRC) on North Ronaldsay on 23rd September 1984.

Pallas's Warbler *Phylloscopus proregulus* A total of seven occurred during October 1982; the only Orkney records.

Yellow-browed Warbler *Phylloscopus inornatus* Scarce visitor but almost regular. Seen on North Ronaldsay in 1968, 1969 and 1970, and between 1972–1983 there were some 20 records, all in September/October. In late September/October 1984 an arrival of at least 15 occurred.

Radde's Warbler *Phylloscopus schwarzi* One trapped near Kirkwall on 10th October 1982 and one trapped in Holm on 17th October 1982.

Dusky Warbler *Phylloscopus fuscatus* Very rare visitor. One on Auskerry on 1st October 1913. The first record for the British Isles.

Wood Warbler *Phylloscopus sibilatrix* Regular passage visitor in very small numbers. A pair bred at Binscarth in 1914 and 1915.

Chiffchaff *Phylloscopus collybita* Regular passage visitor. Often in good numbers. Occasionally stays throughout the summer but so far breeding has not been proved. A small number of birds resembling the Siberian race *P.c. tristis* have been observed in very late autumn and winter.

Willow Warbler *Phylloscopus trochilus* Regular passage visitor and migrant breeder. Usually common in both spring and autumn. Breeds in small numbers in woods and gardens.

Goldcrest *Regulus regulus* Regular passage and occasional winter visitor. Pre-1972 had bred on at least two occasions: at Binscarth Wood in 1945 and at Carrick Wood, Eday in 1962. Apparently now breeding regularly on Hoy and at Binscarth, and occasionally elsewhere.

Firecrest *Regulus ignicapillus* Very rare visitor. One on Auskerry on 13th September 1967.

Spotted Flycatcher *Muscicapa striata* Regular passage visitor and migrant breeder. A small number have bred regularly in woods and gardens in recent years, on Shapinsay, Rousay and at Kirkwall, Binscarth and possibly Berstane on the Mainland; no more than two pairs proved breeding in any one year.

Red-breasted Flycatcher *Fidecula parva* Passage visitor, scarce but more or less regular. Out of 31 documented records since 1972, 27 have been in autumn and four in spring.

Collared Flycatcher *Fidecula albicollis* Very rare visitor. A full plumaged male at Hunscarth, Harray on 30th May 1963, and one on Stronsay on 31st May 1980.

Pied Flycatcher *Fidecula hypoleuca* Regular passage visitor, occasionally in considerable numbers.

Long-tailed Tit *Aegithalos caudatus* Scarce visitor. Two on North Ronaldsay on 20th October 1966 and a party of five at Finstown on 28th and 29th October 1969. Singles were in Kirkwall in October and November 1973, one on Westray in June 1974, four on Eday in October 1975 and three in Stromness in October 1980. Finally, one appeared at Berstane on 20th November 1983 having been ringed at Conon Bridge, Ross-shire in July 1983.

Coal Tit *Parus ater* Scarce visitor. Two at Binscarth Wood on 20th October 1946 and one in the same locality on 20th November 1949.

Blue Tit *Parus caeruleus* Very scarce visitor. There are three 19th century records, and one on North Ronaldsay in May 1912. Then three birds were at Binscarth in May 1969, one on North Ronaldsay on 2nd October 1971, one to two in Kirkwall area in October 1973 and January 1974, one on Stronsay in October 1977 and one on North Ronaldsay in September 1982.

Great Tit *Parus major* Scarce, irregular visitor. Single birds in July 1884 and 1915. One on North Ronaldsay on 9th September 1966. Since 1972 there have been 11 records, 10 of single birds and the other of a party of five on Shapinsay in April 1975. Apart from one in Stromness in January 1974 the others were all March/April or October/December.

Tree Creeper *Certhia familiaris* Scarce passage and winter visitor. Often seen with Goldcrests. The only recent records are of single birds on Shapinsay in December 1980 and at Binscarth in December 1981.

Golden Oriole *Oriolus oriolus* Scarce and irregular passage visitor. Seven recorded 1964–1972 all in May or June except one at St Andrews in mid-September 1965. Has occurred in seven years since 1972 with one to three in each year, all in May/June.

Red-backed Shrike *Lanius collurio* Passage visitor. Fairly regular but in small numbers. A pair was present on Hoy during June 1970 but proof of nesting was inconclusive.

Lesser Grey Shrike *Lanius minor* Scarce visitor. One at Finstown on 11th November 1962, one found drowned in a water barrel on North Ronaldsay on 30th May 1965, and one on North Ronaldsay 27th September 1967.

Great Grey Shrike *Lanius excubitor* Passage visitor. Fairly regular but in small numbers.

Woodchat Shrike *Lanius senator* Scarce visitor. One at Auskerry on 6th June 1913, one at Rendall on 23rd June 1953. One on North Ronaldsay on 8th May 1964, one on North Ronaldsay on 26th May 1971 and one in Orphir from 9th to 16th June 1974.

Jay *Garrulus glandarius* Rare visitor. One on North Ronaldsay, 11th May 1967 is the only record.

Magpie *Pica pica* Rather scarce visitor. Only a few have been recorded; one near Kirkwall Airport from 13th to 26th February 1970, one on North Ronaldsay in October 1976 and another on Rousay in June 1979.

Nutcracker *Nucifraga caryocatactes* Very rare visitor. One shot in Sanday on 1st October 1868 (Buckley and Harvie-Brown).

Chough *Pyrrhocorax pyrrhocorax* Very rare visitor. One on Westray on 19th October 1935 and on 14th May 1942, one at Herston, South Ronaldsay on 10th December 1951, and one on South Ronaldsay 6th January 1965.

Jackdaw *Corvus monedula* Resident breeder and occasional winter visitor. Breeds rather locally in small colonies on cliffs and buildings.

Rook *Corvus frugilegus* Resident breeder. Breeds in a number of colonies where there are plantations of trees. A 1975 survey gave a total of 957 nests; a similar count in 1982 gave 1,347 nests.

Hooded Crow/Carrion Crow *Corvus corone* Resident breeder and occasional winter visitor. The Hooded Crow *C.c. cornix* is the form which breeds in Orkney. It has increased considerably in recent years – a phenomenon perhaps directly related to the rate of moorland reclamation, agricultural land being able to support a larger population. The Carrion Crow *C.c. corone* occurs as an occasional visitor; birds showing the characteristics of Carrion Crows have nested in recent years but always mated with Hoodies.

Raven *Corvus corax* Resident breeder. Regularly distributed on most coastal cliffs. A very few breed on inland sites. Communal winter roosts may comprise up to 60 birds.

Starling (Stirling, Strill) *Sturnus vulgaris* Numerous breeding resident. Breeds commonly in a variety of situations including holes in the ground and among heather.

Rose-coloured Starling *Sturnus roseus* Scarce irregular visitor. Less than ten occurrences in fifteen years up to 1972. Three recent records of birds at Finstown in July 1975, at Skaill in June 1980, on Wyre in August/September 1982 and on Hoy in June 1984.

House Sparrow *Passer domesticus* Common resident breeder. Fairly numerous on most inhabited islands.

Tree Sparrow *Passer montanus* Scarce resident breeder and occasional passage visitor. A small colony became established on Eday in 1961 and continued until at least 1977.

Chaffinch *Fringilla coelebs* Resident breeder, passage and winter visitor. Breeds in limited numbers in woods and gardens. Regular on passage, occasionally in flocks.

Brambling *Fringilla montifringilla* Passage and winter visitor. More or less regular but in varying numbers. Has occasionally been present i nsummer but no proof of breeding.

Greenfinch *Carduelis chloris* Resident and perhaps migrant breeder. Was fairly common up to the late 1940s but breeding numbers now very low; no breeding records reported in 1973–1977. Breeding proved in 1978, 1979, 1980 and 1982 but only at four localities.

Goldfinch *Carduelis carduelis* Scarce and irregular visitor. Only a few recent occurrences, December 1976 and May 1977 with three in May 1981 and one in 1984.

Serin *Serinus serinus* Two on North Ronaldsay on 20th December 1984; record awaiting confirmation.

Siskin *Carduelis spinus* Passage visitor in rather irregular numbers. Large numbers in October 1961 and late September 1984.

Linnet (Lintie) *Carduelis cannabina* Resident and migrant breeder and perhaps passage visitor. Breeds in fair numbers in woods and bushes but also on grassy banks of old quarries.

Twite (Heather lintie) *Carduelis flavirostris* Resident and migrant breeder and passage visitor. Commoner than the Linnet. Breeds on the ground on heather moorland, roadside verge and clifftops.

Redpoll *Carduelis flammea* Fairly regular passage visitor. Usually in small numbers. Pair seen in Hoy in summer of 1971. Bred on Hoy in 1975 and 1976 – the first Orkney breeding records. Autumn 1975 saw a considerable irruption of Mealy Redpolls (*C.f. flammea*); 77 were trapped on North Ronaldsay while up to 100 were present in Kirkwall and 50 at Loch of Sabiston. A similar phenomenon occurred in autumn 1976 and 1984. Birds of the Greenland race (*C.f. rostrata*) occur in small numbers in some years.

Arctic Redpoll *Carduelis hornemanni* Very rare visitor. One adult female caught at North Ronaldsay on 11th October 1970. Additional records of two birds, both on North Ronaldsay, in October 1972 and October 1975. One trapped on North Ronaldsay in October 1980 has not yet been accepted by BBRC, nor has one of the Greenland race (*C.h. hornemanni*) caught at Finstown on 12th October 1984.

Two-barred Crossbill *Loxia leucoptera* Very scarce visitor. One shot on North Ronaldsay in 1894 and preserved as a stuffed specimen at Holland House.

Common Crossbill *Loxia curvirostra* An irruptive visitor. In invasion years passage birds may arrive in small flocks from late June onwards. A recent irruption occurred in June and July 1972 when considerable numbers reached Orkney. Very few in recent years, the maximum being a total of 11 in May/June 1976 and up to 27 on Hoy in October 1982.

Parrot Crossbill *Loxia pityopsittacus* One bird found dead on North Ronaldsay on 18th June 1966 was said to have had the bill measurements of this species. One found dead (prey of Sparrowhawk) on Hoy on 29th October 1982 was the first confirmed record. Another, trapped on North Ronaldsay on 2nd October 1983.

Trumpeter Finch *Bucanetes githagineus* One on Sanday from 25th to 29th May 1981.

Scarlet Rosefinch *Carpodacus erythrinus* Scarce but apparently regular passage visitor. Since 1972 the species has become more common with a total of 33 recorded 1973–1982.

Bullfinch *Pyrrhula pyrrhula* Passage and winter visitor. Occurs in small numbers usually between October and January. Occurrences generally ascribed to the Northern race (*P.p. pyrrhula*). A remarkable invasion of birds of this race occurred in February 1984, as many as 30–40 being recorded.

Hawfinch *Coccothraustes coccothraustes* Rather scarce and irregular visitor. Thirteen records in 1973–1983, all March to May except one in November 1979.

Tennessee Warbler *Vermivora peregrina* One trapped in Holm from 5th to 7th September 1982.

Lapland Bunting *Calcarius lapponicus* Rather scarce passage visitor. More or less regular in variable though always small numbers. Only 13 records in the period 1973–1982, of which one was in May and the rest in September–November.

Snow Bunting *Plectrophenax nivalis* Regular passage and winter visitor. Common in small and large flocks. In the past up to about 5000 but the largest recent flock was 800 on North Ronaldsay in November 1977.

Pine Bunting *Emberiza leucocephala* Very scarce visitor. A male at Papa Westray on 15th October 1943 and another male at North Ronaldsay from 7th to 11th August 1967.

Yellowhammer (Yellow Yarling) *Emberiza citrinella* Scarce resident breeder and perhaps passage and winter visitor. Was formerly a reasonably common breeder but has become increasingly scarce over the past 50 or so years. Bred in Firth in 1974 and at Houton in 1975 but there have been no breeding records since and, in fact, in the period 1976–82 there have been only 10 records, two in March and eight in September–November.

Ortolan Bunting *Emberiza hortulana* Passage visitor. Rather scarce and irregular. Only five records in recent years, two in May, one in June and two in October.

Rustic Bunting *Emberiza rustica* Very scarce passage visitor. One (male) killed by a cat at Finstown 13th October 1927 (Baxter and Rintoul). Three records in recent years; one on Copinsay in June 1976, and singles on North Ronaldsay in October 1976 and September 1979.

Little Bunting *Emberiza pusilla* Very scarce visitor. Two at Pentland Skerries 15th October 1903 and 12th October 1915; one at Sule Skerry 22nd September 1908; one at Auskerry 21st September 1913; and birds on North Ronaldsay on 13th October 1980 and

in September/October 1984, the last not yet being accepted by BBRC.

Yellow-breasted Bunting *Emberiza aureola* Very scarce visitor. One on Auskerry on 22nd September 1964 and one on North Ronaldsay on 18th September 1984.

Reed Bunting *Emberiza schoeniclus* Resident breeder and passage and winter visitor. Was apparently quite scarce in the early part of this century but is now a pretty common breeder and fairly widespread.

Black-headed Bunting *Emberiza melanocephala* Very rare visitor. One on Papa Westray in late June 1967 and one on North Ronaldsay in early August 1967. One on Westray in July 1984 has not yet been accepted by BBRC.

Corn Bunting (Skitter Broltie) *Emberiza calandra* Resident breeder and perhaps passage and winter visitor. Was still fairly common in the 1930s as a breeder (mainly in hay fields). Still breeds regularly on Sanday (eight singing in 1979 and 1982) and Stronsay (ten singing in 1979) but these appear to be the only localities now.

APPENDIX TO BIRD LIST

The Records Committee of the British Ornithologists Union maintain a separate list (Category D) of species reliably identified in the British Isles but not yet fully admitted to the British and Irish list because, among other reasons, they may have been escapes from captivity. Three species listed by Balfour (1972) fall into this category:

Barrow's Goldeneye *Bucephala islandica* Ormond quotes Robinson as stating that the species has occurred in Orkney.

Blue Rock Thrush *Monticola solitarius* One on North Ronaldsay on 29th August to 6th September 1966.

Red-headed Bunting *Emberiza bruniceps* One on

North Ronaldsay on 19th June 1931 was the first British record and several more had occurred up to 1972. Between then and 1979 there were a further seven records of single birds, all May–August.

Balfour (1972) also listed three species which are not admitted to any category of the British and Irish list. They were the Bar-headed Goose (*Anser indicus*) a pair of which was seen on Swona in May 1969 (and one of which has since been recorded on Copinsay in May 1975); the Demoiselle Crane (*Anthropoides virgo*) one of which was shot in Deerness in May 1863; and the Lazuli Bunting (*Passerina amoena*) one of which was seen in Holm in June 1964. Since 1972 the annual bird reports have listed one further species of this nature, the Chilean Flamingo (*Phoenicopterus chilensis*) of which one was present in St Ola in January 1974; a Flamingo (sp) was also present on Westray in June 1979.

MAMMALS

Erinaceus europaeus L. Hedgehog
Sorex minutus L. Pygmy Shrew
Neomys fodiens (Penn.) Water Shrew
Lutra lutra (L.) Otter
Halichoerus grypus (Fab.) Grey Seal   +
Phoca vitulina L. Common Seal
Lepus capensis L. Brown Hare
Lepus timidus L. Mountain Hare
Oryctolagus cuniculus (L.) Rabbit

Apodemus sylvaticus (L.) Long-tailed Field-mouse
Mus domesticus Rutty House Mouse
Rattus rattus (L.) Black or Ship Rat
R. norvegicus (Berk.) Brown Rat
Microtus arvalis (Pallas) Orkney Vole
   M.a. orcadensis Millais
   M.a. sandayensis Millais
   M.a. westrae Miller
   M.a. ronaldshaiensis Hinton
   M.a. rousaiensis Hinton

Index

Only species discussed in the text are listed; other species occurring in Orkney are recorded in the Appendix (pages 236–302).

Aberdeen 18
Agassiz, Louis 40, 198
Agricultural improvements 33, 65, 154, 162, 177f, 183, 200
Alaska 20, 51
Algae 90f, 114, 195, 239–44 (see also seaweed and kelp)
Algal blooms 40, 73, 114
Amphibians 122
Angling 73, 113, 114, 117
Auk, Great 136, 145, 197
Auskerry 95, 97, 145
Ayre 45, 63, 74

Balfour, E. 25, 139, 140, 150f, 159f, 206, 213
Barrel of Butter 95
Barry, George 122, 193
Bats 133
Beaker folk 167
Bede, the Venerable 14, 168
Beetles 261–4
Bere 36, 48, 177, 180
Berriedale 32, 71f, 134, 156
Birch-Hazel scrub 31f
Birds 136–62, 284–302
Birsay 41, 105, 133, 137, 146, 169, 170, 174, 193
Boulder beaches 46, 52
Brand, John 18, 110, 191
Brinkies Brae 36
Brochs 47, 167
Brodgar, Ring of 166
Brown, G. M. 13, 14, 87, 163, 171, 220
Bryophytes 61, 66, 68, 73, 79, 81, 85, 247–9
Burray 42, 59, 127, 134, 184

Caithness 18, 23, 24, 26, 28, 29, 35, 42, 48, 52, 65, 66, 111, 133, 134, 146, 163, 183, 203, 217
Carbon dating 32, 163f, 173
Cathedral 36, 133, 173, 190
Cattle 49, 110, 165, 172, 177f
Chaffinch song 157–8
Chambered cairns 166
Characeae 195, 244–5
Churchill barriers 59, 74, 145
Churchill, Winston 12
Cliffs 29, 47, 53, 56–7, 136f
Clover 48, 178
Colonization 18, 26f, 126f, 134, 170, 200, 223
Communications 18, 179f, 200, 223
Copinsay 52, 137, 142, 144, 192, 219
Copper mines 42
  poisoning in sheep 130

Corries 44, 76
Crofters Act 182
Cubbie Roo's Stone 45
Culling of seals 99f, 217

Deer 49, 133, 172
Deerness 37, 170, 203
Dolphins 105f
Dragonflies 264
Drainage 34, 48, 123, 154, 177, 180, 200, 214
Dunes 58f
Dwarfie stone 44

Eagles 139f, 146, 150, 193, 196, 201
Eday 37, 39, 41, 51, 66, 75, 77, 80, 83, 95, 131, 133, 152, 153, 156, 159, 183, 186
Edinburgh 19, 20, 23, 131, 193, 204
Eels 99, 100, 105, 107, 111, 146f
Egilsay 102, 131, 132, 187
Ephemoptera 265
Erosion 36, 47, 48, 49, 59, 74, 76, 83, 167
Erratic boulders 44–5
Eutrophic lochs 74, 114f
Eynhallow 132, 149, 170, 205

Fair Isle 17, 18, 26, 88, 136, 144, 182, 183
Falkland Islands 20, 21, 106
Faroe 13, 87, 97, 102, 103, 139, 174, 183
Fellfield 77f
Field Club 10, 71, 149, 206, 214, 223
Field mice 27, 131
Finstown 45, 156f
Fishing 73, 117, 172, 181f
Fish farming 218
  fossils 39f
Flagstones 36, 140, 181, 198
Flandrian 31
Flora Orcadensis 203
Flotta 102, 127, 162, 176, 209f
Flowering plants 195, 203–4, 250–61
Forestry 51, 156
Fossils 39f
Foula 18, 136, 152
Founder effect 126
Frogs 122
Frost 20
Fulmars, on Eynhallow 149, 205
Fungi 236–9

Geo 46, 55, 58
Geological Survey 25, 31
Glaciation 44
Glasgow 20, 23

Goats 165
Graemsay 36, 37, 42, 44
Granite 37
Grazing 31, 48, 49, 52, 66, 71, 153
Great Auk 145, 197
Great Glen 37
Greenland 17, 20, 21

Haaf fishing 182
Hammars 76, 78–9
Hares 49, 77, 131
Harray, Loch 73, 74, 113f, 117, 156, 208
Harrier, Hen 14, 51, 72, 127, 150f, 156, 159, 207, 213, 215, 219
Hebrides 13, 18f, 24, 27, 28, 97, 99, 104, 108, 111, 131, 133, 140, 160, 168, 174
Hedgehogs 130f
Hirudinea 261
Hoy 13, 26, 35, 39, 42, 44, 46, 47, 49, 53, 54, 62, 66, 71, 72, 75f, 88, 90, 95, 105, 111, 127, 131, 133, 134, 136, 137, 140, 145, 153, 158, 159, 182, 207, 209
Old Man of 42, 47, 81
Hunting, of whales 102

Ice-ages 15, 26f, 42f
Inverness 18
Iron Age 167, 172, 173
Iron deposits 42
Islands, Orkney see Auskerry, Burray, Copinsay, Eday, Egilsay, Eynhallow, Flotta, Graemsay, Hoy, Longhope, Mainland, North Ronaldsay, Papa Westray, Rousay, Sanday, Shapinsay, Stronsay, Sule Stack and Skerry, Westray, Wyre.
  Other see Fair Isle, Falkland Islands, Faroe, Foula, Hebrides, Mull, Shetland, South Orkney, Stroma, Tiree.

Kelp 91, 195, 218
  harvesting 182, 184f, 200, 218
Kirkwall 17, 18, 19, 45, 117, 131, 132, 133, 137, 156, 166, 183, 184, 186, 195, 223
Knap of Howar 32, 163f

Lagoons 47, 113, 120
Land-bridges 26f, 125, 134
Lapland 20
Lava 42
Lead mines 42
Leeches 261

Lepidoptera 24, 29, 31, 133f, 266–75
Lichens 53, 68, 90, 245–7
Lightning 23, 31
Linklater, Eric 17, 220
Liverworts 79, 249
Lobsters 89, 91, 181
Loch, Echnaloch 116, 117
  Harray 73, 74, 113f, 117, 156, 208
  Kirbister 111, 116
  Stenness 73, 113f, 117, 201, 208
  Swannay 115, 117
Loch Lomond Readvance 29
Lochs, vegetation of 73f, 122
Longhope 102, 131, 181
Low, George 25, 95, 99, 122, 129, 131, 132, 181–2, 191f

Machair 50, 58, 60–1, 74
Maeshowe 14, 166
Mainland (of Orkney) 13, 17, 41, 45, 46, 54, 58, 66, 72, 76, 80, 82, 83, 86, 90, 102, 105, 111, 112, 125, 127, 131, 136, 149, 153, 158, 159, 209, 214
Mammals 93–109, 124–33, 150, 302
Manchester 23
Maps 12, 223
Maritime heath 65f, 75f, 137
Mesolithic 163
Metals 42, 130, 173, 217–18
Migration 134, 156–7, 171, 187, 201f, 203
Millais, J. G. 125, 201
Miller, Hugh 40
Mills 45, 51, 110–1, 118, 119
Mines 42
Mires 86, 137
Mites 135
Molluscs 90f, 114, 116, 119, 122, 124, 181, 191, 195, 205, 218, 278–83
Mosses 61, 66, 68, 73, 79, 85, 247–9
Mull 28
Museum, Stromness 40, 195, 205, 223
  Tankerness House 223
Myxomycetes 236–7

Names meanings of 14, 170
Natural History Society 119, 223
Nature Conservancy Council 10, 11, 25, 99, 207f, 214f, 219–20
Nature Reserves 52, 73, 75, 113, 124, 127f, 172, 180, 208, 214f, 219–20
Neolithic 15, 31, 71, 103, 139, 163f, 181
North Ronaldsay 17, 37, 46, 66, 75, 81, 95, 105, 128, 129, 133, 140, 146, 182
  Sheep 32, 124, 127f, 180, 184
North Sea Oil 9, 37, 42, 102, 109, 150, 162, 209f

Occidental Oil Company 9, 11, 209
Odonata 264
Oil 9, 37, 42, 102, 109, 150, 162, 209f
Old Man of Hoy 42, 47, 81
Oligotrophic lochs 74, 114f
Orkney, Earls of 173
  extent 17, 45
  Field Club 10, 71, 149, 206, 215, 223
  Islands Council 51, 73, 111, 207f, 220
  name 14

Natural History Society 193, 223
vole 14, 27, 28, 49, 124f, 151, 160, 201, 216
Orkneyinga Saga 107, 171, 173
Orthoptera 264
Otter 93, 107f, 213

Papa Westray 39, 66, 75, 113, 131, 133, 137, 140, 145, 146, 153, 163, 170
Paring of turf 79, 177
Peat 29, 32, 33, 45, 48, 49, 52, 75, 77, 82–3, 115, 119, 175–6
Pentland Firth 24, 26, 27, 35, 42, 52, 88, 105, 146, 163, 168, 182
Peregrine Falcon 53, 77, 139, 146, 196
Picts 168f
Pigs 33, 165, 172, 177, 179
Place names 14, 170
Plankton 89, 141
Plantations, forestry 51, 156
Plecoptera 266
Pleistocene 26f, 42f, 134
Pollution 9, 172, 175, 210
Pomona 18
Population 17, 209
Porpoises 105f
Poultry 23, 179, 180
Primula scotica 14, 49, 65, 67f, 203, 214, 216, 219
Pytheas of Marseilles 18

Rabbits 49, 52, 59, 66, 131, 160, 184
Radioactivity 42, 217–18
Radio Orkney 11, 290
Rainfall 18, 22, 23, 135
Rats 132–3, 160
Reclamation 50, 52, 65, 83, 119, 123, 134, 153, 162, 177, 180, 200, 212f
Rendall, R. 25, 35, 91, 188, 203f, 216, 220, 279
Romans 18, 167
Ronaldsay see North Ronaldsay and South Ronaldsay
Rousay 39, 40, 41, 42, 55, 66, 72, 75, 76, 77, 81, 83, 86, 95, 103, 125, 131, 132, 149, 152, 153, 156, 159, 163, 166, 167, 184
Royal Society for the Protection of Birds 10, 74, 136, 151, 159, 206, 214, 284
St Andrews 23, 198, 199
Saltmarsh 63f, 137
Sanday 37, 39, 41, 42, 47, 66, 75, 98, 103, 111, 113, 125, 127, 131, 132, 133, 140, 155
Scapa Flow 13, 26, 29, 35, 46, 52, 54, 55, 60, 71, 83, 88f, 95, 105, 108, 181, 182, 209f
Sea, depth 26, 28, 88
  shore 45, 55, 59, 87f, 148–9, 205
Seals 49, 57, 94f, 207, 219
  cull 98f, 217
Seaweeds 58, 90f, 176, 178, 218, 239–45 (see also kelp)
Shapinsay 37, 39, 45, 51, 121, 127, 131, 156, 158, 193
Sheep 33, 49, 50, 52, 165, 172, 180, 184
  North Ronaldsay 32, 124, 127f, 184
Shetland 9, 10, 13, 17, 18, 20, 21, 22, 23, 26, 28, 42, 48, 54, 76, 83, 88,

91, 102, 104, 106, 107, 108, 111, 117, 129, 131, 133, 136, 138, 139, 140, 142, 144, 148, 153, 154, 169, 182, 198, 203, 212, 276
Silage 159, 179, 180
Sites of Special Scientific Interest 52, 73, 75, 113, 124, 127f, 172, 180, 208, 214f, 219–20
Skara Brae 9, 14, 32, 48, 103, 126, 163f, 173, 223
Skye 13, 28
Snow 20
South Orkney Islands 20, 21
South Ronaldsay 39, 42, 52, 54, 59, 105, 111, 125, 127, 131, 132, 164, 166
Spiders 275–7
Statistical Account 95, 127, 131, 133, 181, 185, 193
Stenness, Loch 73, 113f, 208
  Stones of 166
'Stormay' 187f
Stroma 17, 26, 131
Stromatolites 40, 42
Stromness 18, 36, 38, 39, 40, 41, 46, 53, 88, 91, 106, 109, 133, 205, 217, 223
Stronsay 28, 37, 39, 46, 47, 52, 75, 83, 98, 102, 103, 113, 127, 132, 152, 153, 183, 184, 185, 204
Sule Skerry and Stack 17, 52, 53, 54, 95, 106, 142f, 202
Sullom Voe 109
Sunshine 23, 135
Syrphidae 266

Tankerness House Museum 223
Temperatures 19f
  inversions 23
Tides 88f, 95, 120
Tiree 20, 23
Toads 122
Tomb of the Eagles 165
Tombola 45, 47
Torquay 23
Trichoptera 265
Tudor, John 18
Tundra 32

Ultima thule 18
Uranium 25, 42, 206, 217–8

Vikings 9, 15, 117, 131, 168f, 189
Volcanic rocks 28, 42
Voles 14, 27, 28, 49, 124f, 151, 160, 193, 201, 216

Wallace, John 18, 48, 145, 146
Walrus 102
Warebeth 38, 42
Weather 18f
Westray 24, 28, 39, 45, 46, 55, 64, 76, 77, 79, 82, 95, 111, 113, 125, 127, 131–2, 133, 136, 137, 140, 142, 145, 149, 153, 163, 183, 218
Whales 102f
Wind 19, 23, 24, 135, 175
Wintering birds 148, 207, 218
Woodland 31f, 48, 51, 54, 71, 72, 156f
Wyre 95, 131

Yesnaby 36, 38, 66, 217